On Lincoln

CIVIL WAR HISTORY READERS

Since 1955 the journal *Civil War History* has presented the best original scholarship in the study of America's greatest trial. In commemoration of the war's sesquicentennial, The Kent State University Press presents *Civil War History* Readers, a multivolume series reintroducing the most influential articles published in the journal.

Conflict and Command	Edited by John T. Hubbell
Race and Recruitment	Edited by John David Smith
On Lincoln	Edited by John T. Hubbell

"Some of today's most influential Lincoln historians, including Douglas L. Wilson and Allen C. Guelzo, first introduced their trailblazing findings in *Civil War History*. For inclusion in this anthology, John Hubbell has judiciously selected gems from among the many Lincoln-related articles that ran in that indispensable journal, covering topics ranging from emancipation to military strategy, from important public documents to significant private concerns. Space is granted to both laudatory and critical voices. Lincoln buffs and professional historians alike will welcome the publication of this valuable anthology."

  MICHAEL BURLINGAME, author of *Abraham Lincoln: A Life*

"These extraordinary essays, culled from more than 500 from *Civil War History*'s long-serving editor, are timely and as refreshing as when first published. All are chock-full of information that serves us well. In these beautifully written articles, the authors cover all of the important issues confronted by President Abraham Lincoln, from leadership and the military to race, the first draft in American history, dissent, and the women of the Middle Period. This volume is a major contribution to the more than 16,000 books written about our most respected chief magistrate."

  FRANK J. WILLIAMS, Founding Chair of The Lincoln Forum
  and retired Chief Justice of the Rhode Island Supreme Court

"John Hubbell and the Kent State University Press have brought together and conveniently made available fifteen important articles on Lincoln from past issues of *Civil War History*, the premier journal for the period. Written by leading authorities on Lincoln and the Civil War, most of the articles appropriately focus on the main issues involving Lincoln's presidency. Professor Hubbell, also a prominent historian, provides an insightful assessment of each article's contribution to our understanding of Lincoln's career and role in the Civil War. Readers interested in this great president will want to have a copy of this book on their desk."

  WILLIAM C. HARRIS, Lincoln Prize–winning author of
  Lincoln and the Border States: Preserving the Union

CIVIL WAR HISTORY READERS
VOLUME 3

ON
LINCOLN

Edited by
JOHN T. HUBBELL

THE KENT STATE UNIVERSITY PRESS
Kent, Ohio

© 2014 by The Kent State University Press, Kent, Ohio 44242
All rights reserved
Library of Congress Catalog Card Number 2013042808
ISBN 978-1-60635-200-7

LIBRARY OF CONGRESS CATALOGING-IN-PUBLICATION DATA
On Lincoln / edited by John T. Hubbell
    pages cm — (Civil War history readers)
Includes index.
ISBN 978-1-60635-200-7 (pbk.) ∞
1. Lincoln, Abraham, 1809–1865—Political and social views. 2. United States—History—Civil War, 1861–1865—Biography. 3. United States—Politics and govern-ment—1861–1865. 4. Political leadership—United States—History—19th century. 5. Presidents—United States—Biography. I. Hubbell, John T., editor of compilation. E457.2.O5 2014

973.7092—dc23   2013042808

Contents

Introduction	vii
Abraham Lincoln as Revolutionary	
Otto H. Olsen	1
Lincoln and Van Buren in the Steps of the Fathers: Another Look at the Lyceum Address	
Major L. Wilson	14
On the Verge of Greatness: Psychological Reflections on Lincoln at the Lyceum	
Charles B. Strozier	31
Abraham Lincoln, Ann Rutledge, and the Evidence of Herndon's Informants	
Douglas L. Wilson	43
Abraham Lincoln and "That Fatal First of January"	
Douglas L. Wilson	68
Lincoln and the Mexican War: An Argument by Analogy	
Mark E. Neely Jr.	100
Lincoln as Military Strategist	
Herman Hattaway and Archer Jones	122
Jefferson Davis and Abraham Lincoln as War Presidents: Nothing Succeeds Like Success	
Ludwell H. Johnson	135
To Suppress or Not to Suppress: Abraham Lincoln and the *Chicago Times*	
Craig D. Tenney	151
"A Catholic Family Newspaper" Views the Lincoln Administration: John Mullaly's Copperhead Weekly	
Joseph George Jr.	165

Abraham Lincoln on Labor and Capital
James A. Stevenson ... 187

Lincoln's Calvinist Transformation: Emancipation and War
Nicholas Parrillo ... 201

Only His Stepchildren: Lincoln and the Negro
Don E. Fehrenbacher ... 233

Defending Emancipation: Abraham Lincoln and the Conkling Letter, 1863
Allen C. Guelzo ... 252

The Historian as Gamesman: Otto Eisenschiml, 1880–1963
William Hanchett ... 282

Contributors ... 294

Index ... 296

Introduction

Abraham Lincoln is a historiographical lodestone, the subject of so many books that one feels obliged to cite the number (16,000?). They range from the mythological to the hagiographic to the defamatory, from monographs on any number of topics, often illuminating, and to biographies, all definitive. The articles in the present collection address subjects salient to an understanding of the man. Perhaps salient is a term that carries its own risks, just as a military salient is a tactical circumstance that invites attack. Some may also invite the charge of being dated, having been published in an earlier century! A fair criticism, perhaps, or at least an expected one. On reflection, however, historical writing at its best is long lasting. Consider Lord Charnwood's biography of Lincoln (1917) and Frederick Douglass's speech at the dedication of the Freedmen's Memorial in Washington, D.C. (1876). The Freedmen's monument may elicit an understandable unease among latter-day visitors, but Douglass's words are the most insightful commentary on Lincoln and race, slavery, and emancipation yet written. Charnwood's slender volume, published long before the opening of the expansive public records and correspondence, contains insights into his life, character, and presidency seldom equaled even by his most accomplished biographers. Both Douglass and Charnwood write with an elegance that does justice to the great man. Both agree that Lincoln was a great man and offer no apology for that judgment. In Charnwood's words, the biographer should not "shrink too timidly from the display of partisanship which, on one side or the other, it would be insensate not to feel. The true obligation of impartiality is that he should conceal no fact which, in his own mind, tells against his views." The admirable scholarship, the subtlety of analysis, and the appreciation of context in the following articles are reasons enough for their inclusion. If they inspire further reflection and even a few more publications, so much the better.

Otto Olsen's "Abraham Lincoln as a Revolutionary" is powerfully analytical and occasionally sardonic in tone. The last may stem from the cooling toward Lincoln at the time of publication. Many historians were critical of his persistent advocacy of colonization, his slow path to emancipation, and what may have been an undue "reasonableness and restraint." Some even found fault with his prose! Olsen chooses to underscore what Lincoln did, not his persona or political tactics. The "greatest revolutionary is the one who is most successful, not the one who is most extreme, dramatic, or vocal." Lincoln's "assertive idealism" was evident in his early life, as was his belief in a free society, resting on the essential phrases of the Declaration of Independence. He also recognized the counter arguments. In his 1852 eulogy to Henry Clay, he spoke specifically and pointedly of an "increasing number of men [who] for the sake of perpetuating slavery... were beginning to assail and ridicule the white man's charter of freedom.... So far as I have learned, the first American of any note, to do or attempt to do this, was the late John C. Calhoun." This statement was a departure from and a challenge to a long acceptance of the fact of slavery and the growing power of its adherents.

Slavery, in all its manifestations, was the greatest threat to the ideals and the prosperity of the nation, a point on which Lincoln "displayed as firm a commitment as the abolitionists themselves." Southerners in fact increasingly thought of him as a revolutionary agent, and as the emerging leader of a Northern political party, more dangerous than the abolitionists—who themselves had little regard for Lincoln. The Civil War was a revolutionary event and Lincoln was its guiding hand. In Olsen's words: "His true greatness was not that he had such admirable personal qualities, but that he successfully applied them in a revolutionary way." One might infer from this article that Lincoln's leadership was of consequence, a conclusion strongly challenged by some recent historians.

Lincoln's "assertive idealism," or variations on that theme, has been of interest to any number of biographers, mostly admiring, with a corporal's guard of detractors. Of special interest is his January 27, 1838, address, "The Perpetuation of Our Political Institutions," presented at the Young Men's Lyceum at Springfield, Illinois. In the two following essays, the authors interpret this remarkable speech in the context of national politics and in its ideological and psychological implications. Both give attention to the widely quoted passage: "Towering genius disdains a beaten path. It seeks regions hitherto unexplored. . . . It thirsts and burns for distinction; and if possible, it will have it, whether at the expense of emancipating slaves or enslaving freemen."

Major L. Wilson, in "Lincoln and Van Buren in the Steps of the Fathers," considers Lincoln's twin fears, a growing "mobocratic spirit" and an always present threat of "Caesarism." Political theorists have for centuries argued that democracy, with all its untidiness, is likely to lead to a demand for order, for a strong leader, for a Caesar. And there is always an ambitious sort eager to accept or to seize that role. Lincoln, for his part, pleaded: "Let reverence for the laws become the political religion of the nation." Others have interpreted Lincoln's warnings against the emergence of a Caesar as a not so veiled statement of his own ambitions. This interpretation, most notably by Edmund Wilson, is an example of just how easily theory can "out run the documentation." Lincoln was a Whig and Whigs were given to referring to President Jackson as "King Andrew," and Martin Van Buren as the dutiful son and heir. Lincoln was not above partisan barbs or hyperbole, but his appeal was for a "procedural community," not a deference to popular passion or an invitation to "towering genius." It was also a renewed appeal for a national dimension to politics. Freedom was national; slavery was "accidental, temporary, and local."

Charles B. Strozier, in "On the Verge of Greatness: Psychological Reflections on Lincoln at the Lyceum," grounds his analysis in biography and psychology, approaches that inform his larger and influential studies of Lincoln. At age twenty-eight, Lincoln was already an experienced and well regarded Illinois Whig, who defined its political institutions as the greatest asset of this favored nation. He was also ambitious and trying, as young men will, to find his place in the world. It was his time of self-definition. Strozier suggests that these personal considerations were present in his politics; his critique of the nation may have been an introspective assessment of his own inner conflicts. "Passion. . . will in the future be our enemy. Reason, cold, calculating, unimpassioned reason, must furnish all the materials for our support and defense." The sometimes exalted language, the "most striking and important aspect of the speech," could also be an expression of a "healthy self assertiveness." Ambition, after all, was not an altogether negative trait, as Lincoln later and famously told General Joseph Hooker. But he may have recognized his own ambition and the need to keep it within its proper limits. This self-control, this respect for reason over passion, remained an often noticed characteristic of the man.

Douglas A. Wilson's articles assess two events of Lincoln's personal life, one somewhat misty and one that remains a bit of a puzzle. In "Abraham Lincoln, Ann Rutledge, and the Evidence of Herndon's Informants," he discusses a story long repudiated or dismissed by major historians, most notably James G. Randall.

Randall discounted the widely reported account of a love affair between Lincoln and Ann Rutledge because it rested on the recollections of contemporaries as compiled by William Herndon and Jesse Weik. The story was too problematical to be taken seriously; the "informants" relied on folklore and hearsay. When Wilson examined the Herndon-Weik Collection (and published an edited volume on its contents), he concluded that there was "remarkably little disagreement among the informants on the basic elements of the story." Further, he said, "it is difficult to fault Herndon as an investigator." Why did Randall and others reject the story? They seemed to be guided less by evidence than by an arbitrary point of view. At least some readers will see the irony in dismissing contemporary accounts of events, when most historians search diligently for such documentation.

In "Abraham Lincoln and 'That Fatal First of January,'" Wilson expands on Lincoln's off-and-on courtship of Mary Todd, his tepid pursuit of other women, and a remarkable exchange of letters with Joshua Speed, his closest friend. Lincoln was experiencing a spell of despondency over his rough-edged romances, his equivocation over Mary Todd, his unsteady political prospects and, all the while, empathizing with Speed over marriage and all its implications. By Wilson's calculation, they may have been interested in the same woman for a brief time! His untangling of this particular web again rests on a close reading of the evidence. Not one event, but a series of circumstances combined to leave Lincoln emotionally unsteady. Lord Charnwood may, as usual, have said it best: "[Lincoln] started on manhood with a sound and chivalrous outlook on women in general, and a nervous terror of women when he met them." Indeed.

In "Lincoln and the Mexican War: An Argument by Analogy," Mark E. Neely Jr. addresses the question of why Lincoln did not stand for reelection after only one term in Congress. The most common explanation was that his speech against President James K. Polk's reasons for the war weakened his already tenuous prospects. Neely discounts this notion and posits that Lincoln was neither overly idealistic nor politically maladroit. He had not been opposed to the annexation of Texas and did not argue, as did many Whigs, that the war was a plot to add slave states to the Union. At the same time he did fear that domestic institutions might be adversely affected by the war, a fear shared by other politicians, North and South. He became more anti-expansionist when it seemed that slavery was likely to be introduced into the new territories. A less exalted reason for his lack of enthusiasm for reelection was he had grown a bit jaded with life in Washington. He also had said that he had intended to serve only one term and others in his district believed that it was another's "turn." The Whig party was not a strong element in Illinois, as was evident in his successor's loss in 1848, notwithstanding Zachary Taylor's election as president. Lincoln had followed the interests of party politics and not reluctantly.

If Lincoln as war president was a case of an inexperienced executive leading an inexperienced people, assessments of his record have been positive for the most part. He instinctively understood that organizing a military force was very much like organizing a political coalition. His primary—and continuing—task was to raise and maintain an army while convincing the Northern population that the national cause was a worthy one.

Herman Hattaway and Archer Jones (authors of the influential *How the North Won*, 1983), find much to praise in "Lincoln as Military Strategist." His "ideas were realistic and workable." He "fully shared the ideas" of the West Pointers in command, even if at times he had his doubts about some of them. If he was not unduly deferential to the generals, he expected a great deal from them. His admonition to make Lee's army rather than Richmond the proper focus of the Army of the Potomac was a balance of difficult choices. A correlative fear for the security of Washington may have been overdrawn. (See Thomas J. Rowland, "'Heaven save country governed by such counsels': The Safety of Washington and the Peninsula Campaign," in the March 1996 issue of *CWH*.) If Lincoln was not the ablest strategist of the war, as some admirers have suggested, he was successful, through force of intellect and will, in holding together a fractious people and a powerful army that was too often poorly led.

Ludwell H. Johnson's "Jefferson Davis and Abraham Lincoln as War Presidents: Nothing Succeeds Like Success," is something of a sequel to an earlier article in *Civil War History* ("Civil War Military History: A Few Revisions in Need of Revising," 1971). He chides "writers of history, or what passes for history," who praise Lincoln's "outstanding qualities by pointing to Davis's corresponding deficiencies." As Johnson sees it, "even a brief systematic comparison shows that Davis was clearly superior to Lincoln as a war president." Davis possessed presence and dignity, attributes associated with executive leadership. Lincoln was lacking on both counts. Davis's political and military appointments were at least equal to Lincoln and sometimes superior. His "major military appointments, promotions, and dismissals were remarkably free of politics." In sum, Jefferson Davis was "one of the most remarkable men of his day, and for that matter, in all of American history." The "cult of Lincoln and the fact of Confederate defeat" has denied (and continues to deny) him justice "at the bar of history." There will be no editorial comments on historians and bars and scholarly debate.

Civil liberties during the Civil War have long been of interest to historians. Craig D. Tenney's "To Suppress or Not to Suppress: Abraham Lincoln and the *Chicago Times*" is an analysis of what Lincoln's opponents called an egregious attack upon the First Amendment. The closure of the *Times* on June 1, 1863, which followed by a few weeks the arrest and conviction of Clement Vallandigham, elicited widespread protests by Northern Democrats. Wilbur F. Storey, the editor and publisher of the *Times*, was a vitriolic critic of Lincoln, the Republican Party, emancipation, and the Conscription Law. When soldiers took control of the paper, Democrats charged the president with assuming dictatorial powers. In fact, the decision to lift the suppression order came after some well placed Illinois Republicans, including David Davis, urged Lincoln to do so. Professor Tenney suggests that a "tender regard for the First Amendment" did not influence Lincoln's reluctant decision to revoke the order. Rather, it was "something more basic to the president's nature—a regard for politics." This conclusion is given an extensive and concurring examination in Mark Neely's Pulitzer Prize–winning *The Fate of Liberty: Abraham Lincoln and Civil Liberties* (1991). Political exigency trumped the Constitution. This is not to imply that his "inner Caesar" was emerging.

A graphic example of the opposition press is described in Joseph George's "'A Catholic Family Newspaper': John Mullaly's Copperhead Weekly." Mullaly (1835–1915), an Irish immigrant, was a "leader of Catholic thought and action in the nineteenth century." During the Civil War he was the editor of the *Metropolitan Record*, which, with blessing of Archbishop John J. Hughes, "became the official newspaper" of the New York Archdiocese. It was not meant to associate itself with a political party, an editorial policy that prevailed until the summer of 1862, when the *Record* effectively became an anti-administration publication and lost its standing as the "official organ" of the Archdiocese. Emancipation was the tilting point for Mullaly and conscription sealed his break with Lincoln. In June 1864 he changed the name of the paper to the *Metropolitan Record and New York Vindicator* and declared it to be an advocate of the "principles of Jeffersonian Democracy." The subtext was a full-throated opposition to the war. On August 19, 1864, Mullaly was arrested for "willfully counseling" opposition to the draft. The case was dropped but Lincoln's reelection weakened Mullaly's influence. He continued his opposition to emancipation, his commentary often couched in the vilest of racial terms. His was by no means a solitary voice and still provokes debate over the proper limits, if such exist, of press freedom in wartime.

Abraham Lincoln is the source of many apt quotations, cited in support of or counter to latter-day circumstances and causes. Some authors even create quotations for their own purposes. His comments on economic relationships and religion are helpful in understanding the man and his times and may be helpful in understanding our own.

James A. Stevenson's "Abraham Lincoln on Labor and Capital" contains a striking passage from an 1859 speech at an Agricultural Fair in Wisconsin. He cited, and seemed to agree with, those who believed that "labor is prior to, and independent of capital: that in fact, capital is the fruit of labor, and could never have existed if labor had not first existed—that labor can exist without capital, but capital could never have existed without labor. Hence. . . labor is the superior—greatly the superior—of capital." Lincoln expanded on this theme in his December 1861 Message to Congress, repeating some of the same phrases. His own experiences led him to advocate a free, mobile society. He did not consider the accumulation of wealth to be a proper goal, nor did wealth give one class the right to dominate others. One can only ponder what he would have made of the Gilded Age, trickle-down economics, or Ayn Rand.

Lincoln's religious beliefs and their influence on his politics continue to attract attention and a diverse audience. Nicholas Parillo, in "Lincoln's Calvinist Transformation: Emancipation and War," poses the thesis that "Lincoln's deep commitment to republicanism never lost its motive power, but by the end of the war, his new Calvinist tendencies acquired strength equal to that of his never-changing democratic beliefs." This profound change was "closely interwoven with his policies regarding emancipation and war." Parillo develops this theme in the context of a religious culture that prevailed from the preaching of Jonathan Edwards to Lincoln's own day. In finally confronting, perhaps reluctantly, the unhappy fact of slavery, Lincoln's "political ideals took on the force and weight of religious convictions." Beginning with his election and the consequent demands of office, he "began to consider God as an active agent." This transformation was most evident in his advocacy of emancipation, which demanded a sort of political genius and, increasingly, an appeal to God.

Lincoln's struggle with emancipation became part of a larger struggle to define the meaning of the war itself. In the end, the Civil War "was not a senseless evil but an instrument of expiation," a theme that Lincoln so eloquently posited in his Second Inaugural. It was, says Parillo, "an expression of religious ideas that had been an integral part of Lincoln's leadership throughout the war."

Lincoln's ineluctable connection with race and slavery, slavery and race, has preoccupied historians of all persuasions. Racist nattering, in public and in private, is not rare and is sometimes influential. This may reflect the audience as much as it does the persuasiveness of the writer. Even historians who may be sympathetic to Lincoln question his motives as well as his policies. They are also likely to give small consideration to the political culture in which Lincoln lived. Of course, the element of context may serve to excuse as well as explain.

Don E. Fehrenbacher takes the title of "Only His Stepchildren: Lincoln and the Negro," from Frederick Douglass, who said of Lincoln: "He was preeminently the white man's President, entirely devoted to the welfare of white men.... You are the children of Abraham Lincoln. We are at best only his stepchildren, children by adoption, children by force of circumstances and necessity." Fehrenbacher does not altogether disagree. Rather, he confronts Lincoln's apparent contradictions, the "conflicting qualities" of a remarkable man who was "of the people and yet something more, sharing popular passions and rising above them...." (Perhaps he was understanding of rather than "sharing popular passions.") He could be "tentative and equivocal," yet the intensity of his belief in the evil of slavery and the rightness of emancipation aroused a mix of affection and admiration and outrage and hate. In matters of policy he necessarily considered his constituency. Fehrenbacher seems to say that this was not undue or exaggerated caution but a form of astute political leadership. Douglass recognized this in that same speech in 1876: "... measuring him by the sentiment of his country, a sentiment he was bound as a statesman to consult, he was swift, zealous, radical, and determined." Professor Fehrenbacher, in this intellectual *tour de force*, illustrates this profound truth in the admirable fashion that came to be expected of his writings on Abraham Lincoln.

Lincoln's opponents described the Emancipation Proclamation as a betrayal of those thousands of soldiers who had enlisted in a war for the Union and then found themselves joined in a war for abolition. Lincoln responded with a series of public letters, a defense of his policies in general and, most forcefully, in defense of emancipation. Allen C. Guelzo's "Defending Emancipation: Abraham Lincoln and the Conkling Letter, 1863," is an especially timely analysis of the one such message that addressed the public opposition most directly. It is also a reminder that Lincoln was his own best witness and historians should pay closer attention.

James Cook Conkling and others in Central Illinois had called for the "unconditional Union men in our State to hold a Grand Mass Meeting at Springfield" on September 3. At their invitation Lincoln said that he might attend "or send a letter—probably the latter." He wrote the letter over a period of three days in late August and sent it to Conkling with "but one suggestion. Read it very slowly." One thinks today of sound bites and applause lines.

The meeting was a success in the eyes of the organizers. The letter, as Lincoln intended, was an unequivocal defense of the Emancipation Proclamation and the recruitment of Negro soldiers. Nor did he neglect to appeal to the patriotism of the North. The twin themes of justice (meaning freedom) for the slaves and an exhortation to persevere in the war could not be misunderstood. He reminded the delegates, and the nation, that "Negroes, like other people, act upon motives." If "they stake their lives for us, they must be prompted by the strongest motive— even the promise of freedom." That promise, added Lincoln, "being made, must be kept."

The letter was published in pamphlets and newspapers throughout the North. All, even his opponents, understood that its core, its essence, was the permanence of emancipation. Professor Guelzo defines the Conkling Letter as a "reminder, even as Lincoln's reputation as an emancipator has become clouded over time, that the Emancipation Proclamation had made slaves, not merely pawns in a political game, but 'thenceforwards and forever free.'" And if, in the opinion of Richard Hofstadter, the Emancipation Proclamation had "all the moral grandeur of a bill of lading," those most affected by it found grandeur enough in the words and the intent of its author.

Lord Charnwood has written that Abraham Lincoln "died with every circumstance of tragedy, yet it is not the accident of his death but the purpose of his life that is remembered." The articles in this collection form a commentary on the "purpose of his life," but the "accident of his death" has attracted its own historiography, a coalition of mystery, fraud, and, somewhat belatedly, scholarly attention. In 1937, one Otto Eisenschiml published *Why Was Lincoln Murdered?* It became influential in its own unexamined way. His major theme was that Secretary of War Edwin Stanton was the leader of a cabal of Radical Republicans who welcomed Lincoln's passing and in deliberate and devious ways brought it about. William Hanchett has published two articles in *Civil War History* that challenge this story. In "The Eisenschiml Thesis" (September 1979), he systematically demolished the "thesis." He also noted that professional historians had rejected Eisenschiml's account but without "close critical analysis."

In "The Historian as Gamesman: Otto Eisenschiml, 1880–1963," Hanchett credits the author with assiduously accumulating documents relating to the assassination, but the "evidence" was "stretched and twisted." He posed "dishonest questions deliberately framed to cause the unwary readers to jump to conclusions that Eisenschiml knew were unfounded." Notwithstanding its unfirm foundation, the book was a commercial success. It was a Book-of-the-Month Club selection and reprinted as a paperback. Because of scholarly indifference, by default it found wide acceptance among the public. Eisenschiml charged the historical profession with holding a bias against the outsider, no matter the virtues of his research. These "college Olympians" would never accept the work of the uninitiated (i.e., no PhD). Hanchett notes that the first book on the assassination written by a professionally trained historian appeared in 1982! This curious circumstance allowed Eisenschiml's book, a "deliberate falsification," to receive more attention than it deserved.

On that melancholy note, we are once again reminded that an honest history is the mark of a free people. My thanks to the authors of these essays on Abraham Lincoln.

Abraham Lincoln as Revolutionary

Otto H. Olsen

With the possible exception of his beard, there is little about Abraham Lincoln that fits the modern, popular concept of a revolutionary.[1] Rather, Lincoln has been associated with qualities that are usually perceived, even by many leftists, as the antithesis of revolutionary. Typically these qualities include some combination of moderate, reasonable, kind, liberal, conservative, pragmatic, flexible, pious and law abiding.[2] These hardly accord with the familiar extremism, cruelty, and violence of revolution. And so, the leader of the bloodiest war and one of the most stupendous social transformations in our history endures as a symbol of moderation and the rule of reason and law.

There has been little inclination among the new left to consider Lincoln in any way an exemplar of progressive change. Some have been actually hostile, a

---

1. An earlier version of this essay was delivered at the Fifth Annual Lincoln Symposium, Springfield, Ill., Feb. 12, 1978. I am indebted to William Burr, Larry Lynn, Richard Schneirov, and Paul Wolman, graduate students at Northern Illinois Univ., for inspiring the topic.

2. For example, James G. Randall, *Lincoln the Liberal Statesman* (New York, 1947); T. Harry Williams, "Abraham Lincoln: Pragmatic Democrat" and Norman Graebner, "Abraham Lincoln: Conservative Statesman," both in Graebner (ed.), *The Enduring Lincoln* (Urbana, 1959). Decided exceptions that picture Lincoln as radical or revolutionary are Dwight Lowell Dumond, "Virtually an Abolitionist," in Don E. Fehrenbacher (ed.), *The Leadership of Abraham Lincoln* (New York, 1970), and William Burr and others, "Lincoln & the Second American Revolution," *In These Times*, I (Feb. 9-15, 1977).

reflection of the recent tendency to stress the failures rather than the achievements of the Civil War era and to judge radical Republicans by either lost alternatives or present day standards.[3] Lincoln's concessions to racism, his experiments with colonization, his slow movement toward emancipation, his limited Reconstruction aims, and above all, perhaps, his reasonableness and restraint have encouraged an easy abandonment from the left. Conservatives and moderates, on the other hand, obviously relish the retention of Lincoln as a symbol of their own. But perhaps our concepts have become stereotyped by the troubles of the modern world. After all, if it was a revolution that we celebrated on our bicentennial, we have a goodly number of conservative revolutionaries to account for—George Washington, John Adams, James Madison, and Alexander Hamilton among others. Those revolutionaries not only lacked beards, but they also displayed all the qualities we have just associated with Lincoln; and they, too, proceeded with slow and patient deliberation. Just as it was fifteen months from the bombardment at Fort Sumter to Lincoln's decision to proclaim emancipation, so, too, it was fifteen months from Lexington and Concord to the Declaration of Independence.

A conservative distaste for the concept of revolution in our history also appears to reflect a belief that the American Revolution, together with the Constitution, represented something of a finality in social evolution. Our system is conceived of as eternal. Jefferson's speculation about periodically watering the tree of liberty with the blood of tyrants is dismissed as rhetoric, and we assume that our system of elections and constitutional amendment can solve all our social problems in a rational, legal, and peaceful way.[4] The one insurmountable difficulty with this hope, as far as the Civil War is concerned, is that it was not fulfilled. The discouraging fact is that our system could not deal sensibly with the obvious anachronism of slavery in the modern world. Rational and peaceful evolution did not occur, and the war came.

That war was not only violence incarnate, it had consequences that have been

---

3. Julius Lester, *Look Out, Whitey! Black Power's Gon' Get Your Mama!* (New York, 1968), 58; Louis S. Gerteis, *From Contraband to Freedman: Federal Policy Toward Southern Blacks, 1861-1865* (Westport, 1973), 4-5, 78, 154: William A. Williams, *America Confronts a Revolutionary World: 1776-1976* (New York, 1976), 111-14. Steven Rosswurm drew my attention to the citation from Williams.

4. For example, Phillip S. Paludan's bicentennial Lincoln address, "Lincoln, the Rule of Law, and the American Revolution," *Journal of the Illinois State Historical Society*, LXX (Feb. 1977): 10-17. The emphasis upon Lincoln as a law and order man relies heavily upon a speech very early in his career before the Young Men's Lyceum of Springfield, Ill., on Jan. 27, 1938. This speech was read in its entirety, apparently in response to this essay, at the Abraham Lincoln Association Dinner, Feb. 13, 1978.

considered revolutionary. It radically altered the social order of the South by abolishing race slavery. In so doing it established the power and extended the program of a free labor, capitalist system on a national scale. And it forcefully established the permanence of the Union and the supremacy of the national government.[5]

If any of these conceptions of the Civil War as a revolution are accepted, Lincoln's role respecting that war provides an obvious basis for evaluating him as a revolutionary. This concept is primarily dependent upon Lincoln's contribution to achieving revolutionary results, and not upon any effort to define Lincoln personally as a radical or extremist. By this test, the greatest revolutionary is the one who is most successful, not the one who is most extreme, dramatic, or vocal.

Common to revolutionaries has been a strong commitment to human welfare together with the relentless pursuit of some basic social transformation reflecting that commitment. Lincoln was characterized by both. His conception of justice and progress was based upon the principle that "each man should do precisely as he pleases with all which is exclusively his own,"—in other words upon the basic principles of the free labor-free enterprise system.[6] And judging from Lincoln's limited conception of the inalienable rights of the black slave—that is the right to the fruits of his or her own labor—this economic right stood first among all rights.[7] Lincoln's directly related political ideals were well summarized in the Gettysburg address—a nation "conceived in liberty," "the proposition that all men are created equal," and "government of the people, by the people, and for the people." It was when Lincoln spoke on such things, on Right, Liberty, the Declaration of Independence, said William Herndon, that he was carried away with emotion. "Then he extended out his arms . . . as if appealing to some superior power for assistance and support. . . . It was as such moments that he seemed inspired, fresh from the hands of his creator. Lincoln's gray eyes would

---

5. This concept of revolution has been associated especially with William E. B. DuBois and Charles A. and Mary R. Beard, but its more recent formulation as a capitalist revolution may be found in Barrington Moore Jr., *Social Origins of Dictatorship and Democracy: Lord and Peasant in the Making of the Modern World* (Boston, 1966), 3; Margaret Shortreed, "The Antislavery Radicals: From Crusade to Revolution, 1840-1868," *Past and Present*, XVI (Nov. 1959), 65-89; Raimondo Luraghi, "The Civil War and the Modernization of American Society: Social Structure and Industrial Revolution in the Old South Before and During the War," *Civil War History*, XVIII (Sept. 1972), 242; Eric Foner, "The Causes of the American Civil War: Recent Interpretations and New Directions," *Civil War History*, XX (Sept. 1974), 197-214.

6. Speech, Oct. 16, 1854, Roy P. Basler (ed.), *The Collected Works of Abraham Lincoln* (New Brunswick, 1953), II, 265, hereafter cited as *Works*.

7. Speeches, June 26, 1857, and July 17, 1858, *Works*, II, 405, 520.

flash fire when speaking against slavery or spoke volumes of hope and love when speaking of Liberty—justice and the progress of mankind."[8]

I believe that such values were at the heart of Lincoln's political behavior; they formed his motives and defined his goals. His more frequently lauded personal characteristics determined his manner and his method; but behind those always stood a basic commitment to specific social ideals. The goal that arose in defense of those ideals, and which Lincoln would pursue with unflagging determination, was the destruction of slavery in the United States. In pursuit of that goal he displayed all of the ardor of the abolitionists but always tempered by a different motive and approach. Lincoln's primary concern was not the immediate fate of the slave, the sins of the slaveholder, or abstract matters of religion and morality. His general conception embraced the history and the welfare of all mankind, and his immediate concern was the fate of economic freedom and political democracy in the United States. Unlike the abolitionists, Lincoln stood squarely within, a champion rather than a critic of, the free society of the North. He believed in, participated fully in, and finally assumed the leadership of a society that he envisioned as representing "the last, best hope of earth."[9]

Lincoln's assertive idealism was apparent throughout his early career—in his endorsement of women's suffrage in 1836, his reasoned stance against slavery in the Illinois legislature of 1837, his condemnations of President Polk's war, and his antislavery speeches in the presidential campaign of 1848.[10] All of this was indicative but also preliminary.

By the late 1840s Lincoln obviously had become deeply disturbed by the expansionist demands of the slave states, and he was remarkably, even suspiciously, silent about the Compromise of 1850. In his eulogy on Henry Clay in 1852, Lincoln dwelled upon Clay's devotion to human liberty and opposition to slavery, and he directed public attention to the fact that "an increasing number of men . . . for the sake of perpetuating slavery" were "beginning to assail and to ridicule the white man's charter of freedom—the declaration that 'all men are created free and equal.' So far as I have learned," he concluded, "the first American, of any note, to do or attempt this, was the late John C. Calhoun."[11]

The repeal of the Missouri Compromise and the instituting of popular sovereignty under the Kansas-Nebraska act of 1854 meant that slavery might now

8. Quoted in Randall, *Lincoln the Liberal Statesman*, 179.
9. Second Annual Message to Congress, Dec. 1, 1862, *Works*, V, 537.
10. *Works*, 1, 48, 74-75, 420-22, 431-42, 446-48, 450-52, 501-16.
11. July 6, 1852, *Works*, II, 130.

expand into territory where it had hitherto been banned. For Lincoln, as for many Americans, this was clear proof of the expansive threat of slavery; it crystalized his position and impelled him toward an alliance with those forces that soon formed the Republican party. Initially Lincoln focused upon a possible restoration of the Missouri Compromise, but by 1856 he was a Republican. The basic position of that party was an insistence upon the federal prohibition of any further expansion of slavery. In 1857, the Dred Scott decision by the Supreme Court of the United States declared, in effect, that this position of the Republican party was unconstitutional. In 1860 Lincoln would run for the presidency upon just such a platform.

That sequence of events marked a crucial turning point in the history of the nation, one which, in my estimation, constituted a revolutionary development in national politics. Despite persistent claims to the contrary, Lincoln and his party were radically departing from the principles and practices that had governed the nation since the American revolution. Notwithstanding the Northwest Ordinance of 1787, it can hardly be said that a prohibition against the further expansion of slavery had been national policy since that time. Lincoln appears correct in his insistence that the majority of the founding fathers were ashamed of slavery, hoped for its eventual disappearance, and accepted federal restrictions on its expansion; but he could not well claim to speak for them when he *stressed* that the Declaration of Independence applied to blacks, or when he equated their hope for the disappearance of slavery with his own insistence upon an absolute prohibition of its expansion.[12]

To the contrary, the American Revolution had been followed by a compromise that allowed the spread of both the slave labor system and the free labor system. For the sake of obtaining a national Union, the founding fathers had catered to slavery, discussing it with incredible daintiness and allowing its growth and spread. During succeeding decades, the slave states remained powerful in the national government, the slave population increased eightfold, and a remarkable expansion of slavery occurred. Kentucky, Tennessee, Alabama, Mississippi, Missouri, Louisiana, and Arkansas were admitted to the Union as slave states, and the Missouri Compromise of 1820 explicitly endorsed the spread of slavery into part of the Louisiana territory. It was precisely this tradition of successful expansion that so disturbed Lincoln and the Republicans and led them to risk the Union itself by abandoning the original compromise. Initially the principles of freedom had been sacrificed for the sake of Union; now the Union itself was

12. Speech. Feb. 27, 1860, *Works*, III, 522-35.

to be risked for the sake of curtailing the growing power of slavery.[13] The determination to accept that risk rested, of course, upon the even more successful expansion and maturation of the free labor capitalism of the North.

That slavery violated the rights of the enslaved was of secondary concern to Lincoln and something he had learned to live with. What was of primary concern was his steadily developing conviction that the expansionist demands of slavery were threatening to destroy the prosperity and ideals of the nation. This he would not accept. The expansion of slavery was depriving free citizens of a place "to go to and better their condition" and was encouraging Americans to "'cancel and tear to pieces' even the white man's charter of freedom." Already the liberal world is warning us, noted Lincoln in 1854, "that the one retrograde institution in America is undermining the principles of progress, and fatally violating the noblest political system the world ever saw." Slavery was "the great Behemoth of danger." "Our republican robe is soiled, and trailed in the dust," he lamented. "Let us repurify it. Let us turn and wash it white, in the spirit, if not the blood, of the Revolution. . . . If we do this, we shall not only have saved the Union; but we shall have so saved it, as to make, and to keep it, forever worthy of the saving."[14]

One year later, still a Whig, Lincoln complained in a private letter that thirty-six years of experience had demonstrated "that there is no peaceful extinction of slavery in prospect for us. The signal failure of Henry Clay, and other good and great men . . . together with a thousand other signs, extinguishes that hope utterly. . . . That spirit which desired the peaceful extinction of slavery, has itself become exstinct, with the *occasion,* and the *men* of the Revolution. . . . So far as peaceful, voluntary emancipation is concerned, the condition of the negro slave in America . . . is now as fixed, and hopeless of change for the better, as that of the lost souls of the finally impenitent." "Our political problem now is," he concluded, "Can we, as a nation, continue together *permanently—forever—*half slave, and half free? The problem is too mighty for me."[15]

Of course Lincoln soon concluded that we could not continue—*forever—*half slave and half free because the demands of slavery were eroding the spirit of freedom and threatening to make the entire nation slave. What was at stake was not

---

13. For the question of slavery in our early political history see Staughton Lind, *Class Conflict, Slavery and the United States Constitution* (Indianapolis, 1967); Donald L. Robinson, *Slavery and the Structure of American Politics* (New York, 1971); Duncan J. MacLeod, *Slavery, Race and the American Revolution* (London, 1974).

14. Speech, Oct. 16, 1854, *Works,* II, 268, 270, 276.

15. Lincoln to George Robertson, Aug. 15, 1855, *Works,* II, 317-18.

the fate of the southern slave, nor the danger of secession, but the fundamental economic and social structure of the United States. Two social systems were engaged in a struggle for dominance, and one or the other must triumph. The nation could not continue so divided; it must become all one thing or the other. "Welcome, or unwelcome, agreeable, or disagreeable," Lincoln concluded, "whether this shall be an entire slave nation, is the issue before us."[16] In determining that imperative choice, Lincoln became the prototype and the champion of the free labor system and its principles of competitive equality and freedom. "What is it that we hold most dear amongst us? Our own liberty and prosperity. What has ever threatened our liberty and prosperity save and except this institution of Slavery?"[17] In resisting the threat of slavery, the Declaration of Independence epitomized basic hopes and ideals for all of mankind. It stood, thought Lincoln, as "a standard maxim for free society, which should be familiar to all, and revered by all; constantly looked to, constantly labored for, and even though never perfectly attained, constantly spreading and deepening its influence, and augmenting the happiness and value of life to all people of all colors everywhere."[18]

As Lincoln thus sought national redemption in the principles of antislavery, he insisted that he was seeking a return to the past, and in one very real, but also very limited sense, this was true. It was true in the sense of the antislavery hope, perhaps even intent, of the revolutionary generation. But that traditional antislavery hope was now generating a drastic change away from the programmatic position of all major political parties in the past. The most recent effort to deal with growing sectional discord along traditional lines had been achieved by the Compromise of 1850 and the ill-defined principles of popular sovereignty. That effort had been supported by Lincoln's own Whig party and his declared mentor Henry Clay, and despite the calamitous impact of the Kansas-Nebraska Act, it was still being championed by Stephen A. Douglas as a moderate approach to sectional discord that promised to achieve the ultimate triumph of the free labor system in the only peaceful way possible. That policy certainly did keep slavery out of Kansas, where in 1858 a decisive 85 per cent of the population voted against a proslavery constitution after four years of troubled popular sovereignty. Nevertheless Lincoln, unfairly depicting Douglas as part of a proslavery conspiracy, led the fight against him and popular sovereignty. When the antislavery implications of

16. Speech, May 18, 1858, *Works*, II, 453.
17. Speech, Oct. 15, 1858, *Works*, III, 313.
18. Speech, June 26, 1857, *Works*, II, 406.

Douglas's position began to attract some Republican support, Lincoln steadfastly opposed cooperation with him as something that would destroy the Republican party and turn it into "the tail of Douglas' new kite."[19]

Lincoln and his party proceeded instead to mobilize voters on a moral issue and a sectional base. For the first time in the history of the United States, a political party was to rise to dominance that denounced and indirectly sought to destroy the basic social structure of one major section of the nation while drawing all of its own leadership and all of its votes from the other. It was a sophism to say to the South, as Lincoln did, "the fact that we get no votes in your section, is a fact of your making, and not of ours."[20]

In Lincoln's view "the chief object" of the Republican party was "to prevent the *spread* and *Nationalization*, of Slavery."[21] According to one reporter, Lincoln presented the "underlying principle" of the party as "hatred to the institution of Slavery; hatred to it in all its aspects, moral, social, and political."[22] That moral stance could not be surrendered because "whenever the sentiment, that slavery is wrong, shall give way in the North, all legal prohibitions of it will also give way."[23] "We want, and must have," he insisted, "a national policy, as to slavery, which deals with it as being a wrong." That necessary policy was endangered by "dark and mysterious" doings that were underway to fasten slavery upon the territories and eventually upon all of the free states as well. "To meet and overthrow the power of that [proslave] dynasty, is the work now before all those who would prevent that consummation," he proclaimed in 1858. "That is *what* we have to do." The agitation "*will* not cease, until a *crisis* shall have been reached, and passed." The goal must be to "arrest the further spread of" slavery, "and place it where the public mind shall rest in the belief that it is in the course of ultimate extinction. . . ."[24] Admittedly this was about as conservative a means of destruction as one might envision, but it was destruction nonetheless.

It is not difficult to understand why the South saw in all of this a revolutionary threat. Among Northerners, Stephen A. Douglas perceived the danger well. This new doctrine preached by Lincoln and his party, Douglas warned, was arraying "all the Northern States in one body against the South," was demanding

19. Lincoln to Lyman Trumbull, Dec. 11, 1858, *Works*, III, 345.
20. Speech, Feb. 27, 1860, *Works*, III, 536.
21. Speech, Sept. 16, 17, 1859, *Works*, III, 429.
22. Speech, Oct. 1, 1859, *Works*, III, 482.
23. Speech, Sept. 16, 17, 1858, *Works*, III, 430.
24. Ibid., 435; Speech, June 16, 1858, *Works*, II, 461, 465, 467.

a centralized uniformity of institutions, and was threatening to bring about a disruption of the Union and sectional war.[25]

To recognize the portentuous, even revolutionary, nature of such developments and attitudes is not to say that Lincoln was an extremist, or that he anticipated war. As is often noted, he was such a close-mouthed man that we never will know his expectations, and his concept of change undoubtedly was bounded by his faith in the economic and political characteristics of the society of which he was so much a part. Lincoln rejected the self-righteousness and the political irrelevance of the abolitionists because he believed in the method and the promise of the established political system. He looked to logical persuasion, practical politics, and gradual, peaceful progress.

In his own terms, however, Lincoln displayed as firm a commitment to ideals as the abolitionists themselves. Respecting the wrong and the expansion of slavery he was basically neither moderate, pragmatic, or flexible. His was a hard, even rigid, stance based upon predetermined concepts of social and moral necessity. Extremism in behalf of such concepts was wicked only so long as the political process continued to function properly, and particularly because in such circumstances extremism and violence were positively harmful to the antislavery cause.[26] When the courts or the congresses perverted the imperative antislavery end, Lincoln would appeal to "the people" as "the rightful masters of both congresses and courts. . . ." And when he stood by the Constitution, it was because he had determined that the Constitution itself corresponded to the fundamental first principles of liberty and popular sovereignty. To say as did James G. Randall that Lincoln "believed in evolutionary democratic progress" is hardly the whole truth. He may have hoped for and believed in the promise of peaceful, evolutionary progress, but he believed even more strongly in other fundamentals that he would soon use to justify both revolution and war.

It does not denigrate Lincoln's temperate qualities to note that they were assisted during this crisis by the sectional circumstances as well as the political system involved. Insofar as northern Republicanism was a revolutionary movement, it was one with a uniquely external enemy, and Lincoln enjoyed the advantage of laboring not within, but without, the society he was attacking. What appeared dangerous and revolutionary in the South was reasonable and moderate in the North. Lincoln was defending rather than attacking the dominant ideals

---

25. Speech, Aug. 21, 1858, *Works*, III, 12.
26. Stephen B. Oates, *With Malice Toward None: The Life of Abraham Lincoln* (NewYork, 1977), 123.

of his own society and, therefore, was not subject to the provocative suppression that revolutionaries in a different situation invariably have to contend with. In terms of the dominant values of the free labor North, perhaps Lincoln was not a revolutionary at all. It was in terms of the total national condition and the South that he was. It is precisely this distinction that is the root of a paradox that would continue to haunt the entire revolutionary thrust of the Republican party.

We must also recognize that the very success of Lincoln's reasonable practicality created an ominous contradiction. Such success ultimately undermined moderation by creating a far more serious threat to slavery than abolitionism had ever been. The preliminary triumph of a peaceful movement for fundamental social change often creates a social crisis culminating in violence. In such circumstances, it is a counter revolution by vested interests against the threat of change that initiates a violent revolutionary response and counter revolution came to Republicans in the form of secession. Contrary to Lincoln's hopes, reasonable and practical politics did not mean peaceful progress; they meant secession and war. One may even suggest that the moderate policies of Lincoln were a more significant contribution to the coming of that war than the fanaticism of even abolitionism or of old John Brown.

As the final crisis approached, Lincoln's insistent calls for peace and restraint suggested nothing so much as a full awareness of the risk involved. And yet, he continued to reject any middle ground. "Let us stand by our duty, fearlessly and effectively," he urged in his celebrated Cooper Union speech of February 1860. "Let us be diverted by none of those sophistical contrivances ... such as groping for some middle ground between the right and the wrong, vain as the search for a man who should be neither a living man nor a dead man ... [or] such as Union appeals beseeching true Union men to yield to Disunionists, reversing the divine rule, and calling, not the sinners, but the righteous to repentance...."

"Neither let us be slandered from our duty by false accusations against us, nor frightened from it by menaces of destruction to the Government nor of dungeons to ourselves. LET US HAVE FAITH THAT RIGHT MAKES MIGHT, AND IN THAT FAITH, LET US, TO THE END, DARE TO DO OUR DUTY AS WE UNDERSTAND IT."[27] These were hardly words of temperateness and care.

Lincoln ran for the presidency that year upon a platform the key plank of which, he admitted, "in a sort of way" had been declared unconstitutional by the national Supreme Court.[28] To Southerners this hardly displayed reverence

---

27. Speech, Feb. 27, 1860, *Works*, III, 550.
28. Ibid., 543.

for the law so much as a deliberate flouting of the constitution itself. That fall Lincoln was elected by a totally sectional vote, and as President-elect it was he who defined the Republican stand during the secession crisis of 1860-61.

As David Potter has shown, Lincoln's position during that crisis killed any possibility of compromise on the vital issue of slavery extension. "Let there be no compromise on the question of *extending* slavery," he instructed Republican congressmen. "There is no possible compromise upon it, but which puts us under again, and leaves all our work to do over again. . . . On that point hold firm, as with a chain of steel." "The tug has to come & better now than later."[29]

In taking this stand Lincoln was, of course, remaining true to his campaign platform; but he also was showing no disposition to subject national policy to popular will at a moment of dire crisis. Although Lincoln clearly had obtained a constitutional majority of the electoral college, his popular vote was not only totally sectional, it was a decided minority of the American people. What was at issue was not his claim to the presidency, but a matter of national policy wherein Lincoln's position apparently had been rejected by popular vote. Lincoln had received fewer than two million votes, his opponents almost three million. None of those opponents had favored a ban on the expansion of slavery. Even in the states that remained loyal to the Union, Lincoln's vote had been a minority, and even some Republicans had voted for such other things as the tariff and the homestead rather than against slavery expansion. Finally, there is much evidence to suggest that a large majority of the American people would have endorsed the most promising hope of compromise, the Crittenden proposals, which Lincoln firmly opposed.[30]

It may be doubted that any such compromise would have succeeded or would have altered the outcome, but Lincoln had helped destroy that possibility as the leader of a partisan minority, not a representative of the popular will. David Potter attributed Lincoln's role in this instance to a gross underestimation of the danger of secession and an abiding faith in the good sense and unionism of the white South. But such naivete hardly accords with Lincoln's reputed wisdom, nor does it accord with the concern he expressed at Cooper Union that *"the southern people will not so much as listen to us."*[31] Perhaps more fundamental to

---

29. David Potter, *Lincoln and His Party in the Secession Crisis* (New Haven, 1942), especially chaps. 6-8; Lincoln to Lyman Trumbull, Dec. 10, 1860, to William Kellogg, Dec. 11, 1880, and to Elihu B. Washburne, Dec. 13, 1860, all in *Works*, IV, 149-51.

30. David Potter, *Lincoln and His Party in the Secession Crisis*, 188-200.

31. Ibid., 246-47; Speech, Feb. 27, 1860, *Works*, III, 547. What will appease the South, asked Lincoln in this speech? "This and only this: cease to call slavery wrong, and join them in calling it right. And this must be done thoroughly—done in acts as well as in words."

Lincoln's rigidity was the fact that it was perceived as tactically advantageous to the antislavery cause and that it was consistent with his emphasis over the past several years—consistent with his faith in the political process and with his belief in the necessity for both moral firmness and a national antislavery policy.

Unlike William H. Seward and other conservatives, Lincoln apparently was not convinced that time was so much on the side of the free labor system that it was permissible to compromise. Rather he feared that under existing circumstances compromise constituted appeasement and would seriously weaken the government and the antislavery cause, whereas to stand firm promised to succeed and to discredit the slave power. Lincoln would "suffer death" before he would endorse "buying the privilege of taking possession of this government to which we have a constitutional right. . . ." "If we surrender," he advised Republicans, "it is the end of us, and of the government. They will repeat the experiment upon us ad libitum." Now was the time to hold firm because the interests of slavery could "never have a more shallow pretext for breaking up the government, or extorting a compromise than now." In other words compromise should be rejected on principle and it could be refused because an extremist secessionist response would discredit slavery and expand the base of Republican support. Lincoln conceded the right "of the people" to promote compromise, but he would not lead on that route.[32]

Rather than accept the portent of Lincoln's victory, the South moved to dissolve the Union and go its own way. In so doing it would only accelerate the coming of precisely those revolutionary developments it feared. Lincoln, who had refused to compromise on slavery, refused to accept the disruption of the Union and turned to war. The man who preached reason and peace now grasped the sword.

The impact of the war that resulted was revolutionary, and it was Lincoln who guided that revolution. He led the way to total war and unconditional victory, he thereby established the permanence and supremacy of the nation over the state, and he effectively achieved the destruction of slavery and the total triumph of the free labor system. In attaining those results, Lincoln displayed not only kindness, moderation, and care, but also determination, vigor, and steel. He responded to the initial crisis with such arbitrary promptness that critics soon "cried out against his dictatorship." "For four years he prosecuted the war vigorously, careless of constitutional restraint," bending the law as mercy or the necessities of

---

32. Lincoln to James T. Hale, Jan. 11, 1861, and Remarks, Jan., 10-21, 1861, *Works*, IV, 172, 175-76.

war might demand.³³ He cultivated support for his policies with great energy and skill. Kenneth Stampp is right; when it came to the fundamentals of success, "the radical leaders, rather than Lincoln proved to be the sentimental idealists ... while Lincoln ... was not only the hard headed realist but the most skillful politician of them all."³⁴ It was he who promoted determined and total war. It was he who bypassed the constitutional restraints facing Congress to expropriate billions of dollars in slave property with neither compensation nor due process. It was he who brought former black slaves to fight and kill Confederate whites. It was he who insisted that the Thirteenth Amendment be added to the Union party platform of 1864, and it was his quiet pressure that accomplished its adoption by Congress, early in 1865. Not many weeks later the Confederacy collapsed. The ordeal had ended.

The manner in which all of this occurred was admittedly at variance with Lincoln's humanism and desires. He had hoped that the end could be achieved in a peaceful and orderly fashion, reflecting the merits of the system and the good sense of the American people. But that did not occur. He and all were swept up by those forces he had been so instrumental in creating. When events moved toward a dire resolution, Lincoln stood like steel by the ideology of democracy and free labor capitalism to direct a violent war which overthrew slavery and vitally altered the nation. In so doing he catered to necessity while striving always to lead in a manner which was moderate, reasonable, and considerate of all parties involved. His true greatness was not that he had such admirable personal qualities, but that he so successfully applied them in a revolutionary crisis. However, reluctantly and unconsciously he did so, Abraham Lincoln had served as a most successful promoter and leader of internal revolution in the United States.

33. David Donald, "Abraham Lincoln: Whig in the White House," in Graebner (ed.), *The Enduring Lincoln*, 48–51; Dwight L. Dumond, "Virtually an Abolitionist," in Fehrenbacher (ed.), *The Leadership of Abraham Lincoln*, 128.

34. Kenneth Stampp, *The Era of Reconstruction, 1865–1877* (New York, 1965), 49.

Lincoln and Van Buren in the Steps of the Fathers

Another Look at the Lyceum Address

MAJOR L. WILSON

On January 27, 1838, Abraham Lincoln delivered an address to the Young Men's Lyceum at Springfield, Illinois, entitled "The Perpetuation of Our Political Institutions." Less than a year earlier, on March 4, 1837, President Martin Van Buren dealt with the same matter in his Inaugural Address. Both expressed concerns widely shared at the time and the ambiguous nature of these concerns: they proudly claimed success for the "republican experiment" begun by the fathers, yet warned that it might fail if the present age proved false. "It impresses on my mind a firm belief," the president observed, "that the perpetuation of our institutions depends upon ourselves."[1] To the sons had fallen the solemn duty of preserving the work of the founding fathers.

While both expressed a common concern for preserving the republic, Lincoln and Van Buren differed in their assessment of the specific dangers facing it. One was the widespread incidence of mob action. Deploring "the increasing disregard for law which pervades the country," Lincoln feared the long-run effect of the "mobocratic spirit" would be to erode "the attachment of the People" and destroy

---

1. Roy P. Basler, ed., *The Collected Works of Abraham Lincoln*, 9 vols. (New Brunswick: Rutgers Univ. Press, 1953), 1:108-15; James D. Richardson, *A Compilation of the Messages and Papers of the Presidents*, 20 vols. (New York: Bureau of National Literature, 1897), 4:1530-37, 1532; Rush Welter, *The Mind of America, 1820-1860* (New York: Columbia Univ. Press, 1975), 276-93.

Civil War History, Vol. XXIX No. 3 © 1983 by The Kent State University Press

the basis of self government. "Let reverence for the laws," he urged, "become the political religion of the nation." Van Buren likewise saw how the "ardor of public sentiment" often outran "the regular progress of the judicial tribunals." By wounding "the majesty of the law," moreover, mob action might eventually provide the occasion "for abridging the liberties of the people." On balance, however, Van Buren was far less concerned about mob violence than Lincoln. Reaffirming at this point a Jeffersonian trust in the "generous patriotism" and "sound common sense" of the people, he believed they would soon return to the "landmarks of social order."[2] On two other dangers to the republic the differences were much clearer and sharper. Lincoln devoted only two sentences to the rising voice of abolitionist agitation and expressed no personal opinion on the matter. In a lengthy passage, by contrast, Van Buren condemned abolitionism as the greatest threat to the republic. Regarding the menace of Caesarism Van Buren made no explicit references at all, whereas Lincoln placed central emphasis on it in his address.

The Lyceum Address has been the subject of a considerable number of studies. Done mainly from the perspective of later events—mounting sectional controversy and the Civil War—these studies impute to the young Lincoln prophetic powers of one sort or another. Some argue that he was very ambitious and that he identified with the Caesarian figure he predicted would arise. Other studies see Lincoln as a prophet of "political religion." During the controversy over the expansion of slavery in the 1850s he accordingly held up the principle of equality to judge and redeem a divided nation; after war began he invoked divine providence in behalf of a new birth of freedom.

Relatively little attention, on the other hand, has been given to Van Buren's views and none to a comparison of them with the views of Lincoln. In taking up the matter this essay focuses particularly on the political context of the 1830s, at a time when the system of two-party competition was approaching maturity. If a prophet of some sort, the young Lincoln was also a Whig politician. As a Whig, moreover, his views on the perpetuation of republican institutions surely gained greater clarity and force in dialectical contrast with the party ideology of Democrats. And no other Democrat had contributed more to the organization of his party and its ideological identification than President Van Buren. A closer look at his views will throw further light on the Lyceum Address and, in reciprocal fashion, lend added credence to the anxiety each expressed for the

---

2. Basler, *Works of Lincoln*, 1:109, 111, 112; Richardson, *Messages*, 4:1533.

disorders of the day. The perpetuation of republican institutions was a theme which easily lent itself to political cant and ritual; yet for Lincoln and Van Buren it was a matter of genuine concern.

Underlying the differences between them over the specific dangers facing the republic in the 1830s was a basic difference in attitude toward the fathers. Throughout his Inaugural Address Van Buren invoked the filiopieties of the day and expressed them most dramatically in a striking image he cast of himself as a lesser figure of a later age. Here he pictured himself contentedly treading "in the footsteps of illustrious men, whose superiors it is our happiness to believe are not found on the executive calendar of any country." As "the earliest and firmest pillars of the Republic," the fathers were men of heroic stature who declared independence for the nation, won it on the battlefield, and established "inestimable institutions" for ordering republican freedom. In the ongoing life of the nation it remained only for the sons "sacredly to uphold those political institutions." The age of heroes, of destroyers and creators, was over; the task remaining for their successors was one of preservation. Nor was the role of preserver either ignoble or unrewarding. If a retrospect of the nation was "gratifying" to the patriot, there was a "deeper delight" in contemplating the happiness of a "thousand generations" to come.[3]

Rhetorically, Van Buren had sought for years to assimilate Andrew Jackson to the "illustrious predecessors" of the revolutionary generation. As a military hero, in this view, Jackson regained independence for the nation at the Battle of New Orleans. In the political forum Jackson was seen as a Tribune of the people and not, as Whigs charged, a Caesar. The enhanced power he claimed for the presidency as a "direct representative" of the people was not used to subvert the balances of the Constitution: it was rather used to destroy the national bank, among other enemies of the people, in order to restore the government to its simple republican tack. In this same spirit Van Buren often invoked the judgment of Thomas Jefferson that Jackson was the last of the Romans.

In personal terms Van Buren professed to see his relationship to Jackson as that of a dutiful son. Two earlier statements, made before he became president, defined this relationship and clearly anticipated the self-effacing image he struck in the Inaugural Address. Because the phrasing of these statements soon echoed in Lincoln's Lyceum Address, they are cited here in full. On the eve of being nominated to run for vice president with Jackson in 1832, he protested that

---

3. Richardson, *Messages*, 4:1530, 1531, 1536.

his ambition had already been realized under Jackson as secretary of state and minister to England: "To have served under such a chief, at such a time, and to have won his confidence and esteem, is a sufficient glory; and of that, thank God, my enemies cannot deprive me!" In the same vein was a public letter accepting the nomination of his party to run for president in 1836 as Jackson's successor:

> I content myself, on this occasion, with saying, that I consider myself the honored instrument, selected by the friends of the present administration, to carry out its principles and policy; and that, as well from inclination as from duty, I shall, if honored with the choice of the American people, endeavor to tread generally in the footsteps of President Jackson—happy, if I shall be able to perfect the work which he has so gloriously begun.[4]

Lincoln presented a notable contrast. Sentiments of filiopiety, it is true, can be found throughout the Lyceum Address. Out of "gratitude" for the fathers and a sense of "duty to posterity," he observed, it remained only for the sons to preserve the "political edifice of liberty and equal rights." And reverence for the name of George Washington made the obligation a "sacred" one. Three features of the address, however, set it apart from the conventional piety Van Buren invoked. First of all, Lincoln did not deem the revolutionary fathers as virtuous as the president professed to see them. Far from being disinterested patriots concerned only with the larger good, they were also ambitious men moved by a "ruling passion" for distinction and fame. Nor were the mass of the people at the time particularly intelligent and virtuous. Excited rather by feelings of hatred and revenge against the British, they illustrated how "the force of circumstances" in a revolutionary situation allowed the passions of the people, "the basest principles of our nature," to work in behalf of a noble cause.[5]

Secondly, Lincoln doubted the sons would be as self-effacing as Van Buren prescribed. He did recognize the need for such a posture, to be sure, and closed his address with the thought that the preservation of the temple of liberty required new pillars "hewn from the solid quarry of sober reason." Passion had contributed to the erection of the temple, but now it could only be sustained by "cold, calculated, unimpassioned reason." Yet his entire address assumed that passion was a stronger element than reason and that it was unrealistic to expect

---

4. *Albany Argus*, April 9, 1832; *Washington Globe*, June 12, 1835.
5. Basler, *Works of Lincoln*, 1:108, 113, 114.

of the sons a virtue superior to that of the fathers. With regard to the leadership class Lincoln was totally explicit, outlining at this point his warning against Caesarism. It went against all lessons of history, he argued, to suppose that new men of "ambition and talents" would not arise among the sons with the same "ruling passion" for fame the fathers displayed. Many men in each generation might be contented with "a seat in Congress, a gubernatorial or a presidential chair," but, he added with great emphasis, "such belong not to the family of the lion, or the tribe of the eagle." No new Alexander, Caesar, or Napoleon would be able to gratify his ambition merely by "supporting and maintaining an edifice that has been erected by others."[6]

The third feature of Lincoln's address is the most striking. The crucial sentences in his fuller description of the Caesarian danger echo the very phrases Van Buren had used to define the unheroic role of preserver. "Towering genius," Lincoln thus proceeded,

> disdains a beaten path. It seeks regions hitherto unexplored. It sees no distinction in adding story to story, upon the monuments of fame erected to the memory of others. It denies that it is glory enough to serve under any chief. It scorns to tread in the footsteps of any predecessor, however illustrious. It thirsts and burns for distinction; and, if possible, it will have it, whether at the expense of emancipating slaves or enslaving freemen.[7]

As a dutiful son, Van Buren wanted his and succeeding generations to tread contentedly in the footsteps of illustrious predecessors. With many of the same phrases Lincoln looked rather to the advent of a newborn Caesar.

Lincoln's phrasing of the Caesarian danger, with its echoes of Van Buren, has been totally overlooked in the studies of the Lyceum Address. Between the roles of Caesar and dutiful son, however, lies a world of difference which calls for reexamination. Read in one way, the phrasing of the address gives added support to the view that Lincoln harbored Caesarian ambitions of his own. The image of a weak and unheroic Van Buren, happy to follow the steps of others, thus provided a sharp and dramatic contrast. Seen another way, Van Buren's statements can be dismissed as the utterances of a shameless sychophant of Jackson; and Lincoln's mocking use of them, which assumed any danger of Caesarism

---

6. Ibid., 115, 113, 114.
7. Ibid., 114.

had passed with Jackson, served the political purpose of a young Whig heaping contempt on the Democratic president. A third reading, one which takes the rhetoric of both more seriously, invites a fuller analysis of their concerns for the republic within the context of competing party ideologies. Each of these will now be considered.

One reading of the Lyceum Address has taken the Caesarian warning primarily as an expression of Lincoln's own ambitions. More than two decades ago Edmund Wilson threw out the provocative suggestion that the young Lincoln was very ambitious and that he projected himself into the role of Caesar against which he warned his Springfield audience.[8] Had Wilson been aware of the way Lincoln echoed Van Buren's phrases, he might have stated his position even more strongly. Rhetorically, the unheroic virtues Van Buren ascribed to the dutiful son constituted a dramatic foil for Lincoln's own "ruling passing" for fame. Van Buren was apparently satisfied to serve in turn as senator, governor, and president—to occupy, in Lincoln's terms, "a seat in Congress, a gubernatorial or a presidential chair" in the house the fathers built. But if these positions in government satisfied a sly fox, they clearly could not gratify the towering passions of a lion or an eagle! The contrast of a contemptible Van Buren, in short, served to underscore the Caesarian dimensions of Lincoln's own ambition.

Two recent studies, done in the mode of psychohistory, have built upon Wilson's suggestion; and both could have been strengthened by notice of the Van Buren connection. George B. Forgie has worked out a Freudian interpretation. In this view the young Lincoln loved the fathers, but, because they had preempted him, he also hated them. Only once in the life of a republic, at its founding, was there normally any scope for heroic action. By the 1850s Lincoln resolved the conflicting claims of filiopiety and ambition unconsciously by projecting onto an "evil son," Stephen A. Douglas, a Caesarian design to undermine the work of the fathers. Foiling the efforts of the evil brother would enable a good son to share in the fathers' glory. With the formula of a "house divided," Forgie thus argued, Lincoln defined conflict with Douglas, whose doctrine of popular sovereignty was made to appear an indirect but very real means for extending slavery into new territories and ultimately into the entire Union. By an electoral victory over Douglas on a free-soil platform, Lincoln supposed he could abort the design for "enslaving freemen" and restore the Union to the principle of the fathers. His

---

8. Edmund Wilson, *Patriotic Gore: Studies in the Literature of the American Civil War* (New York: Oxford Univ. Press, 1962), 99–130.

victory led instead to secession and a war for "emancipating slaves"—and the sons from the thralldom of the fathers.[9]

The desire to triumph over Death was, according to Dwight G. Anderson, Lincoln's basic motivation. From the perspective of later events Anderson found in the Lyceum Address "two Lincolns"—a dutiful son and a Caesarian destroyer—both driven by the passion for immortality. The first Lincoln, nurtured on the pieties of Parson Weems, sought glory in preserving the work of the fathers. As a Whig congressman in the late 1840s he accordingly tried with his "spot resolutions" to counter the Caesarian designs President James K. Polk presumably had on Mexico. When this effort brought spectacular failure rather than immortal fame, the second Lincoln emerged in the 1850s bent on destruction. With the formula of the house divided he escalated sectional controversy and enhanced his own chances for the presidency. With the outbreak of war he then proceeded to rebuild the house of the fathers and to claim, as a new sanction for it, the blessings of the Father in Heaven. With such divine endorsement the nation Lincoln consolidated easily embraced the role of lawgiver to the world and, by the end of the century, set itself upon an imperial mission far exceeding the grandest visions of Manifest Destiny held by President Polk.[10]

Any brief summary cannot do justice to these two works—brilliant in conception, sophisticated in argument, rich in new insights about Lincoln and his times. But a number of general criticisms tend, in the view of the present essay, to render the Caesarian interpretation less than convincing. For one thing, it shares with the "needless war" school of Civil War causation the questionable assumption that the issue of slavery expansion was without substance, and that responsibility for the course of events lay with a "blundering generation" of politicians. To Lincoln, in this case, was thus ascribed a truly extraordinary power of manipulating complex events to his own ends. These works also exhibit the perils of any psychohistorical approach. If enormous problems arise in dealing with a living person "on the couch," the difficulties are compounded

---

9. George B. Forgie, *Patricide in the House Divided: A Psychological Interpretation of Lincoln and His Age* (New York: W. W. Norton, 1979).

10. Dwight G. Anderson, *Abraham Lincoln: The Quest for Immortality* (New York: Alfred A. Knopf, 1982). Another work on Lincoln—Charles B. Strozier, *Lincoln's Quest for Union: Public and Private Meanings* (New York: Basic Books, 1982)—skillfully uses a psychohistory approach to illuminate the private life of Lincoln, particularly his less than happy relations with his wife, and to suggest how, after 1854, Lincoln's shift to public concerns found in the "house divided" a metaphor with resonance for articulating these concerns. Little attention, however, is given to the Caesarian theme.

in the case of a historical figure. The temptation becomes almost irresistible to let constructive theory outrun the documentation. Finally, there is a basic question of perspective. From the vantage point of the Civil War, or the turn of the twentieth century, a Caesar is easier to find in the young Lincoln than if one's view is focused on the late 1830s when he spoke to the Lyceum in Springfield.[11]

A second reading of the address, done from the political context of the 1830s, thus tends to discount the Caesarian interpretation. Here, Lincoln's warning, with its echoes of Van Buren, sounds very much like the effusions of a zealous Whig partisan invoking the "standard Whig rhetoric" of the day. Along with their thesis that Jackson was a Caesar, Whig foes had for years been furbishing a public image of Van Buren as a contemptible "politician by trade." With such epithets as "sly fox," the "little magician," a "master spirit," or "Talleyrand" they passed judgment against a political schemer without principles, a member of the "non comittal" tribe who could laugh out of one side of his mouth and cry out of the other. A campaign piece, ghosted under the name of David Crockett, drew out the image most fully.[12]

Meanwhile, the Whig press especially liked to flail Van Buren with his own words; and those with which he defined his relationship to Jackson proved very useful. His protest of a "sufficient glory" serving under "such a chief," along with the vow to tread in the "footsteps" of Jackson, quickly entered the public domain and were made to appear, not as the phrases of a concerned and dutiful son but rather as the flattery of a time server questing for preferment and power. The *National Intelligencer* soon picked up the "glory" and "chief" phrases, combined them with the "footsteps" image and, after Van Buren's inauguration, began to mock his "footsteps administration." Another widely circulated paper, the *Albany Evening Journal*, sounded the same refrain and periodically headed its editorial column with these taunting lines:

VAN BURENISM

---

11. David Brion Davis, "Uncle Oedipus and Ante Bellum," *New York Review of Books*, October 25, 1979, 23–26; George M. Fredrickson, "Lincoln and His Legend," ibid., July 15, 1982, 13–16; Richard O. Curry, "Subconscious Caesarism: A Critique of Recent Scholarly Attempts to Put 'Honest Abe' on the Analyst's Couch," presented at the annual meeting of the Southern Historical Association, Memphis, Tennessee, November 5, 1982, 1–12.

12. Curry, "Subconscious Caesarism," 11; David Crockett, *The Life of Martin Van Buren* (Philadelphia: Robert Wright, 1835).

It is glory enough for me to serve under such a chief. I shall continue to walk in his footsteps.[13]

The lines also echoed widely in congressional debates and the politcal campaigns of the day.

Read in this context, Lincoln's warning loses much of its force. Had the danger of Caesarism been considered real, he might have welcomed Van Buren's prescription of preserver as a perfect antidote. By parroting Van Buren's phrases Lincoln sought instead to ridicule the unheroic president. What kind of leadership was more desirable, Lincoln seemed to ask, the devious ways of a sychophantic fox or the boldness of lions and eagles? As Whigs approached the presidential election of 1840—in which Van Buren was expected to seek reelection—they answered the question by nominating a Caesarian "chieftain" of their own, General William Henry Harrison. In doing so they passed over the claims of Henry Clay, who had contributed more than any other figure to the Whig platform against Caesar. Lincoln enthusiastically welcomed the nomination and assuaged any sense of guilt over the shabby way his "beau ideal" was treated by the reflection that Clay's fame was "already immortal."[14] With their huzzas to Harrison and hoopla for log cabins and cider, moreover, Whig campaigners in 1840 clearly made greater appeal to the "passions" than to the "sober reason" of the people.

A "political" reading of the Lyceum Address, in sum, sees Lincoln as a politician and not a prophet of dire evils to come. His phrasing reflected nothing more than the rhetorical excesses of a young and partisan Whig mocking the Democratic incumbent. But there are problems with such a narrow political interpretation. The Lyceum audience in Springfield was not a political gathering nor the time, January 1838, on the eve of any electoral canvass. Despite the later vagaries of log cabins and cider, many Whig spokesmen did have profound reservations about the regnant principle of popular sovereignty, particularly as it was informed by the 1830s with the spirit of "romantic democracy" and symbolized in the person of Andrew Jackson. A recent study confirms Whig fears that mob action was rising during Jackson's administration; it also suggests a

---

13. *National Intelligencer*, Aug. 13, 1832; June 11, 13. 1835; Nov. 14, 1837; *Albany Evening Journal*, Aug. 9, 18, 1832; May 25, 1835; Aug. 30–Sept. 8, 1837.

14. *Sangamo Journal*, Nov. 3, 1838, cited in William Nisbet Chambers, "The Election of 1840," Arthur M. Schlesinger Jr., ed., *History of American Presidential Elections, 1789-1968*, 4 vols. (New York: Chelsea House, 1971), 1:694; Edwin A. Miles, "The Whig Party and the Menace of Caesar," *Tennessee Historical Quarterly* 27 (1966): 361-79.

relationship between the mobocratic spirit and the popular perception of Jackson as an "anarchic hero" or ultimate expression of the sovereign free individual.[15] Caesarism and the excesses of democracy, in this view, were closely related. In the case of Lincoln, according to another study, the Lyceum Address expressed the outlook of a conservative lawyer and not a politician. As a check on popular passions and towering genius he invoked the power of "procedural community" lodged in the common law tradition and the belief in constitutionalism. Finally, Lincoln tended to downplay the political hoopla of 1840 and to concentrate his campaign efforts mainly on the issue of banking and currency.[16]

A third reading of the Lyceum Address focuses on ideology. If the maturing of the two-party system by the end of the 1830s gave scope for the rhetorical excesses of mere "politicians," it also brought greater coherence to competing party ideologies. Lodged in the rhetoric of political spokesmen were expressions of ultimate concerns—in this case a concern for the perpetuation of the republic. A closer analysis of the views held by the Democratic president will provide a framework for appreciating the outlook of the young Whig from Illinois.

Although historians have made little note of the fact, Van Buren gave to his Inaugural Address a distinct rhetorical form, one which enabled him to express in an effective way his concern for order. Looking back over the half century since the writing of the Constitution, he passed in review the elements of disorder which the fathers themselves had feared might wreck the "republican experiment." On the positive side, he reported, the sons had overcome many of these fears. The people had proved a capacity for self-government by bearing arms and paying taxes to support the government. Greater unity and not dismemberment had come with "the extension of our territory, the multiplication of States, and the increase of population." Collisions had occurred between the central government and the states, but such "vibrations of authority" had in every case been followed by a renewed appreciation for the federative nature of the Union.[17]

Another concern of the fathers, animated by a profound fear of political parties and the disorganizing spirit of faction, had also been overcome. At first, Van

---

15. David Grimstead, "Rioting in Its Jacksonian Setting," *American Historical Review* 77 (1972): 361-97.
16. George M. Fredrickson, "The Search for Order and Community," Cullom Davis, et al., eds. *The Public and the Private Lincoln: Contemporary Perspectives* (Carbondale: Southern Illinois Univ. Press, 1979), 86-98; Gabor S. Boritt, *Lincoln and the Economics of the American Dream* (Memphis: Memphis State Univ. Press, 1978), 63-78.
17. Richardson, *Messages*, 4:1534.

Buren observed, there was a "common sentiment" that only the "great weight" of Washington's character could "bind the discordant materials of our Government" and "save us from the violence of contending factions." But nearly forty years after Washington's death, the president proudly claimed, the republic "still preserves its spirit of free and fearless discussion, blended with unimpaired fraternal feelings." Enhancing the sense of pride in this claim was the fact, left unspoken, that Van Buren himself had contributed a great deal to the organization of the party system which, through its checking and balancing mechanism, provided a valuable means for sustaining political freedom. Also unspoken was the belief that party competition placed limits on personal ambition. The ethos of new party organization stressed the subordination of individual judgment or ambition to the will of the majority collected through party channels. Moreover, regular party contests worked against the force of the mobocratic spirit, for they served at once to excite the "passions" of the people and, by giving vent, to contain them.[18]

In the ambiguous nature of things, however, the president's claim for the success of the fathers' experiment was mingled with an anxious sense that new dangers might yet cause it to fail. To one of these dangers, the incidence of mob action, he devoted a paragraph of his Inaugural Address. But, as noted earlier, he did not deem it a fatal danger. By contrast much more space in the address was given to a second danger, abolitionist agitation, because he saw it as "perhaps the greatest" threat to the republic. As a candidate for president in 1836 Van Buren had taken several steps against it. He encouraged party friends in New York to hold rallies and pass resolutions opposing the abolitionists. As vice president he cast the deciding vote in favor of a bill pushed through the Senate by John C. Calhoun giving postmasters in the South discretionary power to stop the delivery of "incendiary" abolitionist material through the mail. He also helped fashion a compromise formula for dealing with abolitionist petitions addressed to the House. Thereafter called the "gag rule" by its foes, it allowed petitions to be brought into the House chamber but then required that they be laid on the table without further action.

Finally, candidate Van Buren issued a lengthy statement pledging, if elected president, to veto any measure against slavery in the District of Columbia passed without the consent of all the slaveholding states. While not denying a

---

18. Ibid., 1533; James W. Ceaser, *Presidential Selection: Theory and Development* (Princeton: Princeton Univ. Press, 1979), 123–69; Michael Wallace, "Changing Concepts of Party in the United States: New York, 1815–1828," *American Historical Review* 74 (1968): 453–91.

constitutional power in Congress to pass measures against slavery in the District, he professed that his sense of obligation to veto any such measure was as "imperative" as if no power existed at all. Had there been a district at the time the Constitution was written, he claimed, the fathers would have placed an explicit ban on antislavery matters. The spirit and thinking of the fathers in 1787, no less than the letter of the constitutional bond, were to be consulted.[19]

Van Buren repeated the veto pledge in his Inaugural Address, making it in fact the only specific policy issue raised. Critics found in the pledge further evidence that he was a "northern man with southern feelings"; and the charge gained added strength from the fact that he was the first president to use the word "slavery" in an inaugural address. But the president considered himself a northern man with national feelings. Committed to the Union as the indispensable means for the "republican experiment," and therefore as an absolute good, he could only regard abolitionism as a deadly enemy. With "the eyes of statesmen and patriots," he thus argued, the "thoughtful framers of our Constitution" had legislated for the country "as they found it"—diverse in economic interests, divided into distinct sovereignties, and shaped by social habits and institutions "peculiar" to each part. Thus fashioned of plural elements, the Union could only be preserved by "undeviating adherence" to the "sacred instrument" of the Constitution and to "the spirit that actuated the venerated fathers of the Republic."[20] To perpetuate the republic in 1837 meant not only to reaffirm the institutional arrangements of 1787 but also to embrace the opinions of the fathers at the time the arrangements were made.

Van Buren supposed the creed of his party, as taken over from Jefferson, precisely conformed to the plural nature of the Union. From an early day, moreover, he understood how party organization itself, no less than party creed, served as a practicable bond of Union. In the wake of the Missouri controversy he accordingly saw the need for "resuscitating old party feelings" which the "era of good feelings" under President James Monroe had virtually effaced. Without national party competition, he thought, "geographical divisions founded on local interests, or what is worse prejudices between the free and slaveholding states," would inevitably arise. "Party attachments," by contrast, generated "counteracting feelings" which served as a "complete antidote" to the fever of sectionalism. He therefore sought by the end of the 1820s to organize his party on a national basis by reviving what he took to be the old Jeffersonian alliance of "southern

---

19. *Washington Globe*, Mar. 19, 1836.
20. Richardson, *Messages*, 4:1531, 1532, 1535.

planters" and the "plain republicans" of the North. By cutting across sectional lines, party organization thus constituted an institutional bond of Union and gave added security to its plural elements.[21] In this view the monistic impulse of abolitionism clearly violated the essential nature of the Union and, through its politically divisive effect, threatened to dissolve the connecting bands of party.

There was a consistency and a quality of statesmanship in Van Buren's outlook which Whig political rhetoric easily discounted and many historians have overlooked. If a tone of sychophancy sounded in his vow to follow in the steps of others, it also expressed a profound concern for order. While his description of himself as an "honored instrument" of party served to embellish the Whig image of a "politician by trade," it also conveyed his appreciation for party as a new institutional means for securing political order. His strong stand against abolitionism opened him to the political charge of "going South"; yet it ultimately reposed on a plural concept of the Union. Picturing himself a lesser figure of a later age, he wanted his and subsequent generations to assume the same pose. To follow in the steps of illustrious predecessors required loyalty to the institutional arrangements of the fathers and fidelity to their spirit of concession and compromise. In the language of "political religion" he was a priest and not a prophet. Van Buren, in effect, called for a moratorium on change regarding elements he deemed essential to the Union.

Lincoln could not accept a permanent moratorium on change. His emphasis on "procedural community," it was true, did lend itself in some degree to Van Buren's call for following in the fathers' steps. Because the practice of law was Van Buren's chief vocation for a quarter century, he can be regarded as the first lawyer president. His love of the law, moreover, and his appreciation for its British roots tended to place him on the conservative side of his own party, within whose ranks was rapidly swelling the spirit of "romantic democracy." Lincoln's Whiggish sentiment—that veneration for the law become the political religion of the nation—was one with which Van Buren could identify.

But there was another element in the outlook of Whigs profoundly at odds with Van Buren's views. Whigs in far larger numbers than Democrats identified with the evangelical mission to Christianize America and thereby fashion a "moral community" underlying political institutions. For most Whigs a greater degree of moral consensus was desired because it would serve to strengthen the

---

21. Van Buren to Thomas Ritchie, Jan. 13, 1827, cited in Robert V. Remini, *Martin Van Buren and the Making of the Democratic Party* (New York: W. W. Norton, 1970), 130–33.

conservative effects of "procedural community." Since republican government ultimately reposed on the will of the people, the shaping of that will was a matter of utmost importance. There was in the task of creating a broader moral consensus, however, the prospect of change as well as preservation.[22] New values, or older values more widely disseminated, provided a standard with which to judge and improve upon existing arrangements no less than simply to secure them. More fatefully, the national dimension to new consensus, expressing a Whig imperative for unity, potentially threatened Van Buren's view of the Union. His conception of it as a multi-national state was one in which there could never be a uniformity of values. The goal of abolitionism, however radical in formulation, obviously evinced the desire for common national values.

Lincoln was not an abolitionist or, like many other Whigs of the day, formally affiliated with any evangelical religious body. But he did share in a more general way the Whig emphasis on improvement as well as preservation. Indeed, his kind of conservatism, so in contrast to that of Van Buren, held preservation and improvement to be necessarily related. While "bad laws" should be "religiously observed," he believed there was the companion obligation to replace them. That a law was "bad" normally indicated, in a free society, a change in opinion since the law was made and pointed toward some later notion of "good" to which the law should conform.[23] Nor was this a normative judgment only. Realistically, the veneration for law, which Lincoln wanted to become the "political religion" of the nation, ultimately required that the law itself be subject to change and improvement. In this he was only voicing the conventional wisdom of enlightened conservatives since Edmund Burke, namely, that a society without the means of change was without the means of self preservation. Lincoln held, in other terms, that it was not possible, even if desirable, to follow so literally in the steps of the fathers.

It was in these terms that Lincoln's passing reference in the Lyceum Address to the disordering impact of abolitionist agitation can be more clearly understood. Although his reference was brief, compared to the lengthy passage in Van Buren's Inaugural, two facts at the time gave it fuller force. First, much of the mob action by the mid-1830s was directed against abolitionists; secondly, a mob in nearby Alton had lynched an abolitionist editor, Elijah Lovejoy, about two

---

22. The term, "moral community," is found in Fredrickson, "Search for Order and Community," 91; Daniel Walker Howe, *The Political Culture of the American Whigs* (Chicago: Univ. of Chicago Press, 1979).

23. Basler, *Works of Lincoln*, 1:112.

months prior to the Lyceum Address. No mention of the event was made, but it was in the minds of both the speaker and his audience. Lincoln thus proceeded:

> There is no grievance that is a fit object of redress by mob law. In any case that arises, as for instance, the promulgation of abolitionism, one of two positions is necessarily true; that is, the thing is right within itself, and therefore deserves the protection of all law and all good citizens; or, it is wrong, and therefore proper to be prohibited by legal enactments; and in neither case, is the interposition of mob law, either necessary, justifiable, or excusable.[24]

Lincoln at this point withheld any private judgment about what was right and what was wrong in regard to the "promulgation of abolitionism." The significant thing was that he adduced right and wrong as the standard of judgment and deemed the standard a "necessary" one. Without hesitation Van Buren had condemned abolition, not because it was wrong "within itself" but rather because it was totally repugnant to his idea of the Union as an irreducible pluralism of elements. While he would absolutize existing arrangements, Lincoln here appealed to a "higher law." Van Buren's "political religion" would venerate existing law and existing arrangements; Lincoln's involved a standard by which to judge and change. If Van Buren can be seen as a priest of political religion, the position Lincoln defined made room for a prophet.

A number of studies claim to find in the Lyceum Address a foreshadowing of the role Lincoln later played as a prophet of political religion for the nation. By the mid-1850s, according to Harry V. Jaffa, Lincoln articulated the view that the essence of the republic was not to be found in the configuration of arrangements made by the fathers in 1787 but rather in the "central idea" of equality expressed by the Declaration of Independence. It was a transcendent idea which served at once to define the nation and to judge it. When applied to the issue of slavery it supported the position of free soil, which accepted the coexistence of slavery and freedom in the old part of the Union but prescribed only freedom in the new and unsettled part of the Union. Only freedom was "national" and essential; slavery was accidental, temporary, and local.

In this view of things, Jaffa argued, Lincoln saw the doctrine of popular sovereignty, with which Stephen A. Douglas replaced the Missouri Compromise

---

24. Ibid., 113; Leonard L. Richards, *Gentlemen of Property and Standing: Anti-Abolitionist Mobs in Jacksonian America* (New York: Oxford Univ. Press, 1970).

line, as a deadly peril to the republic. By giving to the people in the territory the right to decide the issue, Douglas opened the possibility that slavery might spread into the territory once thought secure for freedom. Morally, the doctrine was totally unacceptable: its "don't care" attitude whether slavery was voted up or down exhibited in naked form the "mobocratic spirit." In an unsettled region, where original perfect freedom of choice obtained, Lincoln did not believe the people had a right to choose wrong. The national idea of equality, he thought, placed a substantive limit on the procedural right of a local majority. The house was divided because Douglas repudiated its essential principle. To reunite the house required, as Lincoln phrased the matter in the 1850s, to "readopt the Declaration of Independence."[25] Following the steps of the fathers meant fidelity to the central idea of the republic.

The Civil War and its train of consequences, in particular the abolition of slavery, saved the edifice of the fathers by rebuilding it. In the perspective of its prior arrangements, which Van Buren wanted to preserve, war transformed a multi-national state into a nation state. The nation, as Lincoln formulated the matter in the Gettysburg Address, experienced a "new birth" of freedom. As president he served as prophet and redeemer, saving the republic by placing it in greater conformity with what he took to be its central idea. A final dimension to his role as prophet was attained in the Second Inaugural; there the results of the war and the sufferings of the whole nation were seen in the perspective of providential judgment. The Almighty, Lincoln averred, had His own purposes. Many studies focus on this point and embellish the view of Lincoln as prophet and theologian for the nation.[26]

It is not the purpose of this essay to assess in any detail the many works dealing with Lincoln and political religion. It is enough to suggest that this interpretation of Lincoln's later career can gain added strength from a new reading of the Lyceum Address in the context of Van Buren's views. His views, so effectively expressed in the "footsteps" metaphor, provided a foil for the young Lincoln

---

25. Harry V. Jaffa, *Crisis of the House Divided: An Interpretation of the Lincoln-Douglas Debates* (Garden City: Doubleday, 1959).

26. Glen C. Thurow, *Abraham Lincoln and American Political Religion* (Albany: State Univ. of New York Press, 1976); Elton Trueblood, *Abraham Lincoln: Theologian of American Anguish* (New York: Harper & Row, 1973); William J. Wolf, *The Almost Chosen People: A Study of the Religion of Abraham Lincoln* (Garden City: Doubleday, 1959); Robert N. Bellah, "Civil Religion in America," *Daedalus* 96 (1967): 1-21; Sidney E. Mead, *The Nation with the Soul of a Church* (New York: Harper & Row, 1975); Russell E. Richey and Donald G. Jones, eds., *American Civil Religion* (New York: Harper & Row, 1974).

which earlier studies have not recognized. To be sure, Van Buren's footsteps image easily lent itself to the uses of "politics," and Lincoln surely enjoyed giving the Democratic president a few rubs. Again, the unheroic model of leadership conveyed in the image was one an ambitious Lincoln condemned, even assuming that his aspirations were less than Caesarian in scope. At the ideological level Van Buren's call to follow in the steps of illustrious predecessors voiced a profound concern for order and essentially prescribed a moratorium on change. With a different and more dynamic outlook, Lincoln simply could not accept as either desirable or possible a tactic for conserving the work of the fathers by following so literally in their steps. Differing ways of perpetuating republican institutions reflected at last profoundly different concepts about the nature of the republic to be saved.

On the Verge of Greatness

Psychological Reflections on Lincoln at the Lyceum

CHARLES B. STROZIER

On a chilly Saturday evening, January 27, 1838, at seven o'clock in Springfield, Illinois, the members of the local Young Men's Lyceum gathered in the Baptist Church at Seventh and Adams Streets, just a block from the new capitol that was under construction in the town's square.[1] Abraham Lincoln, an ardent member of the Lyceum, that evening presented a speech he titled "On the Perpetuation of Our Political Institutions." Just shy of his twenty-eighth birthday, Lincoln chose the opportunity of the speech to reflect broadly on the issues of the day and define his political philosophy. He was by then accustomed to speechmaking, being Whig leader in the state legislature, serving out his third term. He was quite well known for his stand on a strong banking system, had played an instrumental role in moving the capitol to Springfield the previous year, and

---

1. Mark Johnson, of the Illinois Preservation Agency, and Thomas F. Schwartz, Curator of the Lincoln Collection in the Illinois State Historical Library, helped me track down these details, which are based on clues in the *Sangamo Journal*, Paul Angle's *Here I Have Lived: A History of Lincoln's Springfield* (Chicago: Abraham Lincoln's Book Shop, 1935), and a general familiarity with the early history of Springfield. There are no surviving records of these meetings, but the Illinois State Historical Library does have the minutes from the debating society in nearby Petersburg from approximately the same period. One can guess from these minutes the range of topics discussed at the Young Men's Lyceum of Springfield. Note also Donald M. Scott, "The Popular Lecture and the Creation of a Public in Mid-Nineteenth-Century America," *Journal of American History* 66 (1980): 791-809.

was generally bullish, if somewhat naively so, on what were called internal improvements or vast, state-supported projects like building roads and canals. But in none of these early speeches had Lincoln addressed the larger political and ethical meanings of contemporary events, something so characteristic of his later, great speeches, like the House Divided speech in 1858, Cooper Union in 1860, the First Inaugural in 1861, the Gettysburg Address in 1863, and the magnificent parting words of his Second Inaugural of 1865. The speech to the Lyceum is the first in this series of major addresses by Lincoln. For this reason alone, Lincoln's words merit careful attention. The Lyceum speech defines themes that echo throughout Lincoln's life. There he proclaims, perhaps a little grandly, his enduring political values. But there he also, as a young man in some personal crisis, wears his heart on his sleeve and speaks projectively of things outside the self that are in turmoil within.

Perhaps the most important general point to note about Lincoln at the Lyceum is that he chose a speech to express his most profound reflections. It seems to me fairly certain that this mode of creativity derived from his special relationship with his biological mother, Nancy Hanks Lincoln. "God bless my mother," Lincoln told his law partner, William Herndon, in 1850. "All that I am or ever hope to be I owe to her."[2] Though Nancy could only sign a mark for her name, she seemed to have a quality of mind that distinguished her in the frontier settings in which she lived. Lincoln himself, interestingly enough, told his law partner once that his mother was "an intellectual woman, sensitive and somewhat sad."[3] Many of the contemporary observers whom that same law partner, William Herndon, interviewed later also called her "intellectual." For example, Dennis Hanks, Lincoln's illegitimate cousin who lived with the family for about a year before Nancy died in 1818, said: "Lincoln's mother learned him to read the Bible...."[4] All this has influenced people like Carl Sandburg, who would have her reading the Bible to young Abraham—an unlikely though not impossible vision. Many children on the frontier learned to read but not to write. Even some slaves, who

---

2. William H. Herndon and Jesse W. Weik, *Life of Lincoln*, ed. Paul M. Angle (Cleveland: World Publishing, 1930), 2–3. Note also three Herndon letters to Ward Hill Lamon, Feb. 28, 1869, Feb. 25, 1870, and Mar. 6, 1870. The original of these letters are in the Lamon Collection of the Huntington Library, Huntington, California, but they have also been published in Emmanuel Hertz, ed. *The Hidden Lincoln* (New York: Viking Press, 1938), 59, 62–72.

3. Herndon to Jesse Weik, Jan. 19, 1886. The original is in the Herndon/Weik Collection of the Library of Congress, but a published version is available in Hertz, *The Hidden Lincoln*, 139.

4. Dennis F. Hanks statement to William H. Herndon, June 13, 1865. The original is in the Herndon/Weik Collection; see also Hertz, *The Hidden Lincoln*, 276.

almost never learned to write, did learn to read. This quiet, strong woman who had no opportunity to get an education absorbed readily and thoroughly the oral culture of her environment, a culture based much more than today's on the Bible. A smart, receptive person on the frontier could "know" the Bible and still sign with a mark. Nancy must have shared this knowledge with her special son, who in turn was deeply influenced by biblical phrasing, style, and content. He was also, in his style of intellectuality and creativity, much more a listener and speaker than a reader and writer. The Lyceum speech, as well as most of his important and memorable prose, was written to be read aloud.[5]

The speech[6] begins, as is so customary with Lincoln's rhetorical style, by placing us in the context of a continuous historical narrative that has a clear beginning: "In the great journal of things happening under the sun," he says, "we, the American People, find our account running, under date of the nineteenth century of the Christian era." The birth of Christ in this passage begins a historical sequence for Lincoln in a way that parallels the evocation, in another speech, of the signing of the Declaration of Independence: "Four score and seven years ago our fathers brought forth a new nation conceived in liberty. . . ."

Lincoln then moves to a lofty description of the riches and abundance of America. This "fairest portion of the earth," he says, possesses the world's best land, soil, and climate. These are to be treasured, but the country's most important assets are its political institutions, which provide more civil and religious liberty than any other in history. But several potential dangers threaten this national experiment. He dismisses invasion by an outside force from Europe. Shall we expect some "transatlantic military giant," he asks, to "step the Ocean" and "crush us at a blow?" No, never!, Lincoln exclaims. The combined forces of Europe, Asia, and Africa with a Bonaparte at their head could not "take a drink from the Ohio, or make a track on the Blue Ridge, in a trial of a thousand years."

The real danger, on the contrary, is from divisions within the country itself, most of all "the increasing disregard for the law," and what Lincoln calls "the growing disposition to substitute the wild and furious passions" for the "sober judgement of the Courts." In general, the spirit of mob violence often surfaced in Jacksonian America, but what Lincoln here calls the "mobocratic spirit" had been exacerbated by the economic panic of 1837. The event on everyone's mind—

---

5. See Charles B. Strozier, *Lincoln's Quest for Union: Public and Private Meanings* (New York: Basic Books, 1982), 9.

6. All references to the Lyceum speech are to Roy P. Basler, ed., *The Collected Works of Abraham Lincoln*, 8 vols. (New Brunswick, N.J.: Rutgers Univ. Press, 1953), 1:108-15.

which Lincoln tangentially evokes in a phrase about shooting editors—was the recent death of Elijah P. Lovejoy, the abolitionist publicist, who had been shot by a mob in St. Louis as he unloaded his third printing press. But there were other events as well. "Accounts of outrages committed by mobs, form the everyday news of the times," Lincoln says. They are everywhere, from New England to Louisiana, and "neither peculiar to the eternal snows of the former, nor the burning suns of the latter," and thus in both slaveholding and non-slaveholding areas. The problem is basic and national: "Whatever, then, their cause may be, it is common to the whole country."[7]

Mob violence, Lincoln argues, tears apart the fabric of society by weakening the attachment of the people to the laws. All laws, he says, must be obeyed, even bad ones. "There is no grievance," Lincoln states categorically, "that is a fit object of redress by mob law."

Instead of such stability, however, Lincoln finds that the mobocratic spirit prevails throughout the land. The danger the mobocratic spirit poses is amorphous in its general effects and yet surprisingly specific in its political outcome, according to Lincoln. Mob violence thus weakens the attachment of the people to the laws and makes it impossible for the people to govern themselves, that is, for democracy to operate effectively. "Whenever this effect [of weakening the attachment of people for the law] shall be produced among us; whenever the vicious portion of population shall be permitted to gather in bands of hundreds and thousands, and burn churches, ravage and rob provision stores, throw printing presses into rivers, shoot editors, and hang and burn obnoxious persons at pleasure, and with impunity; depend on it, this Government cannot last." In an environment of weakened laws, wild and furious passions, and mobocratic rule, then, "new reapers will arise" and "seek a field," men of "ambition and talent" who will seek the gratification of their "ruling passion." These men—who suddenly become a man in the course of a paragraph as Lincoln talks about them/him—will emerge and overthrow the government and govern by authoritarian rule.

---

7. It would be interesting, though tedious and rather beyond the point of this article, to track down the source of every act of violence Lincoln refers to in his speech. Besides the allusion to the murder of Lovejoy, however, one reference is quite apparent and seemed to cause Lincoln great pain. He says in the speech: "A mulatto man, by the name of Mcintosh, was seized in the street, dragged to the suburbs of the city, chained to a tree, and actually burned to death; and all within a single hour from the time he had been a freeman, attending to his own business, and at peace with the world." Lincoln got the story from the *Sangamo Journal*, May 7, 1836, which had in turn reprinted the entire account from the *St. Louis Republican*, under the title "Horrible Tragedy." St. Louis papers, which may have reached Lincoln directly, regularly ran stories of unruly mobs; e.g., *St. Louis Observer*, Aug. 14, 1834.

Lincoln imagines this new ruler as a man of "towering genius" who "disdains a beaten path." "Many great and good men," Lincoln says, have aspired to a seat in Congress, or a gubernatorial or even presidential chair. But such accomplishments would be too mundane for this new ruler, for such *"belong not to the family of the lion, or the tribe of the eagle."* Alexander, Caesar, or Napoleon would never have been satisfied with such circumscribed titles. On the contrary, this figure Lincoln evokes will add "story to story, upon the monuments of fame"; will deny there is glory in serving anyone else; will scorn to tread in the footsteps of "any predecessor, however illustrious"; and will thirst and burn (Lincoln's verbs) for distinction, even to the point of emancipating slaves or enslaving freemen. Lincoln asks: "Is it unreasonable then to expect, that some man possessed of the loftiest genius, coupled with ambition sufficient to push it to its utmost stretch, will at some time, spring up among us?"

Lincoln concludes his speech with some considerations on preventing the appearance of such a destructive genius in our midst. The answer he offers lies basically in reaffirming the work of the founders, those wise and learned men who created the republic and left us their priceless documents, the Declaration and the Constitution (Lincoln, unlike many of his generation, especially Southerners, always considered the two inseparable founding documents). Our fathers who established this country, he says "were the pillars of the temple of liberty; but now, that they have crumbled away, that temple must fall, unless we, their descendants, supply their places with other pillars, hewn from the solid quarry of sober reason. Passion," he continues, "has helped us; but can do so no more. It will in future be our enemy. Reason, cold, calculating, unimpassioned reason, must furnish all the materials for our future support and defence."

If that, then, is the argument of the speech, presented in some detail to suggest the richness of young Lincoln's impassioned rhetoric—there is no question his style improved with the years—it is open to many interpretations and has in fact occasioned more lively debate in recent years than any other single document in the Lincoln field. One scholar, however, is worried about all the attention many of us have lavished on the speech, since we lack a manuscript of it and have had to rely entirely on the version that appeared in the *Sangamo Journal* on February 3, 1838.[8] That version, of course, could have been altered between delivery and publication, perhaps incorporating suggestions of those who heard and later read the speech. But it should be remembered that the version in the newspaper

---

8. John Y. Simon, Commentary at the Symposium of the Abraham Lincoln Association, Springfield, 1984, later published in *Papers of the Abraham Lincoln Association* 6 (1984): 25-27.

was accompanied by a note suggesting Lincoln had delivered to them an actual copy of his speech; as a text, it is thus more reliable than a large number of Lincoln's speeches, which are only available in newspaper version without any accompanying notes. Or, to take another example, the generally accepted text of the Gettysburg Address is not the one delivered on the battlefield, but the one later corrected by Lincoln for history. All things considered, the Lyceum speech, even though it comes to us via the newspaper, seems to me sufficiently reliable to warrant careful attention to Lincoln's language and images that make possible the kind of psychohistorical exegesis which is my wont.

Some historians have suggested that Lincoln's immediate model for the genius who disdains a beaten path was none other than Andrew Jackson. While such a model for Lincoln's image of the towering genius may have existed in his mind, it is far more likely that, judging from the actual description of this genius, if Lincoln was thinking of anyone in particular, it was Napoleon Bonaparte (who, in fact, is mentioned by name twice in the speech). It also seems to me that Lincoln may well have been thinking more generally about political processes. Keep in mind that the sequence of mobocracy undermining democracy, which then gives way to autocracy or dictatorship, is precisely the model in Plato's *Republic*. Perhaps Lincoln encountered some version of Plato's work in the early grammar books he used in school, which were in fact quite advanced, or he could have read versions of Plato in newspaper stories.

Edmund Wilson was the first to argue that Lincoln's description of the towering genius appears in the speech as the projected image of his own oedipal wishes for greatness. In this influential interpretation, which I am stating more psychologically than Wilson, it was actually Lincoln himself who unconsciously desired to be a towering genius, rising above the emasculated fathers. Having created the image of the towering genius, however, Lincoln shrank from it with a shiver of unacknowledged recognition. But that image endured, and Wilson, whose politics bordered on the anarchic, felt the speech showed Lincoln as a purposeful tyrant whose unconscious strivings were later realized during the war.[9]

We have all been touched, for better for worse, by Wilson. Even the most unpsychological of observers must consider the meaning of the Lyceum's dictator in understanding Lincoln's thought.[10] Psychohistorians especially have

---

9. Edmund Wilson, *Patriotic Gore: Studies in the Literature of the American Civil War* (New York: Oxford Univ. Press, 1962), 107-8.

10. I speak here of the "dictator," for it has become conventional in the literature. It should be noted, however, that nowhere in the speech does Lincoln actually say "dictator."

massaged and elaborated Wilson's ideas. George B. Forgie thus takes Lincoln's image and his ambivalent attitude toward the founders as a cultural metaphor for what he calls the "post-heroic" generation.[11] Three years after Forgie's book appeared (and one month before my own), Dwight Anderson's *Abraham Lincoln: The Quest for Immortality* was published.[12] Anderson argued, among other things, that the Lyceum speech showed Lincoln's desire to slay the founders and take their place, that such feelings profoundly influenced his making of the Civil War, and that he found his immortality by becoming himself the Lyceum tyrant by the end of the war. In such readings of the text, young Lincoln at the Lyceum reveals his dark side—in Jungian terms, his shadow—and aspired to autocratic rule that found realization during his presidency.

Suffice it to say, among its other problems, such an interpretation reads backward from a decidedly negative view of Lincoln's wartime leadership, a view which neither I nor most scholars share, to find justification for it in an offbeat psychological interpretation of an early speech. It is not surprising that several leading Lincoln scholars in the country have come down hard on this line of interpretation, one with Olympian disdain (Don Fehrenbacher), and a second with marked irritation (Richard N. Current).[13]

But to return to the dictator, there is in fact some powerful oedipal imagery in the speech, especially in the contrasting images of the dictator and the idealized founders whose work is trampled underfoot. The evil figure of the dictator—a kind of Jacksonian Darth Vader—is thus vibrant, powerful, unfettered, and above and beyond history itself, while the founders and their work rots, subject to the suggestively castrative abuse of nature: "They [the founders]," says Lincoln, "were a forest of giant oaks; but the all-resistless hurricane has swept over them, and left only, here and there, a lonely trunk, despoiled of its verdure, shorn of its foliage; unshading and unshaded; to murmur in a few more ruder storms, then to sink, and be no more." But what does this imagery mean? It is facile to

---

11. George B. Forgie, *Patricide in the House Divided: A Psychological Interpretation of Lincoln and His Age* (New York: Norton, 1979). In my own 1982 work, *Lincoln's Quest for Union*, I was too brief in my discussion of the speech, and I assumed more psychological knowledge on the part of the average reader than I should have. I have also thought a good deal more about the speech in the decade since I last wrote about it, and I researched several topics, especially in relation to Thomas Lincoln, that have enriched my understanding of Lincoln at the Lyceum; thus this article.

12. Dwight G. Anderson, *Abraham Lincoln: The Quest for Immortality* (New York: Knopf, 1982).

13. Don E. Fehrenbacher, *Lincoln in Text and Context: Collected Essays* (Stanford, Calif.: Stanford Univ. Press, 1987), 222-23; Richard N. Current, "Lincoln After 175 Years: The Myth of the Jealous Son," *Papers of the Abraham Lincoln Association* 6 (1984): 15-24.

suggest that Lincoln in power actually became what he fantasized as a young man. On the contrary, one wants to grasp as deeply as one can its rich meaning in Lincoln's actual life. To do that, one needs, among other things, to go beyond the limited utility of drive theory and oedipal/schmedipal categories, and to see in self-psychological terms a young great man struggling mightily, and tentatively, to orient himself in the public world. Along these lines, I would like to focus on four psychological issues that I think have been seriously misunderstood in the debate surrounding Lincoln at the Lyceum.

First, inherent in the projective image of the dictator, as well as in the implicit identification with the idealized founders, Lincoln at the Lyceum reveals a powerful and largely unacknowledged grandiosity.[14] Read psychologically, that is in fact the most striking and important aspect of the speech. Now most other psychological commentators from Wilson to Anderson have assumed there is something evil in such grandiosity, that if it's there in repressed form at the Lyceum, it must still be lurking in the shadows when Lincoln was president a quarter of a century later. But that is an unwarranted psychological assumption on many levels. It is not that grandiosity is healthy, but that the expression of the grandiose self in an otherwise normal man may be simply a temporary exaggeration of a highly desirable healthy self-assertiveness. One expects, even welcomes, powerful ambition in a young great man. Young Lincoln had to imagine himself as more capable than his accomplishments made visible at the time. This was not an ordinary small-town lawyer. This was a young man of driving ambition, a man who read Shakespeare and surely fantasized himself as one of the poet's troubled kings,[15] a man described by his law partner as having an ambition that was like a little engine that knew no rest.[16] This was a man who really did lift himself out of the backwoods, educate himself against great odds, marry upwards, and endure several political defeats to get elected twice as President of the United States. His terrible dilemma at the Lyceum was the

---

14. The most significant recent commentator on grandiosity is Heinz Kohut, who in several books outlined his psychoanalytic psychology of the self. Note *The Analysis of the Self: A Systematic Approach to the Psychoanalytic Treatment of Narcissistic Personality Disorders* (New York: International Universities Press, 1971); *The Restoration of the Self* (New York: International Universities Press, 1977); and the interviews with me in the posthumously published *Self Psychology and the Humanities: Reflections on A New Psychoanalytic Approach*, ed. Charles B. Strozier (New York: Norton, 1985).

15. See Strozier, *Lincoln's Quest for Union*, 228-30. Note also Fehrenbacher's comments on this issue, "The Weight of Responsibility," Lincoln, 157-63.

16. William H. Herndon and Jesse W. Weik, *Life of Lincoln*, ed. Paul M. Angle (Cleveland: World Publishing, 1930), 304.

discrepancy between fantasy and reality, ambition and fulfillment. Lincoln had done little to justify his own sense of self-worth that ranked him in his mind, unconsciously or not, with Alexander, Caesar, or Napoleon, let alone with his heroes, Washington and Jefferson. His assertiveness, thus frustrated, turned toward a kind of brittle grandiosity that gave voice to some murky images in the speech. In time, Lincoln learned to bridle these needs while simultaneously pushing forward vigorously to realize his ambitions and enormous potential. The United States is a free nation in no small measure because of that change and development within Lincoln.

Second, in my exegesis of the Lyceum speech, I would argue that the evocative (and repeated) images there of the wild and furious passions of the mob, which must in turn be vehemently opposed by "reason, cold, calculating, unimpassioned reason," is a reflection of the tensions within Lincoln's self at the time of the speech. Make no mistake about it: young Lincoln at the Lyceum was in the throes of what Erikson has called an identity crisis.[17] He had just begun to find himself as a lawyer and politician after years of drift, and even these identity elements rested on fragile foundations. He certainly remained confused in love. Some very important new work by John Y. Simon suggests, after a fresh look at the documentary evidence, that Lincoln in fact loved Ann Rutledge deeply and was devastated at her sudden death in 1835.[18] The old myth in this case has proven hardy and at least partially true. Subsequently, Lincoln's ambivalent attempt at romance with Mary Owens went nowhere, as at first was the case in 1839 and 1840 with Mary Todd, largely because with both Marys he was so hesitant in pushing courtship toward consummation.[19]

Behind these relationships with women, however, was Lincoln's then all-

---

17. The most extensive discussion of young Lincoln's identity crisis is Strozier, chapter 2 of *Lincoln's Quest for Union*. For the theory of identity, note especially Erikson's *Childhood and Society*, 2d ed. (New York: Norton, 1963); *Identity: Youth and Crisis* (New York: Norton, 1968); *Insight and Responsibility* (New York: Norton, 1964); *Young Man Luther: A Study in Psychoanalysis and History* (New York: Norton, 1958).

18. John Y. Simon, "Ann Rutledge," *Papers of the Abraham Lincoln Association* II (1989), forthcoming. The most complete—but biased—denunciation of the Ann Rutledge story is James G. Randall, *Lincoln the President: Springfield to Gettysburg*, 2 vols. (Gloucester, Mass.: Eyre and Spottiswoode, 1945), 2:321-42. Note also James Hurt, "All the Living and the Dead: Lincoln's Imagery," *American Literature* 52 (1980):360, in which Hurt argues that the Rutledge story may have originated to explain Lincoln's depression.

19. Jean Baker's revisionist view of the broken courtship in *Mary Todd Lincoln: A Biography* (New York: Norton, 1987) is quite wrong in this regard; note my discussion, "The Psychology of Mary Todd Lincoln," *The Psychohistory Review* 17 (1988): 11-24.

important bond with Joshua Fry Speed, the best friend of his life and the only male he ever got close to. Lincoln had also been sharing a bed with Speed since April 1837 and would continue to do so until December 1840.[20] I have never believed that the evidence suggests a homosexual relationship, but I do think that Lincoln was in a state of some sexual confusion in early 1838, and that the unruly passions of the mob in the Lyceum speech, whatever else they represent, are a direct expression of his own troubled soul. At that point in his life, his repertoire of redemptive cures was limited to a false and empty rationalism: "reason, cold, calculating, unimpassioned reason," he says, "must furnish all the materials for our future support and defence." That Lincoln later found in marriage and fatherhood far broader and more human sources of emotional vitality is yet again a measure of his capacity for growth and change.

Third, Lincoln's idealization of the founders in the Lyceum speech has some fascinating roots in what Stanley Cath and I have recently called a "core fantasy."[21] One part of the idealization seems grounded in Lincoln's degraded image of his biological father, Thomas. The founders provided young Lincoln with a worthy alternative to Thomas. But Lincoln's connection with the founders may well have rested on even deeper psychological foundations. When Lincoln told Herndon about his angelic mother, he also described her as the "illegitimate daughter of Lucy Hanks and a well-bred Virginia farmer or planter" whom Lincoln may have fantasized as Washington or Jefferson, his great heroes of the American Revolution.[22] It was from this Virginian that Lincoln believed he had derived the power of analysis and logic as well as the mental activity and ambition that distinguished him from his low-born family, which it should be noted, included his father.[23] Thomas, in other words, seemed to have been little more than a biological accident in the rich fantasy life of young Lincoln, who, on the contrary, had a direct, blood tie to those wonderful men in frock coats who made revolution and wrote stirring words that formed the basis of our political institutions. They were special because they were, after all, family.

20. For a detailed discussion of the relevant evidence here, note chapter 2, footnote 59, of Strozier, *Lincoln's Quest for Union*.

21. Charles B. Strozier and Stanley H. Cath, "Lincoln and the Fathers: Reflections on Idealization," *Fathers and Their Families*, ed. Stanley H. Cath, Alan Gurwitt, and Linda Gunsberg (Hillsdale, N.J.: Analytic Press, 1989), 285–300.

22. Lincoln often mentioned Washington by name, and once described in detail his childhood fascination for the great hero of the Revolution; see *Collected Works* 4:235–36. There is no such recorded praise for Jefferson, but Lincoln's constant praise for the Declaration of Independence, especially in the 1850s, suggests lifelong fascination with its distinguished author.

23. Herndon and Weik, *Life*, 2.

Finally, there is what might be called a developmental course of Lincoln's political idealizations after 1838. Such idealizations are never fixed. At the Lyceum Lincoln vainly strives to find ways to preserve the founders' sacred work against the rot of time and the degrading effects of mob violence on democratic institutions. He finds the answer basically in a reaffirmation of the Declaration and the Constitution. They, and the men who created them, represent our only hope in troubled times against the danger of dictatorial usurpation.

This theme of idealizing the work of the founders becomes in turn the dominant one in Lincoln's political philosophy, much to our collective benefit. No one preserved the thought of the founders more than Abraham Lincoln as the country hurtled toward civil war. In speech after speech in the 1850s, Lincoln invoked the spirit of the "fathers" as the basis for the salvation and rejuvenation of the country. For example, in 1854 he told a Peoria audience: "Let us re-adopt the Declaration of Independence, and with it, the practices, and policy, which harmonize with it. Let north and south—let all Americans—join in the great and good work. If we do this, we shall not only have saved it, as to make, and to keep it, forever worthy of the saving. We shall have so saved it, that the succeeding millions of free happy people, the world over shall rise up, and call us blessed, to the latest generations."[24]

In time the course of events re-shaped Lincoln's idealizing needs in some fascinating ways. Even as he left Springfield he talked of having a task before him greater than that which rested upon Washington.[25] With dramatic suddenness Lincoln had assumed a position alongside the founders of the republic, taking their measure and looking at them as equals. At Gettysburg, Lincoln subtly indicated his awareness of this change in his own attitude.[26] He invoked the familiar respect for the fathers who had "brought forth, upon this continent, a new nation, conceived in Liberty, and dedicated to the proposition that all men are created equal." But then he stated the momentous issue for himself and the nation: whether the Civil War, symbolized by the battlefield where he spoke, would put an end to this great experiment. He concluded that the deaths were not in vain and that the nation—under his leadership in a war for which he personally assumed responsibility—would have "a new birth of freedom," and whether "government of the people, by the people, for the people" would not "perish from the earth."

---

24. *Collected Works*, 2:276.
25. *Collected Works*, 4:190.
26. *Collected Works*, 7:17–18.

The war and its terrible carnage, however, as well as his own inner needs, created for Lincoln something of a psychological and moral crisis. There seemed no explanation for the suffering, the death, and the destruction. In the past Lincoln had always related the great political issues of the day to the thought of the founders. But the war tore loose his own and the nation's moorings in the past. For security and for meaning, he now turned increasingly to God. One might say Lincoln's gaze drifted upward, and at the Second Inaugural he spoke for God in declaring that His purpose in bringing the war was to punish us for the sin of slavery.

The Lyceum speech is thus a kind of psychologically expressive nodal point in young man Lincoln. It speaks to issues that lay deep in childhood, possibly touching his fantasies of family connectedness with the founders. But the speech also reveals Lincoln's intense, if then confused, ambitions, as well as the struggles with his own "wild and furious passions." It was, however, Lincoln's remarkable capacity for growth and change that drew him toward humane and vitally significant solutions to his inner turmoil, and toward new ideas that helped bind the nation's wounds. None of Lincoln's speeches, it might be said, are so rich in meaning, or have been so sorely misinterpreted.

Abraham Lincoln, Ann Rutledge, and the Evidence of Herndon's Informants

Douglas L. Wilson

The Ann Rutledge story has always sounded like nineteenth-century popular fiction. The most beautiful girl in the village becomes engaged to a rich storekeeper, who admits he has been living under an assumed name and who says he will marry her when he returns from a visit to his aged parents. When he stops writing and shows no sign of returning after two years, the deserted girl accepts the advances of the poor-but-honest postmaster, who has loved her secretly all along. She agrees to marry him, and they plan a bright future, including college for her and a legal career for him, only to have death intervene at the height of their happiness and cancel all their vows. When William H. Herndon came across the Ann Rutledge story unexpectedly after Abraham Lincoln's death, it gradually took possession of his nineteenth-century soul. He came to believe he had found in the tragedy of Lincoln's first romance at least a partial answer to the mystery of his great law partner's chronic melancholy—namely, that the loss of Ann Rutledge had given a permanent wound to his spirit and altered his outlook on life. This theory he laid on in extravagant terms in a lecture in November 1866 and later incorporated in a more measured and moderate form some twenty-three years later in his biography, *Herndon's Lincoln*.[1]

    1. Herndon's lecture, "ABRAHAM LINCOLN. MISS ANN RUTLEDGE. NEW SALEM. PIONEERING AND THE POEM.," delivered on Nov. 16, 1866, and distributed as a broadside,

It was perhaps inevitable that such a story should wear out its welcome, threatening, as it does, to reduce Lincoln's deep inner life—if not the key to his greatness—to a romantic cliché. Novels and popular biographies could not resist the theme that was stated most memorably in Edgar Lee Masters's epitaph for Ann Rutledge in *Spoon River Anthology:*

> Out of me unworthy and unknown
> The vibrations of deathless music;
> "With malice toward none, with charity for all."
> Out of me the forgiveness of millions toward millions
> And the beneficent face of a nation
> Shining with justice and truth.[2]

For the rising generation of twentieth-century Lincoln scholars, the last straw seems to have been Carl Sandburg's *The Prairie Years,* published in 1926, in which the hero's amorous feelings toward the fair Ann are rendered in mawkish scenes and trembling soliloquies. The following year the young Paul M. Angle attacked the Ann Rutledge story as "one of the great myths of American history."[3] All of the evidence in support of it, he argued, was after the fact, with no contemporary evidence of any kind having been produced. He charged Herndon with having chosen his evidence selectively, ignoring and suppressing testimony that cast doubt on the story, and accepting as authentic testimony he should have regarded as suspect. Moreover, Herndon had heedlessly given credence to the doubtful tale of Lincoln's near insanity after the death of Ann Rutledge.

This repudiation of the Ann Rutledge story as a critical event in Lincoln's life, reinforced by Angle's sensational exposure a few years later of an Ann Rutledge hoax, found favor with the community of Lincoln scholars,[4] but there remained one difficulty: the documents upon which Herndon had based his account were not generally available for examination. This was a consideration of some importance in that the position taken by Angle and others was in large part a

---

has been reprinted in *Lincoln and Ann Rutledge and the Pioneers of New Salem* (Herrin, Ill.: Trovillion Private Press, 1945). His biography, co-authored with Jesse W. Weik, appeared in 1889.

2. Edgar Lee Masters, *Spoon River Anthology* (New York: Macmillan, 1964), 219.

3. Paul M. Angle, "Lincoln's First Love?" *Lincoln Centennial Association Bulletin* 9 (Dec. 1, 1927): 1.

4. See, for example, Roy P. Basler, *The Lincoln Legend: A Study in Changing Conceptions* (Boston: Houghton Mifflin, 1935): 147–63, and Louis A. Warren, "The Ann Rutledge Myth," *The Lincoln Kinsman* 35 (May 1941): 1–8.

critique of Herndon's use of evidence they themselves had not seen. Besides Herndon's collaborator, Jesse W. Weik, the only scholar to have full access to this prodigious mass of unique source material was Albert J. Beveridge, who, in writing before Angle's attack, had relied on the Herndon documents extensively in his account of Lincoln's New Salem years and had apparently found nothing to fault Herndon's factual rendering of the Ann Rutledge story.[5] Thus, when the Herndon documents were acquired by the Library of Congress in 1941 and made available to researchers, it was fitting, if not inevitable, that the authoritative "sifting of the Ann Rutledge evidence" should have been undertaken by the most imposing Lincoln scholar of the day, J. G. Randall. Randall's analysis of the Herndon documents appears as an appendix to the first part of his study of Lincoln's presidency. This was, he admits, "something of a digression." "Yet," he noted, "the popular writing has created a stock picture, and the true state of the evidence requires attention."[6] Like Angle, Randall did not attempt to disguise his belief that the Ann Rutledge story, in having "usurped the spotlight," had worked great mischief in the understanding of Abraham Lincoln.

Though much more detailed and fully worked out, Randall's objections to Herndon's evidence are essentially Angle's: that Herndon adduced no contemporary evidence to support his conclusions; that he chose selectively from conflicting testimony; and that he credited dubious and unreliable witnesses. In addition, Randall laid great stress on the problematic character of the evidence, which largely consists of older people's recollections of what happened thirty years before. What Angle had been unable to do without full access to the Herndon documents, Randall here proceeded to do: he closely analyzed the letters and interviews of many of the key informants; he pointed out contradictions and inconsistencies; he called attention to the indirect and hearsay character of some of the testimony. His clear-cut conclusion was that the story of the love affair between Lincoln and Ann Rutledge and Lincoln's subsequent temporary derangement must be regarded as "unproved" and that, as such, "it does not belong in a recital of those Lincoln episodes which one presents as unquestioned reality."[7]

Randall's appendix formed the capstone contribution to the effort to discredit

---

5. See the massive documentation of Lincoln's New Salem years, almost exclusively from Herndon's documents, in Albert J. Beveridge, *Abraham Lincoln 1809-1858* (Boston: Houghton Mifflin, 1928), 1:100-159.

6. J. G. Randall, Appendix: "Sifting the Ann Rutledge Evidence," *Lincoln the President: Springfield to Gettysburg* (New York: Dodd, Mead & Co., 1945), 2:321.

7. Ibid., 341.

the Ann Rutledge story as history, an effort whose success among historians has been virtually complete. Lincoln's first love affair was thus effectively proscribed, and in the nearly half century that has elapsed, no reputable Lincoln biographer has seen fit to treat the Ann Rutledge story seriously. A clear indication of the profound effect these strictures have had is the chastened version of the Ann Rutledge story given by Carl Sandburg in the one-volume edition of his biography published in 1954. In the acknowledgments, he pays tribute to the scholars who "made a strong case that the [Lincoln-Rutledge] 'romance' rested on conjecture and assumption while the often related grief and borderline insanity of Lincoln at her death were improbable."[8] In a completely rewritten account of the New Salem period, Sandburg dropped the mawkish interior monologues and substituted circumspect passages like this: "It was certain that Ann Rutledge and Lincoln knew each other and he took an interest in her; probably they formed some mutual attachment not made clear to the community; possibly they loved each other and her hand went into his long fingers whose bones told her of refuge and security. They were the only two persons who could tell what secret they shared, if any."[9]

But is the Ann Rutledge story, as we have been telling ourselves all these years, mostly a myth—or, as Louis A. Warren has termed it, "pure fiction"? In a recent paper, John Y. Simon has argued persuasively that the critique under review, though it "exposed the shaky underpinnings of any detailed account of the [Lincoln-Rutledge] relationship," has been carried too far. "This commendable correction of the historical record, once valuable, now requires reappraisal, especially as it provoked an overreaction."[10] Simon traces the public career of the Ann Rutledge story from its first appearance in Herndon's 1866 lecture and shows that by mingling evidence with speculation, embellishing the story of Lincoln's derangement, and tastelessly offending Mary Todd Lincoln, Herndon "grossly mishandled a major incident in the Lincoln story," from which "neither

---

8. Carl Sandburg, *Abraham Lincoln: The Prairie Years and The War Years*, one-volume edition (New York: Harcourt, Brace, 1954), 743.

9. Ibid., 44. This is reminiscent of Paul Angle's summary in his 1927 article: "Certainly Ann Rutledge and Lincoln knew each other; probably they formed a mutual attachment; possibly they were in love. But the evidence on which the story has heretofore been based is certainly far from conclusive." Angle, "Lincoln's First Love?" 6.

10. Quoted in John Y. Simon, "Abraham Lincoln and Ann Rutledge," *Journal of the Abraham Lincoln Association* 11 (1990): 19, 28. My study of Herndon's informants was well along when I first learned of this paper through the friendly offices of Roger D. Bridges. I am grateful to the author for generously making available to me a revised draft in advance of publication.

Herndon's reputation nor that of Ann Rutledge ever recovered." His conclusion is that in spite of Herndon's blunders and in spite of the caveats and misgivings of doubting historians, "the reality of the story appears certain," and that Ann "should take her proper place in Lincoln biography."[11]

The discussion that follows comes at the problem from a different direction. It is based on a study of the evidence provided by Herndon's informants, the letters and interviews relating to the Ann Rutledge affair in the Herndon-Weik Collection.[12] At the heart of the controversy, as Simon has shown, is the role of Herndon himself, but beyond that is the standing of the testimony of Herndon's informants. Of Herndon, it has been alleged that he was not an impartial investigator, that he coached his witnesses and guided their responses with leading questions, that he was assiduous only in the pursuit of answers and information that suited him. David Donald, who, in the 1940s, was one of the first (and apparently the last) to survey the Herndon documents for their Ann Rutledge testimony, helped perpetuate the notion that the romance was little short of a collaborative fabrication: "One letter of inquiry followed another, and the more often old men and women repeated their tales the surer they became of the whole story. The hundreds of papers, letters, and interviews on the Ann Rutledge theme preserved in the Herndon-Weik Collection show that the legend grew in color and in detail and that over the years the story crystallized from a floating rumor into a fixed romance."[13] Randall and his wife, Ruth Painter Randall, are especially hard on Herndon as an avowed enemy of Mary Todd Lincoln and are disposed to see his rendering of the Ann Rutledge affair as a deliberate affront in this regard.[14]

Herndon's informants, the former residents of the New Salem neighborhood who offered their recollections of the Ann Rutledge romance, have fared little better. It is charged that their testimony is generally suspect because they were anxious to associate themselves with the early career of a great man, that they

---

11. Ibid., 15, 33.

12. The text of some, but by no means all, of these letters and interviews exist in the form of copies Herndon had made in 1866 and which now repose in the Huntington Library. A small number were printed in the collection of Herndon materials edited by Emanuel Hertz as *The Hidden Lincoln* (New York: Viking, 1938).

13. David Donald, *Lincoln's Herndon* (New York: Knopf, 1948), 187. This characterization ignores the fact that the story of the romance in all its essential features was common knowledge in Petersburg before Herndon had ever heard of it, as evidenced by the article written by John Hill and published in the *Menard Axis* in 1862. Hill supplied Herndon with a copy of the article, which is in the Herndon-Weik Collection, Manuscript Division, Library of Congress, hereafter cited as H-W. See Hill to Herndon, June 6, 1865, H-W.

14. See Simon, "Abraham Lincoln and Ann Rutledge," 19-28.

were therefore easily led to say what his biographer wanted to hear, that their testimony is contradictory and inconclusive, and that they could not be expected to recall with clarity events that happened thirty years earlier. Randall, who is generally condescending about Herndon's informants, pointedly praises one of them, George Spears, for what he calls the "refreshing candor" with which Spears admitted he didn't remember much about the events in question. The clear implication is that other witnesses suffered from a similar inability but lacked the candor to admit it.

Some of these charges were made by critics, like Angle, who did not have access to the documents and were basing their conclusions on portions of the testimony that had appeared in print, on Herndon's tarnished reputation, and on speculation about how and when he developed his information. But strictly on the basis of the documents themselves and what they reveal, it is difficult to fault Herndon as an investigator. They show that his efforts, which began about a month after Lincoln was assassinated, were prompt and prodigious.[15] Within four months, he had opened a correspondence with Lincoln's relatives, with his earliest acquaintances and his oldest friends, and with informants at the scenes of his childhood in Kentucky and Indiana; he had traveled to Chicago to interview Lincoln's cousins, John and Dennis Hanks, to Coles County to interview his step-mother and other relatives, and to Spencer County, Indiana, to question the people with whom Lincoln had grown up. Amidst this flurry of investigative activity that was aimed at the whole span of Lincoln's life, Herndon did not neglect the people who knew Lincoln in New Salem. He traveled to Petersburg to interview residents still on the scene, and he corresponded frequently with them and with others who had moved away. This pattern of energetic, dedicated investigation Herndon kept up for nearly two years, and though his efforts eventually languished, he was still taking interviews about Ann Rutledge as late as 1887.[16] The resulting archive, a cache of primary material containing hundreds of documents, is the richest source of information on Lincoln's life extant, which even at the present day is far from exhausted.[17]

---

15. Horace White's letter of May 22, 1865, H-W, refers to "yours of the 20th" and endorses Herndon as "peculiarly qualified . . . to be his [Lincoln's] biographer."

16. See his interviews with Jasper Rutledge, Lizzie Herndon Bell, James McGrady Rutledge, and Henry Hohimer, all of which date from March 1887, and his letter about them to Jesse Weik, quoted below in note 47.

17. The letters and interviews of Herndon's informants are currently being edited for publication by Douglas L. Wilson and Rodney O. Davis.

When Herndon first heard the story of Lincoln's romance with Ann Rutledge, within days of beginning his inquiries, he, of course, pursued it with other informants, but the responses from this period indicate that he was actually more interested in other matters, such as Lincoln's early movements and his reading. Herndon's cousin, J. Rowan Herndon, who had known Lincoln well in New Salem, sent a torrent of information in response to Herndon's first letter in May 1865, but it was not until the prospective biographer's fourth letter several weeks later that he got around to sounding out his cousin about Lincoln and women. Rowan replied: "You ask about him as Regards women. They all Liked him and [he] liked them as well[.] There was a Miss Rutlege j have know Dout he would have maried iff she had of Lived But Deth Prevented."[18] This indirect way of raising the question initially with his informants is indicative of Herndon's approach. Writing six months later to his father-in-law in Petersburg, who acted as a kind of research assistant, he directed: "If you ever see Mrs Armstrong please get out of her all the facts in reference to Mr. Lincolns life when in Menard—what he did—what he said—when he said it where he said it—before whom—How he lived—his manners—customs—habits—sports, frolics—fun—his sadness—his wit; his humor. What he read—when he read it—How he read—and what and who he loved, etc. etc. and in short all she may know about him in mind—heart—soul—body."[19] These examples show what becomes clear when one reviews the documents, namely, that as an investigator, Herndon's initial approach to informants was typically open-ended, and while it may have prompted informants to respond on certain subjects, it was not calculated to elicit preconceived answers. As Beveridge said of this material: "Everywhere it is obvious that Herndon is intent on telling the truth himself and on getting the truth from those who could give personal, first-hand information."[20]

This is not to say that Herndon did not eventually pursue the Ann Rutledge story with vigor and resourcefulness. But the character of his investigation has often been misrepresented by the critics, who have sometimes assumed that he knew little or nothing of the Ann Rutledge affair until the fall of 1866 and that, once he got wind of it, became obsessed by it.[21] Both of these conceptions

---

18. J. R. Herndon to Herndon, July 3, 1865, H-W.
19. Herndon to G. U. Miles, Dec. 1, 1865, H-W.
20. Albert J. Beveridge, "Lincoln As His Partner Knew Him," *Literary Digest International Review* vol. 1, no. 33 (Sept. 1923):33.
21. Angle assumes that Herndon first heard the story from John McNamar in Oct. 1866. See Angle, "Lincoln's First Love?," 2.

are wrong. Herndon learned of the romance in late May 1865, possibly in an interview on the 29th with Hardin Bale in Petersburg.[22] Although he would accumulate information on the affair for many months, the documents suggest he did not begin to bear down on the matter until early in 1866, when he made some specific inquiries about it.[23] By March 23 his father-in-law and faithful research assistant, G. U. Miles, in sending testimony from Petersburg, would write: "The above Statements I think you may rely on but if you Should undertake to write a history of my life after I am dead I dont want you to inquire So close into my Early courtships as you do of Mr Lincolns."[24]

Herndon had the advantage of knowing the people involved: "I knew Miss Rutledge myself, as well as her father and other members of the family, and have been personally acquainted with every one of the score or more of witnesses whom I at one time or another interviewed on this delicate subject."[25] But at the same time, Herndon was an able and experienced lawyer and was not naive where witnesses were concerned. The responses of his informants show again and again that Herndon checked the information he was gathering, particularly when he noted discrepancies, by trying it out on other informants. Not surprisingly, they frequently disputed each other's recollections. William G. Greene disputed Mentor Graham's claim to have taught Lincoln as a student and advanced his own claim to have loaned Lincoln books with which to study grammar and surveying. James Short in turn disputed this, stating that Greene's father was a drinking and illiterate man and had no books in his house. And so on. Ironically, following up in this way has earned Herndon the accusation of leading his witnesses, while the disputes among the informants have contributed to their testimony being called a "mass of confused and contradictory evidence."[26]

Herndon's reputation as an honest man—as, indeed, a man with a passion for the truth—has been affirmed in all quarters and is not in dispute.[27] But he did

---

22. Bale to Herndon, May 29, 1865, H-W. This, like many of the early documents in the Herndon-Weik Collection, is in the form of a letter addressed to Herndon, though in Herndon's own hand and signed by the informant. One must agree with David Donald that these "should probably be understood as his memoranda of oral interviews, which were read back and approved by his informants." Donald, *Lincoln's Herndon*, 185n.

23. See letters of Henry McHenry, Jan. 8, 1866, and William G. Green, Jan. 23, 1866, H-W.

24. G. U. Miles to Herndon, Mar. 23, 1866, H-W.

25. William H. Herndon and Jesse W. Weik, *Herndon's Life of Lincoln: The History and Personal Recollections of Abraham Lincoln*, ed. Paul M. Angle (Cleveland: World Publishing Co., 1949), 105.

26. Randall, "Sifting the Ann Rutledge Evidence," 324.

27. See Angle, "Lincoln's First Love?" 5; Albert J. Beveridge, quoted in Benjamin Thomas, *Portrait for Posterity: Lincoln and his Biographers* (New Brunswick: Rutgers Univ. Press, 1947), 250; Randall, "Sifting the Ann Rutledge Evidence," 339; and Donald, *Lincoln's Herndon*, 347.

love to analyze and speculate, and he undoubtedly had a romantic disposition to which the Ann Rutledge story appealed, and which led him, especially in his 1866 lecture, to expand on the story and to rhapsodize shamelessly on the lasting effects of this romance on Abraham Lincoln. His informants, though not responsible for most of Herndon's speculations, have suffered because of them. Angle complained that Herndon's testimony "comes either from a member of the Rutledge family—naturally interested in making the attachment between Ann and the martyred President as intimate as possible—or from a one-time resident of New Salem, interested in fastening all possible glamour to that forgotten village."[28] Angle had not seen the documents when he wrote this, but one who had seen them said much the same. "Old-timers dug back into their store of gossip to reproduce, verbatim, conversations held with Lincoln fully thirty years before (and in some cases fifty years before). It was a kind of local contest to see who could remember the most."[29] These characterizations are manifestly unfair. In fact, Herndon's informants are, for the most part, reasonably circumspect in what they say and ready to acknowledge the limits of their own knowledge. Though—as Herndon himself knew—a few of his informants were suspiciously facile and self-important in their testimony, most come across as straightforward and reliable witnesses who exhibit no purpose to exaggerate or deceive.[30]

To be sure, the recollections of the New Salem informants are fragmentary and impressionistic. They remember that Lincoln was a great reader, a good storyteller, a good wrestler; that he was a store clerk, postmaster, and was elected to the state legislature. They remember Lincoln's wrestling match and subsequent friendship with Jack Armstrong; that he was elected captain of a company of volunteers in the Black Hawk war. They recall that Lincoln was great friends with Jack Kelso, and that they loved to recite Burns and Shakespeare; that Lincoln studied first grammar and surveying, and then the law. One of the things they remember and comment on is that he courted Ann Rutledge, who was engaged at the time to another man, and that he went a little crazy at her death.

The condescending treatment of Herndon's informants as unreliable witnesses is a curious business, for even the critics find it impossible not to rely on them. For example, J. G. Randall accepts John McNamar as "Ann's fiancé," not because there is contemporary documentary evidence to this effect, but because Herndon's informants seemed to agree that this was the case. But he is reluctant to accept

---

28. Angle, "Lincoln's First Love?," 5.
29. Donald, *Lincoln's Herndon*, 353.
30. Herndon was especially wary of William G. ("Slicky Bill") Greene and Dennis F. Hanks.

Lincoln's courtship of Ann or his excessive grief and apparent derangement at her death, in spite of the fact that these are just as clearly affirmed by the same group of witnesses. He characterized the Ann Rutledge testimony as "some pro, some con, some inconclusive, all of it long delayed reminiscence, much of it second- or third-hand, part of it consisting of inference or supposition as to what 'must have been' true."[31] But even if these charges are strictly true, does this warrant the conclusion Randall wants us to accept—that Herndon's evidence is a hopeless hodgepodge from which no historical reality can reliably be drawn?

What is most notable in the case of the Ann Rutledge affair—the objections of Angle, Randall, and Donald notwithstanding—is that there is remarkably little disagreement among the informants on the basic elements of the story. Reduced to three essential questions, these may be represented as follows: (1) Did Lincoln love or court Ann Rutledge? (2) Did Lincoln grieve excessively at Ann's death? (3) Did they have an understanding about marriage? In order to gauge the evidence in terms of these questions, the testimony of all Herndon's informants who mention the Ann Rutledge story has been reviewed and a "Yes," "No," or "No Opinion" has been assigned for each question (see Table 1). The witnesses who testified about Ann Rutledge, including those whose testimony was forwarded to Herndon by others, number 24.[32] It is obvious that some of these were clearly not testifying from first-hand knowledge. John Hill, for example, was not yet born when Ann died, and Lizzie Herndon Bell was only a small child. Others, such as B. F. Irwin, William McNeely, and William Bennett testified only as to what they had heard from others. But most of the 24 were contemporaries of Lincoln, or older, were acquainted with Lincoln and Ann, and were well placed in the small circle of neighbors to know something about the events in question.

As Simon has pointed out, none of these informants denied or expressed doubt that Lincoln loved or courted Ann Rutledge.[33] Moreover, all but two affirmed it directly or by implication. One of the two who failed to affirm it, Mrs.

---

31. Randall, "Sifting the Ann Rutledge Evidence," 331; see also 324, 341, and 333.

32. This count must be regarded as minimal and may not be complete. For example, Herndon refers in his biography to a remark of A. Y. Ellis about Lincoln and Ann Rutledge, but I do not find it in Ellis's letters. See *Herndon's Life of Lincoln*, 110.

33. "Loved" is used here in the overt sense, as opposed to worshipping from afar. This is lumped with "courted" to avoid verbal distinctions that are not substantive. Some responses are scored by implication. Informants who testify that they believed the couple engaged to be married ("Yes" to the second question) are counted as "Yes" to the first question also.

E. H. Abell, wrote Herndon: "The Courtship between him and Miss Rutledge I can say but little[.] this much I do know he was staying with us at the time of her death it was a great shock to him and I never seen a man mourn for a companion more than he did for her[.] he made a remark one day when it was raining that he could not bare the idea of its raining on her Grave[.] that was the time the community said he was crazy[.] he was not crazy but he was very disponding a long time." Mrs. Abell may have been reticent or uninformed about Lincoln's courtship of Ann, but she leaves no doubt that his feelings for her were very strong.[34] The tally for the first question—Did Lincoln love or court Ann Rutledge?—is "Yes" 22, "No" 0, "No opinion" 2.

The second question—Did Lincoln grieve excessively at Ann's death?—produces a similar result: no one denied the story of Lincoln's unusual behavior, though the informants who voiced an opinion differed as to the severity of his reaction. Some claimed that he became temporarily deranged, others that his friends feared for his sanity, and others simply that he took Ann's death very hard. The reckoning here is "Yes" 17, "No" 0, "No opinion" 7.

The third question—Did Lincoln and Ann have an understanding about marriage?—is the only one about which there is actual disagreement, and the reason is not hard to understand. At the time of Lincoln's courtship of Ann, she was officially and publicly engaged to another man, John McNamar, who left town soon after their engagement. Ann's family reported that McNamar's long absence from New Salem, his failure to write to Ann, and the discovery that he had been operating under an assumed name caused Ann to accept Lincoln's attentions, which, in the words of Ann's brother Robert, "resulted in an engagement to marry, conditional to an honorable release from the contract with McNamar. There is no kind of doubt as to the existence of this engagement."[35] Few outside the Rutledge family, if any, knew about this understanding between Lincoln and Ann until after her death. James Short was probably typical of the close friends for whom Lincoln's extraordinary bereavement was a revelation: "The Rutledges lived about a half a mile from me. Mr L. came over to see me & them every day or two. I did not know of any engagement or tender passages between Mr L and

---

34. Mrs. E. H. Abell to Herndon, Feb. 15, 1867, H-W. Henry McHenry, the only other informant whose affirmation of the courtship is not explicit, reports that there were two theories in the neighborhood about Lincoln's behavior after Ann's death. One was that he was studying too hard at the law; the other that he was grieving over Ann. McHenry says he subscribed to the latter view. McHenry to Herndon, Jan. 8, 1866, H-W.

35. R. B. Rutledge to Herndon, [Oct. 1866], H-W.

Miss R at the time. But after her death . . . he seemed to be so much affected and grieved so hardly that I then supposed there must have been something of the kind."[36] In these circumstances, it is understandable that some residents, even one as well-placed as Ann's aunt, Mrs. William Rutledge, would think that Ann really preferred the rich storekeeper, McNamar, and would have married him if she had lived.[37] But she is the only one of Herndon's informants to say as much; the only other to dispute the engagement was Lizzie Bell, a child at the time, who was apparently repeating her mother's doubt that the two were "absolutely engaged."[38] Even with these two dissents, the totals for the third question—Did Lincoln and Ann have an understanding about marriage?—are "Yes" 15, "No" 2, "No opinion" 7.

The conclusion one must draw from this reckoning is that on the three basic points at issue in the Ann Rutledge affair—the existence of a courtship, the existence of an understanding about marriage, and Lincoln's excessive grief at the death of Ann Rutledge—the informants are overwhelmingly in agreement.

This tally of the opinions of Herndon's informants, decisive as it appears, gives equal weight to each informant and does nothing to help us sort out those whose testimony is the most probative and thus most important. Nor are we able, in many cases, to find out what the informant's knowledge is based on. Small communities are supposed to be hard places to keep secrets, but they are also notoriously rife with speculative gossip, and some of what Herndon collected is undoubtedly little more than this. But there are at least five witnesses who received information about the love affair between Ann Rutledge and Abraham Lincoln from a prime source—the principals themselves.

There are at least two informants who received information directly from Ann. These are her brother, Robert B. Rutledge, and her cousin, James McGrady Rutledge. Critics of the story have come close to implying that members of the Rutledge family are, *ipso facto*, unreliable witnesses, though this hardly seems warranted.[39] Far from trying to capitalize on Ann's connection to Lincoln, the

---

36. Interview with James Short, July 7, 1865, H-W. This response is tallied as a "Yes" to the second question (about Lincoln's grief) and as a "Yes" by implication to the first question (about Lincoln's love for Ann), but a "No opinion" on the question of an engagement.

37. See G. U. Miles to Herndon, Mar. 23, 1866, H-W. In this letter, Miles reports that Mrs. Samuel Hill thinks that "Lincoln would have got her had She lived," but in her undated interview with Herndon, she says, "If McNamar had got back from NY before Anns death she would have married McNamar." These two views are not strictly incompatible but may show a vacillation on her part.

38. Interview with Lizzie Herndon Bell [March 1887], H-W.

39. See Angle's remark, cited in footnote 28.

Rutledges at first shied away from Herndon. When Herndon approached James McGrady Rutledge, the cousin who was thought to know more about Ann's relations with Lincoln than anyone except her brother David, McGrady evaded him. Ann's brother Robert later advised Herndon to "correspond with [McGrady] and say to him that this is no longer a delicate question, inasmuch as it must of necessity become a matter of history, that I desire the whole truth to be recorded."[40] Apparently, not even this could prompt McGrady Rutledge to answer Herndon's letters. Herndon probably had heard what McGrady would later write in his reminiscences, that he and Lincoln had lived together at Rutledge's tavern and that "while he was boarding there Lincoln became deeply in love with Ann."[41] Robert described McGrady to Herndon as "a cousin about [Ann's] age & who was in her confidence," which adds weight to what he reported to Robert: "Ann told me once in coming from a Camp Meeting on Rock creek, that engagements made too far ahead sometimes failed, that one had failed (meaning her engagement with McNamar) and gave me to understand, that as soon as certain studies were completed she and Lincoln would be married."[42] It was not until 1887 that Herndon caught up with the reluctant cousin, who gave him only a terse summary of what he knew. Herndon asked, "Do you know anything concerning the courtship and engagement of Abraham Lincoln and Ann Rutledge?" McGrady replied, "Well I had an opportunity to know and I do know the facts. Abraham Lincoln and Ann Rutledge were engaged to be married. He came down and was with her during her last sickness and burial. Lincoln was studying law at Springfield Ill. Ann Rutledge concented to waite a year for their marriage after their engagement until Abraham Lincoln was Admitted to the bar. And Ann Rutledge died within the year."[43]

40. See R. B. Rutledge to Herndon, Nov. 21, 1866, H-W: "He [James McGrady Rutledge] says you and Mr. Cogsdell talked with him on this subject, but he did not tell you as much, as he thot you had a design in it." For McGrady's reputed knowledge of the Lincoln-Rutledge affair, see Thomas Reep, *Lincoln at New Salem* (Petersburg, Ill: Old Salem Lincoln League, 1927), 32.

41. Fern Nance Pond, ed., "The Memoirs of James McGrady Rutledge 1814-1899," *Journal of the Illinois State Historical Society* 29 (Apr.-Jan. 1937-38): 88.

42. R. B. Rutledge to Herndon, Nov. 21, 1866, H-W.

43. Interview with James M. Rutledge, undated, H-W. The conjectural date of March 1887 assigned by the Library of Congress seems correct. The manuscript is presumably in the hand of Jesse W. Weik, to whom Herndon addressed a letter on Apr. 22, 1887: "Inclosed you will find some evidence which I took down in writing when I was at Menard. You had better copy the pencil writing before it rubs out: it is important, as I think on the Ann Rutledge question, and it may be on others." The reference is presumably to the interviews with Jasper Rutledge, Caleb Carman, and Lizzie Bell, which are still in Herndon's pencil, and that of James McGrady Rutledge, which apparently exists only in Weik's autograph.

When Herndon finally succeeded in making contact with Ann's immediate family more than a year after first hearing of the romance, it was her brother, Robert B. Rutledge, who agreed to cooperate. Rutledge acknowledged Herndon's letter of July 30, 1866, which he characterized as "Making inquiry as to my knowledge of the early history of our *Martered President*." He told Herndon, "[It] will require some time to answer intelligably, as I will have to consult our Family Record, My Mother and elder Brother, who are in Van Buren Co Iowa."[44] Nearly three months later, Rutledge forwarded to Herndon a twelve-page statement drawn in part from the records and recollections of his family in the form of numbered answers to Herndon's queries. The beginning of his response to Herndon's eighth query tells us something about the man and how he regarded his responsibilities as an informant: "I cannot give you a satisfactory reply to many items embraced in this inquiry for the lack of dates or circumstances corroborating them. Many things said of him and done by him are indelibly fixed in my mind but the absence of the proper surroundings impels me to with hold them."[45]

The fourth query is about Ann: "You make some pertinent inquiries concerning my sister and the relations which existed between herself and Mr Lincoln." Rutledge's straightforward account of Ann's engagement to McNamar, her subsequent disenchantment and engagement to Lincoln, and the "terrible" effect of Ann's death on Lincoln's mind filled out and confirmed what Herndon had been hearing from other informants for more than a year. Rutledge made no attempt to swell the importance of his sister's relationship with Lincoln, and his description of her is rather modest: "My sister was esteemed the brightest mind of the family, was studious, devoted to her duties of whatever character, and possessed a remarkably amiable and lovable disposition. She had light hair and blue eyes."[46] He said nothing in his account of the cause of Ann's death, but when Herndon, in

---

44. R. B. Rutledge to Herndon, Aug. 5, 1866, H-W. The family apparently agreed to speak with one voice on the subject of Ann, for in addition to his lack of success with McGrady Rutledge, Herndon had little luck getting additional information from another brother, John, though he made several attempts. Ann's sister, Nancy Rutledge Prewitt, retold the family version many years later, adding a few details not reported by Robert. See Fairfield (Iowa) *The Inter Ocean*, Feb. 10, 1899, transcribed in Jane E. Hamand, *Memoirs of the Rutledge Family of New Salem, Illinois*. Compiled for the Decatur Lincoln Memorial Collection, Nov. 1921. A typescript copy is on deposit at the Library of Congress. I am grateful to James Gilreath of the Rare Book and Special Collections Division for assistance in locating this document.

45. R. B. Rutledge to Herndon, [Oct. 1866], H-W. Rutledge's letter is replete with information and anecdotes about Lincoln at New Salem and is relied upon extensively by Beveridge in his biography.

46. R. B. Rutledge to Herndon, [Oct. 1866], H-W.

his next letter, tried out on him the theory he had heard repeated by some of the old neighbors, Rutledge demurred: "You suggest that the probable cause of Ann's sickness was her conflicts—Emotions &c, as to this I cannot say. I however have my own private convictions, the character of her sickness was brain fever."[47]

Robert's conscientious consultations with others, which he felt obliged to do to test his own memory and augment the record, are objected to by Randall as violations of "the law of evidence," though he grants that "some investigators might not consider that his product was rendered less valuable by this consultation."[48] While he tries to suggest that Robert is inconsistent and contradictory, that he was obsequious toward Herndon, and purports to be troubled by Rutledge's use of the term "conditional"[49] for the engagement, Randall fails to find substantial fault with Robert's account, which he nevertheless tars as "dim and misty with the years." Of McGrady's testimony through his brother Robert, Randall complains because of its indirectness: "Here is one person reporting what another person had written him concerning what that person recollected he had inferred from something Ann had casually said to him more than thirty-one years before!" Of his direct testimony to Herndon Randall says nothing.[50] On balance, there is little to object to in the responses of these deliberate, straightforward, and relatively modest witnesses.

If there are at least two reliable informants who had knowledge of the love affair directly from Ann, there are at least three whose knowledge of what happened came from Lincoln himself. The first is Mentor Graham, who was Ann's schoolteacher and who helped Lincoln with his studies. He told Herndon: "Lincoln and [Ann] was Engaged—Lincoln told me so—She intimated to me the same: He Lincoln told me that he felt like committing Sucide after...." Though

---

47. R. B. Rutledge to Herndon, Nov. 18, 1866, H-W. For informants offering this interpretation, see the undated interviews with Mrs. Hardin Bale, who said that Ann "died as it were of grief," and Mrs. Samuel Hill, who commented, "Anns sickness was caused by her complications."

48. Randall, "Sifting the Ann Rutledge Evidence," 329.

49. Robert first uses the word "conditional" to describe the understanding that there would be no official "engagement" until Ann had notified McNamar of her decision. He later admits that suggesting the engagement of Lincoln and Ann was dependent upon contacting the lost McNamar was misleading and declares it "not conditional." See R. B. Rutledge to Herndon, Nov. 18, 1866, H-W.

50. Randall, "Sifting the Ann Rutledge Evidence," 330, 328. This is possibly because the transcript does not appear with the other letters and interviews on the microfilm, which was made before the documents were given foliation numbers and placed in the current order. I am grateful to Oliver Orr of the Manuscript Division, Library of Congress, for assistance in examining the Herndon-Weik Collection.

Randall minimizes Graham's testimony as a "meager" contribution, there is no reason to doubt this known friend and counselor of the young Lincoln.[51]

Another witness whose knowledge of the Ann Rutledge affair may be presumed to have come from Lincoln himself is Nancy Green, the wife of Lincoln's close friend, Bowling Green. Mrs. Green told G. U. Miles that "Mr Lincoln was a regular suiter of Miss Ann Rutledge for between two & 3 years next up to August 1835 in which month Miss Rutledge died after a Short ilness that Lincoln took her death verry hard So much So that some thought his mind would become impared." She further confirmed what Herndon had heard elsewhere, that "in fear of it [i.e., of Lincoln's mind becoming impaired] (her husband)] Bolin Green went to Salem after Lincoln brought him to his house and kept him a week or two & succeeded in cheering him Lincoln up though he was quite malencholy for months."[52] The close attachment of Lincoln to Bowling Green is well known, and if there is any cause to doubt the testimony of his wife, who helped care for Lincoln, it has not been advanced.

The third witness, Isaac Cogdal, claimed to have actually asked Lincoln directly about the Ann Rutledge affair in later years and got an answer. Angle and Randall argue that this counts against the credibility of his testimony, principally because of Lincoln's known reluctance to discuss personal matters, but they neglect two important considerations.[53] The first is that Cogdal was a longstanding personal and political friend of Lincoln's, a fellow Whig from Democratic Menard whose friendship went back to the New Salem days and who Herndon himself attests was intimate enough with Lincoln to discuss religious questions with him in his law office.[54] Randall tells us that Cogdal studied law and was granted a license in 1860, not long before the conversation took place, but he does not report that the man who advised him to study law and apparently offered him instruction was Abraham Lincoln.[55] The second thing

---

51. Interview with Mentor Graham, April 2, 1866, H-W. Randall calls attention to the cautionary note Herndon wrote on the margin of his interview with Graham's daughter, Lizzie Bell, describing them both as "cranky—flighty—at times nearly non copus mentis—but good & honest" (326). But this characterization, written no earlier than 1887, is obviously a two-edged sword.

52. Miles to Herndon, Mar. 23, 1866, H-W.

53. See Angle, who tries to dismiss Cogdal as a "mediocre lawyer" with no claim on Lincoln's friendship, "Lincoln's First Love?," 6–7, and Randall, "Sifting the Ann Rutledge Evidence," 333–35. Simon successfully answers other objections, such as the circumstance of Cogdal calling Lincoln "Abe" at a time when he was always called "Lincoln." New Salem residents knew and very frequently refer to Lincoln in their testimony as "Abe."

54. See Herndon's parenthetical note in their second undated interview, H-W.

55. See the biographical account of Cogdal, almost certainly from data supplied by himself,

overlooked in regard to Cogdal's testimony is the context. Cogdal told Herndon that as President-elect, Lincoln had invited him to his office in the statehouse to talk about old times and had asked him pointedly about the Rutledges and other New Salem families. Cogdal's interview reads: "After we had spoken over old times ... I then dared to ask him this question," at which point he relates his question and Lincoln's answer. Herndon, in taking down the interview, realized how critical the context was to the credibility of such an answer. He apparently queried Cogdal about the way in which his question was introduced into the conversation and recorded his response in the margin: "May I now in turn ask you a question Lincoln said Cogdall. Most assuredly. I will answer your question if a fair one with all my heart."[56]

As close friends of Lincoln, Cogdal and Herndon well knew that he did not customarily express himself on personal subjects. The wording of both Cogdal's descriptions of the moment—"I then dared to ask him" and "May I now in turn ask you a question Lincoln"—together with the remembered heartiness of Lincoln's reply, indicate Cogdal's awareness of the rare opportunity that had been given him to confront the reserved Lincoln on the subject of Ann Rutledge. Herndon's marginal addendum shows that he, too, was very much aware of how pertinent the context was to crediting the extraordinary candor of Lincoln's response. In his answer, Lincoln not only admits to having been deeply in love with Ann Rutledge, he acknowledges, when pressed by Cogdal, that he "ran off the track" at her death. Though Herndon had already heard the story many times before, the last thing Cogdal remembered Lincoln saying on that occasion contained something entirely new and seems to have made a particular impression on Herndon: "I did honestly—& truly love the girl & think often—often of her now."[57]

To Randall, Cogdal's testimony "seems artificial and made to order. It was given out after Lincoln's death; it presents him in an unlikely role; it puts in his mouth uncharacteristic sayings."[58] Perhaps so, but this is not testimony about something that happened in the "dim and misty" past; Cogdal is testifying just five or six years after the event, which was not an obscure encounter with an old friend but an extremely memorable one with the President-elect of the United States. And once Lincoln's departure from his usual reserve in personal matters is accounted for, we

---

in [R. D. Miller], *History of Mason and Menard Counties* (Chicago: O. L. Baskin, 1879), 749. Randall cites this source.

56. Interview with Isaac Cogdal, undated, H-W.

57. Interview with Isaac Cogdal, undated, H-W. This is surely the germ of Herndon's theory that Lincoln never got over Ann Rutledge's death and brooded on her all his life.

58. Randall, "Sifting the Ann Rutledge Evidence," 335.

have no more reason to doubt this testimony than did Herndon, who knew Cogdal as a man highly regarded in his community and an old friend of Lincoln's.[59]

The conclusion seems inescapable, that the witnesses who had the best opportunity to know what transpired between Abraham Lincoln and Ann Rutledge tell essentially the same story as the other informants. In spite of the claim of critics that Herndon "collected sharply conflicting reminiscences on the Lincoln-Rutledge idyll," a review of the informants' letters and interviews fails to confirm it.[60] If the testimony on the basic elements of the Ann Rutledge story is thus overwhelming, as it assuredly is, why has the opposite view prevailed in our time? John Y. Simon has offered some cogent insights into this curious state of affairs, one of which is that critics such as the Randalls have, in effect, "reclassified the romance as an accusation requiring proof, something of which Lincoln would be held innocent until proved guilty, rather than a biographical incident in which a preponderance of reliable evidence would prevail."[61] Simon's point is apt, for there can be little doubt that the key to understanding the banishment of the Ann Rutledge story from Lincoln biography is not simply the historical evidence itself but the standards by which the leading critic, J. G. Randall, has insisted that the evidence be judged.

In choosing to address the question of standards, it is by no means conceded that the criticism of Herndon's evidence that has prevailed for sixty years has been always fair, even-handed, or accurate. On the contrary, there is much to dispute. There is Angle, for example, who had not seen anything like the full evidence in 1927 but wrote as though he had. His characterization of Herndon's testimony shows how limited his knowledge was: "The Rutledge-New Salem testimony consists of letters written to Herndon soon after the publication of his lecture, and of signed statements collected by friends at his request." As we have already seen, most of Herndon's testimony, much of it consisting of personal interviews conducted by himself, was assembled before the lecture. Nor was Angle at pains to exercise care in his characterization of Herndon's evidence: "Some thought it amounted to nothing, others felt that Ann cared just as much for McNamar as for Lincoln, while 'Uncle' Jimmy Short . . . wrote that he had never heard of anything

---

59. For Cogdal's standing in his community, see T. G. Onstot, *Pioneers of Menard and Mason Counties* (Forest City, Ill.: T. G. Onstot, 1902), 231.

60. Donald, *Lincoln's Herndon*, 316. Let it be acknowledged that this depends on what is allowed as "sharply" and "conflicting." The variety of testimony that Donald mentions does not seem to me to exhibit serious conflict as to the three basic elements of the story.

61. Simon, "Abraham Lincoln and Ann Rutledge," 27.

of the kind!"⁶² There is no testimony that the love affair amounted to nothing. The only testimony that Ann cared just as much for McNamar is qualified by the phrase, "to appearances," by which Nancy Green clearly meant "as far as outsiders were able to judge by the way things appeared."⁶³ And Uncle Jimmy's testimony, which has already been quoted, shows that he *did* believe in the romance; he came to this belief, he testifies, when he saw the effect Ann's death had on Lincoln. Angle's failure to quote Uncle Jimmy's actual testimony is further explained by his eagerness to discredit what he called "the 'disastrous effect' legend."⁶⁴

In the light of sixty years' hindsight, it seems clear that Angle's position was way out in front of his evidence and that his essay ultimately demonstrated little more than his eagerness to endorse an idea whose time had come. Like Lee on the attack, his aggressive seizure of the moment more than made up for his lack of resources. J. G. Randall's "Sifting of the Ann Rutledge Evidence," written nearly twenty years later, is of an altogether different character. More comprehensive in its scope, it is widely recognized as the most authoritative treatment of the evidence and therefore the prime document in the debunking of the Ann Rutledge story. Randall gives notice at the outset that his taking up the subject is "not for any intrinsic importance at all, but because historical criticism finds here a challenge and a needful task."⁶⁵ It is clear from the start that he means to deal not only with the evidence itself but with broader issues involved in the proper and legitimate use of historical evidence, and he begins with the problem of reminiscence.

> The historian must use reminiscence, but he must do so critically. Even close-up evidence is fallible. When it comes through the mists of many years some of it may be true, but a careful writer will check it with known facts. Contradictory reminiscences leave doubt as to what is to be believed; unsupported memories are in themselves insufficient as proof; statements induced under suggestion, or psychological stimulus, as were some of the stories about Lincoln and Ann,

---

62. Angle, "Lincoln's First Love?," 7, 6.
63. See Miles to Herndon, Mar. 23, 1866, H-W. Randall's discussion also fails to consider Mrs. Green's qualification.
64. Angle, "Lincoln's First Love?," 7.
65. Randall, "Sifting the Ann Rutledge Evidence," 321. It is clear from his letters and papers, now in the Library of Congress, that Randall vacillated between making this essay a chapter in his book, *Lincoln the President*, and printing it as an appendix, which is what he finally did. I am grateful to John Sellers of the Manuscript Division, Library of Congress, for assistance in examining these papers.

call especially for careful appraisal.... When faulty memories are admitted the resulting product becomes something other than history; it is no longer to be presented as a genuine record.[66]

While this has the professorial tone of a lecture on historiography, there can be no doubt that it was intended to present a standard for separating history from non-history that the evidence given by Herndon's informants, all of which can be readily classified as reminiscence, cannot meet. The crux of the matter is that memories of participants or witnesses to historical events, being fallible, are not sufficient, in and of themselves, to constitute proof. Contemporary evidence or "known facts" must exist with which to check them. The student of Herndon's documents knows without reading further that, overwhelming as the Ann Rutledge evidence is, it cannot pass so stern a test.

Randall advances the view that "in the law of evidence . . . it is insisted that testimony ought to come straight," with the implication that testimony at second and third hand is automatically suspect, if not inadmissible. This is why, as we have seen, he draws attention to Robert B. Rutledge's quoting a letter he has solicited from his cousin McGrady, even though what McGrady has to say seems critically relevant to the facts and events in question. In the same vein, this is why Randall finds it less noteworthy that John Jones was an eyewitness to Lincoln's regular visits to Ann Rutledge and that he saw Lincoln in great distress after his last visit to Ann than that this supposed eyewitness should qualify certain statements by indicating that he had them from others.[67] Just as Randall's evidentiary "law" seems modeled on the inadmissibility of hearsay in a court of law, his objection to what he calls "must have been" evidence seems to be based on the courtroom prohibition on questions calling for a conclusion on the part of a witness. James Short's inferring that Lincoln took Ann's death so hard because he had been in love with her is thus a "must have been" conclusion. In a trial, Short could testify that he saw Lincoln come several miles to visit Ann's house every other day or so and that Lincoln appeared to be greatly distressed at her death, but Short's conclusion, which he freely gave to Herndon, would presumably be out of order.

In sum, Randall insists on an extremely high standard for proof: evidence must be contemporary or confirmed by contemporary evidence; it must be first

---

66. Randall, "Sifting the Ann Rutledge Evidence," 325.
67. Ibid., 328n.

hand and direct; it must not be elicited by leading questions; it must be consistent; it must not include inferences drawn by witnesses. Evidence that fails these tests is less than adequate for proof and thus cannot establish historical reality. In requiring standards for proof not unlike those in criminal trial, Randall tends to treat the Ann Rutledge story, as Simon suggests, like an accusation against Lincoln and one that must be proved beyond a reasonable doubt. This is what justifies his conclusion that the love affair of Lincoln and Ann Rutledge is "unproved" and that it therefore "does not belong in a recital of those Lincoln episodes which one presents as unquestioned reality."[68]

So what does it matter, one may ask, if the standards for evidence are kept conspicuously high in judging the Ann Rutledge affair? Are we not then likely to arrive at a more accurate and reliable result? For reasons to question the appropriateness of such lofty standards in judging what happened in the Ann Rutledge affair, one need look no further than the concrete details of Randall's own practice. In his analysis of the Ann Rutledge evidence, he objects to testimony given at second and third hand but uses it without complaint when it serves his purpose.[69] He objects to the use of hearsay, but when Henry McHenry reports that some residents thought Lincoln's mental condition after Ann's death was brought on by his legal studies, Randall cannot resist mentioning it, even though no informant testified to this as his own belief.[70] And he is often "guilty" of accepting the testimony of a single witness even though it is unsupported. For example, on the basis of the unsupported testimony of John McNamar that he had placed a wooden marker on Ann's grave, Randall announces: "It was McNamar, not Lincoln, who marked Ann's grave. As to Lincoln's grief it has been seen that his alleged derangement of mind is without adequate substantiation; in the 'uncolumned air' of Herndon's lecture it is nothing more than fiction."[71] One unsubstantiated word from McNamar is sufficient proof for Randall that McNamar carved Ann's marker, while the combined testimony of more than a dozen eyewitnesses cannot convince him that Lincoln's grief was unusual.

For Randall, a contemporary letter written by Mathew S. Marsh shortly after Ann's death "establishes the fact that Lincoln was attending to his postmaster duties as usual," though the letter writer says Lincoln was absent from the post

---

68. Ibid., 341.
69. See his use of the testimony of Nancy Green and Mrs. William Rutledge as given in G. U. Miles's letter to Herndon, 331.
70. Randall, "Sifting the Ann Rutledge Evidence," 332.
71. Ibid., 340.

office and could be expected, in violation of postal regulations, to frank the letter.[72] Randall thus allows himself a "must have been" inference that he would have found objectionable in Uncle Jimmy Short. Randall, of course, is not a witness, but in the Ann Rutledge dispute he presents himself less as a historian in search of the truth than as an advocate doggedly defending a position. In the early pages of *Lincoln the President,* Randall the historian draws very extensively on Herndon's informants and depends on them for the documentation of Lincoln's personal and political background. There he does not confine himself to testimony that can be checked with contemporary sources or "known facts," nor does he balk at accepting as historical incidents about which the evidence is conflicting, as will be seen in a notable example given below.

That Randall's own practice is at odds with the standards he himself laid down for judging the Ann Rutledge evidence is hardly surprising. Historical scholarship, for whatever similarities it might bear to trying a case in a court of law, is a very different kind of enterprise and employs different methods. Observing the evidentiary safeguards of a criminal trial would, after all, bring a substantial portion of historical inquiry to a halt, for much of what we want to know about the past simply cannot be established on these terms. Abraham Lincoln's early life is a perfect example. Virtually everything we know about Lincoln as a child and as a young man—his incessant reading and self-education, his storytelling, his honesty, his interest in politics, and so forth—comes exclusively from the recollections of the people who knew him. Non-contemporary, subjective, often unable to be confirmed even by the recollections of others, to say nothing of contemporary documents, this evidence is sheer reminiscence. Even Lincoln's own autobiographical statements fall squarely into this category; though he was a man known for his honesty, he was, in the most extensive and valuable of these statements, representing himself and his personal history for political purposes.[73] Randall's caveats about such evidence and the admixture of error and bias it may contain are certainly justified, but the historian or biographer has no alternative but to find a way to work with it and, indeed, with anything that may be indicative of the truth.

Consider as a parallel episode to the Ann Rutledge affair Lincoln's famous

---

72. Ibid., 335. Only Randall's predisposition prompts him to see this letter as casting doubt on the story of Lincoln's excessive grief; it can just as readily be seen as supporting it.

73. For the two most notable statements, those prepared for Jesse W. Fell and John L. Scripps, see *The Collected Works of Abraham Lincoln,* ed. Roy P. Basler et al. (New Brunswick: Rutgers Univ. Press, 1953), 3:511–12 and 4:60–68.

wrestling match with Jack Armstrong, the leader of the Clary's Grove boys. This event was important not only for its role in establishing the young newcomer at New Salem but, as Beveridge and others have observed, in the launching of Lincoln's political career. From the same group of informants who told him about Ann Rutledge, Herndon collected several versions of the event, some of which were wholly incompatible. One version had Armstrong taking unfair advantage of Lincoln, who took it in such good part that he won the admiration of Armstrong and his followers.[74] Herndon favored a version in which Lincoln believed he had been fouled and angrily shook Armstrong by the throat. Beveridge inclined toward the account of Henry McHenry, one of the Clary's Grove boys, in which Lincoln and Jack agreed that neither could throw the other and shook hands.[75] Benjamin Thomas opted for a version printed by William Dean Howells in which the Clary's Grove boys threatened to intercede when their champion began to get the worst of it, at which point Lincoln offered to fight them all one at a time.[76] While it is true that there is no contemporary evidence of Lincoln's match with Jack Armstrong, several old residents did claim to have seen it. And while it is true that Henry Clark, James Short, Henry McHenry, and R. B. Rutledge disagree substantially about what happened in the match, they do agree, as Beveridge has noted, "that it ended in such fashion as to win the friendship of Armstrong and the allegiance of his band."[77]

If we treat this episode as Randall treats the Ann Rutledge affair, we must declare the evidence hopelessly contradictory and find Lincoln innocent of wrestling Jack Armstrong. The famous match might be granted the status of folklore, but, as Randall wrote of the Ann Rutledge story, it would "not belong in a recital of those Lincoln episodes which one presents as unquestioned reality." But Beveridge sees in the conflicting accounts of the wrestling match some

---

74. See James Short to Herndon, July 7, 1865, H-W.

75. Herndon and Weik, *Herndon's Life of Lincoln*, 70; Beveridge, *Abraham Lincoln*, 1:111. Beveridge's text names Rowan Herndon as the source of the account he favors, but this is a mistake for Henry McHenry.

76. Benjamin Thomas, *Lincoln's New Salem* (Chicago: Americana House, 1954), 65–66. Howells's version seems to be based on interviews by James Quay Howard with William G. Greene and Royal Clary. See David C. Mearns, *The Lincoln Papers* (Garden City: Doubleday, 1948) 1:152–57. Thomas notes that Lincoln let this version stand uncorrected in the copy of Howells's campaign biography he annotated for Samuel Parks. The assumption that whatever Lincoln left uncorrected in the Parks copy of Howells may be relied on as accurate is a very dubious one, not only in light of the known errors Lincoln thus "endorsed" but in light of the distinctly political context in which the corrections were sought and rendered.

77. Beveridge, *Abraham Lincoln*, 1:111.

Table 1. Herndon's Informants on Lincoln and Ann Rutledge

Informant	Loved or Courted AR?	Grieved at AR's Death?	Understanding About Marriage?
Abell, Mrs. E. H.	No Opinion	Yes	No
Bale, Hardin	Yes	Yes	Yes
Bale, Mrs. Hardin	Yes	No Opinion	No Opinion
Bell, Lizzie	Yes	No Opinion	No
Bennett, William	Yes	No Opinion	Yes
Carman, Caleb	Yes	No Opinion	No Opinion
Cogdal, Isaac	Yes	Yes	Yes
Graham, Mentor	Yes	Yes	Yes
Green, Mrs. Nancy	Yes	Yes	Yes
Greene, L. M.	Yes	Yes	Yes
Greene, William G.	Yes	Yes	Yes
Herndon, J. Rowan	Yes	No Opinion	Yes
Hill, John	Yes	Yes	Yes
Hill, Mrs. Samuel	Yes	Yes	Yes
Hohimer, Henry	Yes	No Opinion	Yes
Irwin, B. F.	Yes	Yes	Yes
Jones, John	Yes	Yes	Yes
McHenry, Henry	No Opinion	Yes	No Opinion
McNeely, William	Yes	Yes	No Opinion
Rutledge, James McGrady	Yes	No Opinion	Yes
Rutledge, John M.	Yes	Yes	Yes
Rutledge, Robert B.	Yes	Yes	Yes
Rutledge, Mrs. William	Yes	Yes	No
Short, James	Yes	Yes	No Opinion

critical points of agreement. His approach, in which the discrepancies are not allowed to overshadow more important considerations, preserves the incident as an important part of the biographical record. To accept the essentials of the Jack Armstrong story as proved—which Randall himself does[78]—and dispute the basic elements of the Ann Rutledge story as "unproved" is to operate with a double standard. More importantly, of course, it works to withhold from consideration an incident in Lincoln's early life which is at least as important.

John Y. Simon has sensibly suggested that the Ann Rutledge story should be regarded not as an "accusation requiring proof" but as "a biographical incident in which a preponderance of reliable evidence would prevail." This calls to mind Herndon's story of Lincoln pleading a case in Coles County in which the jury

---

78. Randall, *Lincoln the President*, 1:31n.

returns for further elucidation of the phrase "preponderance of evidence." After the explanations of the judge and the opposing attorney only add to the confusion, Lincoln asks the jury to picture a pair of scales such as they were used to seeing in stores and think of the evidence introduced by each side in the suit as being placed in the scales and weighed. If either side has even the slightest bit more evidence than the other, he tells them, it will cause one side of the scales to go down and that will determine the preponderance of evidence.[79] The jury understood, and Lincoln won. In the case of Ann Rutledge, it is utterly clear where the preponderance of evidence lies, but it hardly follows, as his defenders seem to have feared, that Lincoln is thereby the loser. The restoration of his love affair with Ann Rutledge to Lincoln's biography must be regarded as a positive gain for all who seek to understand the man and the circumstances that brought him forth.

---

79. See Herndon to Jesse W Weik, Nov. 11, 1885, H-W.

Abraham Lincoln and "That Fatal First of January"

Douglas L. Wilson

Abraham Lincoln's courtship of Mary Todd, while one of the most colorful and dramatic episodes in his early life, is also one of the least understood. What obscures this critical chapter in Lincoln's maturation and emergence, and in turn hampers our ability to assess its character and importance, is the fragmentary and incoherent form in which the story of the courtship has come down to us. The crux of the problem of what happened to Lincoln over the course of his courtship is the mysterious broken engagement. Lincoln became engaged to Mary Todd in 1840, but by "that fatal first of Jany. '41" the engagement had been abruptly broken. How it came to be broken, by whom, and under what circumstances have long been subjects of speculation, but much of the mystery remains. What follows is an attempt to shed light on the broken engagement, and thus on Lincoln's development, by relating the testimony of the most knowledgeable witnesses to Lincoln's own letters and other contemporary evidence.

The biographer with the best opportunities for determining what happened in the broken engagement, William H. Herndon, ingloriously failed, for he ultimately opted for an account of the affair that does not stand up. After questioning many witnesses and puzzling over the problem for several years, he decided to accept as true the story of Lincoln's failure to appear at his own wedding on the "fatal first of January" 1841.[1] Though some later biographers were still to give it credence, by 1900 Ida M. Tarbell had effectively undermined its credibility by showing that of the surviving friends and relatives—some of the very people who were presumably left waiting with Mary at the altar—none had ever heard of such a thing, and all denounced it as false.[2]

Paul M. Angle tackled the broken engagement in collaborating with Carl Sandburg on *Mary Lincoln: Wife and Widow* (1932), making it the subject of a special appendix, but he lacked full access to the letters and interviews of Herndon's informants (whom he mistrusted), and tried, with inconclusive results, to clarify the picture through reliance on contemporary letters. The most detailed investigation of Lincoln's courtship was made by Ruth Painter Randall. Her rationale of the courtship was part of a highly partisan and self-conscious effort to rescue the character and reputation of Mary Todd Lincoln, but in spite of a prodigious program of research, her account is essentially that of Mary's family as first put forward by Elizabeth Edwards and later refined by Frances Wallace, Albert S. Edwards, and Katherine Helm[3]: that Lincoln loved Mary from the beginning and that she returned his love; that because of family opposition and Lincoln's doubts about his ability to be a suitable husband to Mary, their engagement was broken through a confrontation on January 1, 1841, and a letter of release sent by Mary shortly thereafter; and that in spite of an estrangement of a year and a

---

1. Herndon's earliest theory regarding the broken engagement is detailed in the letter to Ward Hill Lamon, Feb. 25, 1870, Lamon Papers, Huntington Library, and it is printed in Emanuel Hertz, ed., *The Hidden Lincoln* (New York: Viking, 1938), 62-69. A later and much-altered version occurs in his manuscript account titled "Lincoln & Mary Todd" in the Herndon-Weik Collection, Manuscript Division, Library of Congress (hereafter cited as H-W). His final version appears in the biography on which he collaborated with Jesse W. Weik, *Herndon's Life of Lincoln*, ed. Paul M. Angle (Cleveland: World Publishing, 1949), 166-71.

2. See Ida M. Tarbell, *The Life of Abraham Lincoln* (New York: Lincoln Memorial Association, 1900), 1:176-80. Albert J. Beveridge is the most prominent of later biographers to adopt Herndon's account of the aborted wedding.

3. See Angle's appendix in Carl Sandburg and Paul M. Angle, *Mary Lincoln: Wife and Widow* (New York: Harcourt, Brace, 1932), 329-50; Randall had three tries at it, first in collaboration with her husband in the account given in J. G. Randall, *Lincoln the President: Springfield to Gettysburg* (New York: Dodd, Mead, 1945), 51-62, then in a full-length biography, *Mary Lincoln: Biography of a Marriage* (Boston: Little, Brown, 1953), 36-51, and finally in a popularized account, *The Courtship of Mr. Lincoln* (Boston: Little, Brown, 1957), 111-30; Elizabeth Todd Edwards's account is given in two interviews with William H. Herndon, H-W; Wallace's appears in *Lincoln's Marriage: Newspaper Interview . . . Springfield, Ill., Sept. 2, 1895* (Privately printed, 1917); Albert S. Edwards's is given in Walter B. Stevens, *A Reporter's Lincoln* (St. Louis: Missouri Historical Society, 1916), 73-79; and Katherine Helms's appears in her biography of her aunt, *The True Story of Mary, Wife of Lincoln* (New York: Harper & Brothers, 1928), 86-91.

half, the residual love on both sides eventually triumphed over these obstacles, resulting in the quickly arranged marriage on November 4, 1842. As we shall see, this family version is very difficult to reconcile with the testimony of competent witnesses, but for Mrs. Randall, it was a classic American love story, "where a girl of the aristocracy remained loyal to her lover of log-cabin origin, meeting him secretly and defying family opposition to her marrying a man 'on a different social plane.'"[4]

Mrs. Randall's account of the broken engagement in her biography of Mary Todd Lincoln has long been considered standard, if not definitive, but as Charles B. Strozier has urged, her "explanation of Lincoln's motivation is naive." He calls her smiling version of this troubled courtship "Romeo and Juliet, American style" in that it "posits an external force [the family's disapproval] to explain Lincoln's breaking the engagement." Strozier himself has argued forcefully that Lincoln's broken engagement is related to his "inner conflicts over intimacy [which] cannot be fully grasped by examining his courtship of Mary Todd." This provocative thesis may have dampened the incentive for a fresh consideration of the factual history of the courtship, for Strozier accepted Mrs. Randall's account of the factual details as "not likely to be surpassed." But while acquiescing in Mrs. Randall's factual account of what happened, Strozier opened up an original and fruitful venue by emphasizing the crucial role played by Lincoln's friend Joshua E. Speed, "whose patient friendship during these crucial years first aggravated Lincoln's conflicts, then served as the vehicle for their resolution."[5] The present discussion, accordingly, takes as its starting point Joshua Speed's own account of the broken engagement.

Joshua Speed was a well-to-do and well-educated young Kentuckian, a friend of Mary Todd and her Springfield circle, and by all accounts he was the closest friend Abraham Lincoln ever had. Even Herndon, who yielded to no one in overall knowledge of Lincoln, conceded, on the basis of what Speed told him and the copies of Speed's letters from Lincoln, that Speed had Lincoln's confidence in something he rarely discussed with others, namely his relations with women. "Lincoln loved this man [Speed] more than any one dead or living; and it may truthfully be said that Lincoln 'poured out his whole soul['] to Speed in his love scrapes with Miss Todd."[6]

4. Randall, *Mary Lincoln*, 64.
5. Charles B. Strozier, *Lincoln's Quest for Union: Public and Private Meanings* (Urbana: Univ. of Illinois Press, 1987), 39, 41.
6. "Lincoln & Mary Todd," H-W.

In sending Herndon copies of his letters from Lincoln during this period, Speed explained that a special relationship had existed between himself and Lincoln in the matter of courtship. "In the winter of 40 & 41, he was very unhappy about his engagement to his wife—Not being entirely satisfied that his heart was going with his hand. How much he suffered then on that account none know so well as myself. He disclosed his whole heart to me." We have no reason to doubt what Speed says, but for confirmation that Speed knew the intimate details of Lincoln's ordeal, we have Lincoln's explicit acknowledgment of it. Speaking of the personal difficulties surrounding his courtship as a failure "to keep my resolves when they are made," Lincoln wrote Speed in July 1842: "In that ability, you know, I once prided myself as the only, or at least the chief, gem of my character; that gem I lost—how, and when, you know too well."[7]

What was it that Speed knew? This was the question asked by Herndon in an interview with Speed, and his response deserves careful attention. In the original manuscript in the Herndon-Weik Collection, Herndon's notes on what Speed told him about the broken engagement are recorded in two separate entries on different sheets of paper but have been marked by Herndon with carets, indicating that the two were part of the same narrative and were intended to be woven together.[8]

This is what Herndon first wrote, apparently at white heat, either as Speed spoke or as Herndon remembered his testimony.

J. F. Speed

In 1840 Lincoln went into the southern part of the state as Election Canvasser debator Speaker—Here first wrote his Mary—She darted after him—wrote him—Lincoln—seeing an other girl—& finding he did not love his wife wrote a letter saying he did not love her—Speed saw the letter—tell the Conversation—between Lincoln & Speed—Went to see "Mary"—told her that he did not love her—She rose—and said "the deciever shall be decieved wo is me," alluding to a young man she fooled—Lincoln drew her down on his knee kissed her—& parted—He going one way & she an other—Lincoln did love Miss Edwards—"Mary" saw

---

7. Joshua F. Speed to Herndon, Nov. 30, 1866, H-W; AL to Speed, July 4, 1842, Roy Basler et al., eds., *The Collected Works of Abraham Lincoln* (New Brunswick, N.J.: Rutgers Univ. Press, 1953), 1:289; hereafter cited as *Collected Works*.

8. It should be noted that Herndon refers in his biography to at least one letter from Speed bearing on the broken engagement that does not appear to be in the Herndon-Weik Collection, that dated Jan. 6, 1866 (*Herndon's Life of Lincoln*, 170), but the substance of the testimony is very close to what is given in the undated interview.

it—told Lincoln the reason of his change of mind—heart & soul—released him—Lincoln went crazy—had to remove razors from his room—take away all knives and other such dangerous things—&c—it was terrible—was during the Special session of the Ills Legislature in 1840 Lincoln married her for honor—feeling his honor bound to her—[9]

The second part, written on a separate sheet, apparently represents Herndon's effort to "tell the Conversation—between Lincoln & Speed" about the proposed letter to Mary Todd:

Speed saw the letter to "Mary" written by Mr Lincoln. Speed tried to persuade Lincoln to burn it up. Lincoln said—"Speed I always knew you were an obstinate man. If you won't deliver it I will get some one to do it. I should not deliver it nor give it to you to be delivered: Words are forgotten—Misunderstood—passed by—not noticed in a private Conversation—but once put your words in writing and they stand as a living & eternal monument against you. If you think you have will & manhood enough to go and see her and speak to her what you say in that letter, you may do that. Lincoln did go and see her—did tell her &c—Speed said—Lincoln tell me what you said and did"—Lincoln told him—Speed said—The last thing is a bad lick, but it cannot now be helped—Lincoln kept his promises and did not go to see her for months—they got together somehow.[10]

It is clear that this second part was intended to go into the narrative at the point where Herndon had written, and then struck out, "Speed saw the letter," as these are the first words of the second passage, and the first passage is marked at that place with a caret.[11] But simply inserting the second passage at the point indicated has the unfortunate effect of confusing the chronology, because the second passage, which was originally intended to "tell the conversation" of Speed and Lincoln, actually continues the narrative beyond the time of the conversation and thus, when inserted as indicated, gets ahead of the story. If we attempt to

---

9. The passage "Lincoln went crazy . . . 1840" is written vertically on the same sheet in the left margin, with carets indicating its insertion point; undated interview with Herndon, H-W.

10. Undated interview with Herndon, H-W. In his biography, Herndon expands on the exchange between Lincoln and Speed over the letter and fills in details as to what transpired between them when Lincoln returned. See *Herndon's Life of Lincoln*, 168-69.

11. Such an insertion is precisely what was done by the copyist, John G. Springer, presumably under Herndon's supervision, in transcribing Herndon's "Lincoln Records," now part of the Ward Hill Lamon Papers at the Huntington Library.

rectify this editorially, by putting the narrated events from the second passage in sequence, we arrive at the following (second-passage material italicized):

> J. F. Speed
>   In 1840 Lincoln went into the southern part of the state as Election Canvasser debator Speaker—Here first wrote his Mary—She darted after him—wrote him—Lincoln—seeing an other girl—& finding he did not love his wife wrote a letter saying he did not love her—*Speed saw the letter to "Mary" written by Mr Lincoln. Speed tried to persuade Lincoln to burn it up. Lincoln said—"Speed I always knew you were an obstinate man. If you won't deliver it I will get some one to do it. I should not deliver it nor give it to you to be delivered: Words are forgotten—Misunderstood—passed by—not noticed in a private Conversation—but once put your words in writing and they stand as a living & eternal monument against you. If you think you have will & manhood enough to go and see her and speak to her what you say in that letter, you may do that. Lincoln did go and see her—*... told her that he did not love her—She rose—and said "the deciever shall be decieved wo is me," alluding to a young man she fooled—Lincoln drew her down on his knee kissed her—& parted—He going one way & she an other—*Speed said—Lincoln tell me what you said and did"—Lincoln told him—Speed said—The last thing is a bad lick, but it cannot now be helped*—Lincoln did love Miss Edwards—"Mary" saw it—told Lincoln the reason of his change of mind—heart & soul—released him—Lincoln went crazy—had to remove razors from his room—take away all knives and other such dangerous things—&c—it was terrible—was during the Special session of the Ills Legislature in 1840 *Lincoln kept his promises and did not go to see her for months—they got together somehow.*—Lincoln married her for honor—feeling his honor bound to her—[12]

This seems to represent Herndon's intention, as nearly as it can be inferred, and has the fortunate effect of resolving the chronological discrepancies.[13] Here then, in Herndon's abbreviated and sometimes telegraphic report, is what Speed told him about Lincoln's courtship: Lincoln took up with Mary by letter during his campaign excursion into Egypt (in August and September of 1840), and she responded eagerly. Through his interest in another woman, he discovered that

---

12. Note that in this conflated version the crossed-out material, the instruction ("tell the conversation—between Lincoln & Speed"), and the overlapping phrases ("did tell her&c—" and "Went to see 'Mary'—") have been eliminated.

13. Mrs. Randall's failure to sort these matters properly leads her to accuse Herndon of deliberate misstatements. See Randall, *Mary Lincoln*, 45.

he did not love Mary. He wrote this in a letter to Mary but was persuaded by Speed to tell her its import in person. When he confronted her, she reproached herself and wept, at which point he comforted and kissed her, a gesture that Speed put down as a "bad lick." Later, seeing that Lincoln was in love with Matilda Edwards, Mary confronted him, telling him she knew how things stood, and released him. This happened during the special session of the legislature in 1840 (November 23 to December 5) and caused Lincoln to go crazy and appear suicidal. Having made a promise (either to himself, to Mary, or to the Edwards family), he did not call on her for many months. When he finally married her, it was to satisfy his sense of honor, presumably because he felt bound by the commitment he had originally made.

Speed's version of what happened between Lincoln and Mary Todd contains at least two elements that stand out as striking departures from the versions of Mrs. Randall and most authoritative biographers. The first is the date of the confrontation with Mary that precipitated Lincoln's temporary derangement. The documentary record of Lincoln's prolonged bout with the "hypo" in January 1841, of which his own letters are a telling portion, has suggested to all biographers from Herndon onward that any suicidal behavior must have come then. But Speed, his closest friend and confidant, is quite specific that the break with Mary and the consequent "crazy spell" happened during the special session of the legislature, which he correctly places in 1840. We shall return to the matter of chronology in due course. The second thing that stands out in Speed's account is the crucial role played by Lincoln's feelings for Matilda Edwards in his relations with Mary Todd. Matilda was the eighteen-year-old daughter of the prominent Whig politician, Cyrus Edwards, of Alton, who had brought his daughter along with him in mid-November when he came to Springfield to attend the upcoming sessions of the legislature.[14] She stayed in the home of her cousin, Ninian W. Edwards, the same household in which Mary Todd was living, and she remained there for many months.

Ninian W. Edwards was also Mary Todd's brother-in-law, and his version of what brought about the broken engagement accords with Speed's. As the

---

14. The Edwards's arrival in Springfield must have occurred sometime prior to the opening of the special session of the legislature on Nov. 23, 1840. Her first letter home, addressed to her brother Nelson, is dated Nov. 30. A photostat of this letter is in the Randall papers, Library of Congress; it is quoted by Ruth Painter Randall in *The Courtship of Mr. Lincoln*, 69–70. For permission to examine the Randall papers, I am grateful to David H. Donald, and for assistance in using them, to John R. Sellers.

head of the household to which Mary Todd belonged and one who considered himself responsible for her welfare, he was in a position to know a good deal of what went on between Mary and Lincoln, especially from Mary's point of view. Herndon's notes on his interview with Edwards are given in full:

> Says—Sept 22d 1865—That during Lincoln's Courtship with Miss Todd—afterwards Lincoln's wife—that he, Lincoln, fell in Love with a Miss Edwards—daughter of Cyrus Edwards, who was brother of Govr N. W. Edwards—Matilda Edwards was her name: she subsequently became the wife of Mr. Strong of Alton. Lincoln did not ever by act or deed directly or indirectly hint or speak of it to Miss Edwards: she became aware of this—Lincoln's affections—the Lincoln and Todd engagement was broken off in consequence of it—Miss Todd released Lincoln from the Contract, leaving Lincoln the privilege of renewing it (poor fellow H.) if he wished—Lincoln in his conflicts of duty—honor and his love went as crazy as a *Loon*—was taken to Kentucky—by Speed—or went to Speed's—was kept there till he recovered finally—(unfortunate man! H) He was cured—Edwards admits that he wanted Speed to marry Miss Edwards and Lincoln Miss Todd: He gave me policy reasons for it—the substance of which I give in an other place—Matilda Edwards refused Speed—(J. F. Speed of Louisville Ky) as she refused S. A. Douglas—she refused Douglas on the grounds of his bad morals. Lincoln did not attend the Legislature in 1841 & 2 for this reason—so is Mrs Wm Butler correct as to her suspicions.[15]

When taking down this interview, which came fairly early in his investigations, Herndon affects never to have heard of Matilda Edwards, but he was eventually to hear a good deal more.[16] Elizabeth Edwards, the wife of Ninian and the elder sister of Mary Todd, had her own version of what happened. Her testimony Herndon took down in unusual detail. This was doubtless for the reason that Mrs. Edwards was in an even better position to know what was going on between Lincoln and Mary, inasmuch as she had been something of a mother to her younger sister and had taken a close personal interest in her

---

15. Edwards's account of the marriage he wanted of Speed and Miss Edwards has not been located; interview with Herndon, Sept. 22, 1865, H-W.
16. Though Herndon writes as though he had never heard of Matilda Edwards, this seems merely to be a style of reporting followed early in his investigations in which he affects to be an unknowing recorder of information. Some of his early interviews he wrote out as though they were letters to himself and had the interviewees sign them.

affairs. Elizabeth was particularly at pains to explain her own and her husband's role in the affair, first encouraging and then discouraging the match, and her account contained an even more startling assertion.

> I knew Mr L well—he was a cold man—had no affection—was not social—was abstracted—thoughtful—I knew he was a great man long years since Knew he was a rising man and nothing else modifying this, desired Mary at first to Marry L. L. could not hold a lengthy conversation with a lady—was not sufficiently educated & intelligent in the female line to do so—He was charmed with Mary's wit and fascinated with her quick sagacity—her will—her nature—and culture. I have happened in the room where they were sitting often & often and Mary led the conversation—Lincoln would listen & gaze on her as if drawn by some superior power, irresistably so: he listened—never scarcely said a word. I did not in a little time think that Mr. L. and Mary were suitable to each other and so said to Mary. Mary was quick, lively, gay, frivolous it may be, social and loved glitter, show & pomp & power. She was an extremely ambitious woman and in Ky. often and often Contended that she was destined to be the wife of some future President—Said it in my presence in Springfield and Said it in earnest. Mr. Speed came to see Miss Matilda Edwards—left & went to Ky—Miss Edwards staying. Mr Lincoln loved Mary—he went crazy in my opinion—not because he loved Miss Edwards as Said, but because he wanted to marry and doubted his ability & Capacity to please and support a wife. Lincoln and Mary were engaged—Every thing was ready & prepared for the marriage—even to the supper &c—. Mr L. failed to meet his engagement—Cause insanity. In his lunacy he declared he hated Mary and loved Miss Edwds. This is true, yet it was not his real feelings. A crazy man hates those he loves when at himself—often—often is this the Case. The world had it that Mr L backed out and this placed Mary in a peculiar situation & to set herself right and to free Mr. Lincoln's mind she wrote a letter to Mr L stating that she would release him from his engagements. Mr Edwards & myself after the first crush of things told Mary and Lincoln that they had better not ever marry—that their natures, mind—Education—raising &c—were so different they could not live happy as husband & wife—had better never think of the subject again. However all at once we heard that Mr L & Mary had secret meetings at Mr S. Francis'—Editor of the Sprfgd Journal. Mary said the reason this was so—the cause why it was—that the world—woman & man were uncertain & slippery and that it was best to keep the secret courtship from all Eyes & Ears. Mrs L told Mr L that though she had released him in the letter spoken of—yet she said that

she would hold the question an open one—that is that she had not changed her mind, but felt as always. The whole of the year the crazy spell Miss Edwards was at our house—say for a year. I asked Miss Edwards subsequently Mrs Strong if Mr Lincoln ever mentioned the subject of his love to her. Miss Edwards said— "On my word he never mentioned such a subject to me: he never even stooped to pay me a compliment."[17]

Ninian and Elizabeth Edwards clearly had different interpretations of Matilda Edwards's role in what occurred between Lincoln and Mary Todd in the winter of 1840–41, but they agreed that Matilda and Lincoln's supposed love for her had been spoken of.[18] For Ninian, Lincoln's "affections" for Matilda were the cause of the broken engagement, and he probably regarded Lincoln's telling Mary that he loved Matilda as the precipitating factor; for Elizabeth, this outburst was merely a manifestation of Lincoln's insanity. They agreed that Mary gave Lincoln an open-ended release and that he went crazy, but while Ninian's account seems to support Speed's in having the lunacy come after the release, Elizabeth clearly believed the release came by letter after Lincoln's derangement.

What struck Herndon most forcefully in Elizabeth Edwards's testimony was, of course, the sensational story of Lincoln's failure to appear at his own wedding. Herndon may have been skeptical at first, but Mrs. Edwards repeated her story independently to his collaborator, Jesse W. Weik, and Herndon eventually decided to accept it.[19] Herndon's decision to accept Elizabeth Edwards's story of the defaulting bridegroom as authentic had important consequences: it not only skewed his entire conception of the courtship, but it eventually cost him much in the way of credibility as a biographer.

In addition to the testimony of Speed and the Edwardses, Herndon heard about the role of Matilda Edwards from yet another well-placed member of

---

17. Herndon's notes for this interview in H-W are undated, but in the original edition of *Herndon's Lincoln* (p. 227), they are dated Jan. 10, 1866.

18. It is clear from his solo interview and from other testimony referred to later that Ninian W. Edwards disagreed with his wife's view of what happened but acquiesced in her version when they were interviewed together. Mrs. John T. Stuart told Ida M. Tarbell: "The late Judge Broadwell told me that he had asked Mr. Ninian Edwards about [the aborted wedding ceremony], and Mr. Edwards told him that no such thing had ever taken place." Tarbell, *Life of Lincoln*, 1:177–78.

19. Herndon may have questioned Mrs. Edwards again about this years later, though his notes, written after the interview on July 27, 1887 (H-W), make no mention of it. Weik's diary entry of his interview on Dec. 20, 1883, is given in Jesse W. Weik, *The Real Lincoln* (Boston: Houghton Mifflin, 1922), 63.

Lincoln's early Springfield circle, James H. Matheny, who was chosen to stand up with Lincoln when he finally married Mary Todd. Some of the details of Matheny's testimony must have horrified Ninian and Elizabeth Edwards when they appeared in Ward Hill Lamon's biography in 1872,[20] but Matheny's testimony corroborates important parts of Ninian's testimony and supports Speed's belief that the ultimate reason Lincoln married Mary Todd was to preserve his honor. In recording his interview with Matheny, Herndon noted:

> That Lincoln and himself in 1842 were very friendly—That Lincoln came to him one evening and said—Jim—"I shall have to marry that girl." Matheny says that on the same evening Mr & Mrs Lincoln were married—That Lincoln looked and acted as if he were going to the slaughter—: That Lincoln often told him directly & indirectly that he was driven into the marriage—said it was concocted & planned by the Edwards family—: that Miss Todd—afterwards Mrs Lincoln told L. that he was honor bound to marry her—: That Lincoln was crazy for a week or so—not knowing what to do—: that he loved Miss Matilda Edwards and went to see her and not Mrs. Lincoln—Miss Todd.
>
> Matheny further says that soon after the race—the political friendly race between Baker & Lincoln—which was in 1846 or 7 and after Lincoln was married that Lincoln took him—Matheny to the woods and there and then said in reference to L's marriage *in the aristocracy*—"Jim—I am now and always shall be the same Abe Lincoln that I always was"—Lincoln said this with great Emphasis—The cause of this was that in the Baker & Lincoln race it had been charged that L had married in the aristocracy—had married in the Edwards—Todd & Stuart family.[21]

Herndon's notes suggest a credible context for Lincoln's having spoken candidly to Matheny on so personal, and presumably so painful a subject—the galling imputation that he had married for social position when he had actu-

---

20. See Ward Hill Lamon, *The Life of Abraham Lincoln; From his Birth to his Inauguration as President* (Boston: James R. Osgood and Co., 1872), 243. Herndon sold copies of his Lincoln materials to Lamon in 1869 and provided explanations and interpretations by letter that were incorporated into the biography by Lamon's ghost, Chauncey Black.

21. Interview with Herndon dated May 3, 1866, H-W. Curiously, Matheny is the only witness to support Mrs. Edwards's story of the aborted wedding. Jesse W. Weik says he spoke several times with Judge Matheny about the broken engagement and concluded: "The marriage was originally set for a day in the winter of 1840–41, probably New Year's Day, and Judge Matheney [sic] always insisted that he had been asked to serve as groomsman then." *The Real Lincoln*, 60.

ally been maneuvered into a commitment he could not honorably evade. At the same time, it should be noted that Lincoln had a political motive for putting this construction on his marriage, for Matheny was one of a group of young Sangamon Whigs who resented the aristocratic wing of the party and whose support was apparently shifting from Lincoln to Edward D. Baker.[22] Matheny's other testimony shows that he was not an admirer of Mary Todd, but he seems to be clear in stating that Lincoln told him on several occasions that the Edwards family—presumably Ninian and Elizabeth—had connived at his engagement, and that afterwards Mary told Lincoln that "he was honor bound to marry her." He also seems clear that Lincoln told him he had loved and wished to court Matilda Edwards, not Mary Todd.

Those familiar with these witnesses and their relationships to Lincoln will realize that there are many complications to be sorted out in all this testimony. The Edwardses, whose political and personal relations with Lincoln were often strained and who were still chafing at their treatment during Lincoln's presidency when they gave their testimony, were presumably well aware of the charge that Matheny referred to—that Lincoln married into their family for social position. In their testimony, the Edwardses were at pains to emphasize their discouragement of the match, though when he spoke to Herndon alone, Ninian had admitted that he originally wanted Lincoln to marry his sister-in-law for "policy reasons." For his part, Lincoln may well have come to see this original encouragement in a different light, and thus told Matheny that he had been lured into an engagement that Mary had subsequently told him he could not bow out of with honor. Sensitivity to this charge, along with the rumors that Lincoln had backed out, were surely reasons the Edwardses both stressed Mary's letter of release and its generous, open-ended character.

But the point to be made here is that the four principal accounts of the courtship collected by Herndon—those of Joshua F. Speed, Ninian W. Edwards, Elizabeth Todd Edwards, and James H. Matheny—all implicate Lincoln's feelings for Matilda Edwards as a prime factor in the breaking of the engagement. And what is noteworthy about all this testimony naming Matilda Edwards is that it cannot be classified as gossip.[23] All of these informants were either intimates of

---

22. This circumstance is explicitly spelled out by Herndon in his manuscript account, "Lincoln & Mary Todd," H-W.

23. Mrs. Randall's depiction of Ninian W. Edwards as merely retailing the Springfield gossip about his sister-in-law strains belief and is perhaps understandable only in terms of her undisguised wish to undermine his testimony. See Randall, *Mary Lincoln*, 49.

Lincoln or close relatives of Mary. They are presumably describing for Herndon what they witnessed and were told by the principals themselves, as opposed to what was speculated by others. And though they have varying perspectives and interpretations of what they saw and heard, all of these informants indicate that Lincoln's attraction for Matilda Edwards was a factor in the broken engagement of Lincoln and Mary Todd, for even Elizabeth Edwards, who thought Lincoln did not love Matilda, acknowledged that he told Mary he did.

Though recent biographies of Lincoln or Mary Todd fail even to mention the name of Matilda Edwards, there is a surprising amount of other evidence that supports the testimony that Lincoln had romantic inclinations toward her and that she was at least a passive player in what one contemporary called "the Mary Todd 'embrigglement.'"[24] Herndon himself was for several years persuaded of its truth, with the result that Chauncey Black adopted this interpretation in scripting Ward Hill Lamon's biography. A niece of Matilda's, Alice Edwards Quigley, bore witness to the tradition in her family: "Tradition tells us that Lincoln and Douglas were both in love with her." Ninian Edwards' son, Albert S. Edwards, also reported that his "family thought that Lincoln was much taken with Matilda, but nothing came of it beyond story-telling and fun-making." Sarah Rickard, herself the object of Lincoln's attentions during this period, remembered something similar.[25]

There are, as Mrs. Randall acknowledges, indications that Matilda Edwards was accounted the cause of Lincoln and Mary's breakup in Springfield gossip. An example appears in the tradition handed down in the Springfield family of Octavia Roberts, in which Matilda's actual relationship to Ninian Edwards (she was his cousin) has been confused. Roberts, who interviewed many people who had known the Lincolns, wrote: "That [Lincoln's] attraction for [Mary Todd] suddenly ceased all the world knows, but the reasons given for his change of heart differ. My Grandmother, who was Mrs. Lincoln's contemporary, always told

---

24. Attributed to Uncle Jesse Dubois in Milton Hay to John Hay, Feb. 8, 1887, in "Recollection of Lincoln: Three Letters of Intimate Friends," *Bulletin of the Abraham Lincoln Association* 25 (Dec. 1931), 9.

25. Lamon, *Life of Abraham Lincoln*, 239–41; reproduced in H. O. Knerr, *Abraham Lincoln and Matilda Edwards*, mimeographed typescript (Allentown, Pa., n.d.), Illinois State Historical Library; Walter B. Stevens, *A Reporter's Lincoln* (St. Louis: Missouri Historical Society, 1916), 75; see the long interview with Sarah Rickard Barret and her husband Richard F. Barret reported by Nellie Crandall Sanford for the *St. Louis Globe-Democrat*. A clipping of this article, datelined Kansas City, Mo., Feb. 9, without heading or page number but dated in pencil 1907, is in the files of the Lincoln Collection, Illinois State Historical Library.

her family that it was owing to the visit of Ninian Edwards' own sister, who was a beautiful girl, and won Lincoln's love."²⁶ But in addition to family traditions and gossip, there is also a contemporary document that strikingly confirms the recollections of Speed, Ninian Edwards, and Matheny. This is a letter from Jane D. Bell in Springfield to Ann Bell in Danville, Kentucky, dated January 27, 1841, which reads in part:

> Miss Todd is flourishing largely. She has a great many Beaus.
> You ask me how she and Mr. Lincoln are getting along. Poor fellow, he is in rather a bad way. Just at present though he is on the mend now as he was out on Monday for the first time for a month dying with love they say. The Doctors say he came within an inch of being a perfect lunatic for life. He was perfectly crazy for some time, not able to attend to his business at all. They say he don't look like the same person. It seems he had addressed Mary Todd and she accepted him and they had been engaged some time when a Miss Edwards of Alton came here, and he fell desperately in love with her and found he was not so much attached to Mary as he thought. He says if he had it in his power he would not have one feature in her face altered, he thinks she is so perfect (that is, Miss E.) He and Mr. Speed have spent the most of their time at Edwards this winter and Lincoln could never bear to leave Miss Edward's side in company. Some of his friends thought he was acting very wrong and very imprudently and told him so and he went crazy on the strength of it so the story goes and that is all I know . . . [torn off] No one but Speed . . . [torn off]²⁷

While Jane D. Bell does not claim to be offering a firsthand account or even to know more than a few details, her source of information seems to be close to Lincoln's circle of friends, the coterie that frequented the Edwards home. Mrs. Randall scorns the testimony in this letter as mere gossip, citing the expression

---

26. Octavia Roberts, "We All Knew Abr'ham," *Abraham Lincoln Quarterly* 4, no. 1 (Mar. 1946):
27. The mistake of identifying Matilda as the sister of Ninian occurs in Ward Hill Lamon's biography and may have worked its way into Springfield traditions from that source. See Lamon, *Life of Abraham Lincoln*, 239.
27. This text is taken from a copy of the letter supplied to Prof. John B. Clark of Lincoln Memorial University in 1948 by Mary B. E. (Mrs. Henry) Jackson, a relative of the writer of the letter, identified as Jane Hamilton Daviess Bell, and in turn copied and supplied to James G. Randall by R. Gerald McMurtry on Nov. 7, 1950 (Randall Papers, Manuscript Division, Library of Congress). This text varies slightly from the extract printed in the *Lincoln Herald*, 50:4-51:1 (Dec. 1948-Feb. 1949), 47, which omits the final fragment. The original of this letter has not been located.

"they say" as indicative of its being little more than "wagging tongues." But Jane D. Bell would appear to have been much better connected in such matters than the typical Springfield gossip. She was another Kentuckian, related by marriage to James Bell, the proprietor of James Bell & Co., over whose store Lincoln shared a bed with Bell's first cousin and business partner, Joshua F. Speed.[28] Writing to the sister of James Bell, Jane D. Bell was not so much spreading idle gossip as responding, as the letter clearly shows, to a request for information about the status of a match that must have been of particular interest to Kentuckians—that of the upstart politician, Abraham Lincoln, and the aristocratic Kentucky belle, Mary Todd. Her source is not named, but it seems likely that the most intimate details of the story she sketched were known, in the words of her fragmentary sentence, to "no one but Speed."

Jane D. Bell's pointed reference to the admonitions of Lincoln's friends concerning his behavior points to an issue that requires attention: the possibility that Speed and Lincoln were both in love with Matilda Edwards at the same time. Speed's account is silent on the subject, but both Ninian and Elizabeth Edwards testified explicitly that Speed courted Matilda, and Ninian told Herndon that Speed went so far as to propose marriage and was refused. Elizabeth's testimony even hints that his lack of success with Matilda had something to do with his decision to return to Kentucky: "Mr. Speed came to see Miss Matilda Edwards—left & went to Ky—Miss Edwards staying." Speed himself, though he did not name the woman involved, described his feelings as a failed suitor in a letter to his sister in March 1841 and talked about leaving Illinois for Kentucky.[29] But perhaps the most vivid and telling proof of Speed's pursuit of Matilda Edwards in the winter of 1840–41 is found in another contemporary document, a letter written by Mary Todd about two weeks before the "fatal" first of January 1841. In this letter, Mary briefed her close friend, Mercy Levering, on the newest arrival on the Springfield social scene: "I know you would be pleased with Matilda Edwards, a lovelier girl I never saw. Mr Speed's ever changing heart I

---

28. For an account of the relationship of Bell and Speed (their mothers were sisters), see George W. Frye, *Colonel Joshua Fry of Virginia and Some of his Descendants and Allied Families* (Cincinnati: n.p., 1966), 39, 103–4, 169–70. I am indebted to Thomas F. Schwartz and Jeffrey Douglas for assistance in establishing the relationship of Bell and Speed.

29. "I have been most anxiously in pursuit of one—and from all present appearances, if my philosophy be true I am to be most enviably felicitous, for I may have as much of the anticipation and pursuit as I please, but the possession I can hardly ever hope to realize." Joshua Speed to Eliza Speed, Mar. 12, 1841, Illinois State Historical Library.

suspect is about offering its young affections at her shrine, with some others."³⁰ "With some others" confirms what Mary had written earlier and others were to remark, that Matilda had many admirers.

If the testimony detailed above may be credited, Speed and Lincoln were both in love with Matilda Edwards. Whether they were both in love with her at the same time returns us to the first point raised by Speed's own account of Lincoln's broken engagement—its chronology. Herndon's ultimate decision to accept Mrs. Edwards's version of the broken engagement seems to have affected his entire conception of the courtship and caused him to ignore much of what Speed and others had told him, including the recurring testimony about the role of Matilda Edwards. Though he and Weik say little about the chronology of the courtship in their biography, Herndon had blocked one out in a manuscript drafted in the 1880s titled "Lincoln & Mary Todd." Here he worked backwards from the supposed wedding day, January 1, 1841, and reasoned that the letter to Mary Todd "was handed to Speed about August 1840 probably a little before."³¹

What might be called the accepted chronology of the courtship, inasmuch as it is employed by virtually every modern biographer, features an extended acquaintance and courtship beginning in 1839, an engagement sometime in 1840, an incident involving another suitor that provokes a jealous reaction from Lincoln, and a confrontation on the first day of January 1841 that sunders the engagement. When we compare this to the account given by Joshua Speed, whose familiarity with the facts is attested by Lincoln himself, we are presented with a very different picture. Speed implies that Lincoln first made romantic overtures to Mary by mail during his electioneering trip to Southern Illinois in August and September 1840. Since Lincoln left for the circuit almost immediately upon returning from his electioneering junket in September, he and Mary could have had very few days together before the special session of the legislature, which opened November 23.³² This session only lasted two weeks and was marked at the end by Lincoln's famous leap from the church window on the final day,

---

30. Mary Todd to Mercy Levering, Dec. [15?] 1840, Justin G. Turner and Linda Levitt Turner, eds., *Mary Todd Lincoln: Her Life and Letters* (New York: Alfred A. Knopf, 1972), 20.

31. Herndon believed for some time what his informants had told him, that Lincoln's love for Matilda was a factor in the broken engagement, but he later acceded to Mrs. Edwards's contention that it was not a factor and so left Matilda out of *Herndon's Lincoln*. See his statement in "Lincoln & Mary Todd," H-W.

32. See *Lincoln Day by Day: A Chronology 1909-1865*, ed. Earl Schenck Miers and William E. Baringer (Washington: Lincoln Sesquicentennial Commission, 1960), 1:147.

December 5. Speed says that it was during this special session that Lincoln had his final interview with Mary Todd and subsequently went crazy and became suicidal, at least four weeks prior to the first of January 1841. Of course, Speed could have been mistaken or he could have confused the special session with the regular one, which began two days later on December 7. But he does make a point of its being the special session, presumably in order to distinguish it from the regular one and to place the incident more precisely in time, and he does date it correctly in 1840. And surprising as it may seem, this dating fits very well with the other testimony and contemporary evidence.

If Speed's dating is accurate, the events he recounted happened in a fairly short period of time. Except for two brief stopovers between trips, Lincoln was absent from Springfield between August 18 and November 7 or 8. Matilda Edwards probably arrived about a week later. In Herndon's notes, Speed says that "Lincoln—seeing an other girl—& finding he did not love his wife wrote a letter saying he did not love her." It would seem an obvious inference that Matilda Edwards, whom Speed later names and says Lincoln did love, is the other girl that Lincoln was attracted to, especially in light of the testimony of Mr. and Mrs. Edwards and Judge Matheny. According to Speed, Lincoln's first confrontation with Mary, in which he told her he did not love her and Mary reproached herself and wept, not only failed of its intention but actually had the opposite effect of renewing the engagement.[33] But a second confrontation, Speed told Herndon, in which Mary acknowledged Lincoln's love for Matilda, brought the engagement to an end.

Speed's account of the second confrontation is capsulated in Herndon's notes thus: "Lincoln did love Miss Edwards—'Mary' saw it—told Lincoln the reason of his change of mind—heart & soul—released him." Speed here has Mary confront Lincoln with his love for Matilda Edwards, but it is quite possible that her remarks about Matilda may have come in response to something offered by Lincoln. There is a persistent and widespread tradition that Mary's flagrant attentions to another suitor—most likely Edwin B. Webb—was the cause of an angry remonstrance by Lincoln at their last interview. Though Speed's and Ninian Edwards's testimonies suggest that she may have given Lincoln his release at this second encounter, Matheny testified that Lincoln told him of a confrontation

---

33. This is spelled out in Herndon's biography, where he quotes Speed as telling Lincoln, "You not only acted the fool, but your conduct was tantamount to a renewal of the engagement, and in decency you cannot back down now." *Herndon's Life of Lincoln*, 169.

in which Mary told him "that he was honor bound to marry her." But all three of these informants told Herndon that the breakup precipitated in Lincoln a spell of temporary insanity, which, by Speed's dating, would have had to occur no later than December 5, 1840.

As we have seen, there was certainly a good deal of talk at the time and subsequently about Lincoln's attentions to Matilda Edwards, and while Ninian and Elizabeth Edwards admitted that her name was mentioned by Lincoln in the course of the breakup, they both insisted that he never addressed her directly in romantic terms. (It is, of course, an indicative circumstance that Elizabeth felt called upon to ask her about it.) Indeed, Matilda's reported denial has been offered as proof that Lincoln could not have been a serious admirer whose partiality brought about the end of his engagement.[34] Matilda was, by all accounts, a beautiful young woman whose presence in Springfield was immediately felt. One of the most revealing documents that confirms this state of affairs is Mary's letter to Mercy Levering, referred to earlier. Internal references date this letter about December 15, 1840, or ten days after the special session of the legislature ended. Speed's version of what happened between Lincoln and Mary casts this letter in an entirely new light, for if Lincoln and Mary had broken their engagement during the special session, then some long-standing puzzles about this letter, written ten days later, are explained. Mary's letter reads in part:

> Mr Edwards has a cousin from Alton spending the winter with us, a most interesting young lady, her fascinations, have drawn a concourse of beaux & company round us, occasionaly, I *feel as Miss Whitney*, we have too much of such useless commodities, you know it takes some time for habit to render us familiar with what we are not greatly accustomed to—Could you step in upon us some evenings in these 'western wilds' you would be astonished at the change, time has wrought on the hill, I would my Dearest, you now were with us, be assured your name is most frequently mentioned in our circle, words of mine are not necessary to assure you of the loss I have sustained in your society, on my return from Missouri, my time passed most heavily, I feel quite made up, in my present companion, a congenial spirit I assure you. I know you would be pleased with Matilda Edwards, a lovelier girl I never saw. Mr Speed's ever changing heart I suspect is about offering its young affections at her shrine, with some others, there is considerable acquisition in our society of marriagable gentlemen, unfortunately only 'birds of

---

34. Herndon, in "Lincoln & Mary Todd," Angle, and Ruth P. Randall all take this position.

passage.' Mr Webb, a widower of modest merit, last winter is our *principal lion*, dances attendance very frequently.[35]

When she first introduces the subject of Matilda, Mary becomes vaguely defensive and circumspect; she wanders off the topic, but later recovers, reintroducing Matilda by name and praising her. Students of this letter have been puzzled that Mary, while writing to Mercy about the recent and prospective marriages of mutual friends and joking about the "crime of matrimony," says nothing about her own engagement. In fact, in a long letter giving the news of her circle, she pointedly singles out Edwin B. Webb as "our *principal lion*." His position as Mary's most attentive suitor becomes more interesting later on in the letter when she describes a prospective outing: "we have a pleasant jaunt in contemplation, to Jacksonville, next week there to spend a day or two, Mr Hardin & Browning are our leaders the van brought up by Miss E [dwards] my humble self, Webb, Lincoln & two or three others whom you know not."[36] Since the two leaders of this pleasant jaunt were married men, and Webb's attentions might be expected to be directed toward her, Mary seems to be anticipating the prospective pairing of Lincoln and Matilda Edwards.

Speed's version of the breakup provides a ready explanation for these supposed anomalies, namely, that Mary was no longer engaged to Lincoln and that she had been eclipsed in Lincoln's affections by Matilda Edwards. She betrays no outright jealousy, nor would an overt display be expected, but the curious passage that apparently describes her reaction to Matilda's popularity—"occasionaly, I *feel as Miss Whitney*, we have too much of such useless commodities, you know it takes some time for habit to render us familiar with what we are not greatly accustomed to"—suggests that she was less than happy yielding the social spotlight to a newcomer. Whatever awkwardness she may have felt about Matilda, Mary represents her to Mercy Levering as "a congenial spirit" and a surpassingly lovely girl. Having said that Matilda had attracted "a concourse of beaux," Mary apparently felt obliged to tell Mercy just who among their circle had demonstrated romantic interest in this new sensation. She names Joshua Speed, whose "ever changing heart" she suspects is about to be committed, "with some others." The "others," according to Herndon's principal informants and other witnesses, included Abraham Lincoln.

---

35. Mary Todd to Mercy Levering, Dec. 1840, Turner and Turner, eds., *Mary Todd Lincoln*, 20.
36. Ibid., 22.

Jane D. Bell's letter, written the following month, reports that Lincoln "and Mr. Speed have spent the most of their time at Edwards this winter and Lincoln could never bear to leave Miss Edwards's side in company. Some of his friends thought he was acting very wrong and very imprudently and told him so and he went crazy on the strength of it." Lincoln's going crazy because he was criticized by his friends for imprudent behavior seems hardly credible, but this report takes on a different meaning when one considers that Lincoln and Speed, who slept in the same bed and were on the most intimate terms, were at this time both in love with the same woman. This meant that they were, inescapably, rivals for the attentions of Matilda Edwards, and as such had to experience some degree of tension. Speed apparently did not mention any of this to Herndon, and whatever tension there was obviously did no permanent damage to their friendship, but Speed *did* describe a fairly heated argument over whether or not it was manly for Lincoln to send Mary Todd a letter, rather than tell her face-to-face that he didn't love her. Speed represents himself as having had Lincoln's best interests at heart, which may have been the case, but he does not relate what appears likely from other testimony—that Lincoln was trying to free himself from his engagement to Mary Todd in order to court the woman at whose shrine Speed would soon be observed offering his own affections.[37]

That Speed, in these circumstances, should reproach Lincoln for his unseemly attentions to Matilda Edwards—which surely must have been painful and humiliating to Mary Todd—is well within the realm of probability. And that Lincoln should react emotionally to a charge of ungentlemanly behavior from his closest friend, even as he was trying to live down the imputation that his change of heart was dishonorable, is tellingly consistent with what we know about his vulnerabilities at this stage in his life. In a letter to Speed written over a year later, Lincoln apparently refers to this episode in justifying his prodding counsel about Speed's own love affair: "Perhaps this point [the constancy of Speed's love for Fanny Henning] is no longer a question with you, and my pertenacious dwelling upon it, is a rude intrusion upon your feelings. If so, you must pardon me. You know the Hell I have suffered on that point, and how tender I am upon it. You know I do not mean wrong."[38] In this light, Mrs. Bell's

---

37. Consider, in this light, Lincoln's remark to Speed eighteen months later: "I believe now that, had you understood my case at the time, as well as I understood yours afterwards, by the aid you would have given me, I should have sailed through clear." AL to Speed, July 4, 1842, *Collected Works*, 1:289.

38. Ibid., Feb. 3, 1842, *Collected Works*, 1:268.

report about Lincoln's behavior toward Matilda and the censure of his friends is entirely plausible, if not as an explanation of his temporary insanity, at least as an indication of relevant factors in a complex situation.

Mrs. Randall argues that if Matilda Edwards had come between Lincoln and Mary Todd, the latter would not have remained her friend. But what saved Matilda Edwards from the jealous wrath of Mary Todd is reasonably discernible from the evidence. In the first place, Matilda herself does not appear to have been seriously interested in the Springfield beaux she attracted in such profusion. It is clear from her letter to her brother on November 30 that she welcomed the attentions of Newton D. Strong, who had accompanied her on the stage from Alton and whom she eventually married: "Tell [CaI] that I praised her very much to Mr S and said nothing for myself except that I had very Strong attachments." The letter further reveals that, unlike Mary Todd, she was decidedly unworldly.[39] Her cousin Ninian's pleading that she attend a ball she seems to have resisted on grounds of religious piety, and she was later said by Ninian to have rejected the advances of Stephen A. Douglas because of his bad morals, something Mary Todd was not heard to complain about. Speed was also said to have suffered rejection, but his active pursuit of Matilda in December 1840 may well have effectively blocked that of his more inhibited and self-conscious friend, Abraham Lincoln. And this helps to explain, if true, Lincoln's reported failure to address Matilda directly on the subject of his feelings toward her.

Though upstaged by his socially accomplished rival in Springfield, Lincoln had at least one outing with Matilda that month in which Speed was not present. The excursion to Jacksonville mentioned in Mary Todd's letter to Mercy Levering came off as projected, as is evident in an unpublished letter from Matilda's father, Cyrus Edwards, in Springfield to his son Nelson in Alton: "Your Sister started with Miss Todd for Jacksonville on Thursday morning under the protection of Mr Hardin, accompanied by Gillespie, Lincoln, Webb and Brown of Vermilion. They will return on Monday. We miss them very much." There is only one Thursday-to-Monday weekend in the latter half of December in which Lincoln might have been absent from Springfield, Christmas weekend from Thursday the 24th to Monday the 28th.[40] Though Lincoln and John J. Hardin

---

39. ME to Nelson Edwards, Nov. 30, 1841, photostat in Randall Papers, Library of Congress; see excerpts from this letter quoted by in Randall, *The Courtship of Mr. Lincoln*, 70.

40. Cyrus Edwards to Nelson G. Edwards, Dec. 1840. I am grateful to Mrs. R. H. Chrisco and Mrs. Elise Nelson Quigley for permission to examine and quote from the Edwards family papers, now in the Knox College Library, Galesburg, Ill.; see *Lincoln Day by Day*, 1:149–50.

were back in Springfield attending the legislature the following Tuesday, the postmark of Edwards's letter, which is dated the same Tuesday, December 29, suggests that Mary Todd and Matilda Edwards may have remained behind. If Cyrus Edwards meant that the young women who were so much missed were to be in Jacksonville until the Monday following the 29th, or January 4, then it is possible that Mary Todd was in Jacksonville on the fatal first of January 1841, and could not have had an acrimonious confrontation with Lincoln, who was in Springfield.

Speed's version of what happened between Lincoln and Mary Todd, together with the evidence that he himself was in pursuit of Matilda Edwards, also puts some other contemporary documents in a different light. Mary's friend Mercy Levering was carrying on a romantic correspondence with a member of Mary's Springfield circle, James C. Conkling, whom she would soon marry. Their letters are a prime source of contemporary information about the affairs of Lincoln's Springfield, but they, too, have had their puzzling aspects. In first publishing excerpts from these letters, Paul M. Angle noted that they make it "obvious that the general impression among friends of the couple was that Lincoln had been jilted." Since a letter from Mary in June 1841 showed that she "was anxious that their former relations be resumed," and Lincoln's letter of March 27, 1842, to Speed indicated "that the break between Lincoln and Mary Todd came on Lincoln's initiative," it was somewhat puzzling to Angle that these contemporary letters should "picture him quite clearly as a *rejected lover*."[41]

That he is pictured as the victim of disappointment in love is beyond dispute. The most relevant passages are these:

JCC to ML, Springfield, Jan. 24, 1841:
Last evening I spent upon the Hill [the site of the Edwards and Levering homes]. Mrs. L. informed me she had lately written you and had given you some particulars about Abraham, Joshua and Jacob. [Mrs. Lawrason Levering writing about Lincoln, Speed, and Conkling (Jacob Faithful)] Poor L! how are the mighty fallen! He was confined about a week, but though he now appears again he is reduced and emaciated in appearance and seems scarcely to possess strength enough to speak above a whisper. His case at present is truly deplorable but what prospect there may be for ultimate relief I cannot pretend to say I doubt not but he can declare 'That loving is a painful thrill, And not to love

---

41. Sandburg and Angle, *Mary Lincoln: Wife and Widow*, 330, 331.

more painful still' but would not like to intimate that he has experienced 'That surely 'tis the worst of pain To love and not be loved again.'

And Joshua too is about to leave. I know not what dreadful blow may be inflicted upon the interests of our State by his departure.[42]

These letters would be even more revealing had not Mrs. Levering already written an account of the "particulars," as will be seen in Mercy's reply:

ML to JCC, Baltimore, Feb. 7:
Yesterday I wrote a long letter to Bri [Mrs. Lawrason Levering] in answer to her particulars about Abraham, Joshua, and Jacob to which you refer. Poor A I fear his is a blighted heart! perhaps if he was as persevering as Mr. W he might be finally successful. And Joshua too, he has left the prairie state, really I think the citizens of S seem to be deserting it. But what more can one expect when the *Patriarchs* are beginning to move!

JCC to ML, Springfield, March 7:
The Legislature have dispersed. Whether any persons regret it I cannot pretend to say. Miss Todd and her cousin Miss Edwards seemed to form the grand centre of attraction. Swarms of strangers who had little else to engage their attention hovered around them, to catch a *passing smile*. By the way, I do not think they were received, with even ordinary attention, if they did not obtain a *broad grin* or an *obstreperous laugh*. And L. poor hapless simple swain who loved most true but was not loved again—I suppose he will now endeavor to drown his cares among the intricacies and perplexities of the law.[43]

Read in the light of Speed's version of what happened and the evidence of his and Lincoln's mutual attraction to Matilda Edwards, these letters take on a very different meaning from the one offered by Angle and others. What Conkling and Levering were discussing involved not just Abraham, but Joshua as well. And not just Mary Todd, but Matilda Edwards. The "particulars" are not revealed, but the outcome involves Lincoln's disappointment in love and subsequent despondency, and Speed's decision to leave the state. If Lincoln and Mary had not

---

42. Ibid., 178-79.
43. "Mr. W___" is usually taken to be Edwin B. Webb, Mary's most attentive suitor, but later references make it appear that he was a persistent suitor of Mercy's in Baltimore; Sandburg and Angle, *Mary Lincoln*, 179-80.

kept company since early December 1840 and he had thereafter been attentive mainly to Matilda Edwards, and if, as Elizabeth Edwards testified, the word had gotten around Springfield that Lincoln had backed out on his engagement, it passes belief that Conkling and Levering could have connected his despondency in mid-January with rejection by Mary Todd. His depiction as a victim of disappointment in love in their letters could only have reference to what is spelled out explicitly in Jane D. Bell's letter of precisely the same period—his hapless pursuit of Matilda Edwards.

In fact, Conkling's letter points to a more complicated situation than simple rejection, which is what one would expect if several persons were involved. Of Lincoln's "deplorable" case, Conkling says, "I doubt not but he can declare 'That loving is a painful thrill, And not to love more painful still' but would not like to intimate that he has experienced 'That surely 'tis the worst of pain To love and not be loved again.'" In other words, while he acknowledges that Lincoln has experienced the painful thrill of loving and not loving (falling in and out of love with Mary), it is doubtful to Conkling that Lincoln can claim that he does not know what it is to have his love returned (since Mary returned his love even though Matilda didn't). Speed's involvement was presumably as the rival whose active courtship had frustrated the chances of his best friend but resulted in a more definitive form of rejection for himself. In the aftermath, both of these prominent young men were observed by their peers as having suffered a serious comedown but with differing results: Lincoln lapsed into despondency, and Speed resolved to sell his business and leave town.

In tracking the critical phase of Lincoln's courtship, it becomes necessary to sort out the reports of Lincoln's temporary insanity. If Speed is right that Lincoln went crazy and became suicidal during the special session of the legislature, then there were at least two distinct episodes: a brief but violent one precipitated by the breakup with Mary Todd in late November or early December 1840, and a longer period of deep despondency that became noticeable and debilitating in January 1841. That the two were related or even parts of the same illness seems quite likely, especially in view of Speed's testimony that Lincoln wrote a long letter to Dr. Daniel Drake about his mental condition in "Decr 40 or early in January 41,"[44] a period that would appear to fall between the two episodes and that may well have been recalled by Speed on that basis.

If the first episode occurred when Speed says it did, the contemporary record shows no evidence of it, for Lincoln's attendance at the special session of the

44. Joshua F. Speed to Herndon, Nov. 30, 1866, H-W.

legislature was nearly perfect, and no document or testimony has come to light to confirm Speed's dating. But precisely the same may be said for the first day of January 1841, the date usually assigned for the onset of Lincoln's derangement, as the contemporary record shows no sign of anything unusual having occurred on this date. But this lack of contemporary evidence is perhaps only puzzling because an interested posterity has made so much of what would otherwise be rather obscure and distinctly private personal matters.

The second "crazy spell" is the one most often referred to, and it is well documented. During early January Lincoln began to miss roll calls in the legislature, was finally reported ill, and was definitely absent from January 13 until the 19. He refers to his "hypochondriaism" and unshakable depression in his own letters to his partner, John T. Stuart: "I am now the most miserable man living. If what I feel were equally distributed to the whole human family, there would not be one cheerful face on the earth. Whether I shall ever be better I can not tell; I awfully forebode I shall not." The distraught Lincoln is described in Conkling's letter cited above as visibly altered: "reduced and emaciated in appearance and seems scarcely to possess strength enough to speak above a whisper." Lyman Trumbull recalled that the Lincoln of this period (in language that is worth noting) "was engaged in love affairs which some of his friends feared had well-nigh unsettled his mental faculties."[45]

Apparently not all his associates thought of this January episode as desperate. H. W. Thornton, who was a fellow member of legislature, told Ida M. Tarbell: "Mr. Lincoln boarded at William Butler's, near to Dr. Henry's, where I boarded. The missing days [when Lincoln was absent from the legislature], from January 13th to 19th, Mr. Lincoln spent several hours each day at Dr. Henry's; a part of these days I remained with Mr. Lincoln. His most intimate friends had no fears of his injuring himself. He was very sad and melancholy, but being subject to these spells, nothing serious was apprehended." One of Lincoln's closest friends, Orville H. Browning, said of this episode: "I think it was only an intensification of his constitutional melancholy; his trials and embarrassments pressed him down to a lower point than usual."[46]

---

45. Randall, *Mary Lincoln*, 41; *Lincoln Day by Day*, 1:151–52; AL to John T. Stuart, Jan. 20, 23, 1841, *Collected Works*, 1:228, 229; James C. Conkling to Mercy Levering, Jan. 24, 1841, in Sandburg and Angle, *Mary Lincoln*, 179; Horace White, *Life of Lyman Trumbull* (New York: Houghton Mifflin, 1913), 426–27, qtd. in Paul Simon, *Lincoln's Preparation for Greatness: The Illinois Legislative Years* (Urbana: Univ. of Illinois Press, 1971), 238.

46. Qtd. in Tarbell, *Life of Abraham* Lincoln, 180. Thornton believes this refutes Herndon's report that Lincoln was suicidal, but it obviously does not speak to the issue of suicidal behavior

We have seen that Lincoln's "trials and embarrassments" were vaguely amusing to James C. Conkling and Mercy Levering, and contemporary letters show that some of his other acquaintances were actually light-hearted about his situation. In late December 1840, John J. Hardin's family had hosted the Jacksonville excursion party referred to earlier and must have had some familiarity with how things stood regarding Lincoln, Mary Todd, and Matilda Edwards. Very soon thereafter they came to make the social rounds in Springfield, returning to Jacksonville on January 14, about the time of Lincoln's seclusion. Writing back to her brother from Jacksonville, John J. Hardin's sister Martinette expressed curiosity and amusement: "We have been very much distressed, on Mr Lincolns account; hearing he had two Cat fits, and a Duck fit since we left. Is it true? Do let us hear soon." Hardin must have responded reassuringly, as four days later, Hardin's wife Sarah told her husband: "I am glad to hear Lincoln has got over his cat fits we have concluded it was a very unsatisfactory way of terminating his romance he ought to have died or gone crazy we are very much dissapointed indeed Jane Goudy has made him the hero of a tale but she say it will never do for him to get well." The quip about dying or going crazy may have already made the rounds, for John T. Stuart seems to have written something of the sort to Lincoln in late January, to which Lincoln replied on February 3, "You see by this, that I am neither dead nor quite crazy yet."[47]

Sarah Rickard reported in later life that her sister, Mrs. William Butler, took Lincoln into her home and cared for him during the worst of his illness. "Mr Lincoln did not seem to recover, and my sister, who had watched him closely, decided that he had something on his mind. At last she decided upon a plan of action, and one day went into Mr. Lincoln's room, closed the door, and walking over to the bed, said: 'Now, Abraham, what is the matter? Tell me all about it.' And

---

in November or early December; qtd. in John G. Nicolay and John Hay, *Abraham Lincoln: A History* (New York: The Century Co., 1914), 1:187.

47. Martinette Hardin to John J. Hardin, Jan. 22, 1841, Hardin Family Papers, Chicago Historical Society. Martinette, known as "Netty," later married Alexander R. McKee, which is why the manuscript of this letter is misleadingly labeled and its contents attributed to "Martin McKee" by the editors of the *Collected Works* (1:229n) and subsequent writers. Mrs. Randall, for example, refers to the writer as a "slangy gentleman" in *The Courtship of Mr. Lincoln*, 114; Sarah E. Hardin to John J. Hardin, Jan. 26, [1841], Hardin Family Papers. Jane Goudy was the daughter of the Jacksonville printer, Robert Goudy, and wrote verse romances, at least two of which were published by her brothers in 1842: *Minstrel: A Tale in Verse* and *Woman's Pride: A Metrical Romance*. I am grateful to Terence A. Tanner for this and much other useful information; AL to John T. Stuart, Feb. 3, 1841, Roy P. Basler, ed., *The Collected Works of Abraham Lincoln: Supplement 1832–1865* (Westport, Conn.: Greenwood Press, 1974), 6.

he did. Suffering under the thought that he had treated Mary badly, knowing that she loved him and that he did not love her, Mr. Lincoln was wearing his very life away in an agony of remorse. He made no excuse for breaking with Mary, but said, sadly, to my sister: 'Mrs. Butler, it would just kill me to marry Mary Todd.'"[48]

Most modern biographers seem to agree with Paul M. Angle that Lincoln's admission to Speed in 1842 that he continued to suffer for having contributed to someone's unhappiness implies that it was he that broke the engagement with Mary Todd. The nature of the evidence makes it possible to argue the question either way or even to conclude that the engagement simply did not survive whatever occurred at the second confrontation, with neither party having decisively broken the engagement.[49] Recent biographers assume, as did Herndon, that the engagement was broken on the first day of January because of Lincoln's famous reference to "that fatal first of Jany. '41" in his letter to Speed. But it is important to note that none of the witnesses that were close to Lincoln and Mary Todd says anything about this date, and there is evidence, as we have seen, to suggest that Mary Todd may not even have been in Springfield on the first of January. Placing the aborted wedding on that date is part of the speculative chronology worked out by Herndon, but it is no more speculative than the assumption of modern writers that the engagement of Lincoln and Mary Todd was broken off on that day. In fact, the only thing that happened on January 1, 1841, that may well have had a bearing on the affair for which there is hard evidence is Speed's liquidation of his interest in James Bell & Company's store.[50]

But if the fatal first of January 1841 does not refer to the traumatic breaking of the engagement of Lincoln and Mary Todd, what does it refer to? For that we must go back to the letter and the context in which the phrase occurs. Lincoln's letter containing the famous phrase, "that fatal first of Jany. '41," was written on March 27, 1842, nearly a month after Speed's marriage to Fanny Henning. In sending Herndon copies of Lincoln's remarkably revealing letters, Speed explained: "In the summer of 1841, I became engaged to my wife. He [Lincoln]

---

48. For the source of this testimony, see note 25 above. There seems to be no reason to dispute this particular story, and the letter from Speed to William Butler cited below lends confirmation.

49. There is at least one witness, A. Y. Ellis, who testified that it was his understanding that Mary broke the engagement. Ellis to Herndon, written on Herndon's letter to Ellis of Mar. 24, 1866, H-W.

50. AL to Speed, Mar. 27, 1842, *Collected Works*, 1:282; for example, the editors of the *Collected Works* confidently identify "that fatal first of Jany. '41" as "the date on which Lincoln asked to be released from his engagement to Mary Todd"; "I sold out to Hurst 1 Jany 1841. and came to Ky in the spring—" J. F. Speed to Herndon, Sept. 17, 1866, H-W.

was here on a visit when I courted her. And strange to say something of the same feeling which I regarded as so foolish in him took possession of me—and kept me very unhappy from the time of my engagement until I was married. This will explain the deep interest he manifested in his letters on my account."[51] Speed's unhappiness, which apparently amounted to a disposition to back out on his own engagement, is the subject of three letters from Lincoln to Speed prior to Speed's marriage on February 15 and two more in the immediate aftermath.

In these intensely personal letters, Lincoln counsels Speed to put aside his doubts and see the marriage through, arguing that Speed's love of his fiancé is genuine, while his doubts and apprehensions are merely transitory. The letter of March 27 containing the reference to that fatal first of January is Lincoln's response to Speed's acknowledgment a month after the wedding that he has weathered the storm and is "far happier than [he] ever expected to be." Lincoln's jubilation is so unbridled as to seem excessive and serves to demonstrate what has been obvious in his letters, namely that Lincoln has been so deeply involved vicariously in the progress of Speed's ordeal that he experiences Speed's happiness (or lack of it) as his own. In an earlier letter, Lincoln had told Speed: "You well know that I do not feel my own sorrows much more keenly than I do yours, when I know of them." When he received the much-anticipated letter from Speed confirming the fact of his marriage, Lincoln confessed: "I opened the [letter], with intense anxiety and trepidation—so much, that although it turned out better than I expected, I have hardly yet, at the distance of ten hours, become calm."[52]

This is the background and context for Lincoln's seemingly extravagant response to Speed on the subject of his marriage:

> But on that other subject, to me of the most intense interest, whether in joy or sorrow, I never had the power to withhold my sympathy from you. It can not be told, how it now thrills me with joy, to hear you say you are *"far happier than you ever expected to be."* That much I know is enough. I know you too well to suppose your expectations were not, at least sometimes, extravagant; and if the reality exceeds them all, I say, enough, dear Lord. I am not going beyond the truth, when I tell you, that the short space it took me to read your last letter, gave me more pleasure, than the total sum of all I have enjoyed since that fatal first of Jany. '41.[53]

---

51. Joshua F. Speed to Herndon, Nov. 30, 1866, H-W.
52. AL to Joshua F. Speed, Feb. 3, 1842, *Collected Works*, 1:267, and Feb. 25, 1842, 1:280.
53. Ibid., Mar. 27, 1842, *Collected Works*, 1:282.

It is evident that Lincoln's allusion to that fatal first of January was intelligible to Speed. Though readers of this passage have assumed that Lincoln's phrase refers to a notable event in his own life, the context of the passage, and indeed the context of the entire series of letters up to this point, suggests that it refers to an event in the life of Speed. The predominant theme of this and the other letters is Lincoln's empathy, an extreme empathy in which the emotional polarity of one directly relates to that of the other. When Lincoln had been despondent and in the throes of an irresolvable dilemma about his situation in the winter of 1841, Speed had been his counselor. Speed tells of admonishing Lincoln "in his deepest gloom" that he must get a grip on himself or die.[54]

But just as Lincoln was finally showing signs of recovering in the sanctuary of Speed's home in Kentucky in the summer of 1841, Speed was entering into an engagement that almost immediately began to make him "very unhappy." Now the polarity reversed itself and Lincoln became the mainstay and counselor of Speed. This state of affairs continued through the fall of 1841, as Lincoln remained, as he says, free of the "hypo," and Speed, who had accompanied him back to Springfield, became increasingly more apprehensive. Lincoln kept up a steady barrage of counsel and encouragement before and after the wedding until he finally received word in March that Speed was happier than he ever expected to be. The reference to "that fatal first of January" is problematical because its appearance in Lincoln's letter of March 27 marks the exact point at which the polarity is again reversed.

What has obscured the reference to that fatal first of January, and obscures it still, is that it appears in the correspondence at precisely the point where Lincoln switches from celebrating and basking in Speed's good fortune to reflecting on the uncertain state of his own emotions. After the "fatal first" passage, the letter of March 27 continues: "Since then, [that is, since receiving Speed's letter] it seems to me, I should have been entirely happy, but for the never-absent idea, that there is *one* still unhappy whom I have contributed to make so. That still kills my soul. I can not but reproach myself, for even wishing to be happy while she is otherwise."[55] After months of absorption in Speed's anxieties, Lincoln acknowledges the inexorable presence and reemergence of his own.

---

54. Joshua F. Speed, *Reminiscences of Abraham Lincoln and Notes of a Visit to California. Two Lectures* (Louisville, Ky., 1884), 39.

55. AL to Speed, Mar. 27, 1842, *Collected Works*, 1:282.

In a shrewd characterization of the Lincoln-Speed relationship, Gary L. Williams observes that the two men had been trading off on the roles of doctor and patient and that this letter constitutes the turning point in the correspondence—that Lincoln, who had been playing the doctor, "showed signs of renewed weakness,"[56] and that in the next exchange of letters we find the roles have again been reversed and Speed is again advising Lincoln. Whatever figure one uses, emotional polarity or doctor and patient, it seems clear that the mention of that fatal first of January invoked, perhaps quite inadvertently, the specter of Lincoln's own troubled conscience. It is this invocation that suggests to the reader that Lincoln must have been referring to an event in his own life, and while it would be idle to suggest that this possibility is without merit, due account must be taken of the fact that the sentence to which the phrase belongs, and the letter itself and, indeed, the entire correspondence up to that point, is not concerned with Lincoln's own personal affairs or state of mind but is rather sharply focused on his emotional involvement on Speed's behalf. The critical sentence and phrase are cast in the spirit of sympathy that Lincoln, "whether in joy or sorrow," says he is powerless to withhold: "I am not going beyond the truth, when I tell you, that the short space it took me to read your last letter, gave me more pleasure, than the total sum of all I have enjoyed since that fatal first of Jany. '41."

Reinforcing the notion that the event referred to is an untoward event in the life of Speed is the strange case of Sarah Rickard. In sending copies of Lincoln's letters, Speed told Herndon: "I have erased a name which I do not wish published. If I have failed to do it any where, strike it out when you come to it—That is the word Sarah." There are three references to Sarah in the surviving correspondence, and though her name has been romantically connected to Lincoln, these references make it appear that there had been a relationship between Sarah and Speed.[57] This is especially evident in the last of the references, which comes shortly after the "fatal first" passage, and in the context of Lincoln's continuing concern for his friend's fears and apprehensions:

---

56. Gary Lee Williams, "James and Joshua Speed: Lincoln's Kentucky Friends," Ph.D. diss., Duke University, 1971 (University Microfilms), 30.

57. J. F. Speed to Herndon, Nov. 30, 1866, H-W; I agree with Paul M. Angle, Ruth P. Randall, and Gary L. Williams, who argue that the references in these letters to Sarah suggest a romantic connection with Speed rather than Lincoln. Certainly Sarah's own account of Lincoln's attentions to her, which she gave to reporter Nellie Crandall Sanford at great length later in life (see note 25), is entirely consistent with a friendly relationship that was attentive but only teasingly hinted at courtship.

You know with what sleepless vigilance I have watched you, ever since the commencement of your affair; and altho' I am now almost confident it is useless, I can not forbear once more to say that I think it is even yet possible for your spirits to flag down and leave you miserable. If they should, dont fail to remember that they can not long remain so.

One thing I can tell you which I know you will be glad to hear; and that is, that I have seen Sarah, and scrutinized her feelings as well as I could, and am fully convinced, she is far happier now, than she has been for the last fifteen months past.[58]

Here the context indicates that Sarah's feelings are still a matter of concern to Speed. Lincoln's references to Sarah, which Speed pointedly told Herndon to delete, suggest that he may have been acting in Speed's behalf, either as his emissary or his confidential agent. And in reporting on the state of her feelings, Lincoln refers to something that caused her pain or unhappiness fifteen months earlier. This is another reference that is obviously intelligible to Speed, and it implies quite clearly that whatever happened to adversely affect Sarah's feelings in such a way as to be of continuing concern to Speed happened at the beginning of January 1841. It seems clear that the reference to "that fatal first of Jany. '41" and the reference that follows shortly to "fifteen months past" are certainly to the same time period and perhaps to the same date.[59] Does this imply that the fatal first of January refers to something that involved or affected Sarah Rickard?

A contemporary letter from Speed to William Butler may bear on the question. As previously related, it was Butler and his wife Elizabeth who reportedly took Lincoln in and cared for him in the depths of his despondency the previous January. And Sarah Rickard, for whom Lincoln seems at one time to have had a mild attraction, was the sister of Elizabeth Butler and was frequently a member of the Butler household. In his letter to Butler, dated May 18, 1841, Speed writes: "I am glad to hear from Mrs Butler that Lincoln is on the mend. Say to him that I have had but one attack since I left Springfield and that was on the river as I came here—I am not as happy as I could be and yet so much happier than I deserve to be that I think I ought to be satisfied—"[60] Here we see how their

---

58. AL to J. F. Speed, Mar. 27, 1842, H-W.
59. Paul M. Angle points out these implications in his appendix to Sandburg and Angle, *Mary Lincoln*, 346ff.
60. J. F. Speed to William Butler, May 18, 1841, William Butler Papers, Chicago Historical Society (photostat in Illinois State Historical Library).

"hypochondriaism" was regarded by Speed and Lincoln as a bond between them, and we see further that Speed represents himself to Butler as being happier than he deserves to be. This reference was doubtless meaningful to Butler and may have referred to Speed's guilt over the unhappiness of his friend's sister-in-law. Could Speed have been in the same situation with Sarah as Lincoln was with Mary—having hurt her feelings by declaring his love for another? If so, it seems likely, if acutely ironic, that the "other" in both cases was Matilda Edwards.

Abraham Lincoln's courtship of Mary Todd remains an incomplete tableau, and the events surrounding the broken engagement still comprise a mystery. But certain elements in the story are clarified in the evidence adduced above, and their significance may now be better understood. First, the accepted chronology of the courtship and Lincoln's "crazy spells" must be revised and the effects thereof on his behavior reassessed. For example, the actual breaking off of the engagement may now be seen as more closely related to the leap from the church window at the end of the special session than to Lincoln's collapse as an effective political leader in January 1841. Next, Lincoln's well-attested attraction for Matilda Edwards and its effect on his engagement to Mary Todd need to be acknowledged and taken into account. This means, for example, that Mrs. Randall's Romeo and Juliet model will have to be drastically altered or dispensed with entirely. Third, a hitherto hidden element in Lincoln's emotional crisis—his romantic rivalry over Matilda Edwards with his closest friend, Joshua Speed—must now be weighed in the biographical balance. This has obvious implications for a psychological line of inquiry, such as that pursued by Strozier, for example, but should prove of interest and importance to all biographers. Finally, the provocative phrase, "that fatal first of January," needs to be recognized as an ambiguous reference, at the very least, and a problematical one at best, that may well relate less to Lincoln than to fateful developments in the life of his intimate friend, Joshua Speed. These substantial changes in the accepted account of Lincoln's courtship may not yield all the answers that students of his early life and career are seeking, but they do present some interesting new questions.

Lincoln and the Mexican War

An Argument by Analogy

MARK E. NEELY JR.

Since Albert Beveridge's *Abraham Lincoln, 1809-1858* (1928), historians have regarded Lincoln's opposition to the Mexican War as a unique mistake, an ordinarily practical politician's case of political suicide. The unseasoned Sucker, they say, went to Washington for his first and only fling at national office (other than the Presidency fourteen years later), was dazzled by the shining brilliance of his great Eastern Whig heroes, forgot the simple patriotic sentiments of his expansionist Midwestern constituents in Illinois's Seventh Congressional District, and opposed the war. The consequence was bipartisan outrage among his constituents and a tactical decision on Lincoln's part not to face the voters again for years. Indeed, his record in Congress was so odious to the voters that it doomed the next Whig to run for the District's congressional seat to defeat anyway—and that too in the only safe Whig district in this overwhelmingly Democratic state.

G. S. Boritt has entered an important challenge to the reigning interpretation. He notes that there is almost no evidence of popular disagreement with Lincoln's stand except in Democratic newspapers. Among Whigs who lived in the Seventh District, only two left evidence of dissent. One was Albert Taylor Bledsoe, who recalled decades later that Lincoln had made a political mistake by opposing the war. In the meantime, however, Bledsoe had been Assistant Secretary of War in the Confederacy and had become, for obvious reasons, a

Lincoln-hater. The other was Lincoln's law partner, William H. Herndon, a witness who must be contended with. Boritt suggests that Herndon exaggerated the importance of his influence on the great man by claiming greater political wisdom. Boritt hints at a complete reversal of the older view, seeing Lincoln's opposition not as opportunistic but as "the politics of morality" and seeing it as politically palatable to his constituents as well.[1]

The reappraisal of Lincoln's opposition to the Mexican War is only just beginning and needs a great deal of refinement. There is still a tendency to grant too much of the case to those who say he was politically maladroit and, therefore, to leap to the defensive position that he was being idealistic. The challenge to the older view is not based on any large body of evidence unavailable to Beveridge and his followers, and there may be some temptation to look upon the debate as a draw. This article will attempt to approach the problem by indirection, adding the weight of the actions of Lincoln's analogous peers in Congress to the balance and providing some refinements based on reading the documents in the light of post-Beveridge scholarship.

The first refinement that needs urgently to be made regards the interpretation of William Herndon's contemporary warnings to Congressman Lincoln that he had strayed onto dangerous ground in opposing the Mexican War. In his 1889 biography, Herndon recalled: "I warned him of public disappointment over his course, and I earnestly desired to prevent him from committing what I believed to be political suicide."[2] Even Lincoln's defenders have taken Herndon at his word on this point, and the term "political suicide" has influenced the literature ever since.[3]

Only Lincoln's letters to Herndon have survived, and one must infer what Herndon told Lincoln from the nature of Lincoln's responses. Though this leaves room for doubt on some points, happily it leaves no room for doubt in regard to the nature of Herndon's warning. Herndon wrote Lincoln on January 19, 1848, as soon as he heard that he had voted for George Ashmun's amendment (to a resolution of thanks to General Zachary Taylor for his victory at Buena Vista) which called the

---

1. G. S. Boritt, "A Question of Political Suicide: Lincoln's Opposition to the Mexican War," *Journal of the Illinois State Historical Society*, LXVII (Feb., 1974), 79–100, also includes an exhaustive historiographical discussion which makes the customary review of the literature superfluous here.

2. Paul M. Angle (ed.), *Herndon's Life of Lincoln* (Cleveland, 1965), 226.

3. Boritt, for example, claims that "The extant half of the Lincoln-Herndon correspondence on the subject suggests that Lincoln discounted his law partner's evaluation of Illinois sentiment on the war." "A Question of Political Suicide," 92.

Mexican War "unconstitutional and unnecessary." Lincoln answered Herndon's letter the next day after he received it, saying: "The only thing in it that I wish to talk to you about at once, is that, because of my vote for Mr. Ashmun's amendment, you fear that you and I disagree about the war. I regret this, not because of any fear we shall remain disagreed, after you shall have read this letter, but because, if you misunderstand, I fear other good friends will also."[4] Thus it was Lincoln who suggested that the disease of political error might spread to Whig friends; Herndon had uttered only a personal disagreement with Lincoln's stand on the war.

Herndon complained again on January 29, and Lincoln again answered the next day after receiving the letter: "Your letter of the 29th. Jany. was received last night. Being exclusively a constitutional argument; I wish to submit some reflections upon it in the same spirit of kindness that I know actuates you."[5] Herndon seems to have quibbled with his partner on a constitutional point exclusively; he had apparently said nothing about the political effect of Lincoln's error on the district.

In his later biography, Herndon made his claim to superior "political" wisdom seem plausible by quoting Lincoln's letter in response to still another letter written on June 15th, over four months after their disagreement over the Mexican War. In this letter, Lincoln did say "how heart-sickening it was to come to my room and find and read your discouraging letter of the 15th." The discouraging news, if one judges from what followed in Lincoln's letter, however, had nothing to do with popular reactions to Lincoln's stand on the Mexican War. Answering Herndon's despair over the loss of certain men to the Whig cause in the district, Lincoln explained the cause of the problem:

> Baker and I used to do something, but I think you attach more importance to our absence than is just. There is another cause. In 1840, for instance, we had two senators and five representatives in Sangamon; now we have part of one senator, and two representatives. With quite one third more people than we had then, we have only half the sort of offices which are sought by men of the speaking sort of talent. This, I think, is the chief cause.

The letter went on to discuss the discontent of young men in the party (like Herndon) who felt they were being held back by the old fogeys. In fact, the

---

4. Lincoln to Herndon, Feb. 1, 1848, in Roy P. Basler (ed.), *The Collected Works of Abraham Lincoln* (New Brunswick, N.J., 1953), I, 446. Hereafter cited as Lincoln, *Coll. Works.*

5. Ibid., Feb. 15, 1848, ibid., 451.

problem, as Herndon obviously described it—far from being Lincoln's unpopularity—was the lack of his (and Edward Baker's) popular presence as political speakers to rouse the Whigs to an election effort. Herndon also asked for information about the Mexican War, but the discussion remained unrelated to the political problems mentioned earlier in Lincoln's letter. Surely Herndon would not bemoan Lincoln's absence from the campaign and accuse him of driving voters away in the same letter.[6]

Remove William Herndon's claim to speak for disaffected Seventh District Whigs, and the evidence in regard to the political wisdom of Lincoln's opposition to the Mexican War is moot. Democratic newspapers attacked Lincoln for his stand, Whig newspapers defended him, and no editor broke partisan ranks. Lincoln did not stand the test of the voters in the next election (August 1848), and the man who did lose the seat, Stephen T. Logan, was a notoriously poor campaigner fully capable of losing the district on his own.[7]

To evaluate the political wisdom of Congressman Lincoln's stand, one can only compare it to the course taken by similar men in similar circumstances. Unfortunately, Illinois affords no analogs, for Lincoln was the only Whig in the Illinois delegation to the Thirtieth Congress. Neighboring Indiana offers the nearest available basis for comparison. Politically and socially, the states were much alike, carved as they were out of the Old Northwest Territory by settlers from the same areas of the eastern and southern United States. The Democracy dominated both states by the time of the Mexican War; in 1846, Illinois had one Whig Congressman out of seven and Indiana, two of ten. The Whig party was stronger in Indiana, where it contested elections in every congressional district (though in two districts Whigs occasionally claimed a "no party" status in their campaign rhetoric); in Illinois, Whigs gave up the fight in some districts altogether. Nevertheless, the two delegations recognized their kinship and often cooperated (and competed) as the representatives of the interests of the Old Northwest.[8]

The comparison is complicated by the peculiarly unregularized status of American elections at that time. For the same Congress in which Lincoln served, elections were held in various states at various times over a period of a year and three months. Lincoln was elected in August 1846, and then waited more than a

---

6. Lincoln to Herndon, June 22, 1848, ibid., 490-91.
7. Boritt, "A Question of Political Suicide," 93.
8. Such regional cooperation is evident, for example, in Lincoln's quest for appointive office from the Taylor administration. See Donald W. Riddle, *Congressman Abraham Lincoln* (Urbana, 1957), 214-15.

year to go to Washington to take his seat in the Thirtieth Congress, which convened in December 1847. Indiana's delegation to the same Congress was elected in August 1847, a full year later.[9]

Indiana's Whig congressmen thus stood election at the height of the Mexican War, during a period in which Congressman-elect Lincoln could, and did, remain silent on the issue. The Indiana Whigs could not remain silent, though they knew it was a thorny issue in the expansionist West. John D. Defrees, who edited the largest Whig newspaper in the state, thus advised a would-be Whig congressman from South Bend:

> This war questions rather a dangerous one to handle. It requires much prudence in its management. That the war is an outrage—and will forever be so regarded cannot be doubted. Corwin's speech on the subject, was pure, unadulterated Christianity, but, unfortunately, *that* has very little to do in determining elections.
>
> I think the true policy for you to take would be . . . "that Congress should declare that, in the prosecution of the war, it was not our intention to . . . dismember the Republic of Mexico, or to demand any portion of her territory, as the terms of a treaty of Peace—& that we were at all times ready to open negoti[ati]ons to conclude peace." . . . So long as the War lasts,—our *flag* and those who uphold it *must* be sustained—while, at the same time, those who placed that flag where it is, must be denounced &c. The doctrine of withholding supplies—proper enough in England where it always produces a change of Ministers, will not answer here, however it may be in theory.[10]

Of the two incumbent Whig congressmen in Indiana in 1847, only Caleb Blood Smith regained nomination. By far the most vociferous opponent of the war in the state, Smith came from a safe Whig district; Fayette, Henry, Union, and Wayne counties had consistently given majorities to Whig congressional candidates since 1837. When Smith ran for reelection against Democrat Charles Test in the summer of 1847, he described his campaign to Joshua Giddings this way: I am "in the field and canvassing the district in opposition to the war." The Democratic paper in Richmond, Indiana, called for Test's election "not because

---

9. Brian G. Walton, "The Elections for the Thirtieth Congress and the Presidential Candidacy of Zachary Taylor," *Journal of Southern History*, XXXV (May 1969), 186-87.

10. John D. Defrees to Daniel D. Pratt, Apr. 17, 1847, Daniel D. Pratt Papers, Indiana Division, Indiana State Library, Indianapolis.

he is a democrat, not because he has claims on the democracy of the 4th district, but merely, because he is the advocate of his country's cause, the vindicator of her honor, the sworn foe of her enemy, and the supporter of her rights." In the issue immediately preceding the election, the rival Whig paper asked simply, "Are we for peace or war?" Smith won, 4,988 to 3,540, a better margin than in 1845. He even brought scorching Tom Corwin from Ohio to Richmond after the election. Three weeks after Lincoln gave his anti-war address in Congress, Smith gave his third anti-war speech in Congress.[11]

The other Whig incumbent chose not to run, and Terre Haute Whig Richard W. Thompson ran in his stead. Thompson's was a safe Whig district also, and this dictated an anti-war campaign. Thompson explained his strategy to a nervous supporter this way:

> Of course, the *Whigs* have power to beat me—the *Locos* have not. Why should *Whigs* vote against me? There are a few *here* who do it from *personal* considerations—say 10 in this County. There are also 3 in Vermillion—but I know of no others of *this* sort in the district. Then, all other *Whigs* who vote against me must do it because of my *anti-war* notions—The question then resolves itself into this—is the District *for* the war or *against* it. . . . I do not think the district in favor of the war—and shall think it *Whig* until *I am beaten*.[12]

A constituent agreed, noting that "the war, . . . was the only question of the canvass (of which any notice was taken)."[13] Thompson was running against a popular candidate who gave the Democracy confidence even in the Whiggish district. Whig J. S. Harvey, fretting about Thompson's campaign, advised Thompson that in Putnum county one "Captain Roberts was buried . . . lately, and they have been raising the very devil over there out of your opposition to the war. A whig from there the other day says he can count 20 Whigs in that vicinity who will not vote for you; I did not know the man, but there are those here (your friends) who say he is to be believed."[14]

---

11. Hal W. Bochin, "Caleb B. Smith's Opposition to the Mexican War," *Indiana Magazine of History*, LXIX (June 1973), 98–99, 107, 109, 110.

12. Richard W. Thompson to H. G. Hilton, July 16, 1847, Richard W. Thompson MSS, Lilly Library, Indiana University, Bloomington.

13. R. L. Hathaway to Abiathar Crane, Aug. 3, 1847, Crane Papers, William Henry Smith Memorial Library, Indiana Historical Society, Indianapolis.

14. J. S. Harvey to Richard W. Thompson, July 15, 1847, Illinois State Historical Society, Springfield.

Thompson's judgment was vindicated, for he defeated the popular Joseph A. Wright by some two hundred votes. This was a considerably smaller margin than that by which Whig Edward McGaughey had won the district two years previously, but factionalism in Whig ranks may have been a problem. H. G. Hilton wrote Thompson about two weeks before election day to warn him that he was in trouble because of his war stand and that, if Thompson would just give the word, McGaughey would save him. Thompson answered, "If I am to be beaten, because of my anti-war opinions, McGaughey would himself be equally objectionable—and I should scarcely think it probable that he could operate upon *war* men." Thompson added only a polite interest in having "the *active* support of McGaughey."[15] R. L. Hathaway was euphoric about Thompson's victory and argued that the Democrats' "defeat has shown them that the war is unpopular in this country and they now, for the *first time*, admit it. Not even the leaders deny it & some of the democrats this morning declare that they have always been anti-war men."[16] Thompson himself gave a more measured and temperate analysis of his victory to fellow Whig Elisha Embree just after the election:

> ... I never doubted of my own success—although I ran against one of the most unscrupulous men in the State. My position in regard to the war was a very bold one, and kept some Whigs, who would not vote for Wright, away from the polls. But I was determined to carry it through. I knew my vote would be less than the usual Whig vote, but preferred to have it so, rather than to be elected by a different course. Hence my majority is only about 200—while I might have had, by a different course, a much larger one.[17]

Thompson's course of action in Congress was much like Lincoln's. Within days of arriving (on December 21, to be exact, the day before Lincoln introduced his famous "Spot Resolutions"), Thompson submitted a series of resolutions calling on the President to tell Mexico that peace could be settled on these terms: establishment of a boundary line in Texas that included the settlements south and west of the Nueces; purchase from Mexico of the territory west of the Rocky Mountains and north of the line 36° 30'; settlement of United States

---

15. Richard W. Thompson to H. G. Hilton, July 16, 1847, Thompson MSS.
16. R. L. Hathaway to Abiathar Crane, Aug. 3, 1847, Crane Papers.
17. Richard W. Thompson to Elisha Embree, Aug. 14, 1847, Lucius C. Embree Papers, Indiana State Library.

claims against Mexico, and the surrender of all claims by the United States for indemnity for the expenses of war. On January 3, Thompson voted for resolutions to withdraw the army to the east bank of the Rio Grande and to make peace with no indemnity and with payment of all just claims due American citizens before the war. He voted for the Ashmun amendment. Then on January 27, just two weeks and a day after Lincoln's, Thompson gave a speech which argued that the United States had had no right to march troops as far as the Rio Grande, more or less the point of Lincoln's speech."[18]

Two other Indiana districts sent Whigs to Congress in 1847. In the First District, on the Ohio River, Elisha Embree upset Robert Dale Owen, a three-term Democratic incumbent of national reputation. George G. Dunn won a startling victory in the counties directly north of the First District. Winning by twelve votes out of almost fifteen thousand, he reversed a 64 per cent Democratic landslide of 1845.

Dunn and Embree behaved differently than Thompson and Smith, probably because they did not come from safe Whig districts. Embree's campaign stressed the issue which had bred factionalism in the local Democratic party and which brought defeat to Robert Dale Owen: one-man power and its everpresent accompaniment, nepotism. Owen was making his fourth consecutive run for Congress, and he had given too many patronage plums to too narrow a clique, including his brothers David and Richard (appointed director of the geological expedition to Wisconsin and captain of infantry, respectively) and his brother-in-law Robert Fauntleroy (as astronomer on the Coast Survey).[19]

Embree apparently dodged saying whether he admired Thomas Corwin's famous anti-war speech or not and answered most questions about his platform by saying that he would support Zachary Taylor's course—a dodge as well because no one knew clearly where Taylor stood either. Democrats accused Embree of hypocrisy in crying over widows and orphans, some of whom were made by the very victories of Zachary Taylor he otherwise celebrated. He could not dodge the war issue altogether. Embree supported Taylor's defensive-line strategy, a plan to withdraw United States troops to a certain limited territory and leave it

---

18. *Congressional Globe*, 30 Cong., 1 sess., 61, 94, 95; *Appendix*, 263-67.

19. Factionalism is apparent in articles quoted in the *Princeton Democratic Clarion*, Mar. 13, 1847, and March 27, 1847. See also Richard William Leopold, *Robert Dale Owen: A Biography* (Cambridge, 1940), 234-35. The need for rotation in office as a cause of Democratic loss of the district is discussed in the *Madison Courier*, Aug. 7, 14, and 21, 1847. See also, Lawrence N. Powell, "Rejected Republican Incumbents in the 1866 Congressional Nominating Conventions," *Civil War History*, XIX (Sept. 1973), 219-37.

to Mexico to attack or sue for peace. He also gave a speech in the campaign in which he said it was not right to annex Texas because annexation brought on war. He did not stress the boundary issue, as Lincoln would later, but he did stress the war's origins. Avoiding an anti-expansionist position of any substance, Embree compared the situation of Texas to that of an underage youth wishing to marry. The United States, he said, should have got Mexico's consent. However, once the marriage was consummated, a parent need not annul it merely because the consent was not originally obtained, and Texas should be retained now.[20]

When he went to Congress, Embree avoided the war issue for a time and failed to be present at the vote on the Ashmun amendment. Finally, however, on May 3, 1848, amidst rumors of peace, he gave a speech on a Bounty Land Bill, in the course of which he called the Mexican War "a war of invasion and conquest, in opposition to the wishes and against the desires and interests of the great body of the people; a war, ... of the President, and those of his party who expect to profit by it as individuals."[21]

George G. Dunn won in a traditionally Democratic district because the Democratic party there split and had two candidates in the field against him until rather late in the contest. He apparently did not oppose the war in canvassing his two-thirds Democratic district. One constituent transmitted a Democratic dare to the new Congressman: "If you have an opportunity to make a speech on the war question, you ought to do it, for the Loco's, say that you will not take the same ground on the war, in Congress, that you took last summer, when you canvassed the district."[22] Dunn did not take the dare; he made no speech on the war. When he did make his maiden speech (on the Oregon question) weeks after the war was over, Dunn carefully included a disapproval of dissent. "Some may have greatly *erred* in their views and expressions," the Congressman said of Polk's opponents on the war issue, "—in my humble judgment, did; for when the war was recognized by Congress, it was then the lawful war of the country, whatever improprieties and irregularities may have previously existed, and as such demanded the united purposes and efforts of that country to ensure a speedy and honorable peace."[23]

---

20. Embree's speeches are known principally from hostile reports in the *Princeton Democratic Clarion*, June 12, 1847, June 26, 1847, and July 10, 1847.

21. Speech of Hon. Elisha Embree of Indiana, on Bounty Land Bill, Delivered in the House of Representatives, Wednesday, May 3, 1848 (Washington, 1848). Pamphlet in Lucius Embree Papers, Indiana State Library.

22. Isaac E. Johnson to George G. Dunn, Apr. 17, 1848, George G. Dunn MSS, Lilly Library.

23. *Cong. Globe, Appendix*, 30 Cong., 1 sess., 973.

Yet in the same speech Dunn treated the war with abusive language. He said the country was "improvidently and unnecessarily involved" in the war, a war rooted in "an insane and maddened avarice" and in "cupidity." He sneered at "high national considerations" as "the pretence for every international absurdity and insolent assumption of right to interfere in the affairs of others, on our part." He added mocking phrases reminiscent of Tom Corwin: "We are resolved that henceforth there shall be no butchers upon this continent but ourselves."[24] Even in the midst of the war, Dunn had not deemed it inappropriate to vote for the Ashmun amendment, to send his constituents Albert Gallatin's *Peace with Mexico* (an anti-war pamphlet which only grudgingly admitted that the United States might ask to adjust the Texas border and settle outstanding prewar claims against Mexico), or to frank John C. Calhoun's dissenting speeches, doubtless thought to be good anti-war medicine for a Democratic district.[25]

Abraham Lincoln did not share Smith's or the Whig party's concerns about expansion. When the issue first surfaced in the form of the proposal to annex Texas in 1844, Lincoln called annexation on John Tyler's terms merely "inexpedient."[26] In a letter written to Williamson Durley in 1845, Lincoln left the only lengthy consideration of expansion which survives in his early correspondence. He denounced the "whig abolitionists of New York" for refusing to vote for Henry Clay in 1844 and thus making it possible for a Democratic President to annex Texas. But, Lincoln continued, "individually I never was much interested in the Texas question." On the one hand, he "never could see much good to come of annexation; inasmuch, as they were already a free republican people on our own model." On the other hand,

> ... I never could very clearly see how the annexation would augment the evil of slavery. It always seemed to me that slaves would be taken there in about equal numbers, with or without annexation. And if more *were* taken because of annexation, still there would be just so many the fewer left, where they were taken from. It is possibly true, to some extent, that with annexation, some slaves

---

24. Ibid., 969, 971.
25. See Williamson Dunn to George G. Dunn, Feb. 4, 1848; Austin Ward to George G. Dunn, Feb. 8, 1848; and J. G. McPheiters to George G. Dunn, Apr. 20, 1848, George G. Dunn MSS. The popularity of Gallatin's pamphlet is discussed in John H. Schroeder, *Mr. Polk's War: American Opposition and Dissent, 1846-1848* (Madison, 1973), 144-45.
26. "Speech on Annexation of Texas," May 22, 1844, in Lincoln, *Coll. Works*, I, 337.

may be sent to Texas and continued in slavery, that otherwise might have been liberated. To whatever extent this may be true, I think annexation an evil.

Lincoln did "hold it to be ... clear, that we should never knowingly lend ourselves directly or indirectly, to prevent ... slavery from dying a natural death—to find new places for it to live in, when it can no longer exist in the old." This did not apply to Texas, which was already a slave republic. Therefore, Lincoln could conclude, "Liberty [party] men ... have viewed annexation as a much greater evil than I ever did."[27]

Acquisition of territory from Mexico was a different proposition. Slavery was forbidden by law there, and acquisition by the United States might give American slavery new areas to live in. On the other hand, the theory that expansion thinned the concentration of slave population elsewhere and did not in and of itself increase total slave population was as applicable to New Mexico and California as it had been to Texas. Lincoln's ideas about the expansion of slave territory were not yet well thought out, and he would be challenged anew by the actions of the Polk administration in 1846.

Lincoln's ideas about expansion were not trammeled by any Federalist or Eastern residue of fear of expansion per se. Thus Texas annexation was largely a matter of indifference to him. He voiced no opposition to expansion of American territory into Texas as a policy which weakened the country's ability to improve and cultivate existing United States territory.[28]

Lincoln opposed expansion which would help slavery, but he never claimed that the Mexican War was a conspiracy to extend slave territory. In his famous congressional speech against the war, he refused to speculate about President Polk's motive for aggression against Mexico; he devoted the speech to proving simply that Polk was the aggressor. Campaigning for Taylor in the summer of 1848, Lincoln said he "did not believe with many of his fellow citizens that this war was originated for the purpose of extending slave territory." Rather, "it was his opinion, frequently expressed, that it was a war of conquest brought into existence to catch votes."[29]

---

27. Lincoln to Williamson Durley, Oct. 3, 1845, ibid., I, 347-48.
28. Frederick Merk says that "Whigs, as a party, were fearful of spreading out too widely." See his *Manifest Destiny and Mission in American History: A Reinterpretation* (New York, 1966), 40. See also Major L. Wilson, *Space, Time, and Freedom: The Quest for Nationality and the Irrepressible Conflict, 1815-1861* (Westport, Conn., 1974), 108, 115-16, 118.
29. "Speech at Wilmington, Delaware," June 10, 1848, in Lincoln, *Coll. Works*, I, 476.

Qualms about expansion itself would be a new development in Lincoln's thought. He had concentrated in the past on mastering the arguments for the Whig domestic program, which he felt underdeveloped Illinois needed badly; the party's foreign policy views were not stock parts of his political arsenal. It was the autumn of 1848 before Lincoln voiced a basically anti-expansionist position. In a campaign speech for Taylor Lincoln claimed to be at one with "all those who wished to keep up the character of the Union; who did not believe in enlarging our field, but in keeping our fences where they are and cultivating our present possession, making it a garden, improving the morals and education of the people."[30] Significantly, Lincoln was speaking to citizens of Worcester, Massachusetts, where the heritage of Federalist anti-expansionism among Whigs was as strong as any place in the Union. This partisan audience was the first to elicit anti-expansionist remarks from Lincoln.

Like most Western Whigs, Lincoln was better able to compromise with expansionism than the rest of the party. Since he did not oppose expansion properly achieved, it was easier to compromise with expansion brought about by improper means. Lincoln protested those means—Polk's aggression—but expansion came to seem a sort of inevitability to him. In fact, that was the way he expressed his views in the spring of 1848:

> As to the Mexican war, I still think the defensive line policy the best to terminate it. In a final treaty of peace, we shall probably be under a sort of necessity of taking some territory; but it is my desire that we shall not acquire any extending so far South, as to enlarge and agrivate the distracting question of slavery.[31]

One reason for this position was that Lincoln apparently shared the view of many that war between the United States and Mexico had been an inevitability even without the border incident involving Zachary Taylor on the Rio Grande. Such would appear to be the meaning of this remonstrance to John Peck, an Illinois Baptist minister who had written what Lincoln deemed as "a laboured justification of the administration on the origin of the Mexican War":

> ... you say "Paredes came into power the last of December 1845, and from that moment, all hopes of avoiding war by negociation vanished." A little further on,

---

30. "Speech at Worcester, Massachusetts," Sept. 12, 1848, ibid., II, 4.
31. "Fragment: What General Taylor Ought to Say," [March?] 1848, ibid.

refering to this and other preceding statements, you say "All this transpired three months before Gen: Taylor marched across the desert of the Nueces." These two statements are substantially correct; and you evidently intend to have it infered that Gen: Taylor was sent across the desert, in *consequence* of the destruction of all hope of peace, in the overthrow of Herara of Paredes. Is not that the inference you intend? If so, the material fact you have excluded is, that Gen: Taylor was *ordered* to cross the desert on the 13th of January 1846, and *before* the news of Herara's fall reached Washington. . . .[32]

On one occasion, Lincoln even uttered what was a typical apology for expansion—that the territory was better off in the hands of those who really knew how to put it to use for human advantage. In a lecture on discoveries and inventions in 1859, Lincoln sneered at Manifest Destiny, but he also praised the yankee "*habit* of observation and reflection." "But for the difference in *habit* of observation," he said, "why did yankees, almost instantly, discover gold in California, which had been trodden upon, and over-looked by indians and Mexican greasers, for centuries?"[33] These remarks came more than ten years after the Mexican War, but they serve to remind us that Lincoln was not even at this late date an internationally-minded man and that his dislike of that war stemmed mostly from a dislike of Democrats, from fears of the corruption of the Constitution's limits on executive war-making, and from fears that some territorial acquisitions would aggravate the slavery question. He worried not about Mexico and Mexicans but about the impact of the war on the domestic future of the United States.

Lincoln seems to have accepted the concept of territorial indemnity. Surely that concept underlay any belief that territorial acquisitions were "a sort of necessity." Moreover, in a speech in Wilmington, Delaware, on June 10, 1848, Lincoln chose to focus his criticism of the Democrats on the administration's desires for "a large sum of money to gain more territory than will secure 'indemnity for the past and security for the future.'"[34] This was a way to attack the administration for seeking something more than its announced war aim, indemnity, but it is worth noting that Lincoln nowhere questioned the concept of indemnity itself, which was surely an absurdity if the war were strictly a product of American aggression.

When Lincoln embraced the "defensive-line" strategy, he was embracing a plan

---

32. Lincoln to John M. Peck, May 21, 1848, ibid., I, 472.
33. "Second Lecture on Discoveries and Inventions," [Feb. 11, 1859], ibid., III, 358.
34. "Speech at Wilmington, Delaware," June 10, 1848, ibid., I, 476.

that included, by 1848, considerable acquisitions of Mexican territory. Originally formulated by Taylor in 1846, it had been strictly a military strategy designed to achieve victory by putting the burden of attack on the Mexican army. Taylor had thought his small army incapable of invading central Mexico from the north because immense stretches of desert separated them from the prize, Mexico City. In a letter made public in January of 1847, Taylor had advocated the military virtues of assuming the defensive in the territory the United States already controlled.[35]

On February 9, 1847, John C. Calhoun gave a speech before the United States Senate which formulated the defensive-line strategy as a political rather than purely military plan. Calhoun transformed the idea into a stopgap against any movement to acquire all of Mexico: "Mexico is to us the forbidden fruit; the penalty of eating it would be to subject our institutions to political death." He feared that an invasion of central Mexico would change the war from one for limited territorial indemnities to an unlimited war of conquest. He urged the United States to assume a stationary position running along the Rio Grande to the southern border of New Mexico and from there due west along the thirty-second parallel to near the head of the Gulf of California and then south through the Gulf to the Pacific. Thus Calhoun's defensive-line strategy would acquire all the sparsely settled northern territories of Mexico which were said to be of great potential value to the United States and of little or no value to non-commercial Mexico. Taylor's plan was no longer a military strategy. Calhoun's version gained a maximum amount of territory into which Calhoun believed slavery would not enter because the land was too arid, and avoided the question of slavery expansion which would rock the Union if territory further south were acquired.[36]

Lincoln embraced the strategy in all its guises. On the one hand, he said that territorial acquisitions were a necessity, and the strategy was a way of accepting them without agitating the slavery question. On the other hand, he once chided Whig Usher F. Linder, who had his doubts about opposing the war, this way: "By justifying Mr. Polk's mode of prossecuting the war, you put yourself in opposition to Genl. Taylor himself, for we all know he has declared for, and, in fact originated, the defensive line policy."[37] Thus it could be only a "mode of prosecuting the war."

That Lincoln regarded taking some territory as a "necessity" may have meant not that he endorsed the concept of indemnity but that he bowed to the political

---

35. See Otis Singletary, *The Mexican War* (Chicago, 1964), 45.
36. See Schroeder, *Mr. Polk's War*, 69-71.
37. Lincoln to Usher F. Linder, Feb. 20, 1848, Lincoln, *Coll. Works*, I, 453.

realities in the United States, where too many people wanted some sort of expansion for any realistic politician to resist. Such is the most charitable way to interpret Lincoln's vote *against* a resolution which called for ending the war by withdrawing the army to the east bank of the Rio Grande, relinquishing indemnity claims, settling the Texas boundary in the desert between the Nueces and the Rio Grande, and forcing Mexico to pay pre-war claims adjudicated by a joint convention of the two nations. This was a no-territory resolution, in other words, and Lincoln voted against it even though it championed a boundary line for Texas which Lincoln felt very strongly to be correct. The resolution lost by a staggering 137–41 margin, and Lincoln, sensing the probable loss of the measure, may have seen nothing to be gained from hopelessly challenging the will of the congressional majority. The Hoosier Congressmen from Democratic districts, Embree and Dunn, also voted against it. On the other hand, Caleb Smith and Richard W. Thompson voted for the resolution. If one assumes that these votes were meant to appeal to the constituents of their Whig districts, one can also assume that Lincoln's Whig district may have had more Democratic tendencies in rabidly expansionist and solidly Democratic Illinois. Whatever the reason, Lincoln was certainly among those Western Whigs who were most willing to compromise on expansion.[38]

In spite of the appearance of disunity in the vote on the no-territory resolution, Whigs in the Old Northwest reached near unanimity on the issue of expansion. Thompson had endorsed expansion (north of the 36° 30' line) previously in his own series of resolutions. Caleb Blood Smith came around reluctantly to supporting some expansion (just as he came around reluctantly to supporting Taylor for President). Although Smith supported the "no territory" idea in the Twenty-ninth Congress and in the campaign for reelection that followed, he grudgingly changed his mind.[39] Recognizing the strength of the administration, he acknowledged, under the circumstances, the "wisdom and sound policy in the course marked out by the distinguished Senator from South Carolina, [Mr. CALHOUN]":

> If, however, the Administration intends to hold and retain permanently New Mexico and California—acknowledging, at the same time, that they constitute a larger measure of indemnity than we have any just right to demand—why not hold those provinces, and withdraw our forces from the other portions of Mexico? Why shall we keep an army of fifty thousand men in the heart of

---

38. *Cong. Globe*, 30 Cong., 1 sess., 94.
39. Bochín, "Caleb B. Smith's Opposition to the Mexican War," 99, 105, 108.

Mexico, preying upon the vitals of the country, when with ten thousand men we can hold all that the Administration pretends it wishes to retain? Five thousand troops in New Mexico, and an equal number of Upper California, would hold those provinces against all the force which Mexico can bring into the field.[40]

Embree, Dunn, and Lincoln voted against the no-territory resolution. Embree had supported the moderately expansionist defensive-line strategy in the midst of his campaign for the House. Dunn distributed Calhoun's speeches to his constituents, and those documents were the locus classicus of the defensive-line strategy. Lincoln looked upon the defensive-line strategy as a near panacea.

Though all of the Western Whig congressmen made compromises in keeping with their expansionist constituencies, Western Whiggery also showed an impressive level of agreement in opposing the war. The Ashmun Amendment took a position most could agree with: the war was unconstitutional and unnecessary. Only Embree failed to vote for this; he was absent. All agreed that the war was a war of conquest. All five men made their dissent from Polk's policies a matter of public record. The three from Whig districts made speeches directly on the subject of the war and proudly sent them home to their constituents. Dunn and Embree, in more delicate positions than Lincoln, Smith, and Thompson, commented on the war only in speeches on other subjects. Smith, Thompson, and Embree had criticized the war in their campaigns to get to the Thirtieth Congress. Only Dunn seems to have disapproved of far-reaching criticism of the war once it was declared, and he managed to join the rest in terming its declaration unconstitutional and unnecessary.

Lincoln, then, did not behave in an eccentric fashion for a Whig in a Western expansionist state. He bowed more to expansionist sentiment than any Whig from a Whig district, though his choice to make a speech directly on the war issue differed from the course followed by the two most conservative Whigs from basically Democratic districts. He was a mainstream Western Whig who exercised normal caution; why, then, did he not run again?

The principal reason, he said, was in order "to deal fairly with others, to keep peace among our friends, and to keep the district from going to the enemy." When Herndon wrote just after Lincoln's arrival in Washington that some hoped for his reelection, Lincoln replied that he would not object to reelection "although I thought at the time, and still think, it would quite as well for me to return to

---

40. *Cong. Globe, Appendix*, 30 Cong., 1 sess., 325.

the law at the end of a single term." If, however, no one else wished to run, he "could not refuse the people the right of sending me again." Most often, historians have interpreted this only as the obligatory coyness of a man who always lusted after office, but there is reason to believe Lincoln's relative indifference to serving in the House and to believe that it increased through his term.[41]

Lincoln had left the state legislature in March of 1841. It was a long wait through the "turns" of John Todd Stuart, John J. Hardin, and Edward D. Baker to become the district's candidate in 1846. By 1843, he was openly voicing his desire to run.[42] Like many things long awaited, success seemed anticlimactic. Less than three months after his election, Lincoln wrote his close personal friend Joshua Speed, "Being elected to Congress, though I am very grateful to our friends, for having done it, has not pleased me as much as I expected."[43] No doubt the prospect of well over a year's wait to go to Washington served to make the impact on his life less dramatic.

Yet Lincoln could have gone to Congress sooner than he did, and, he did not lift a finger to try to do so. Seventh District Congressman Edward D. Baker, who chose to go to Mexico to fight, was criticized for maintaining his military rank while a member of the House. In December of 1846, he resigned his seat, leaving two months of his term to be filled by another man. A special election to fill the seat was announced for January 20, 1847. Whig members of the state legislature from the Seventh District caucused to choose a nominee. Previous to the meeting, William Brown of Morgan County called on John Henry, the state senator from Morgan, expressing his interest in filling the vacancy and requesting his support. Henry rather disingenuously promised his support, thinking all along that Congressman-elect Lincoln would surely be a candidate for the nomination. At the meeting, Lincoln was present but declined consideration as a candidate. Shortly thereafter, Henry changed his mind, and Brown was forced by Whig leaders to withdraw his candidacy out of the consideration that Henry, if angered, could cause the Whigs to lose Morgan, Scott, and Cass Counties (the two latter were formerly parts of Morgan County and all had only slim Whig majorities).[44]

What is of interest in all this, of course, is that Abraham Lincoln, in what would seem to be an uncharacteristic lack of zeal for elected office, declined

---

41. Lincoln to Herndon, Jan. 8, 1848, Lincoln, *Coll. Works*, I, 431.
42. Donald W. Riddle, *Lincoln Runs for Congress* (New Brunswick, 1948), 9-10.
43. Lincoln to Joshua Speed, Oct. 22, 1846, Lincoln, *Coll. Works*, I, 391.
44. *Sangamo Journal*, Jan. 14, 1847.

to run. John Henry indicated that most people expected Lincoln would want to run as a matter of course. "It was then supposed that Mr. Lincoln would be a candidate for the nomination," Henry said in a letter to the *Sangamo Journal* defending his original willingness to support Brown. Lincoln certainly stood to lose nothing by going to Congress early. The mileage allowance given Congressmen en route to and from Washington was so generous that Henry laid his whole claim to the Whig nomination on the fact that he was a poor man who needed the money from the mileage allowance (Brown was a well-to-do man). Nor was it inordinately troublesome to travel to the capital in such a short period of time. When Lincoln finally went to Congress, he came home in September after a recess and a campaign tour in Massachusetts, campaigned on a moderate schedule in October and returned to Congress by the first week in December for the short lame-duck session which ended the first week in March.[45]

Washington life did not appeal to Mary Todd Lincoln. After about four months she packed up her children and went home to Kentucky. On April 16, 1848, Lincoln wrote her:

> In this troublesome world, we are never quite satisfied. When you were here, I thought you hindered me some in attending to business; but now, having nothing but business—no variety—it has grown exceedingly tasteless to me. I hate to sit down and direct documents, and I hate to stay in this old room by myself. You know I told you in last Sunday's letter, I was going to make a little speech during the week; but the week has passed away without my getting a chance to do so; and now my interest in the subject has passed away too.[46]

Most historians have disregarded this letter, dismissing it as a function of momentary loneliness, but there is good reason to believe that it betrays a more fundamental boredom with the tedium of being an obscure Western Congressman. Although he nowhere else expressed dismay with the elaborate etiquette of sending documents (compiling a list of constituents in a book and not missing anyone of importance), Lincoln did in another letter say that giving speeches in Congress was no special thrill. Of his very first speech in the United States House of Representatives, Lincoln said to Herndon, "I find speaking here and elsewhere about the same thing. I was about as badly scared, and no worse, as

---

45. Ibid.; Riddle, *Congressman Lincoln*, 137–40.
46. Lincoln to Mary Todd Lincoln, Apr. 16, 1848, Lincoln, *Coll. Works*, I, 465.

I am when I speak in court."⁴⁷ Unless they had long tenure in the House and the power consequent to it, nineteenth-century congressmen did only three things. They sent documents and newspapers home to important constituents; they made speeches (intended, like Lincoln's, as much for home consumption as for influence on other Congressmen); and they handled patronage (which was scarce when the President was of the other party). Of these three essential activities, Lincoln was bored by two.

One can add to the tedium of powerlessness the insecurity of identity for Western Whigs. Critics of Lincoln's stand on the Mexican War have recognized this insecurity as a force which could make even a customarily canny politician like Lincoln forget his constituents by cringing before the whims of the party's Eastern power-brokers. There is some truth in this, perhaps, but it is no reason to condemn Lincoln. Nor did cringing before the East necessarily lead to opposition to the war.

Edward D. Baker took a very different course in regard to the Mexican War from that one taken by his friend and fellow Whig. Congressman Baker's response to the war was unreservedly patriotic and a function of his long-standing military interests and aptitudes.⁴⁸ He resigned his seat in the House to become the Colonel of the Fourth Illinois Regiment of Volunteers for the Mexican War. Though his response thus contrasted with Lincoln's, Baker still carefully consulted the wishes of the powers in the Eastern wing of the party, even going so far as to ask Daniel Webster whether it was all right to go. Webster replied on May 18, 1846:

> In reference to our conversation this morning, I am quite free to say, that I approve your purpose of entering into the military service of the country, if your inclination & circumstances prompt such a design. We are in a state of war, that war must be fought thro'; the more vigorously it shall be prosecuted, the shorter it will probably prove. Whig young men, like other young men, may well bear a part in the service which the exigency of the country demands. A son of mine would take a commission tomorrow if he could obtain it. An existing public foreign war, is a subject equally interesting and important, to all parties; all should be equally desirous of carrying their country honorably through it, without sacrificing its honor or interests or tarnishing its military renown.⁴⁹

---

47. Lincoln to Herndon, Jan. 8, 1848, ibid., I, 430.
48. Harry C. Blair and Rebecca Tarshis, *Colonel Edward D. Baker: Lincoln's Constant Ally* (Oregon Historical Society, 1960), 21.
49. Daniel Webster to Edward D. Baker, May 18, 1846, Anson Miller Papers, Illinois State Historical Society.

So much for the vaunted independence of Westerners! Whoever they were, they were not powerful voices in the Whig party and they knew it. Nor should it be ignored that service in the Mexican War failed to make Baker any less a Whig than Lincoln in his views of the origins of that conflict. Lincoln told Herndon on February 1, 1848, that Baker was in Washington again and that the Colonel agreed with the mass of Whigs that the President's conduct "in the beginning of the war" was "unjust."[50]

Nor must one infer Lincoln's lack of taste for his job only from casual references in his own correspondence. Outside corroboration comes from a fragment of a manuscript on Lincoln, written after his death, by his old House colleague Richard W. Thompson. Thompson recalled the similarities in the positions of Congressmen Lincoln and Thompson:

> We were within two months of the same age—our districts were not far apart—our constituents were the sharers of common interests—and we were members of the Whig party, alike impressed by the wonderfully magnetic influence of Henry Clay....

About Lincoln's decision not to run again for Congress, Thompson said this:

> At the close of his only term in Congress he hesitated somewhat as to his future course of life. He had made up his mind not to seek re-election. He did not doubt about his success, but found a Congressional life uncongenial to him. This I personally know, for being of the like opinion with regard to myself, we frequently conversed upon the subject. Having withdrawn from his profession he apprehended that possibly his practice might not be recovered as speedily as his circumstances demanded—....

And, therefore, Thompson said, Lincoln sought a lucrative appointment in the land office.[51]

There are reasons to mistrust the document. Thompson was reminiscing about events of as much as two decades earlier, and he was probably wrong about Lincoln's decision not to run at the end of his term. Lincoln had decided long before, and there was no congressional election in Illinois in 1849 to provoke a

---

50. Lincoln to Herndon, Feb. 1, 1848, Lincoln, *Coll. Works*, I, 447.

51. Richard W. Thompson, MS on Abraham Lincoln, Thompson MSS, Illinois State Historical Society.

new decision. Still, it confirms reliable strands from Lincoln's own letters and does constitute a memoir of an eyewitness whom Lincoln remembered as an "old friend" in 1860, though he had not seen him since their days in the Thirtieth Congress. Thompson had been a genuine friend, too, the only man outside Illinois to put substantial effort towards getting Lincoln an appointive office from the Taylor administration in 1849.[52]

Finally, a brief footnote to the question whether Lincoln caused Stephen Logan's defeat in the congressional election in 1848 seems in order. Defenders of Lincoln's political prowess say Logan was a poor campaigner and by implication concede the facts in the other side's case, namely, that the Democrats tarred Logan with Lincoln's record on the Mexican War.

In truth, this is more a matter of assumption on the historians' part than of evidence of the campaign as seen in local newspapers. In May 1848, over two months before the election, the *Illinois State Register* accused the Whigs not of being traitors but of taking a vacillating and opportunistic approach towards the war. At first they condemned it; when Taylor's popularity rose, they supported it; when Taylor faded a bit and Clay made his anti-war speech, they criticized the war once more. The *Register* termed Logan's position on the war "equivocal" and predicted that he would eventually oppose it because Lincoln and John Henry had not made up their minds before they left, and they eventually opposed it.[53]

By mid-July Suckers knew the war was over; Mexico City had fallen on September 14, 1847. Gradually, other issues replaced the Mexican War in the columns of Seventh District newspapers. By the third week in June, still over a month before the election, the *Register* began to attack Logan as a pro-British Whig. Logan had criticized Democrat Lewis Cass for opposing a quintuple treaty against the slave trade. The *Register* defended Cass on the grounds that the treaty was really aimed at making Great Britain the "mistress of the seas" because it allowed British ships to stop and search American ships suspected of engaging illegally in the slave trade. These charges mounted in a steady crescendo up to election time. Just two weeks before the election, a long article on Logan in the *Register* mentioned Lincoln and John Henry in passing but focused most of its attention on Logan and England. This issue, rather than Lincoln's record, received the lion's share of Democratic attention in the newspaper and ignoring

---

52. Lincoln to Schuyler Colfax, May 26, 1860, Lincoln, *Coll. Works*, IV, 54; Riddle, *Congressman Lincoln*, 214.

53. *Illinois State Register*, Mar. 3, 1848 and May 14, 1848.

it grants too much to the case against Lincoln and slights the degree to which Logan made his own issues.[54]

The comparative method makes Lincoln's opposition to the Mexican War more understandable and makes our descriptions of its nature and tone more precise. He did not err politically, for virtually every Whig Congressman (and candidate, for that matter) in Indiana and Illinois acted as he did. Opposition to the war was a party issue; therefore, Whigs went to Congress and opposed the war, no matter where they came from. There were concessions, of course, to local feelings. Whigs in the Old Northwest compromised easily with expansion; there was no residue of Federalist non-expansionism in this wing of the party. Lincoln was more willing to compromise on expansion than Hoosier Whigs from similarly safe districts. In other words, his dissent was not the least bit shrill under the circumstances, and he picked his way through the political solutions to the Mexican War with a politician's care. On the other hand, then, his stand on the war was not idealistically principled or internationally minded. It was a party stand, it was not an anti-expansionist stand, and his major concern about the war's result was what it would do to the domestic peace of the United States.

The episode gives a surprising insight on Lincoln's biography. In one case for certain, he failed to pursue an office, and there is some evidence that he did not care for the duties of an obscure Western Whig congressman. Lincoln did not fear his constituents, but he did tire of serving them in return for little thanks. It exasperated him to find, after his diligent and tedious efforts at franking, that only two of the five Whig newspapers in the district published his speech. It made him "a little impatient" that no paper carried "a single speech, or even an extract from one" of the others he had sent.[55] When David Davis wrote him near the end of his term, a weary and frustrated Lincoln answered his letter by saying, "I have more cause to thank you for it, than you would suppose. Out of more than three hundred letters received this session, yours is the second one manifesting the least interest for me personally."[56]

Lincoln contentedly returned to Springfield and his law practice. The lesson of his congressional career was doubtless plain to him but misunderstood by most historians since. He had tried to distinguish himself by speaking up in Congress. His constituents had not rejected his message: they simply had not heard it at all.

54. Ibid., June 26, 1848, and July 21, 1848.
55. Lincoln to Herndon, June 22, 1848, Lincoln, *Coll. Works*, I, 491-92.
56. Lincoln to David Davis, Feb. 12, 1849, in Roy P. Basler (ed.), *The Collected Works of Abraham Lincoln: Supplement, 1832-1865* (Westport, Conn., 1974), 14.

Lincoln as Military Strategist

HERMAN HATTAWAY AND ARCHER JONES

The thesis of this paper is that Abraham Lincoln was a conventional mid-nineteenth-century military strategist who fully shared the ideas of Henry W. Halleck, George B. McClellan, and his other West Point–trained generals. These generals, like von Moltke in Prussia, analyzed operations in terms of lines of operations, believed in the superiority of the defensive over the offensive, and saw in turning movements the only way to overcome the power of the rifle-strengthened defensive. Lincoln derived his ideas primarily from his generals and from military realities as exhibited in the course of the war. It is not material to the thesis whether or not the generals derived their ideas from Jomini and whether or not Jomini was an exponent of Napoleonic or eighteenth-century Austrian strategy. It is significant that Lincoln's ideas were realistic and workable.

The president was early indoctrinated by McClellan with the concept of the power of the defense when, in January 1862, the General-in-Chief explained that the "history of every former war" had "conclusively shown the great advantages which are possessed by an army acting on the defensive and occupying strong positions." McClellan had found at the beginning of the war that "but few civilians in our country, and indeed not all military men of rank, had a just appreciation of that fact." If "veteran troops frequently falter and are repulsed with loss," then "new levies ... cannot be expected to advance without cover" against the "murderous fire" of intrenched defenders. He would solve this problem by turning the enemy, for "the effect of this movement" to the enemy's rear "will be to reverse the advantages of position. They will have to seek us in our own works, as we sought them at Manassas." The strength of the defense meant that offensive battles against an enemy with his back to his communications implied a victory which "produces no final results, & may require years of warfare & expenditure to follow up."[1]

With the aid of McClellan and other generals, Lincoln early became fully at home with his generals' military conceptions. To the question as to why "the North with her great armies" so often faced the South in battle "with inferiority of numbers," the President explained "that the enemy hold the interior, and we the exterior lines." Along with understanding lines of operations he fully grasped the logistics of field armies and the significance of intrenchments and had learned to attach great importance to the turning movement or to any chance "to get in the enemies' rear" or to "intercept the enemies' retreat."[2]

The military sophistication which the President had acquired in less than a year and a half extended to a clear understanding of the significance of battles and appreciation of the limited degree to which the Confederates had defeated McClellan at the Seven Days Battles. Grasping that "the moral effect was the worst" aspect of those battles, he thought it probable that, "in men and material, the enemy suffered more than we in that series of conflicts; while it is certain that he is less able to bear it." Lincoln wrote that he saw the psychological "importance to us, for its bearing upon Europe, that we should achieve military successes;

---

1. McClellan to Stanton, Feb. 3, 1862, *The War of the Rebellion: A Compilation of the Official Records of the Union and Confederate Armies* (Washington, 1880-1901), V, 42-45 (all references are to Series I unless otherwise noted; these *Official Records* will hereinafter be cited as *OR*) and Roy P. Basler, (ed.), *Collected Works of Abraham Lincoln* (New Brunswick, N.J., 1953-1955), V, 120-25 (reproduced here in part, including portions omitted in the *Official Records*); Lincoln to McClellan, Feb. 3, 1862, *OR*, V, 41-42; President's Special War Order No. 1, Jan. 31, 1862, ibid., 41; McClellan to Lincoln, Aug. 4, 1861, ibid., 6-9; McClellan to W. Scott, Apr. 27, 1861, ibid., LI, part 1, 338-39; Scott to Lincoln, May 2, 1861, ibid., 339; Scott to McClellan, May 3, 1861, ibid., 369-70; McClellan's report to L. Thomas, Aug. 4, 1863, ibid., V, 54; J. Shields to McClellan, Jan. 10, 1862, ibid., 700-702; J. G. Barnard to Jos. Totten, Dec. 10, 1861, ibid., 683.

For Field Marshal Count Helmuth von Moltke's comparable analysis of tactical power of the defense and his similar reliance on turning movements in 1870, see Michael Howard, *The Franco-Prussian War* (New York, 1961), 7.

2. Lincoln to Agenor-Etienne de Gasparin, Aug. 4, 1862, Basler, *Collected Works*, V, 355; Lincoln to John A. Dix, June 30, 1862, ibid., 194; Lincoln to McClellan, Apr. 9, May 24, 25, 1862, ibid., 184-85, 232, 236. See also Lincoln to Halleck, May 24, 1862, ibid., 231; Lincoln to McDowell, May 30, 1862, ibid., 252.

and the same is true for us at home as well as abroad." Yet, comparing western triumphs at Ft. Donelson, Shiloh, and Corinth with the popular fixation on the East, Lincoln felt that "it seems unreasonable that a series of successes extending through half-a-year, and clearing more than a hundred thousand square miles of country, should help us so little, while a half-defeat" at the Seven Days Battles "should hurt us so much" in morale.[3]

Often criticized for an exaggerated fear for the safety of Washington, Lincoln had realized that "Jackson's game" in the Valley Campaign had been to "keep three or four times as many of our troops away from Richmond as his own force amounts to." During the Seven Days Battles, Lincoln again showed his firm grasp of the significance of lines of operations when he wrote McClellan that "we protected Washington and the enemy concentrated on you; had we stripped Washington, he would have been upon us before the troops sent could have got to you.... It is the nature of the case."[4]

Lincoln thus grasped that battles were unlikely to be decisive and that the means of victory lay in occupying the enemy's territory and breaking his lines of communications. To do this it was necessary to overcome the enemy's advantage of interior lines. Early he explained that his "general idea of the war" was that "we have the greater numbers, and the enemy has the greater facility of concentrating forces upon the points of collision; that we must fail unless we can find some way of making our advantage an overmatch for his; and that this can be done by menacing him with superior forces at different points, at the same time; so that we can safely attack one, or both, if he makes no change, and if he weakens one to strengthen the other, forebear to attack the strengthened one, but seize, and hold the weakened one, gaining so much." To illustrate the simultaneous advance, which would be a controlling idea in Union strategy, Lincoln cited the campaign of First Bull Run when the Confederates used their interior lines to move troops from Winchester to Manassas. "Suppose," Lincoln wrote, when the Confederates at "Winchester ran away to re-enforce Manassas, we had foreborne to attack Manassas, but had seized and held Winchester."[5] This was the concept upon which Lincoln based the policy of simultaneous advances, abortively begun with his 1862 order for all armies to advance on Washington's birthday. There followed three simultaneous Union advances:

3. Lincoln to de Gasparin, Aug. 4, 1862, Basler, *Collected Works*, V, 355.
4. Lincoln to Fremont, June 15, 1862, Basler, *Collected Works*, V, 271; Lincoln to McClellan, June 28, 1862, ibid., 289-91.
5. Lincoln to Buell and Halleck, Jan. 13, 1862, Basler, *Collected Works*, V, 98.

Halleck and McClellan in the spring of 1862, Grant, Rosecrans, and Burnside in the fall, and Grant and Hooker in the spring of 1863.

President Lincoln's attention was still riveted upon operations in Virginia when Lee crossed the Potomac in what Halleck, Lincoln's new General-in-Chief, termed a raid. Rather than being alarmed by any possible threat which Lee's raid might pose, Lincoln perceived it as an opportunity to circumvent the power of the defense and have a battle where the enemy's rear was not toward his communications. The optimistic Lincoln not only did not see Philadelphia as "in any danger," but he even explained lines of operations to the anxious governor of Pennsylvania. If half of McClellan's army moved to Harrisburg, "the enemy will turn upon," wrote Lincoln, "and beat the remaining half, and then reach Harrisburg before the part going there, and beat it too."[6]

More significant for Lincoln than the absence of any real threat from the raiders, was that the situation presented a golden opportunity for the concentrated forces under McClellan. In their flank position northwest of Washington, McClellan's men precluded an enemy advance northward, because Lee "dares not leave them in his rear." Perceiving Lee to be in a potentially serious predicament, Lincoln urged McClellan not to "let him get off without being hurt" and to "destroy the rebel army if possible." His belief in a chance for hurting the enemy rested on his hope that Lee would raid farther north and McClellan could get in his rear.[7]

After the disappointing Battle of Antietam Lincoln again showed his understanding of the strategy of maneuvering an army to turn the enemy from his position. Writing McClellan, the President quoted Jomini when he reminded the general of "one of the standard maxims of war, . . . 'to operate upon the enemy's communications as much as possible without exposing your own.'" McClellan, Lincoln said, acted "as if this applies against you, but cannot apply in your favor."

Before explaining the vulnerability of Lee's position, Lincoln pointed out that McClellan should not "dread his going into Pennsylvania." If he did, he would give up his communications and the Army of the Potomac would "have nothing to do but follow and ruin him." Lee, on the other hand, could easily be turned because the Union army was "nearer Richmond by the route you can, and he

---

6. Wool to Lincoln, Sept. 7, 1862, *OR*, XIX, pt. 2, 207; Lincoln to Buell and Wool, Sept. 7, 1862, Basler, *Collected Works*, V, 409; Lincoln to Webster, Sept. 9, 1862, ibid., 412; Lincoln to Curtin, Sept. 12, ibid., 417.

7. Lincoln to McClellan, Sept. 12, 15, 1862, Basler, *Collected Works*, V, 418, 426; Lincoln to Treat, Nov. 19, 1862, ibid., 501-2.

must take." The President asked McClellan, "why can you not reach there before him" when Lee's route would be the "arc of a circle" and McClellan's the chord? Logistics would be no problem on this march for "the facility of supplying from the side away from the enemy is remarkable—as it were, by the different spokes extending from the hub towards the rim."

Then Lincoln explained what had come to be and would remain his fundamental analysis of the problem posed in Virginia by the tactical power of the defense. It was best to fight the enemy far from Richmond, because, "if we cannot beat him when he bears the wastage of coming to us, we never can when we bear the wastage of going to him." Because of the wastage for Lee of long lines of communication, "in coming to us, he tenders us an advantage which we should not waive." Reminding McClellan of his own point about the importance of not trying to tackle the enemy in intrenchments, the President emphasized that not only was beating the enemy "easier near to us than far away," but "if we cannot beat the enemy where he now is, we never can, he being within the entrenchments of Richmond."

Thus did Lincoln analyze the problem posed by the well-demonstrated primacy of the defensive. Unless there were to be a stalemate, with the Union army sitting in futility before the intrenchments of Richmond, something must be accomplished at a distance from those intrenchments. Lincoln did not subscribe to the thesis that Richmond, like Sebastopol, would fall if besieged. Nor did he have any high expectations of what might be accomplished away from intrenchments. But he hoped that his army would fight if a "favorable opportunity" presented itself.[8]

As Lincoln was evolving a doctrine for dealing with the stalemate in Virginia, he was also maturing a strategy for the operations of all of the armies. By late fall, in collaboration with General-in-Chief Halleck, Lincoln had assigned first priority to opening the Mississippi River and second to cutting the East Tennessee and Virginia Railroad. "To take and hold the Railroad at, or East of Cleveland in East Tennessee, I think fully as important as taking and holding Richmond,"

---

8. Lincoln to McClellan, Oct. 13, 1862, Basler, *Collected Works*, V, 460–62. The maxim quoted by Lincoln is from Jomini. See Baron de Jomini, *The Art of War*, G. H. Mendell and W. P. Craighill, translators (Westport, Conn., 1971, a reprint of the 1862 edition), 80. Here Jomini is quoting from ch. 14 of his *Taite des grandes operations militaire*. Jomini did not use the term turning movement, treating it instead under the concept of base of operations. Lincoln's exposition here and the situation itself are perhaps more consistent with Jomini's base of operations approach than with the turning movement. See *Art of War*, 77–84.

Lincoln wrote. The strategic importance of that railroad had impressed Lincoln early and this conviction intensified because of the belief that Beauregard had reinforced Lee for the Seven Days Battles.[9]

In the new Union priorities, the indecisive Virginia theatre ranked third, ahead only of Missouri and Arkansas. In the fall of 1862 Lincoln and Halleck limited their expectations in Virginia to the hope that Burnside's army could advance and "occupy the rebel army south of the Rappahannock." The objective, explained Halleck, was to enable the Army of the Potomac to detach sufficient forces "to place the opening of the Mississippi beyond a doubt." Burnside's failure to push Lee's army far enough "from the vicinity of Washington and the upper Potomac" meant that Lincoln and Halleck could spare no troops from Virginia for the Mississippi campaign.[10] Even so, two divisions under Burnside were sent to strengthen Kentucky in March 1863.

Thus Lincoln and Halleck stressed the West and accepted a stalemate in Virginia. Yet the strategy for the West differed from that in the East. It aimed at territorial and logistical objectives, seeking to control the Mississippi, eventually to dominate Arkansas, and occupy East Tennessee as well as to cut the East Tennessee and Virginia Railroad in the West. Pursuing the opposite policy in the East, the President avoided seeking to capture or besiege the rebel capital. Instead he wished to aim at Lee's army, albeit with the feeble blows befitting a tertiary objective. Why was Lincoln apparently so inconsistent in his objective for the Army of the Potomac? The principal reason was the tremendous difficulty of taking Richmond. The keys to this problem were in the power of the intrenched defense and the obstacle presented by Richmond's elaborate communication system of three trunk line railroads and a canal.

Even before the defeat at Fredericksburg and the essential failure of the fall campaign, Lincoln had come fully to realize the ascendancy of the defense and the relative indecisiveness of military operations. In late November he explained: "I certainly have been dissatisfied with the slowness of Buell and McClellan; but before I relieved them I had great fears I should not find successors to them, who would do better; and I am sorry to add, that I have seen little since to relieve those fears." Pointing out that this situation really inhered in the constraints of logistics and the strength of the defensive, he indicated: "I do not clearly see the

---

9. Stanton to Mitchell, June 21, 1862, *OR*, XVI, pt. 2, 246; Lincoln to Halleck, June 30, 1862, Basler, *Collected Works*, V, 295; Lincoln to Seward, June 28, 1862, ibid., 292; Write to Halleck, Nov. 7, 1862, *OR*, XX, pt. 2, 24.

10. Halleck to Rosecrans, Jan. 30, 1863, *OR*, XXIII, pt. 2, 23.

prospect of any more rapid movements. I fear we shall at last find out that the difficulty is in our case rather than in particular generals."[11]

None of the many plans to take the Confederate capital presented a really plausible means of interdicting Richmond's communications. The consequences of such a failure were particularly evident to Halleck, an engineer who had published on fortification. He was aware that the Crimean city of Sebastopol had, like Richmond, been largely defended by field, rather than permanent, fortifications and he knew how long it had held out against the experienced, professional forces of the combined armies and navies of Britain, France, Sardinia, and the Ottoman Empire. If Sebastopol could hold out for more than a year against such a formidable attack, there was no hope that they could conquer Richmond sooner, and probably little that they could capture it at all. Halleck also knew that defensive fortifications so economized on men that one man in fortifications equaled six in the attack.[12] Such a favorable ratio for the defenders of fortifications in a siege would enable the rebels actually to reduce their forces in the Richmond vicinity.

If, as the operations in 1862 indicated, they could not beat the enemy in the field, it was clear, as Lincoln had pointed out early in the fall, the enemy surely could not be beaten "within the entrenchments of Richmond." Lincoln and Halleck adopted the obvious solution: avoid a siege. The alternative to a siege, as explained by the General-in-Chief and endorsed by the President, was to abandon Richmond as an objective. The "first object" of a Virginia campaign was no longer to be Richmond "but the defeat or scattering of Lee's army, which threatened Washington and the line of the Upper Potomac." Halleck ordered the Army of the Potomac "to turn the enemy's works, or to threaten their wings or communications; in other words, to keep the enemy occupied till a favorable opportunity to strike a decisive blow." Other measures against Lee's army were to use "cavalry and light artillery upon his communications, and attempt to cut off his supplies and engage him at an advantage."[13]

The ideas Halleck expressed harmonized with and in truth merely extended those expressed by Lincoln in September and October 1862. Lincoln had "confidently believed last September that we could end the war by allowing the

---

11. Lincoln to Schurz, Nov. 24, 1862, Basler, *Collected Works*, V, 509-11.
12. Halleck, *Elements of Military Art and Science* (New York, 1862), 71-87, 374, 439-41.
13. Halleck to Burnside, Jan. 7, 1863, *OR*, XXI, 953-54; Lincoln to Burnside, Jan. 8, 1863, Basler, *Collected Works*, VI, 46.

enemy to go to Harrisburg and Philadelphia, only that we could not keep down mutiny, and utter demoralization among the Pennsylvanians." Just as he had tried to trap Jackson with Fremont's and McDowell's forces the previous May, so also had Lincoln yearned to be able to allow Lee to go too far and block his retreat from Pennsylvania. He had still hoped that the Antietam campaign would at least present an opportunity to "hurt" Lee.

Having thus decided on concentration in the West and settled on the futility of attempting to reach and besiege Richmond, Lincoln and Halleck sought to guide the commander of the Army of the Potomac to adopt the unconventional and unpromising objective assigned him.

The new commander, Joseph Hooker, received from the President a general charge to seek "military success" but to "beware of rashness. Beware of rashness, but with energy and sleepless vigilance go forward and give us victories." Lincoln was in a sense echoing his earlier instructions to Burnside to "be cautious," and, though victories were needed, he may well have meant for Hooker, like Burnside, not to "understand that the government, or the country, is driving you" to seek these victories rashly. Halleck's instructions were more explicit in that he sent a copy of his last instructions to Burnside, which made clear that the "first object was, not Richmond, but the defeat or scattering of Lee's army." Hooker was directed "to keep the enemy occupied till a favorable opportunity offered to strike a decisive blow." Keeping the enemy occupied had another significance, for the "great object" was "to occupy the enemy, to prevent his making large detachments or distant raids, and to injure him all you can with the least injury to yourself." In spite of strong words about "the defeat or scattering of Lee's army," Halleck's instructions were well tempered with realism, Hooker only being told "to act against the enemy when circumstances will permit."[14]

Later Lincoln would reiterate these points when he explained to Hooker that there was "*no* eligible route for us into Richmond; and consequently a question of preference between the Rappahannock route, and the James River route is a contest about nothing." Since it was futile to attempt to take the rebel capital, what was to be the mission of the Army of the Potomac? Lincoln explained: "Hence our prime object is the enemies' army in front of us," and against him there was one definite advantage. "Our communications are shorter and safer than are those of

14. Lincoln to Hooker, Jan. 26, 1863, Basler, *Collected Works*, VI, 78-79; Lincoln to Burnside, Jan. 8, 1863, ibid., 46; Halleck to Burnside, Jan. 7, 1863, OR, XXI, 953-54; Halleck to Hooker, Jan. 31, 1863, ibid., XXV, pt. 2. 12.

the enemy. For this reason, we can, with equal powers fret him more than he can us. . . . While he remains in tact, I do not think we should take the disadvantage of attacking him in his entrenchments; but we should continually harass and menace him, so that he shall have no leisure in sending away detachments. If he weakens himself, then pitch into him."[15]

When, in June 1863, Lee began an advance, Hooker thought it might present him with an opportunity to take Richmond. Lincoln strongly dissented and pointed out to Hooker: "If you had Richmond invested to-day, you would not be able to take it in twenty days; meanwhile, your communications, and with them, your army would be ruined. I think Lee's Army, and not Richmond, is your true objective point."[16] Seeing in Lee's movement the Antietam campaign opportunity reappearing, Lincoln wrote Hooker: "I believe you are aware that since you took command of the army I have not believed that you had any chance to effect anything until now." Hooker, understanding that he was to seize any chance to strike Lee's army in the open, proposed to attack Lee's rear units, intrenched near Fredericksburg. To this Lincoln promptly objected, pointing out that Lee's detachment "would fight in entrenchments, and have you at a disadvantage, and so, man for man, worst you at that point, while his main force would in some way be getting an advantage of you Northward."[17]

The best way to exploit the situation, wrote Halleck, was "to fight his movable column first instead of first attacking his intrenchments." As Lee advanced, Lincoln explained, "follow on his flank, and on the inside track, shortening your lines, whilst he lengthens his." Then, the General-in-Chief advised, when Lee left "part of his forces in Fredericksburg, while with the head of his column, he moves . . . toward the Potomac," there would be an opportunity "to cut him in two, and fight his divided forces." The President, deploring that Hooker's later plan looked "like defensive merely," echoed Halleck's earlier point; if the head of Lee's column was near the Potomac and the tail near Fredericksburg, "the animal must be very slim somewhere. Could you not break him?"[18]

Though the public in the Northeast panicked at Lee's advance and Lincoln called

---

15. Lincoln Memorandum on Joseph Hooker's Plan of Campaign Against Richmond, Apr. 6-10, 1863, Basler, *Collected Works*, VI, 164.

16. Hooker to Lincoln, June 10, 1863, OR, XXVII, pt. 2, 34; Lincoln to Hooker, June 10, 1863, *Collected Works*, VI, 247. See also Halleck to Hooker, June 5, 1863, OR, XXVII, pt. 1, 31-32.

17. Lincoln to Hooker, June 5, 16, 1863, *Collected Works*, VI, 249-50, 281.

18. Lincoln to Hooker, June 10, 14, 16, 1863, *Collected Works*, VI, 257, 273, 280-81; Halleck to Hooker, June 5, 1863, OR, XXVII, pt. 1, 31.

out 100,000 militia, the President nevertheless remained calm, reassuring his wife that he did "not think the raid into Pennsylvania amounts to anything at all." Rather than a menace, Lincoln perceived the Confederate raid, like Lee's previous advance to Antietam, as an opportunity to strike the enemy when vulnerable and far from their base, "the best opportunity we have had since the war began."[19]

It must have been with reluctance that Lincoln had adopted such a pessimistic evaluation of military realities on the Virginia front as to abandon hope of taking the rebel capital. But realizing the defensive power of fortifications and the virtual impossibility of interdicting Richmond's communications, he and Halleck had concluded that there should be no siege of Richmond. Such an operation would simply confer on the rebels all of the advantages of the use of fortifications in the defense, not only making their army as well as their capital invulnerable to attack, but permitting them so to economize on troops in their defense that they might well be able to spare reinforcements for their other armies. The best Union strategy in Virginia was, therefore, to keep away from Richmond and concentrate on Lee's army rather than on the counterproductive objective of the rebel capital. This unconventional assessment, soundly based in both military history and engineering, did not promise success in Virginia because a well-led, veteran army is a most unpromising objective. Yet the alternative was clearly fruitless and the concept was to count on superior numbers and wait for the audacious Lee to make a mistake.

The second conclusion reached by Lincoln and Halleck was that there should be no major operations from southeast of Richmond in spite of the vast superiority of the communications there and the advantage which the rivers offered for turning the enemy's defensive positions. Not only was this line of operations interdicted for striking at Lee's army, it was equally prohibited in the event there was a siege, perhaps imposed by Lee's withdrawal to the defenses of Richmond. Any siege must be carried out from the north side of the city for the same reason that the southeast line of operations was interdicted. The defensive efficiency of the fortifications of Richmond, in the event of a siege from the southeast, was such that the rebels would be able to reduce their troops defending their capital to a very low level and suddenly concentrate the bulk of their forces on the northern Virginia line of operations.

Thus Lincoln's strategy for Virginia differed fundamentally from his strategy

---

19. Lincoln to Mary Todd Lincoln, June 16, 1863, *Collected Works*, VI, 283; Lincoln to Parker, June 30, 1863, ibid., 311.

for the other theatres. There has long been a tendency, however, to generalize from the Virginia theatre all interpretations of Lincoln and his generals. Conscious and unconscious partisans of what might be called the Peninsular school have interpreted Lincoln as interfering with field commanders who knew better how to conduct the war in Virginia and have generalized this to cover Lincoln's conduct of operations in all theatres.

Conscious and unconscious opponents of the Peninsular school have stressed McClellan's weakness in execution to say that his strategy was faulty. Lincoln's stress upon the enemy army as an objective seemed orthodox and modern, whereas a preoccupation with territory and a place, the enemy capital, seemed to reflect that the field commanders had a less sophisticated understanding of strategy than did Lincoln, the generals' strategy even smacking of an archaic, pre-Napoleonic view. Many of the exponents of this point of view wrote after World War II when military operations seemed decisive and armies vulnerable. Some of these post–World War II critics blamed Jomini for teaching the West Point generals a faulty strategy and praised Lincoln for seeing the flaws.

Like the Peninsular school, the proponents of Lincoln also have difficulty generalizing their interpretation to the other theatres of the war. Nowhere else did Lincoln advocate the enemy army as an objective. His objectives in other theatres were not armies, the East Tennessee railroad and the Mississippi being the most obvious examples of Lincoln's goals.

The interpretation here proposed has the opposite difficulty in that, having a generalized explanation for all operations outside of Virginia, the explanation must also include the special case of Virginia, where Lincoln was apparently inconsistent with the strategy advocated elsewhere when he preached attack on Lee's army, a strategy which he did not advocate for other theatres. Lincoln's emerging feeling that lack of success was not due to the generals but to the "case," i.e., the military realities, and his subsequent reactions to the operations of Hooker and Meade indicated that Lincoln shared the generals' skepticism about the annihilation or even the disastrous defeat of an enemy army. What Lincoln meant seems, then, to be that action against Lee in the field was preferable to the futility of a siege against a well-fortified enemy in a city whose communications could not be interdicted. Of course, he hoped for a blunder by Lee which would provide an opportunity to hurt the rebel army.

Lincoln's strategy was thus Scott's anaconda plan, as the President sought to open the Mississippi and strengthen the blockade. Two other measures were also part of his overall strategy. In late 1863 his policy of amnesty and reconstruction sought to lure rebels away from their Confederate allegiance and he hoped, by a combination of political and military action, to reconstruct all of the peripheral areas of the Confederacy.

Before he implemented his matured political strategy he had already moved to adopt a measure which was an extension and logical consequence of his Emancipation Proclamation, at the end of which he announced that those blacks freed by the proclamation would "be received into the armed service of the United States to garrison forts, positions, stations, and other places." Skepticism as to whether blacks could be adequate soldiers did not extend to their manning rear area fortified points or guarding railways, thus "leaving the white forces now necessary at those places, to be employed elsewhere." In this way Lincoln planned for manpower difficulties to be significantly eased by tapping this new source of soldiers, "the great *available* and as yet *unavailed* of, force for the restoration of the Union."[20]

Arming Southern blacks most effectively harmonized with the basic anaconda strategy because Lincoln saw that it worked "doubly, weakening the enemy and strengthening us," because it took "so much labor from the insurgent cause, and supplying the places which otherwise must be filled with so many white men."[21]

But Lincoln believed the program weakened the enemy in another way—psychologically. He thought that "the bare sight of fifty thousand armed, and drilled black soldiers on the banks of the Mississippi, would end the rebellion at once." He did not believe that the rebellion could survive if such a black military force could "take shape, and grow, and thrive, in the South." As the recruiting went forward during the spring and summer of 1863, Lincoln, by then envisioning one hundred thousand black troops, believed that they were a "resource which, if vigorously applied now, will soon end the contest."[22]

Lincoln as strategist was orthodox militarily, relying on professional military advice. In his arguments with McClellan and Meade, he had the advice and full agreement of Halleck, an orthodox soldier and leader of the Western group of generals who ultimately dominated the Union high command. Like his professional advisors, the President understood the power of the defense and the futility

---

20. Emancipation Proclamation, Jan. 1, 1863, Basler, *Collected Works*, VI, 30; Lincoln to Dix, Jan. 14, 1863, ibid., 56; Lincoln to Andrew Johnson, Mar. 26, 1863, ibid., 149. For Lincoln learning of the role of blacks as soldiers in the Revolution, see Benjamin Quarles, *Lincoln and the Negro* (New York, 1962), 155.

21. Lincoln to Grant, Aug. 9, 1863, Basler, *Collected Works*, VI, 374; Annual Message to Congress, Dec. 8, 1863, ibid., VII, 50.

22. Lincoln to Andrew Johnson, Mar. 26, 1863, Basler, *Collected Works*, VI, 149-50; Lincoln to Hunter, Apr. 1, 1863, ibid., 158; Lincoln to Grant, Aug. 9, 1863, ibid., 374.

of trying to destroy an enemy army in the open field. That Grant failed for so long to take Richmond fully vindicated the pessimistic assessment which Lincoln had made in late 1862. That Lee's army remained intact in spite of Grant's direct assaults upon it further confirmed the assumption of the President and his generals about the superiority of the defense.

After some groping and false starts the President had settled on Scott's western offensive. But he added to the purely military strategy a political dimension with his reconstruction policy and a significant political-logistical aspect in his policy of arming Southern blacks. In his active role and military orthodoxy Lincoln resembles Roosevelt; in his political warfare he is far closer to the Fourteen Points than to unconditional surrender.

Jefferson Davis and Abraham Lincoln as War Presidents

Nothing Succeeds Like Success

Ludwell H. Johnson

We are all familiar with the scene on that gloomy, cold, and rainy Washington's Birthday when Jefferson Davis, pale and haggard from the strain of illness and recent military defeats, took the oath of office under the permanent Confederate Constitution. On her way to the ceremony, Mrs. Davis discovered to her consternation that her carriage was escorted by four Negroes in "somber broadcloth and top hats and wearing white cotton gloves. She asked the coachman what they were doing there. 'Well, ma'am,' he said, 'you told me to fix everything up like it ought to be, and this yere's the way we do in Richmond at fun'rals an' sich-like.'"[1]

These circumstances were ominous in the strict meaning of the word, and especially so as to the way Davis was to be judged as president of the Confederacy. I am not referring to his contemporary critics—the Stephenses, the Wigfalls, the Footes, the Keans, the Pollards—but to the writers of history, or what often passes for history. Not that historians have been unanimously uncomplimentary or uncharitable. In his study of Davis and his cabinet, Rembert Patrick rendered a favorable verdict.[2] More recently Raimondo Luraghi, a modern Italian scholar who has put the War for Southern Independence in an even broader perspective

---

1. Allen Tate, *Jefferson Davis, His Rise and Fall* (New York, 1929), 126.
2. Rembert W. Patrick, *Jefferson Davis and His Cabinet* (Baton Rouge, 1944), 45 and passim.

than did Charles A. Beard some fifty years ago, is most impressed by Davis's ability. In speaking of the mobilization of Southern resources, Luraghi writes:

> It is amazing to see how clear-mindedly, how creatively Southern leaders discovered this direction [i.e., "state socialism"], previously unknown, and followed it. The man who, more than any other, embodied this stroke of genius was President Jefferson Davis. Be it only for this, he should rank among the major statesmen in history. His intelligence, his iron will, his capability in facing and solving such appalling problems were indeed amazing.[3]

Many students of the war may find such an opinion almost shocking, so striking is its contrast with the historical consensus on Davis, so at odds with the time-honored stereotype. They are much more accustomed to hearing such statements as the late David Potter's: the Confederate president, he wrote, "faced many obstacles which even the most gifted leader could not have overcome except in part, but the question is whether he dealt with them as effectively as an able leader could. There is no evidence that he did."[4] Weighed in the balance and found wanting—such has been Davis's fate. Perhaps the most representative and sweeping indictment of Davis by a modern historian was handed down by George M. Fredrickson in a recent collection of essays. After extolling the virtues of Abraham Lincoln as a war leader, he goes on to say that "the leadership of Davis was of a very different caliber. The Confederate president was a proud, remote, and quarrelsome man" who "fought constantly with his cabinet," and replaced able men with second-class lackeys. He was tactless, uncompromising, and opinionated, and "acquired bitter enemies in Congress, among the Confederate governors, and among the most competent southern generals." He believed he was a military genius and interfered excessively with his generals, besides adhering rigidly to a "policy of troop dispersal and departmentalization of command. Davis seemed to believe that the heavens would fall if the bureaucratic rules of a peacetime army were violated." Furthermore, he favored generals that he liked at the expense of better commanders who had offended him. "Unlike Lincoln, he lost touch with the political situation, and he failed to provide leadership in the critical area of economic policy. In the end one has a picture of Davis tinkering ineffectually with the South's military machine while

---

3. Raimondo Luraghi, *The Rise and Fall of the Plantation South* (New York and London, 1978), 151.
4. David Potter, *Division and the Stresses of Reunion, 1845-1876* (Glenview, Ill., 1973), 123.

a whole society was crumbling around him."⁵ This passage should be read in its entirety to be appreciated. It is a classic of its kind.

Like Fredrickson, historians often compare Lincoln and Davis as war presidents so as to illuminate the former's outstanding qualities by pointing to Davis's corresponding deficiencies. Lincoln emerges as a paragon of moral grandeur, political sagacity, and strategic intuition, all wrapped up in an appealing humility and kindliness. An almost religious reverence seems to grip some historians when they approach this man (a noun that scarcely seems adequate) who has been likened to Moses and Jesus, among other notables. For example, Allan Nevins observed that "the South in this life-and-death struggle failed to produce a Pericles or Winston Churchill—not to mention another name that springs to every mind. But to ask for this [i.e., another Lincoln], as human history goes, is to ask for a great deal."⁶ One is reminded of the ancient Hebrews, who feared to speak the name of God aloud.

To measure up to someone like this would be impossible for most of fallible mankind, and it is not surprising that Davis has had the worst of it. Perhaps it is not too cynical to suggest that because nothing succeeds like success, the comparison would have come out quite differently had the South won its independence. Suppose the French had not come to the rescue of the Patriots, and the British had crushed the American bid for independence? What would be George Washington's reputation?

Nor is it surprising that so many historians have compared Davis and Lincoln; in writing about the war, it is almost impossible not to do so. Far more remarkable is the fact that Davis always comes out second best, for it seems to me that even a brief systematic comparison shows that Davis was clearly superior to Lincoln as a war president. This is what I propose to undertake here, "with malice toward none; with charity for all; with firmness in the right as God gives [me] to see the right." The admirers of Mr. Lincoln should not be offended, for it was they who started this business of comparisons.

In one way or another, a great many of Davis's alleged sins concern the way

---

5. George M. Fredrickson, ed., *A Nation Divided: Problems and Issues of the Civil War and Reconstruction* (Minneapolis. 1975), 63-64. More recently Paul D. Escott, in his *After Secession: Jefferson Davis and the Failure of Confederate Nationalism* (Baton Rouge, 1977) claimed that Davis was largely responsible for the failure "to build a spirit of Confederate nationalism" (p. ix), and thus was responsible for the collapse of morale and the will to fight.

6. James D. Richardson, ed., *The Messages and Papers of Jefferson Davis and the Confederacy, Including Diplomatic Correspondence, 1861-1865* [Introduction by Allan Nevins] (New York, 1966), 1:xxii.

he dealt with individuals; his personality has been seen as a grave weakness that damaged the Confederate cause. He has been characterized, or caricatured, as cold, super-dignified, haughty, unapproachable, inaccessible. He was contentious, bore grudges, played favorites, was a poor judge of men, and could not brook contradiction or accept advice. This does not exhaust the litany of customary criticisms, but it will serve for the present. It is true that occasionally someone has said something complimentary about his personality, but this only irritates his detractors. David Potter complained that Davis "has been indiscriminately praised . . . for such irrelevant qualities as dignity and looking the part of a leader—something which was also said of Warren G. Harding."[7] Without searching for all that indiscriminate praise, one might observe that dignity is not always irrelevant to effective leadership. Much is made of Lincoln's folksiness and humility, which are said to have enabled him to handle people so much better than did Davis. But in fact Lincoln's not infrequent lack of dignity and presence, what might even be called his obsequious manner, led many powerful men, including some of his own party, sometimes to treat him with contempt. Legions of historians have rushed to evaluate the effects of Davis's aloofness, but who has thought to estimate the cost to the Union cause of Lincoln's lack of dignity? Wendell Phillips's famous gibe at Lincoln as "a first-rate second-rate man" expressed the view of many Northerners of high and low degree, who were certainly influenced at least in part by Lincoln's unpresidential demeanor.

A favorite target of Davis's critics is the Confederate cabinet. He picked men of poor quality, they say, because he was a bad judge of talent and because he wanted only yes-men, and having selected his mediocrities, his personality prevented his working with them efficiently or harmoniously. Look at the turnover: fourteen men passed through six offices. But who has complained that a total of thirteen individuals passed through Lincoln's cabinet? In fairness, two should be deducted for the Interior Department, which the Confederacy did not have; that brings the odds down to fourteen to eleven—surely not a very telling discrepancy. Then take the four most important departments: War, Navy, Treasury, and State. Lincoln had only one secretary of state, it is true, but Judah P. Benjamin served Davis in that capacity for more than three years, so the State Department was scarcely a revolving door. Davis had two treasury secretaries, one of whom served from the beginning until June 1864; Lincoln had three. Each president had only one secretary of the navy. Ah, but look at the War Department, say

---

7. Potter, op. cit., 123.

Davis's critics. Lincoln had only two men in that position, whereas Davis had five. That is quite true, of course, but one of the five held office from November 1862 until February 1865—twenty-six and a half months.

As to the quality of the two cabinets, much might be said. Leaving aside the minor offices, there is little to choose between Seward and Benjamin, taking into account their respective problems and advantages. Taking the same things into account, Secretary of the Navy Mallory was at least the equal of Welles, and the much-abused Memminger probably understood financial matters better than Chase, but was faced with a set of circumstances that no one could have overcome. As for the War Department, presumably no great claims will be made for Simon Cameron, whom Lincoln appointed as his reward for helping to bring the Pennsylvania delegation into line at the 1860 Republican convention. But the consensus has it that Cameron's successor, Edwin M. Stanton, did a first-rate job. This is, in my view, one of those revealed truths handed along unquestioningly from one historian to another, one that has yet to be substantiated. That he was superior to James A. Seddon, who served Davis for more than half the war, certainly remains to be proved. James Ford Rhodes, who was never accused of being pro-Confederate, wrote that "if the frequently superfluous controversial letters of the Confederate President and Secretary of War be excepted, a study of the papers of Davis, Seddon, and Judge Campbell [assistant secretary of war], will give one a high idea of their executive talents; indeed any government might be proud of the ability shown in these documents. A certain class of facts if considered alone can make us wonder how it was possible to subjugate the Confederates."[8]

Much of what has been written about the Confederate War Department is an extrapolation of the opinions of men like the captious Robert G. H. Kean of the Bureau of War. Those who leave diaries have a disproportionate influence on historians, for Kean was in no position to know everything that Davis and Seddon knew, and his opinions should be considered accordingly. People like Kean gave birth to the tediously repeated accusation that Davis reduced his cabinet officers, especially the secretary of war, to mere clerks. So far as Kean is concerned, this notion may have something to do with the fact that his uncle by marriage, Secretary of War George W. Randolph, abruptly resigned from that position in November 1862. This is indeed the favorite illustration of the cabinet-clerk theory. Davis allegedly provoked Randolph's huffy departure, when in reality Randolph

---

8. James Ford Rhodes, *History of the Civil War, 1861–1865* (New York, 1917), 396.

had grossly overreached his authority and resigned without giving the President a chance to discuss the matter with him.[9]

How efficiently did the Confederate cabinet function? There were complaints. Mallory said that Davis "neither labored with method or celerity himself, nor permitted others to do so for him," and observed that although cabinet meetings were often prolonged, the amount of business transacted was often small.[10] But Mallory also came to regard Davis "as a man of will and energy, patience and industry, possessing a knowledge of men and public affairs and an analytical and comprehensive judgment, to all of which were added the prompt business habits of a merchant."[11] Postmaster General Reagan recalled that the cabinet was "so much of one view as to the necessities of our situation, that, while there were occasional differences of opinion among them . . . there was no passion or strife."[12] Reagan categorically denied that Davis was self-willed or arbitrary or that he refused to accept advice. When compared with all the men he had known in public life, said Reagan, Davis was the ablest: "thoughtful, prudent, and wise."[13]

The relative harmony of Davis's official family would have seemed a haven of rest to the beleaguered Lincoln. A secretary of war who acted behind his back, feeding confidential War Department documents to the president's critics in Congress, a treasury secretary who used his department's payroll to build a political apparatus to enable him to oust Lincoln as the Republican candidate in 1864, a secretary of state who helped his alter ego (Thurlow Weed) to arrange illicit trade with the Confederates—these were but a few of Mr. Lincoln's travails. Nor was there any Confederate counterpart to Lincoln's great cabinet crisis of December 1862. Nor did Davis have to ease out a department head for gross mismanagement, or dismiss another to pacify a disgruntled political faction.[14]

---

9. Edward Younger, ed., *Inside the Confederate Government: The Diary of Robert Garlick Hill Kean, Head of the Bureau of War* (New York, 1957), 30; Patrick, op. cit., 126-31.

10. James G. Randall and David Donald, *The Civil War and Reconstruction* (Lexington, Mass., 1969), 270-71.

11. Patrick, op. cit., 43.

12. John H. Reagan, *Memoirs, with Special Reference to Secession and the Civil War* (New York and Washington, 1960), 162.

13. Ibid., 252.

14. For illustrative citations, see T. Harry Williams, *Lincoln and the Radicals* (Madison and Milwaukee, 1965), 93-94, 110-12, 115-16, and passim; Benjamin P. Thomas and Harold M. Hyman, *Stanton, The Life and Times of Lincoln's Secretary of War* (New York, 1962), 259-60; Salmon P. Chase Papers, Library of Congress, 1863-64, passim; Erwin S. Bradley, *Simon Cameron, Lincoln's Secretary of War* (Philadelphia, 1966), 418, 422. For Weed's trading activities, see L. H. Johnson, "Northern Profit and Profiteers. The Cotton Rings of 1864-1865," *Civil War History*, 12 (1966): 102-3, 105-9.

But even if one concedes that a case can be made for Davis's ability to pick capable civilian advisers and work with them amicably, what of Davis and his generals? What of charges such as those of Fredrickson, for example, that Davis was "offended by the independence of Beauregard and Joseph E. Johnston" and so "deprived these generals of important commands and failed to make good use of their talents"?[15] Or this remark of a Davis biographer: "It is hard to imagine Davis saying of a general what Lincoln said of McClellan, who had grossly insulted him: 'Never mind. I will hold McClellan's horse if he will only give us victory.'"[16] In doing a skit about Lincoln, Bob Newhart called this sort of thing "the old humble bit," along with the shawl and string tie, but it is the kind of anecdote that is related *ad nauseam* as if it contained some profound historical insight.

It is interesting to compare Davis's handling of Johnston and Beauregard with what Lincoln did to McClellan. Johnston commanded the Virginia army from First Manassas until he was wounded at Seven Pines—more than ten months. Upon his recovery in November 1862, Davis assigned him to the largest and most important command in the Confederacy, the Department of the West, a position he held until July 1863 when, at his request, Tennessee was removed from his jurisdiction. Then in December, in spite of all the difficulties Davis had had with Johnston, in spite of the disastrous Vicksburg campaign, the President yielded to his cabinet's advice and gave Johnston the Army of Tennessee. Davis relieved him of command in July 1864 only after Johnston had retreated to the outskirts of Atlanta and then refused to assure Davis that he would not abandon the city without a fight. Finally, against his better judgment, Davis recalled Johnston to field service in February 1865.[17]

Now it is true that Davis never offered to hold Johnston's horse. But compare Davis's so-called neglect of Johnston with what happened to McClellan. Lincoln restored "Little Mac" to command after John Pope's resounding defeat at Second Manassas and sent him to repel Lee's invasion of Maryland. McClellan did just that at Sharpsburg, a major strategic victory for the North. Then, when

---

15. Fredrickson, op. cit., 63.
16. Tate, op. cit., 149.
17. For Johnston and Davis, consult, inter alia, Joseph E. Johnston, *Narrative of Military Operations* . . . (New York, 1874); Jefferson Davis, *Rise and Fall of the Confederate Government* (2 vols., New York, 1881); Douglas S. Freeman, *Lee's Lieutenants: A Study in Command* (3 vols., New York, 1942-44); Archer Jones, *Confederate Strategy from Shiloh to Vicksburg* (Baton Rouge, 1961); Alfred P. James, "General Joseph Eggleston Johnston, Storm Center of the Confederacy," *Mississippi Valley Historical Review*, 14 (1927): 342-59; James W. Livingood and Gilbert E. Govan, *A Different Valor: The Story of General Joseph E. Johnston, C.S.A.* (New York, 1956).

McClellan had crossed into Virginia and was moving against the Confederates along the line recommended by Lincoln, the president abruptly removed him. Unlike every other unsuccessful commander of the Army of the Potomac, McClellan never saw active duty again. In other words, Lincoln restored McClellan to command after his losing campaign on the Peninsula and sacked him after his winning campaign in Maryland. What would be said of Davis if he had dismissed Lee permanently after he drove the Federals away from Richmond in the Seven Days' Battle?[18]

Take the other victim of Davis's alleged neglect, P. G. T. Beauregard. Beauregard held an important command in Virginia until early 1862, when he was given another very responsible position under Albert Sidney Johnston. His Virginia career had been marked by gasconading and glory-seeking that make the late Douglas MacArthur seem the model of shy modesty by comparison. He succeeded to the command of the Western army after Johnston's death at Shiloh. Then in June 1862, when the whole Western front was collapsing about his ears, he turned his army over to Braxton Bragg and took an unauthorized sick leave of indefinite duration—for laryngitis! When Beauregard reported himself fit for duty some weeks later, he was assigned to command the Department of Georgia and South Carolina. There he stayed until 1864, when he was ordered to Virginia to aid in the defense of Richmond and Petersburg, which he did brilliantly. In October Davis put him in charge of the Military Division of the West, the biggest territorial command east of the Mississippi.[19]

In the light of the plain facts, what can be said of the persistent charge that Davis refused to give these two generals important commands? One is reminded of Lincoln's advice: argue with a man as long as he will talk sense, and when he stops talking sense stick a corncob in his mouth. The Johnston-Beauregard matter is offered as an illustration of the great clutter of gratuitous misconceptions that will have to be cleared away before an attempt can be made to draw an accurate picture of Jefferson Davis.

The question still remains, of course, as to whether Davis *should* have put men like Beauregard and Johnston in such powerful positions. Could he have found better men? How good was the quality of Davis's military appointments

---

18. The best military biography of McClellan is Warren W. Hassler's *General George B. McClellan: Shield of the Union* (Baton Rouge, 1957).

19. For Davis and Beauregard, see especially T. Harry Williams, *P. G. T. Beauregard, Napoleon in Gray* (Baton Rouge, 1954) and Alfred Roman, *The Military Operations of General Beauregard . . .* , 2 vols. (New York, 1884).

generally? About one there should be little dispute. Only the professional iconoclast, of whom there are a few in active practice, would argue that Davis was mistaken in his choice of Robert E. Lee. In the West Albert Sidney Johnston was an almost inescapable selection, so distinguished was his reputation as a man and a soldier, although he died before he could prove his capacity for high command. On the South Atlantic coast Beauregard performed well. As for the Trans-Mississippi Department, no one will contend that Theophilus H. Holmes was the best choice, but E. Kirby Smith discharged the duties of that difficult assignment with efficiency and intelligence during the last half of the war. Besides Beauregard, the Western Department commanders who followed A. S. Johnston were Bragg, Joseph Johnston, and John Bell Hood, and then Beauregard again. A good case can be made for removing Bragg long before the disaster at Missionary Ridge (there is, incidentally, a case to be made *for* Bragg), and in fact Davis tried to do so in March 1863, but he was thwarted by Johnston's refusal to take field command of the Army of Tennessee. The relief of Johnston before Atlanta and the selection of Hood as his successor are usually given as the classic instance of Davis's poor judgment of military talent. But given the critical situation in Georgia—the long retreat from Dalton to the outer defenses of Atlanta, together with Johnston's inexcusable sulkiness and reticence—Davis had to do *something*. It is not easy to see what he could have done except to remove Johnston, which he did with great reluctance.[20] As to his replacement, an outsider was not to be thought of, with the army pinned between Sherman and Atlanta. A. P. Stewart had only recently assumed corps command, and so the choice was between W. J. Hardee and Hood. The latter was famous for his aggressiveness, something conspicuously lacking on the Confederate side thus far in the campaign, while the former was a close friend of Johnston and bore the honorable but uninspiring nickname, "Old Reliable." That Davis chose Hood under these circumstances does not seem so misguided as is sometimes represented.[21]

How does Lincoln compare with Davis in staffing the high command? The title of Kenneth P. Williams's massive work, *Lincoln Finds a General*, has always struck me as an amusing unintentional lampoon of Lincoln as a general-picker, the implication being that there was only one general to be found and that it took the president three years to locate him. When the roll of Union commanders

---

20. For Davis's reluctance to relieve Johnston, see his *Rise and Fall*, 2:561.
21. See Nathaniel C. Hughes Jr., *General William J. Hardee: Old Reliable* (Baton Rouge, 1965), 215–16, for Hardee's failure to be selected.

in Virginia is called, it is customary to murmur sympathetically about Lincoln's rotten luck in taking up one loser after another and to admire his persistence in hiring and firing. But what would historians have said about Jefferson Davis if the Army of Northern Virginia had undergone seven changes of commanders, five of them after major defeats? One can also imagine their cutting remarks if Davis's ranking field commanders from November 1862 until March 1864 had been, let us say, Louis T. Wigfall and Robert Toombs, who would have been roughly equivalent to Benjamin F. Butler (assuming that Butler could have an equivalent) and Nathaniel P. Banks, two politicians who outranked every field commander from the relief of McClellan until Grant's promotion to lieutenant general.[22] The stock defense of Lincoln's loyalty to such political stumble-bums is that such was the price he had to pay for consolidating Northern support for the war; if so, there could be no more devastating a commentary on the political dynamics of Northern society. But this defense of Lincoln has to be taken on faith in accordance with the rule that if Lincoln did it, it must have been right.

By contrast, Davis needs little defense on this score. When compared to Lincoln, his major military appointments, promotions, and dismissals were remarkably free of politics. As Ezra Warner says in his introduction to *Generals in Blue*, "To a much greater extent than in the Confederate Army, high command was intrusted to individuals whose chief claims to preferment rested exclusively upon political considerations. . . . If based upon the performance in the field of battle the results of these selections reflect most unfavorably in retrospect when compared to the choices of Jefferson Davis."[23] No one would deny that Davis made mistakes, such as his strange and enduring confidence in John C. Pemberton and his loyalty to Bragg, and it may be that in these cases he should have given more weight to public opinion. But as Warner says, the results showed that in building a high command, too little politics was far better than too much.

The considerations that often influenced Lincoln's military appointments are part of the larger subject of how the Republicans sought to politicize the war for partisan advantage. It is a subject too large and complex to be pursued in a brief essay, unfortunately, for it would show, as military appointments illustrate, the great difference between Davis and Lincoln as war presidents. The major war aim of Lincoln and the Republican party generally was, it seems to me, to make that party a permanent majority in the nation; this was the hard core of meaning in the

---

22. For some comments on Northern political generals, see L. H. Johnson, "Civil War Military History: A Few Revisions in Need of Revising," *Civil War History*, 17 (June 1971): 128–30.

23. Ezra Warner, *Generals in Blue: Lives of the Union Commanders* (Baton Rouge, 1964), xviii–xix.

policy of "preserving the Union." The objective of party supremacy could dictate not only the choice of generals, but many other decisions that directly affected the conduct of the war. Political organizations lived on patronage, and patronage meant not only the bestowal of offices, whether civil or military, but a multitude of favors that translated into money or political advancement, or both. The war gave the Republicans incomparably more patronage to distribute than any party had ever enjoyed, and this bloody conflict was seen by an astonishing number of people as a golden opportunity to strike it rich. Unfortunately, the men in the ranks paid the price when they were ordered into battle by incompetent political generals, or sent on bootless campaigns for merely political reasons, or were killed by Confederates who were being fed and clothed by Northern merchants bearing trade permits signed by Lincoln. Such matters call for a comparison of the motives that actuated Lincoln and Davis. Motives can never be known with certainty; perhaps Ben Butler really was a Puritan idealist, as one of his biographers claims. But sometimes educated guesses must be made about why people act as they do. Davis and Lincoln are interesting subjects for such speculation, and there is little reason to believe that the former would suffer by comparison with the latter.

Another familiar charge often directed at Davis is that having picked his generals he then proceeded to interfere harmfully with operations in the field. One historian has claimed that Davis would "sometimes visit battlefields and change the disposition of regiments while combat raged."[24] It is true that the president was on the field at First Manassas (though only at the end of the engagement), Seven Pines, and the Seven Days, but except for two trivial episodes at Seven Pines, I am unaware of any instance of Davis giving such orders. Indeed, during the Seven Days he was shooed away from the front first by Lee and then by A. P. Hill.

Far more important were the strategic decisions that Davis made and for which he has been roundly criticized. His record here is mixed, but it is by no means a tale of unrelieved failure. Davis was largely responsible for Johnston's shift from the Shenandoah Valley to Manassas, a movement that made possible the Confederate victory on July 21. After the loss of Forts Henry and Donelson, Davis stripped much of the Confederate coastal defenses to reinforce A. S. Johnston—a daring, even desperate attempt to prevent the Western front from caving in. Had these reinforcements allowed Johnston to crush Grant at Shiloh, as he very nearly did, the wisdom of Davis's strategy would be beyond dispute, and even though Shiloh was lost, he clearly did the right thing.

In the late fall of 1862, just before the battle at Murfreesboro, Davis detached

24. David Donald, ed., *Why the North Won the Civil War* (Baton Rouge, 1960), 107.

9,000 troops from Bragg's army to strengthen Southern forces in Mississippi. This is usually called a serious mistake, but how often does anyone point out the part played by those troops in repulsing Sherman's attack on Chickasaw Bluffs, the key to Vicksburg? On the other hand, Davis is criticized for not detaching troops from Lee's army to help defend Vicksburg, allowing instead the invasion of the North that came to its dismal climax at Gettysburg. And yet no one can be sure that Bragg, with his penchant for losing won battles, would have crushed Rosecrans at Murfreesboro if he had had Stevenson's division with him, or that Vicksburg would have been saved by troops from Lee's army, or that weakening Lee might not have had serious repercussions in Virginia. The results of the costly victory at Chickamauga are not likely to persuade anyone that ad hoc inter-theater troop transfers were the key to victory, given the feebleness of Confederate logistics and the great disparity in numbers in almost every theater. During 1864 Davis made two strategic decisions of great importance. First, he refused to gather up all the cavalry in the West, put them under Forrest, and send them against Sherman's dangerously attenuated rail lines—the thing that Sherman most feared. Davis persisted in his refusal despite the advice of Johnston, Polk, Hardee, Governor Brown of Georgia, and Lee, and I am unaware of any exculpating circumstances. If anything could have defeated Sherman, it was this, and the defeat of Sherman doubtless would have meant the defeat of the Republicans in the 1864 elections. And with the Democrats in power, the chances of a negotiated peace would have been enormously enhanced. This was, in short, by far Davis's worst mistake of the war.[25]

The other decision was to send Hood against Sherman's rail lines after Atlanta had fallen, hoping to draw Sherman out of Georgia, but by then it was too late for such strategy to work. Sherman had been able to accumulate a reserve of supplies and, since he was no longer heavily engaged, was able to detach troops to guard the railroads. Should Sherman not pursue, the Confederate plan called for Hood to turn back so that Sherman would not be left unopposed in central Georgia. But when Sherman gave up chasing Hood and returned to Atlanta, Hood decided to advance into Tennessee. Davis apparently gave at least tacit approval.[26] The result was a Confederate disaster in Tennessee and Sherman's virtually unimpeded

---

25. For a discussion of this point, see Robert S. Henry, *"First with the Most" Forrest* (New York, 1944), 307-10.

26. William J. Cooper, "A Reassessment of Jefferson Davis as War Leader: The Case from Atlanta to Nashville," *Journal of Southern History*, 36 (1970): 203-4.

march from Atlanta to the sea. Almost certainly nothing could have retrieved the Southern cause in the West at that late date, but Davis nevertheless must bear the responsibility for permitting a campaign that was so radically defective from a strategic point of view.

So even though Davis proved himself to be a remarkably talented commander-in-chief, he did make mistakes. But given the huge disparity in resources, the Confederacy had to fight a near-perfect war if it was to have any hope of maintaining its independence. It had—Davis had—no margin for error. Lincoln, however, did have such a margin; that was lucky for the North, because he was forever making mistakes, either by trading military for political advantage, or simply by interfering in matters he did not understand. In fact, in strategic sense and logistical judgment, Davis was so far superior to Lincoln that any extended comparison would be needlessly cruel. Sometimes Lincoln played a major role in controlling operations in the field, the best (or worst) example being the Peninsula campaign of 1862. On other occasions he tried to avoid taking responsibility for decisions because he feared the political consequences of failure. This political dimension to Lincoln's search for a successful general has not been recognized fully, and it helps to explain, for example, his unhappiness with General-in-Chief Henry W. Halleck, who bitterly disappointed Lincoln by being equally adept at dodging responsibility. Davis's directness, decisiveness, and willingness to accept the consequences of his actions are qualities that are conspicuously rare in the case of Mr. Lincoln. As Stephen A. Douglas said of the latter, "he [is] preeminently a man of the atmosphere that surrounds him."[27] Decisiveness is not the mark of such a man.

To turn from military to political matters, both the Confederate Congress and Davis's relationship with Congress are usually condemned, Congress for being little better than a "bear garden" where the solons threw inkwells at one another, and Davis for tactless and inept handling of the legislators. Yet it is difficult to understand how anyone who has examined the large body of legislation passed by Congress and who has read Davis's correspondence and messages to that body could subscribe to either opinion. The effectiveness of Davis's leadership and his extraordinary grasp of a wide range of subjects are apparent. As for Congress, James Ford Rhodes wrote that a study of Confederate legislation "cannot fail to convey the idea that there was much political capacity" in the legislative branch. Furthermore, he attributes the skillful drafting of many laws

---

27. Richard Hofstadter, *The American Political Tradition* (New York, 1948), 129-30.

to executive officials, especially to Assistant Secretary of War John A. Campbell,[28] until 1861 a justice of the United States Supreme Court. It would be absurd to deny, of course, that some Congressmen detested Davis and repeatedly tried to thwart him, but specimens such as Henry S. Foote, who some believed should have been exposed on a hillside at birth, have been quoted all out of proportion to their importance. And often even those who criticized or opposed Davis's policies finally voted for them. His success with the Provisional Congress and the First Congress was greater than with the Second (and last) Congress, elected in the grim summer of 1863. But all things considered, William B. Yearns, in his study of the legislative branch, concluded that "the Confederate government ran more smoothly than did that of the United States and Lincoln was far more bothered with politics than was Davis."[29]

Davis's role in managing the Confederacy's legislative program was so large, and the sweep of his policies so broad, that a comparison with Lincoln is difficult to make, for Lincoln's interest in legislation was quite restricted. Many of the major laws passed by the Federal Congress were in fulfillment of Republican party promises, and Lincoln was not disposed to meddle in these matters.[30] This is understandable, but it certainly made Lincoln's job simpler and less difficult politically. Instead he concentrated on measures having to do in one way or another with slavery or reconstruction. Yet within this limited though extremely important sphere, Lincoln was not able even to control his own party in Congress. His repeated and earnest proposals for gradual, compensated emancipation accompanied by colonization were largely ignored. As for reconstruction, Lincoln's failure was even more profound. Congressional Republicans were never reconciled to the system proclaimed by Lincoln in December 1863, a system for which the president was still soliciting support on the day before he was shot. In short, Lincoln's task in managing the legislative branch was not as demanding as Davis's, nor was his success nearly as great.

The degree to which Congress cooperated in implementing executive policies tells nothing about either the wisdom or the success of those policies. In a

---

28. James Ford Rhodes, *History of the United States from the Compromise of 1850* (8 vols., New York, 1893-1906), 5:479.

29. William B. Yearns, *The Confederate Congress* (Athens, Ga., 1960), 234.

30. This is conceded even in G. S. Boritt's *Lincoln and the Economics of the American Dream* (Memphis, 1978), 227-31. For example (p. 230): "Thus even if the President had desired to play a truly major part in the Civil War economic revolution, and even if Congress had acquiesced in this, we can be reasonably certain that he could not have mustered the psychic energy for the task."

brief essay one can only mention the two things that are usually pointed to as the great failures of Confederate governance: finances and foreign policy. The two are not unconnected, because for the first year of the war financial policy was predicted on the belief that European powers, especially England, would demand access to Southern cotton early in 1862. Had this occurred, monetary inflation would probably not have exceeded (if it equaled) the inflation of Northern greenbacks. But King Cotton failed, and historians have often been ready to scoff at Davis's belief in the "delusion." There is no doubt that he did confide in the power of King Cotton,[31] but what is rarely noticed is that many outside the South were similarly misled. Early in 1861 both the British and Russian ministers to Washington expected that the economic pressures of a blockade would compel European intervention.[32] In the summer of 1861 Lincoln told his old friend Orville Hickman Browning that "in his opinion they were determined to have the cotton crop as soon as it matured."[33] The whole of Seward's diplomacy was based on the fear of intervention, and strenuous efforts were made to secure cotton and tobacco for the English and French markets. And as everyone knows, in 1862 the British came very close indeed to intervening, only to pull back when McClellan forced Lee to retreat from Maryland to Virginia. It is no wonder that King Cotton, in combination with other factors that the Confederates took into account, was regarded as a real and deadly danger by the North. King Cotton as a "delusion" is an idea born of historical hindsight; according to this use of the word, any unfulfilled expectation, however reasonable, is ipso facto a delusion. The failure of Confederate diplomacy to secure foreign assistance or intervention was not caused by a radically defective policy—a delusion. The reason for failure was external: the hard facts of national interest and international dangers facing European powers meant that the Confederacy would have to win its independence on the battlefield before anyone would recognize it. There was nothing that diplomacy could do.

The collapse of Confederate finances was the direct result of the interdiction of foreign trade. The amount of specie in the South at the outbreak of the war

---

31. So said his wife: Varina Howell Davis, *Jefferson Davis, Ex-President of the Confederate States of America* (New York, 1890), 2:160. See also Frank L. Owsley, *King Cotton Diplomacy* (rev. ed., Chicago, 1959), chapter 1.

32. Lynn M. Case and Warren F. Spencer, *The United States and France: Civil War Diplomacy* (Philadelphia, 1970), 46.

33. James G. Randall and Theodore C. Pease, eds., *The Diary of Orville Hickman Browning* (Springfield, Ill., 1925), 1:489 (July 28, 1861).

was utterly inadequate either to make essential purchases overseas or to support a convertible currency. Since the South could not get its great cash crops to market, financing the war with the printing press was inevitable in the long run. Davis and Memminger were acutely conscious of the dangers of inflation and tried various expedients to slow it down,[34] but Congress did not always cooperate fully, and the pressure of events simply overwhelmed Confederate finances. As Charles Ramsdell wrote a generation ago: "But if you ask me how, under the conditions which had existed in April, 1861, the Confederate government could have avoided this pitfall [i.e., excessive paper money inflation], I can only reply that I do not know."[35] Given Ramsdell's encyclopaedic knowledge of the Confederacy, it is not strange that no one has since been able to suggest a satisfactory alternative.

Far from being the death-rattle of a moribund and archaic society, Confederate financial policies exhibited extraordinary imagination and daring, and Davis's messages to Congress reveal a leader struggling manfully with a problem that was inherently insoluble. Furthermore, as Luraghi has emphasized, financial failure is more than offset by the Davis administration's trade policies and its remarkable mobilization of the Confederacy's economic resources. Accused of being hostage to the past, of being rigid, inflexible, and unimaginative, Jefferson Davis presided over a government-managed industrial system totally without precedent in American history.

The purpose of this brief and incomplete essay has been to suggest that the full story, the correct story of Jefferson Davis, has yet to be told. When it is, he will be seen for what he was, one of the most remarkable men of his day, and for that matter, in all of American history. For many years his talents and character have been obscured by the cult of Lincoln and the fact of Confederate defeat. But Davis was sure that justice would ultimately be done, and that neither he nor his fellow Southerners should fear to stand at the bar of history and hear the final verdict.

---

34. For example, see *The War of the Rebellion: A Compilation of the Official Records of the Union and Confederate Armies* (Washington, D.C., 1880-1901), Series 4, 2:312-23, 1039; 3:159-61, 367, 795.

35. Charles W. Ramsdell, *Behind the Lines in the Southern Confederacy* (Baton Rouge, 1944), 85.

To Suppress or Not to Suppress

Abraham Lincoln and the Chicago Times

Craig D. Tenney

A great deal has been said and written in recent years about governmental attempts to restrain the press. A roughly equal amount has been said and written about press responsibility. It might be well to remember that, when viewed against other periods of national history, recent attempts to influence, if not dictate, press treatment of the government are comparatively mild. The physical operation of the press is not threatened or affected directly as it was in earlier periods when national concern about the First Amendment was considerably less intense than it is presently and an administration's willingness to move, oftentimes harshly, against its journalistic opponents was not nearly so restrained. A case in point is the suppression of the *Chicago Times* in 1863 at the height of the Civil War. No sooner had Major General Ambrose E. Burnside imposed the suppression than President Abraham Lincoln ordered him to lift it, and followed that directive with yet another telling Burnside he might let the suppression stand temporarily. While a few historians have mentioned the *Times* affair and the first Lincoln directive to Burnside,[1] none has mentioned the second.

---

1. See, for example, Justin Walsh, *To Print the News and Raise Hell—A Biography of Wilbur F. Storey* (Chapel Hill, 1968), 174-83; Robert S. Harper, *Lincoln and the Press* (New York, London, Toronto, 1951), 258-62; Harold L. Nelson, ed., *Freedom of the Press from Hamilton to the Warren Court* (Indianapolis, New York, 1967), 230-32.

Civil War History, Vol. XXVII No. 3, © 1981 by The Kent State University Press

Professor James G. Randall, who made a thorough and careful study of the constitutional problems besetting the Civil War president, seemed notably impressed by Lincoln's restraint in dealing with opposition newspapers and by his overall respect for press freedom. Instances of administration activities against the press, Randall said, "were not sufficiently numerous to argue a general repressive policy."[2] But of the newspapers against which action was taken, and there were many,[3] Randall observed that their utterances "were so vicious that suppression or the arrest of their editors seemed but mild forms of punishment."[4] Journalism historians Edwin and Michael Emery, in taking much the same approach, observe that Lincoln had "definite ideas about freedom of expression" when he rescinded the suppression of the *Times*.[5]

Study of the suppression, however, indicates it was not a tender regard for the First Amendment that guided Lincoln's hand in signing the order lifting the suppression. It was something more basic to the president's nature—a regard for politics. One would think that had the president been even moderately favorable toward general press freedom, he would have acted much earlier in the war when Secretary of State William H. Seward, Secretaries of War Simon Cameron and Edwin M. Stanton, and Postmaster General Montgomery Blair, as presidential agents or surrogates, were moving decisively against the opposition press.[6] That Lincoln did not act then would easily and naturally be viewed by cabinet officers, other bureaucrats and by generals in the field as a tacit approval of future repressive action against those publications and editors who bitterly opposed the administration and its war policies. Lincoln apparently never did anything generally to stifle such perceptions, choosing instead to handle such matters on a case-by-case basis.

With Burnside, one case involved the arrest of former Ohio congressman Clement L. Vallandigham in May 1863. Another involved the suppression of the *Times* less than a month later. That the two cases were part of the same cloth is indicated in a report Burnside submitted some time after taking command

---

2. James G. Randall, *Constitutional Problems Under Lincoln*, rev. ed. (Urbana, 1964), 46.

3. Records of many government actions against the press may be found in *The War of the Rebellion: A Compilation of the Official Records of the Union and Confederate Armies* [cited hereafter as O.R.] (Washington, 1880-1901), ser. 2, 2: passim.

4. James G. Randall, "The Newspaper During the Civil War," *American Historical Review* 23 (Jan. 1918), 316.

5. Edwin and Michael Emery, *The Press and America, An Interpretative History of the Mass Media*, 4th ed. (Englewood Cliffs, N.J., 1978), 169-70.

6. See fn. 3, supra. For Blair's involvement, see U.S., Congress. House, *Postmaster General's Authority Over Mailable Matter*, 37th Cong., 3d sess., 1863. Misc. Doc. No. 16.

of the Military Department of the Ohio in late March 1863.[7] He had, he said, been appalled to find that "newspapers were full of treasonable expressions, and large public meetings were held, at which our Government authorities and our gallant soldiers in the field were openly and loudly denounced for their efforts to suppress the rebellion."[8] Within three weeks of taking command, Burnside moved to quash such "disloyalty." On April 13, he issued General Orders, No. 38, which among other things mandated that anyone within the borders of his command who declared sympathy for the enemy would be subject to arrest and trial and that those convicted were to be subject to the death penalty or expulsion beyond federal lines. It was to be distinctly understood, the order held, "that treason, expressed or implied, [was] not to be tolerated in the department."[9]

On May 1, Vallandigham, who had been unseated in the previous fall's election, delivered a fiery anti-Lincoln speech at Mount Vernon, Ohio, and Burnside's troops arrested him at his Dayton home three days later. Taken to department headquarters in Cincinnati, Vallandigham was convicted by a military commission on charges of violating General Orders No. 38.[10] Soon after the arrest, both Lincoln and Stanton wired their support for Burnside: "In your determination to support the authority of the Government and suppress treason in your Department, you may count on the firm support of the President."[11] Under the circumstances, the message clearly implied presidential agreement with Burnside in equating strongly stated opposition with treason. Three weeks later, by which time Vallandigham had been transferred to the Confederacy,[12] the presidential tone had changed perceptibly. The entire cabinet regretted the necessity for the Vallandigham arrest, Lincoln wired the general, but now that the action had been taken, all were for seeing Burnside through with it. Lincoln refused Burnside's offer to resign.[13]

---

7. *O.R.*, ser. 1, vol 23. pt. 2:147. Burnside moved to the Department of the Ohio after being relieved of command of the Army of the Potomac, which he had led to defeat in the battle at Fredericksburg, Va., the previous Dec. 13. The new command comprised the states of Ohio, Indiana, and Illiniois, and parts of Kentucky and Tennessee. Departmental headquarters was at Cincinnati.

8. Ibid., ser. 1, vol. 23. pt. 1:12.

9. Ibid., pt. 2:237.

10. The Vallandigham arrest and trial are covered in *O.R.*, ser. 2, 5:633-46, 656-58, 665-66.

11. Lincoln to Burnside, May 8, 1863, Burnside Papers. General's Papers and Books, Record Group 94, National Archives Building. Washington, D.C.; Stanton to Burnside, May 8, 1863, *Telegrams Collected by the Office of the Secretary of War* [cited hereafter as *War Dept. Telegrams*], *Telegrams Sent by the Secretary of War*, Record Group 107, National Archives Microfilm Publication M473, roll 82, vol. 173, frame 390.

12. *O.R.*, ser. 2, 5:705-6.

13. Lincoln to Burnside, May 29, 1863, ibid., 717.

The tone of the brief message perhaps indicated a lessening of presidential support, and Burnside could certainly discern in the two telegrams more than tacit presidential sanction for violating freedom of expression in the Department of the Ohio where Copperheadism was strong.[14] Burnside's chief concern seems to have been the effect anti-government orators and publications were having on troop morale.[15] Recruiting figures were dropping steadily; desertions were increasing as troop disaffection for war policies grew with the mounting casualty lists. Wood Gray has contended that there was danger of the war's being lost by the disintegration of the armies.[16] Lincoln himself credited Vallandigham with "laboring with some effect to prevent the raising of troops, to encourage desertions from the army, and to leave the rebellion without an adequate military force to suppress it."[17]

Much the same complaint could be made against Wilbur F. Storey, the editor and publisher of the *Chicago Times*. Assuredly there was justification in feeling that Storey was acting to discourage enlistments and was, in fact, encouraging desertions. In the spring of 1863, the *Times* frequently carried purported letters from men in the army, letters reflecting discontent and disgust with abolitionist war goals. One such letter received page one prominence on March 31, 1863, a week after Burnside assumed command of the Department of the Ohio.

> All the privations of a soldier's life could be easily borne—the long, weary march through mud and rain, dust and heat—the blistered feet and aching bones—with no provision other than hard bread of full age and rusty bacon—with no resting place but the damp earth, full of fevers, pain, and death, of which thickly-strewn graves, wherever our armies go, rise up to bear witness—yes, all of this the noble sons and daughters of our unhappy land could bear, were it the precursor of resuming peace and the restoration of our old Union. But alas! the great bulk of the northern army have been most grossly deceived. They were sworn to support the constitution of the United States and the government as guided by it. This

---

14. In support of this assertion, see Mayo Fesler, "Secret Political Societies in the North During the Civil War," *Indiana Magazine of History* 14 (Sept. 1918); Frank L. Klement, *The Copperheads in the Middle West* (Chicago, 1960).

15. The whole tone of Burnside's letter to the U.S. Circuit Court for Southern Ohio, written prior to a hearing of Vallandigham's civil court appeal from his trial before the military commission, supports the statement. See *O.R.*, ser. 2, 5:575-76.

16. Wood Gray, *The Hidden Civil War: The Story of the Copperheads* (New York, 1942), 132. See also Klement, *Copperheads in the Middle West*, 78.

17. Lincoln to Erastus Corning and Others, June 12, 1863, O.R., ser. 2, 6:7.

the army in good faith agreed to do; but I now know that it was only a trap by which to get an immense army of patriotic men, who, once in the clutch of an abolition administration, would be used by it, against their will, to carry on an abolition crusade against the South. I can look at it in no other light. Every passing event confirms it. Each day sheds new light upon the darkness of the plot.[18]

On the following day, April 1, Storey editorialized that every conscript into the army would be "sacrificed uselessly if the imbecile management that has distinguished the conduct of the war hitherto continues."[19] Twelve days later he wrote that Union soldiers were "indignant at the imbecility that has devoted them to slaughter for purposes with which they have no sympathy."[20] It was hardly writing calculated to encourage a rush on enlistment offices.

Storey had moved from a position as owner, editor, and publisher of the *Detroit Free Press*, buying the *Times* from Cyrus McCormick for $23,000 in May 1861.[21] To his new acquisitions Storey brought a hatred of the Negro and abolitionism, a hatred matched, or nearly so, by his attitude toward the Republican party in general and Lincoln in particular. To him, Negroes were destined to be "mere hewers of wood and drawers of water to a superior and dominant race." Referring to efforts at colonization, he maintained that Negroes lacked "manhood to govern and energy to work."[22] He perceived that under abolitionism, "everything—government, constitution, law, order—is subjected to the negro," and that given the opportunity, abolitionists would employ "an Inquisition, a Bastile [*sic*], and a Guillotine to enforce their opinions and desires."[23] Lincoln's signing of the Emancipation Proclamation was a "monstrous usurpation . . . a criminal wrong and an act of national suicide."[24] It was simply a license to depraved Negroes to commit all sorts of unspeakable acts. All that remained to

---

18. *Chicago Times*, Mar. 31, 1863, 1.
19. *Chicago Times*, Apr. 1, 1863, 2.
20. *Chicago Times*, Apr. 13, 1863, 2.
21. Frank W. Scott, *Newspapers and Periodicals of Illinois, 1814-1865*, 2 vols. (Springfield, 1910), 1:65-66; Alfred T. Andreas, *History of Chicago from the Earliest Period to the Present Time* (Chicago, 1885), 2:396; John Moses and Joseph Kirkland, *Aboriginal to Metropolitan, History of Chicago, Illinois* (Chicago and New York, 1895), 3:54.
22. *Chicago Times*, Sept. 13, 1862, 2. For other *Times* articles and editorials on the Negro, see the issues for Sept. 27, 1862, 2; Oct. 1, 1862, 2: Oct. 11, 1862, 1; Oct. 20, 1862, 1.
23. *Chicago Times*, Sept. 8, 1862, 2. For other *Times* diatribes against abolitionists at about this time, see issues for Sept. 5, 1862, 2; Sept. 13, 1862, 2. Sept. 23, 1862, 2; Sept. 24, 1862, 2; Oct. 8, 1862, 1.
24. *Chicago Times*, Sept. 23, 1862, 2.

make the abolitionists' program complete, Storey said, was to arm the slaves and direct them to "commence the work of massacre and pillage" of their masters and their masters' property.[25]

Not without a touch of peevish humor, Storey noted that abolitionist clergy were viewing the war as "a punishment for some great national sin." It was his theory "that the great national sin for which heaven is punishing the American people is the election of Lincoln to the presidency." And Storey conceded that it was a sin "for which the American people ought to be punished."[26] The only way to right the wrongs of the administration, he advised *Times* readers in late February 1863, was "for the democracy of the country to absolutely and unqualifiedly refuse" to support the administration's policies.[27] On March 17, he called for "a united, bold, vigorous, unyielding opposition to the prosecution of the war." Such opposition to Lincoln's issue of the preliminary Emancipation Proclamation, would, he argued, have prevented issuance of the final proclamation in January "and compelled Congress and the administration to go back to the original policies of the war"—peace and reunion.[28]

Vallandigham's arrest, trial, and transfer through southern lines seemed to Storey "like the funeral of civil liberty."[29] The Ohioan, he wrote, had been guilty only of criticizing "those who daily pollute their souls with perjury in breaking their solemn oaths to 'preserve, protect and defend the Constitution of the United States.'"[30] On May 30, another *Times* editorial likened the situation to the period of the Alien and Sedition Acts, with the American public discovering that "however disreputable and contemptible [the administration's] measures, our people might be imprisoned or banished for truly, candidly and intelligently discussing them."[31] The same issue carried a page one article in which the paper's Washington correspondent assigned to Lincoln the physical appearance and demeanor of a lunatic. The president's face was haggard and careworn in the extreme, the report had it. "His eye is restless, and is constantly wandering; at most times with a vacant expression; at others in a manner indicative of positive terror." The same article called Burnside "The Butcher of Fredericksburg" and

---

25. *Chicago Times*, Sept. 24, 1862, 2.
26. *Chicago Times*, Nov. 15, 1862, 2.
27. *Chicago Times*, Feb. 28, 1863, 2.
28. *Chicago Times*, Mar. 17, 1863, 2.
29. *Chicago Times*, May 27, 1863, 2.
30. Ibid.
31. *Chicago Times*, May 30, 1863, 2.

disparaged what the writer regarded as the malignant influence on the president of Senators Benjamin Wade, Zachariah Chandler, and Charles Sumner.[32]

Whatever his provocation, Burnside acted late in the evening of June 1, ordering suppression of the *Times* "on account of the repeated expression of disloyal and incendiary statements."[33] The same order banned circulation of the *New York World* in the department. In Washington, the president apparently was visiting the War Department's telegraph office that evening of June 1, while Stanton was writing Burnside a letter on another matter. It seems likely that a copy of the suppression order moved on the wire at that time, for Stanton appended a postscript to the letter saying that Lincoln had been apprised of the suppression order and that in the president's judgment Burnside would do well to "take an early opportunity" to revoke the order. The reason, Stanton wrote, was Lincoln's feeling that: "The irritation produced by such acts is . . . likely to do more harm than the publication would do. The Government approves of your motives and desires to give you cordial and efficient support. But while military movements are left to your judgment, upon administration questions such as the arrest of civilians and the suppression of newspapers not requiring immediate action, the President desires to be previously consulted."[34]

One would think that had there been any element of urgency in transmitting the president's message, Stanton would have telegraphed Burnside. Apparently he chose to mail the letter instead, and then only after a few days had passed. The delay meant Burnside had no immediate knowledge that his action against the *Times* had evoked Lincoln's displeasure. With no feeling of restraint, he telegraphed Storey, notifying him of the suppression order. "You will please govern yourself accordingly," the telegram concluded.[35] To Jacob Ammen, commanding the District of Illinois, Burnside wired an order to stop publication of the *Times* and "if necessary [to] take military possession of the office." Ammen ordered Captain

32. Ibid., 1.
33. *O.R.*, ser. 1, vol. 23, pt. 2:381.
34. Ibid., ser. 2, 5.723-24. For Lincoln's habit of visiting the telegraph office, see David Homer Bates, *Lincoln in the Telegraph Office* (New York, 1907), 40-42, 154-55. See also John G. Nicolay and John Hay, *Abraham Lincoln, A History* (New York, 1890), 141-42. Under Army regulations, copies of all orders were to be forwarded "at their dates or as soon thereafter as practicable" to the War Department. *Revised U.S. Army Regulations of 1861* (Washington, 1867), 65. Thus, a copy of Burnside's suppression order was probably included in the telegrams arriving in the telegraph office the night of June 1.
35. Burnside to Storey, June 2, 1863, *Department of the Ohio Order Book*, Mar. through June 1863 [cited hereafter as *Order Book*], 152. The book is in the manuscript section of the Rhode Island State Historical Society Library, Providence. To confirm receipt of the message, see *Chicago Times*, June 3, 1862, 2.

James S. Putnam, commanding Camp Douglas just outside Chicago, to enforce the suppression.[36] When Storey and his partner, Ananias Worden, defied the order and began printing the issue of the following morning, Putnam dispatched troops who broke into the building and took all available copies of the offending issue into the streets and tore them to shreds.[37] The action attracted an angry crowd which grew as word of the action spread. An indignation meeting was called for that evening,[38] and rumors were widespread that if the *Times* were not allowed to publish, militant *Times* supporters would see to it that the bitterly anti-*Times* (and ardently pro-Republican) *Tribune* would not be allowed to publish either.[39] At the *Tribune*, preparations were begun to meet any such attack.[40]

A reputed stockholder in the *Tribune*, Judge Van Higgins, summoned a group of business and political leaders to a meeting at the courthouse. The group included Congressman I. N. Arnold, Senator Lyman Trumbull, Mayor F. C. Sherman and former Mayor William B. Ogden, now president of the Chicago and Northwestern Railway. It was Ogden who offered a resolution requesting that Lincoln suspend or rescind the suppression order. The motion was passed and several participants in the meeting were dispatched to gather additional endorsements.[41] Fourteen signatures in all were affixed to the resolution which was telegraphed to the president. A concluding line from Trumbull and Arnold read: "We respectfully ask for the above the serious and prompt consideration of the President."[42] It would prove to be an uncomfortably embarrassing note for Trumbull and Arnold, disastrously so for the latter.

It was one of two telegrams on the subject which the president received from Illinois. The other came from Springfield where Supreme Court Justice David Davis, a former political advisor, and William Herndon, Lincoln's former law partner and future biographer, had, upon hearing of the suppression order on

---

36. Burnside to Ammen, June 1, 1863, O. R., ser. 2, 5:726. See also *Chicago Times*. June 3, 1863, 2; *Chicago Evening Journal*, June 3, 1863, 1.

37. *The Suppression of the Times*, 13. The publication was issued by Storey shortly after the suppression furor had subsided. A copy is in the Newberry Library in Chicago.

38. *Chicago Post*, June 4, 1863, 1.

39. Frederick Francis Cook, *Bygone Days in Chicago* (Chicago, 1910), 52.

40. Ibid., 57; Lloyd Lewis and Henry Justin Smith, *Chicago. The History of Its Reputation* (New York, 1919), 103; *Indianapolis Weekly Sentinel*, June 8, 1863, 1.

41. Cook, *Bygone Days*, 56; Horace White, *The Life of Lyman Trumbull* (Boston and New York, 1913): 207. The resolution, referred to hereafter as "the businessmen's petition," is in O.R., ser. 1, vol. 23, pt. 2:385.

42. O.R., ser. 1, vol. 23, pt. 2:385.

June 2, telegraphed Lincoln saying, "We deem it of the highest importance that you revoke the order . . . suppressing the Chicago *Times*."⁴³ In Washington, Secretary of the Navy Gideon Welles, having learned of the order, lamented military officers' "without absolute necessity disregard[ing] those great principles on which our government and institutions rest." Welles said that he, the president, and probably every cabinet member regretted what had been done in the Vallandigham and *Times* matters, "but as to the measures which should now be taken there are probably differences."⁴⁴ It would appear from Welles's diary entry and the Davis-Herndon telegram that Lincoln, even before reading the telegram from Chicago, had already felt what to him would be rather weighty political pressure to negate Burnside's action against the *Times*.

Political pressures were also being directed against Trumbull and Arnold. Word of their part in the courthouse meeting of June 3 seems to have reached Chicago Republicans in rather short order. On the evening of the third, a group of party members supporting Burnside's order met in Warner's Hall to discuss strategy. Arnold seemingly attracted the most direct wrath. A committee of five was appointed to visit the congressman and persuade him to send a second telegram to the White House, this one seeking to blunt any effect the first might have had. Failing in this, the group was to ask for Arnold's resignation.

The committee arrived at Arnold's home late in the evening. Arnold told the members that his addition to the telegram to Lincoln had been given out of fear that violence would ensue if the suppression was not countermanded. But he said that he could send the president another message that should satisfy his visitors. That message was sent at about one o'clock on the morning of the fourth. In it, Arnold said he had not meant in the earlier message to "express an opinion that the order suppressing the Chicago *Times* should be abrogated."⁴⁵ The message was so short and undetailed as to be anything but forceful.

---

43. Davis and Herndon to Lincoln, June 2, 1863, *War Dept. Telegrams, Telegrams Addressed to the President*, roll 2, vol. 4, frame 72.

44. Gideon Welles, *Diary of Gideon Welles* (Boston and New York, 1911), 421.

45. The account is taken from a pamphlet, *General Burnside's Order, No. 84, Suppressing the Chicago Times, and Its History*, probably printed in 1864 by Arnold's opponent for the congressional nomination. The pamphlet may be suspect as evidence because of its obvious motivation, but the assertions it makes fit the verifiable facts and, inasmuch as Arnold never disputed the allegations publicly, are accepted here. It is known, for example, that Arnold sent Lincoln two telegrams at this time. The first was the one sent jointly with Trumbull at the end of the businessmen's petition. The second denied any intent to endorse the resolution or petition. Roy P. Basler, ed., *The Collected Works of Abraham Lincoln* (New Brunswick, N.J., 1953), 7:363–64.

It could hardly have been an accident or coincidence that Arnold and Trumbull felt constrained shortly thereafter to issue a joint public statement. In it they said that they had refused to sign the request for revocation of the Burnside order. They had, however, asked the president for serious and prompt consideration for the request—the normal method, they explained, of calling citizen grievances to presidential attention. Such action, they said, usually was taken without regard to the writer's opinion of the merits of the case.[46] Their statement appeared in the *Chicago Evening Journal* on June 4. Why the statement made no mention of Arnold's second wire to Lincoln—the one sent early that morning—is not known. It is barely possible, though highly unlikely, that Arnold had not told the senator of his visitors of the night before and that Trumbull consequently had not yet heard of Arnold's second telegram to the president. It appears that the president had not heard of it by the afternoon of the fourth; indeed, it seems likely he had barely heard of the businessmen's petition sent on the third. Upon receipt of the latter message, Lincoln would recall nearly a year later, he was "embarrassed with the question between what was due the military service on the one hand, and liberty of the press on the other." The seeming Arnold-Trumbull endorsement of the petition, he wrote, had persuaded him to revoke the suppression.[47]

Accordingly, on June 4, he wrote to Stanton: "I have received additional dispatches which with former ones [the Davis-Herndon message?] induce me to believe we should revoke or suspend the order suspending the Chicago *Times*, and if you concur in [this] opinion, please have it done."[48] Stanton ordered Assistant Adjutant General E. D. Townsend to send the message verbatim to Burnside, now at Hickman Bridge, Kentucky, directing troops toward General U. S. Grant near Vicksburg.[49] Burnside instructed his staff in Cincinnati to relay the president's order to Storey and the troop commanders in Chicago.[50] But at 6:00 P.M., half an hour before the order lifting the suppression arrived in Storey's office, the

46. The statement was all but buried on page 4 of the *Chicago Evening Journal* of June 4, 1863. White—Trumbull's biographer—makes no mention of it.
47. Basler, *Collected Works*, 364.
48. Lincoln to Stanton, June 4, 1863, O.R., ser. 3, 3:252.
49. Halleck to Burnside, June 3, 1863, Burnside Papers. For some reason, a second copy of this order, dated June 8, is also in the file. See also O.R., ser. 1, vol. 24, pt. 3:383.
50. Two copies of the order, General Orders, No. 91, are found in O.R., one from Assistant Adjutant General N. H. McLean (ser. 1, vol. 23, pt. 2:386), the other from Assistant Adjutant General W. P. Anderson (ser. 2, 5:741). The reason for the duplication is not known. It may have been that one copy was intended for circulation to the affected generals, the other for transmission to the War Department. Original drafts of the wires to the editor of the *Times*, the *New York World* and General Ammen are in the *Order Book*, 165.

slowness of telegraph service became apparent. Obviously having received Arnold's latest telegram in late afternoon, Lincoln was ready to change or modify his earlier instructions to Cincinnati. He instructed Stanton to send Burnside another telegram. The message was terse and scarcely bore any breath of urgency: "The President directs me to say that if you have not acted upon the telegram from Adjutant General Townsend of this date you need not do so but may let the matter stand as it is until you receive a letter by mail forwarded yesterday."[51]

The word "if" was an important modifier. The president did not say what Burnside was to do if he had already lifted the suppression. Certainly no presidential directive could be implied that Burnside reimpose the original suppression order: to rescind an order rescinding another would hardly reflect decisiveness on the administration's part. If Burnside were to wait to act until Stanton's letter arrived, the wait might be as long as twelve days, perhaps longer. (Burnside would note subsequently—on June 12—that a letter sent on the first had "only come to hand today."[52]) Such a delay would mean continued violation of Storey's First Amendment rights for a period determined by the efficiency of mail deliveries. It would allow Lincoln ample time to test more extensively the political waters swirling about the *Times* affair and then take whatever administrative or political action might seem prudent—even letting the suppression order stand. It also would give the president time to reopen the political options he ostensibly had closed with his first telegram to Burnside on June 4.

That his actions to this point had not generated much Republican enthusiasm in Chicago would soon be quite clear. No Chicagoan had heard of Lincoln's second telegram to Burnside on June 4. Most had heard of a mass meeting of Democrats where, on the evening of the third, as many as twenty thousand persons had heard speakers roundly condemn the suppression order and resolve that Illinoisans would, so long as they could, maintain their liberties peacefully, soberly, and loyally, but would have them "at every hazard by some means."[53] The president, many Chicago Republicans felt, had caved in to this pressure. His revocation of the suppression was "humiliating and disgraceful," the *Tribune*

---

51. Stanton to Burnside, June 4, 1863, *War Dept. Telegrams, Telegrams Sent by the Secretary of War*, roll 82, vol. 174, frame 72. It is not known if the letter to which Stanton referred was the same letter he had written Burnside on June 1. If it was, Stanton obviously and for some reason had held onto it for two days before sending it. Why he would have done so is not hinted at in the evidence, but no other Stanton letter bearing on the situation was found in the Burnside Papers for the period.

52. Burnside to Fry, *Order Book*, 201.

53. *Chicago Times*, June 5, 1863, 1.

fulminated on June 5, adding, "The anger of the Copperheads at the first [order] scarcely equalled the indignation of the Unionists at the last."[54] The politically potent Union Leagues of the city and county were among the most indignant, accusing Arnold, Trumbull, and Judge Higgins of taking "counsel of their fears" and of using their official positions to persuade the president to revoke the Burnside order. The result, according to Union League members, had been "a tendency to humiliate the loyal people of the country by an exhibition of weakness, vacillation and timidity."[55]

It would seem that neither the *Tribune* nor the Union Leagues had learned of the second Lincoln-to-Burnside message of June 4. Indeed, neither the president nor Burnside appears to have been anxious to disclose its existence. Stanton had dispatched the message both to Cincinnati and to Lexington, near Hickman Bridge, but it was two o'clock in the morning on June 5 before Burnside replied. The message had arrived too late, he said; he had already countermanded the suppression order. "I am very much embarrassed," he added, "and beg to ask for specific instructions in such cases."[56] He thought of sending more. The *Order Book* shows he had added and then crossed out, " . . . or be allowed to resign my commission. The latter will be most agreeable to me if it is for the interest of the public service, and I really believe that it is."[57] No record has been found of a presidential reply.

Arnold, despite his second telegram to Lincoln on the fourth, was apparently still feeling the wrath of the Republican organization, for he issued a public letter on June 9. In it, he repeated much of what he had told his visitors the night of

---

54. *Chicago Tribune*, June 5, 1863, 1. The more moderate *Evening Journal*, in a front page article on the sixth, noted, "The *Tribune* . . . is saying much that is foolish just now, and all for buncombe. It assails the President for having revoked Burnside's order . . . utterly regardless of the fact that the especial friends of the *Tribune*, with the understood sanction of its editors, telegraphed to the President, asking him to revoke that order." The *Tribune*, on the fifth, had called any claim of its involvement "a point blank fabrication."

55. The Union Leagues held a joint meeting at Warner's Hall on the sixth, two days after Lincoln had set aside the *Times* suppression. Copies of their resolutions were sent to Lincoln, Burnside, Trumbull, Arnold, and Judge Higgins. Burnside's copy, from which these passages are quoted, is in the collection of the general's Civil War papers in the Rhode Island State Historical Society Library. See also *General Burnside's Order, No. 84, Suppressing the Chicago Times, and Its History*, 6. The tone of the resolutions suggests strongly that those attending the meeting had not heard of Arnold's second telegram to Lincoln on the morning of the fourth, or of the president's response. It would seem, in fact, that the publishers of *General Burnside's Order, No. 84.* had not heard of Lincoln's reply.

56. Burnside to Stanton, June 5, 1863, *War Dept. Telegrams. Telegrams Received by the Secretary of War*, roll 109, vol. 228, frame 440.

57. *Order Book*, 166.

June 3 and had said in the joint public statement with Trumbull on the fourth. Furthermore, he declared, without a declaration of martial law, the suppression's constitutionality was suspect and the party might suffer as a consequence.[58] The elections were scheduled for a little more than a year hence, and it is not too much to suspect that Arnold knew that he could be among the chief sufferers. Indeed, in the following April, Arnold wrote the president saying that the principal charge his opponents in the current congressional campaign were using against him was that he was responsible for the order revoking suppression of the *Times*. Would Lincoln, he asked, write a note stating the extent of Arnold's responsibility in the matter?[59] Lincoln's reply, written on May 25, 1864, could hardly have stimulated Arnold's confidence. "I believe it was the dispatch of Senator Trumbull and yourself, added to the proceedings of the meeting which it brought me, that turned the scale in favor of my revoking the order," wrote the president in reference to the businessmen's telegram of the previous June 3. "I am very sure the small part you took in [the proceedings] is no just ground to disparage your judgment, much less to impugn your motives."[60] Roy Basler suggests that Arnold, dissatisfied with the Lincoln note, prevailed upon the president to write another, even going so far as to edit and revise the initial reply.[61] The new message, dated May 27, did not mention the influence which the Arnold and Trumbull names on the businessmen's petition had had on the decision to revoke the suppression order. This new letter mentioned only in barest detail both telegrams and attributed to neither of them any influence on the lifting of the suppression.[62]

All evidence clearly supports the conclusion that, in the *Times* case at least, Lincoln appeared ready to be guided by political considerations—the Davis-Herndon telegram, the cabinet reactions as related in the Welles diary, and the Arnold-Trumbull message affixed to the businessmen's petition of June 3. When Arnold found himself in a painful political position, Lincoln was ready to help a staunch political supporter and to do so at the expense of compromising any First Amendment principles he may have held. Indeed, at only one point in the entire *Times* episode—the May 25, 1864, note to Arnold—did the president so much as mention freedom of the press. Both in that message and the one two days later, the president expressed an uncertainty about the handling of the whole affair.

58. *Chicago Evening Journal*, June 9, 1863, 1.
59. Arnold to Lincoln, Apr. 24, 1864, Basler, *Collected Works*, 7:361.
60. Lincoln to Arnold, May 25, 1864, ibid.
61. Ibid., 364.
62. Lincoln to Arnold, May 27, 1864, ibid., 363-64.

He was, he said, "far from certain today that the revocation was not right."[63] This uncertainty, or ambivalence—taken with his tacit acceptance of press suppression early in the war, his implicit support of Burnside in the Vallandigham proceedings, and his willingness to delay lifting of the suppression order while Storey continued to chafe under loss of his press freedom—does not argue in favor of characterizing Lincoln as a friend of the press. The evidence presented here suggests he was much more ready to accommodate political cronies than opposition editors.

---

63. The Lincoln notes to Arnold did not help the congressman. So bitter were the denunciations against him that Arnold finally withdrew from the race. J. G. Randall, *Mr. Lincoln* (New York, 1957), 319. Interestingly enough, in neither of his books—*History of Abraham Lincoln* (Chicago, 1866) or *Life of Abraham Lincoln* (Chicago, 1885)—did Arnold mention the *Times* affair or his part in it.

"A Catholic Family Newspaper" Views the Lincoln Administration

John Mullaly's Copperhead Weekly

JOSEPH GEORGE JR.

When he died in 1915, John Mullaly was an almost forgotten man. Few were still alive to remember that he had played a prominent role in the intellectual life of New York's Irish during the era of the Civil War. New Yorkers had forgotten that he had become a Copperhead editor in the 1860s, denouncing the Lincoln Administration and even on occasion advocating in his newspaper, the *Metropolitan Record*, that the South should be granted its independence. But he was much better known to earlier generations.

John Mullaly was born in Belfast in 1835 or 1836. He migrated to the United States in the early 1850s, and, before he became editor of the *Metropolitan Record* in January 1859, when he was about 24 years old, he had already enjoyed an interesting career. He had served as a reporter for Horace Greeley's *New York Tribune*, William Cullen Bryant's *New York Evening Post*, and for six years on James Gordon Bennett's *New York Herald*. He acted as special correspondent for the *Herald* on the expeditions which laid the first cable across the Gulf of St. Lawrence. He was also special correspondent on the first three Atlantic cable expeditions of 1857 and 1858, at which time he also served as secretary to the inventor, Samuel F. B. Morse, and to Cyrus W. Field, manager of the company laying the cable.[1]

---

1. *Catholic News* (New York), Jan. 9, 1915; Thomas F. Meehan, "Early Catholic Weeklies," Historical Records and Studies of the United States Catholic Historical Society, XXVIII (1937).

Civil War History, Vol. XXIV No.2, © 1978 by The Kent State University Press

On January 29, 1859, Mullaly published the first issue of the *Metropolitan Record*, commonly referred to as the *Record*, and continued publication until 1873. He then became Commissioner of Health for the city of New York for one term and later a member of the Board of Assessors for two terms. He also played an important role in having the city acquire 4000 acres of land in the Bronx for the purposes of parks and parkways.²

Always interested in science, Mullaly invented, while editor of the *Record*, a process he called Aluminography, used in the printing of aluminum plates. Later he became president of the United States Aluminum Printing Plate Co. As an author Mullaly had works published on the Atlantic cable, New York City's impure milk, and the public parks program in the Bronx. Toward the end of his life, from 1892 to 1896, Mullaly served as editor of *Seminary*, a monthly printed for the new seminary building of the New York Catholic Archdiocese at Dunwoodie, in Yonkers. He died in his eightieth year on January 2, 1915, a forgotten "leader of Catholic thought and action during the nineteenth century," a man who "had outlived his generation."³

But there was nothing obscure about John Mullaly during the Civil War. After six years' service on the *New York Herald*, Mullaly was described by the managing editor of that newspaper as an accomplished reporter. This reputation

---

244–45. Mullaly's name was misspelled in the obituary appearing in the *New York Times*, Jan. 5, 1915. Mullaly's account of the laying of the Atlantic cable appeared in letters to the *Herald* in 1857 and 1858, and also in John Mullaly to Archbishop John J. Hughes, Mar. 30, 1858, John J. Hughes Papers, St. Joseph's Seminary, Yonkers, New York, 112.

2. *Catholic News*, Jan. 9, 1915; Meehan, "Early Catholic Weeklies," 245. As early as 1861 Mullaly had obtained the lucrative right to print public documents. He also served as municipal court attendant while still editor of the *Metropolitan Record*, a political plum obtained by his connections in the Tweed Ring. Like twenty-six other newspapers, the *Record* apparently folded in 1873 after reformers had destroyed Tweed's power and cut the advertising of the city government in these papers, a saving to New York City of $900,000 a year. See manuscript titled "Copy to Mr. Mullaly approving of his application for the printing of public documents, June 5, 1861," Hughes Papers; Mullaly to Hughes, Dec. 17, 1861; *New York Times*, June 27, 1875; *Report of the New York City Council of Political Reform, for the Years 1872, '73, and '74* (New York, 1875), 31, pamphlet in the New York Historical Society.

3. Meehan, "Early Catholic Weeklies," 245; *Catholic News*, Jan. 9, 1915; *New York Freeman's Journal and Catholic Register*, Jan. 9, 1915; *Historical Records and Studies of the United States Catholic Historical Society*, VIII (June 1915), 260; John Mullaly to Rev. J. N. Connolly, Sept. 16, 1895, St. Joseph Seminary Archives. Mullaly's books were *The Milk Trade Of New York And Vicinity, Giving An Account Of The Sale Of Pure And Adulterated Milk* (New York, 1853); *A Trip To Newfoundland; Its Scenery And Fisheries; With An Account Of The Laying Of The Submarine Telegraph Cable* (New York, 1855); *The Laying Of The Cable, Or The Ocean Telegraph . . .* (New York, 1858); and *The New Parks Beyond The Harlem* (New York, 1887).

and the young newspaperman's acquaintance with Archbishop John J. Hughes of New York made possible the launching of Mullaly's newspaper venture, the *Metropolitan Record*.⁴

As early as 1858 Mullaly had determined to publish his own newspaper for New York's Irish Catholics. Archbishop Hughes endorsed his efforts and agreed to advance some money for the enterprise. Mullaly envisioned his *Record* as a weekly journal confining itself to news about and of interest to the city's Catholics. He planned to "give the Catholics a better paper than they ever had in this country," and hoped to begin publication before the Christmas holidays of 1858. However, Mullaly did not have enough money. He estimated that he needed a sum of $5000 to begin publication of the *Record*, but as of December 6, 1858, he had about half that amount. Archbishop Hughes, assuring Mullaly of his continued support, nevertheless discouraged his young friend from beginning publication in time for Christmas. Noting the lack of sufficient capital, Hughes recommended that Mullaly remain as a reporter on the *Herald*. "The best season of the year to commence 'The New York Metropolitan Record,'" the Archbishop advised, "will be when you shall have capital to carry it on for at least one year...."⁵

Although he missed the Christmas season, Mullaly apparently did have enough money shortly afterward because he issued the first number of the *Metropolitan Record* on January 29, 1859. The proprietor assured his readers that the new journal would be a Catholic family newspaper and published a letter from Archbishop Hughes promising his support. Although the newspaper contained some articles written by Hughes during this first year of publication, and although it received some financial assistance from the New York archbishop, it was not until the end of 1859 that Mullaly's journal became the official newspaper of the New York Archdiocese.⁶

In making its appearance in New York the *Record* was joining the *New York Tablet* and the *Freeman's Journal*, two other Catholic weeklies in that city. To win its share of readers, the *Record* announced in its initial number that its first

---

4. Frederic Hudson, *Journalism In The United States, From 1690 to 1872* (New York, 1873), 299; Mullaly to Hughes, Mar. 30, 1858, Hughes Papers, 113.
5. Mullaly to Hughes, Dec. 6, 1858, Hughes to Mullaly, Dec. 6, 1958, Hughes Papers.
6. *Metropolitan Record*, Jan. 29, 1859, 8. Mullaly to Hughes, July 12, 1860; Hughes to Mullaly, July 12, 1860, Hughes Papers; Hudson, *Journalism In The U.S.*, 299; Apollinaris W. Baumgartner, *Catholic Journalism: A Study Of Its Development In The United States, 1789-1930* (New York, 1931), 19; John R. G. Hassard, *Life Of The Most Reverend John Hughes, D.D., First Archbishop Of New York, With Extracts From His Private Correspondence* (New York, 1866), 495.

object was to be a "good Catholic family paper," one that would supply readers "with all the important church news of the world and of the Metropolitan See of New York." It invited parish priests throughout the country to send it information regarding confirmations, church dedications, and other like items for its columns. These items, along with sermons and reviews of religious books, became a staple of the *Record*. Circulation apparently was more than adequate by nineteenth-century standards although competition was fierce because of the large number of newspapers in existence. In 1867, for example, there were two hundred and sixty-nine newspapers, periodicals, and magazines published in New York City alone. Under these circumstances Mullaly was not unreasonable when he estimated that he needed a circulation of "four or five thousand" to meet expenses and earn "a handsome surplus." He obviously obtained an adequate circulation despite the formidable competition. In 1864, the *Times* described the *Record* as a newspaper with "a large circulation among our Roman Catholic citizens." Certainly, Archbishop Hughes had much to do with this success, especially when he made the *Record* his official newspaper. In the December 31, 1859, issue of the newspaper appeared the statement of the Archbishop designating the *Record* as "official organ" of the New York Roman Catholic Archdiocese. "We do this," Hughes noted prophetically, "on condition . . . that this paper shall not at any time identify itself with any political party in the United States."[7]

Mullaly honored the Archbishop's restriction during 1860. As it had in its first year of publication, the *Record* limited its political views to support of the Pope against Italian nationalists and denunciation of British policy dealing with Ireland; but it eschewed all domestic political affairs. However, by the end of 1860 the political crisis in the United States could not be ignored. The Democratic party had already split into two factions and in November the Republicans had captured the White House for the first time. By December there was serious talk of secession. The destruction of the Union was a real possibility. The *Record* had avoided discussion of the political conventions of 1860 and the presidential campaign of that autumn, but now it spoke out in the hope of helping "preserve the integrity of the United States." Mentioning Lincoln's name for the first time, the *Record* printed a letter of a Southerner who predicted that South Carolina would secede as a result of Lincoln's election. Beginning with the secession crisis of 1860–61 and until the issuance of the Emancipation Proclamation in September

---

7. *Metropolitan Record*, Jan. 29, 1859, 8; Dec. 31, 1859, 1; Public Ledger (Philadelphia), Mar. 23, 1867; Mullaly to Hughes, Dec. 6, 1858; Mullaly to Hughes, Dec. 17, 1861, Hughes Papers; *New York Times*, Mar. 17, 1864.

1862, the editorial position of the *Record* was moderate and consistent with the views of Archbishop Hughes; that is, it distrusted abolitionists but denounced secession and supported President Lincoln and the Union.[8]

For example, when the venerable Catholic journal, *United States Catholic Miscellany*, of Charleston, South Carolina, came out in support of that state's decision to secede, the *Record* regretted what it considered a "premature" and "precipitous" action. Although in the *Record*'s view the people of the South had much to complain of, secession appeared to be a "doubtful contingency."[9]

When the firing on Fort Sumter brought about civil war, the *Record* announced its support of the Lincoln government and the Constitution.

> Our loyalty, our fealty, our allegiance is due to the Government of the United States, and in this country we recognize none other. The Constitution under which the nation has marched in a most unexampled career of prosperity is good enough for us, and will remain so until in accordance with its own provisions, such changes may be effected in it as the required majority of the people may deem necessary. We have always loved the flag of the Union, we have seen it wave over stormy and tranquil seas; it has ever been to us the emblem of popular freedom and self-government; we have glorified in its triumphs, and we trust . . . it will once more be the flag of a united and prosperous people.[10]

Mullaly also reminded Southerners that Lincoln was constitutionally elected President, in part because Southerners had failed to support Douglas. Even after Lincoln's election, had the South remained in the Union, it would have had the power in Congress to restrain a Republican President. Southerners foolishly had determined before the election that they would secede in event of a Lincoln victory.[11]

During the first year and a half of the war, the *Record* considered secession as unfortunate. Lincoln's policy was that of a moderate, not an abolitionist, and this policy was acceptable to both Mullaly and his patron, Archbishop Hughes. The prelate, although suspicious of abolitionists, loyally supported the government, going abroad in late 1861 as an unofficial diplomat who worked hard in Paris, especially, to keep Europeans out of the American war. The editor, also distrustful

---

8. *Metropolitan Record*, Dec. 8, 1860, 9.
9. Ibid., Jan. 5, 1861, 12.
10. Ibid., April 27, 1861, 269.
11. Ibid., May 18, 1861, 316-17.

of abolitionists, was satisfied, before the autumn of 1862, that Lincoln was not waging an unconstitutional war against Southern property, Negro slaves. The *Record* was pleased to observe in December of 1861 that the President's annual message to Congress was conservative in nature. The part of that report prepared by Simon Cameron, Secretary of War, and leaked to the press was changed. In that section Cameron had advocated the arming of slaves as soldiers and using them against "rebellious traitors." The President had the offending passages deleted. Mullaly approved. The thought of arming the slaves frightened him. He wrote that "pride of race forbids it, and humanity turns from it." "We want no second edition of St. Domingo here," he warned. "We must take care that this war for the Union does not degenerate into a war for emancipation, in other words a war of extermination."[12]

When General David Hunter issued a proclamation freeing slaves in his military district—South Carolina, Georgia, and Florida—Lincoln publically revoked the order, reserving emancipation policy to himself. Again Mullaly supported the President. "That is the right way," he said, "to treat the usurpation by generals of power that does not belong to them." Lincoln demonstrated in this action that he was a "national man." If he continued this anti-abolition policy, the *Record* predicted that the President would be "sustained by the vast majority of the people. . . ."[13]

In the Fourth of July 1862, edition of the *Record* Mullaly applauded Lincoln's moderate policies and hoped that these past actions could be considered "proof of the conservatism" of Lincoln's "future course." Although the President had retained radical generals, Hunter and Fremont, and had not fired E. M. Stanton, now Secretary of War, who interfered with the "plans of that true patriot, that great conservative Union leader, General McClellan," Mullaly still believed in the "sincerity and patriotism of the President." But there was a hint that the *Record* would perhaps not be able to support Lincoln in the future.

But let us tell him and his advisers that if the war is to be perverted from its original purpose, if this war is to be waged in the interest . . . of abolitionists,

---

12. *Brownson's Quarterly Review*, 3d Ser., III (Jan. 1862), 34–36; Rena Mazyck Andrews, *Archbishop Hughes And The Civil War* (Chicago, 1935), 4–14; James G. Randall, *Lincoln The President* (New York, 1945–1955), II, 26–27, 55–61. Lincoln's annual message for 1861 appears in Roy P. Basler (ed.), *The Collected Works Of Abraham Lincoln* (New Brunswick, 1953), V, 35–53, hereafter cited as Lincoln, *Works*; *Metropolitan Record*, Dec. 14, 1861, 796.

13. Ibid., May 24, 1862, 328. Hunter's proclamation and Lincoln's revocation appear in Lincoln, *Works*, V, 222–24.

he will find himself sadly mistaken; he will find that white men are not willing to become the tools of sectional agitators. . . . [14]

Mullaly's uneasiness with Lincoln's policies was noticed by his Republican contemporaries. Both he and his patron, Archbishop Hughes, opposed abolitionists and showed little antipathy toward the institution of slavery. These feelings brought denunciation from Republican writers, Catholic as well as secular. Orestes A. Brownson, who had become a Catholic in 1844 and an anti-slavery advocate by 1861, described the *Record* in the October 1861 issue *of Brownson's Quarterly Review* as a journal "striving hard to be on both sides" of the secession issue. A few months later, however, Brownson was much less friendly. He apologized to his readers for calling this "weekly sheet" to their attention. He did so because it was the "Official Organ" of the Most Reverend Archbishop of New York. Brownson then complained that Hughes was the author of the article, "The Abolition Views of Brownson Overthrown," which appeared in the *Record* of October 12, 1861, and which defended the institution of slavery.[15]

Horace Greeley's *New York Tribune* was also becoming dissatisfied with the editorial slant of the *Record*. In April 1862, the *Tribune* reminded its readers, under a heading of "Secessionism in New-York," that the *Record* advertized itself as "Official Organ of the Most Rev. Archbishop of New-York" and thereby acquired "an importance which it would not otherwise command." The *Tribune* also recalled that the *Record* had agreed not to participate in "political controversy." Because of its "official" pretensions and non-partisan premises, Catholics "of all parties and of none" were induced to subscribe to this newspaper. For their money, subscribers received, in the opinion of the *Tribune*, "a journal which is violently anti-Republican and practically semi-Secession." Rebel sympathizers were advised to "produce a few thousand copies of this treacherous *Record* and distribute them among the low grogshops of our city."[16]

---

14. *Metropolitan Record*, July 5, 1862, 424.

15. *Brownson's Quarterly Review*, 3d Ser., II (Oct., 1861), 510-526; and II (Jan. 1862), 34-36. Brownson's first article was published as a pamphlet and appears in Frank Freidel (ed.), *Union Pamphlets Of The Civil War: 1861-1865*, (Cambridge, 1967), 128-65. Hughes' article was reprinted in the *New York Herald*, Oct. 8, 1861. Privately, Mullaly stated that he found Brownson's article "vicious" and "bad spirited." He also speculated that Brownson was "in the pay of the Abolitionists," and was "endeavoring to use his supposed influence with . . . Catholics to further the designs" of the Republican party. Mullaly to Hughes, Jan. 13, 1862, Hughes Papers. Publicly, Mullaly described *Brownson's Quarterly Review* as a "*soidisant* Catholic periodical" and accused Brownson of "Abolitionism, streaked with Know-Nothingism." *Metropolitan Record*, Jan. 18, 1862, 40.

16. *New York Tribune*, Apr. 3, 1862.

Mullaly responded in an article titled, "Onslaught of the New York *Tribune* on the Conservatism of the *Record.*" He called the *Tribune* article "malicious" and "unprovoked," defended the "conservatism" of the *Record* and reminded readers that Greeley and the *Tribune* had favored secession during 1861. Privately, Mullaly informed Archbishop Hughes that he believed he was standing on "firm ground" and that he did not expect Greeley to continue the controversy.[17]

But both Brownson and Greeley were correct. The "Official Organ" of the New York Archbishop was becoming less and less non-political and more and more anti-Republican. In February of 1862, Mullaly had written: "I wish the President would issue one good conservative proclamation to the Southern people. It would be worth a dozen victories." In April, Mullaly sensed a "strong conservative feeling springing up among the people in regard to ... abolitionism." By June he was denouncing bills introduced in Congress enabling confiscation of Confederate property—slaves. On this occasion he wrote:

> That confiscation of so-called rebel property is unconstitutional there cannot be the slightest doubt; and we insist upon it, that according to this principle, the emancipation even of the slaves of rebel masters is also a violation of [the Constitution] ... [The Abolitionists'] grand project of social amalgamation and equality between blacks and whites is, to use a popular and expressive phrase, about "played out." Hereafter the policy of the North should be the policy of conciliation and compromise.[18]

By the summer of 1862 Mullaly's *Record* had come to resemble an anti-administration journal. Lincoln's Emancipation Proclamation in September would cause the *Record* to surrender its claims to non-partisanship, lose its status as Archbishop Hughes' "Official Organ," and become one of the leading, or notorious, Democratic newspapers of the North.

Mullaly's attitudes were shared by most of the Catholic press in the United States, and, according to *Brownson's Review* and the *New York Tablet*—journals published by Catholics—by the majority of Northern Catholics. Brownson, who tended to equate the Democratic opposition with disloyalty, found in 1861 only two of the twelve journals "professedly devoted to Catholic interests" as "decidedly loyal." In 1863 he complained that only three Catholic journals were

---

17. *Metropolitan Record*, Apr. 12, 1862, 232; Mullaly to Hughes, Apr. 10, 1862, Hughes Papers.

18. *Metropolitan Record*, June 28, 1860, 409; Mullaly to Hughes Feb. 12, 1862; Mullaly to Hughes, Apr. 10, 1862, both in Hughes Papers. Randall, *Lincoln the President*, II, 225-29, contains a good description of the Confiscation Act.

occasionally anti-slavery and occasionally loyal. And they were at best "only exceptions," and "by no means fair exponents of the sentiments and opinions of the Catholic body in the United States." Brownson titled this 1863 article, "Are Catholics Pro-Slavery and Disloyal?" and answered the question in the affirmative. Pointing out that many Catholics were fighting bravely for the Union army, the *New York Tablet* deplored the publication of Brownson's article, but nevertheless conceded that the "majority" of American Catholics were "pro-slavery." At the very least the editor of the *Record* belonged to this majority.[19]

Although moving in the direction of opposition to the Administration, Mullaly was lulled, in the summer of 1862, by Lincoln's response to Horace Greeley's letter known as "Prayer of Twenty Million." The *Tribune* editor wanted Lincoln to move more quickly in destroying the peculiar institution. Lincoln's published reply, in which he stressed that his paramount object was to save the Union and not to save or destroy slavery, was printed in the *Metropolitan Record*. Mullaly praised Lincoln for "the sincerity of his intentions and the honesty of his convictions." It was about the last time the President would receive unqualified praise from his pen.[20]

When faced with the preliminary Emancipation Proclamation in September 1862, the *Record* was unhappy with the President's action but still hopeful that a basically conservative President did not have his heart in emancipation schemes and did not expect them to succeed. On September 24, 1862, the President issued another proclamation suspending the writ of habeas corpus in certain cases. Persons resisting the draft or discouraging enlistments would be subject to martial law and trial by court martial without the right of appeal to civilian courts. These two proclamations signalled a new direction, a route that would lead, according to the *Record*, to an "emancipation Crusade" and ultimately a war between the races. Mullaly hoped that Lincoln would not go through with his announced policy. Citing Lincoln's "conservative course" on slavery before the Emancipation Proclamation, Mullaly was able to delude himself. He guessed that the proclamation was forced on a reluctant President by Northern extremists, that Lincoln was convinced the Union would never be restored by such action and that the proclamation would prove the impracticality of such a course.[21]

19. *Brownson's Quarterly Review*, 3d Ser., II (Oct., 1861), 522-23; IV (July 1863), 371-73; *New York Tablet*, July 18, 1863, 8.
20. *Metropolitan Record*, Aug. 30, 1862, 552. Greeley's "Prayer of Twenty Million," dated Aug. 19, appears in the *New York Tribune*, Aug. 20, 1862. The president's reply is in Lincoln, *Collected Works*, V, 388-89.
21. *Metropolitan Record*, Oct. 4, 1862, 631, 632-33.

When New Year's Day, 1863, came and with it Lincoln's final proclamation freeing slaves in those territories still under control of the Confederacy, Mullaly still would not face reality. He hoped that "the threat contained in the document will never be executed," and that the war would be continued "for the restoration of the Union," and that "when the Southern States again become integral parts of the one great nation, they will possess all their rights intact." A week later, however, Mullaly was no longer ambivalent about the President or his emancipation policy. He denounced Lincoln and predicted a war of the races in the United States similar to, if not worse than, the earlier carnage in San Domingo. Lincoln's Emancipation Proclamation was a "disgraceful admission to the world" that twenty-two million Northerners with their "unlimited resources" could not put down the rebellion. Since the firing on Fort Sumter, Mullaly now claimed, the conflict was carried on not so much for reunion as for "abolition of slavery." Proof of this policy could now be found in Lincoln's "favoritism toward certain pet abolition generals" and his unjustifiable removal of General McClellan, "a great conservative military leader." Finally, demonstrating his racial prejudices, Mullaly concluded that it was a "sad commentary" on the conduct of the war that the North was unable to suppress the rebellion *"without the assistance of the negroes."*[22]

As he became more critical of the administration, Mullaly tended to ignore his agreement with Archbishop Hughes that the official newspaper of the New York Archdiocese would not identify itself with any political party. As late as April 1862, he wrote of his agreement to avoid partisan politics, but his opposition to Lincoln's policies had now become too strong. A break with Archbishop Hughes, who remained loyal to the Lincoln government, became inevitable as Mullaly increased the bitterness of his invective against the President. For example, in denouncing efforts in Congress to permit Negroes to fight for the Union, Mullaly suggested that Wendell Phillips or President Lincoln should take the field as their commander. He reprinted the cruel and erroneous report in the *New York World* that Lincoln had asked for a joyful tune while visiting the battlefield at Antietam, still strewn with the dying, and unburied dead. In an article titled, "Irish Soldiers and the Union Army," Mullaly wanted all enlistees to have a "thorough understanding that they were to be employed in an abolition crusade." Such partisanship would lead to a disagreement with the Archbishop. The final break involved the views of the editor and his patron on the draft.[23]

22. Ibid., Jan. 3, 1863, 839; ibid., Jan. 10, 1863, 24–25.
23. Ibid., Jan. 24, 1863, 56; Feb. 7, 1863, 83; Feb. 14, 1863, 104–5; Mullaly to Hughes, Apr. 10, 1862, Hughes Papers. For the Antietam incident see Kenneth A. Bernard, *Lincoln and the Music of the Civil War* (Caldwell, Idaho, 1966), 243–76.

In 1861 Hughes' views on slavery and especially abolitionists, were, as Brownson later noted, conservative, and most likely similar to those of Mullaly. But during the war Hughes tended to move toward the support of the Administration while his editor drifted toward opposition. After defending the Union cause in Catholic Europe, especially in Paris and Rome, Hughes returned to the United States in August 1862, and he delivered a famous sermon, supporting the government in general and its policy of conscription specifically.

If I had a voice in the councils of the country, [he announced], I would say, let volunteering continue; if the three hundred thousand on your list be not enough this week, next week make a draft of three hundred thousand more. It is not cruel, this. This is mercy; this is humanity. Anything that will put an end to this drenching with blood the whole surface of the country, that will be humanity. . . . It is not necessary to be true, to be patriotic, to do for the country what the country needs, and the blessing of God will recompense those who discharge their duty without faltering, and without violating any of the laws of God or man.[24]

This widely reprinted sermon gained Hughes the hostility of many Roman Catholics, even, apparently, among fellow bishops. "No act of the Venerable Archbishop's life ever cost him so much popularity with his own people," noted Brownson. Hughes later repeated his support of the draft in a letter to Seward, dated November 1, 1862, and published in the *Record*. Although the letter said nothing about the government's new emancipation policy, it stated bluntly that Hughes considered "conscription, sometimes called drafting, . . . the only fair, open, honest mode by which a nation can support its rights, and in case of danger, its own independence." The Archbishop's position was unequivocal. His editor, however, could not subordinate his own views for the sake of loyalty to the Administration. A break was inevitable.[25]

In the March 14 issue of the "Official Organ of the Most Rev. Archbishop of New York" appeared an article with the self-explanatory title: "The United States Converted Into a Military Despotism—the Conscription Act the Last Deadly Blow Aimed at Popular Liberty." This bitter denunciation was in the last issue of the *Metropolitan Record* that advertised itself as Hughes' "Official Organ." Hereafter, the *Record* only identified itself as "A Catholic Family Paper." Its special connection

---

24. Hassard, *Hughes*, 487.
25. *Brownson's Quarterly Review*, 3d Ser., IV (July, 1863), 370; Hassard, *Hughes*, 487; *Metropolitan Record*, Nov. 15, 1862, 728.

with Archbishop Hughes was ended. He had accepted "unquestioned loyalty to the party in control of the government," but his editor would not follow him.[26]

An unsigned letter to the *Tribune* at that time might have mirrored the Archbishop's feelings. That the *Record* would no longer be identified as the "Official Organ" of the Archbishop

> will be a great relief to his Grace . . . as well as to thousands of loyal Catholics . . . who were scandalized by the open and avowedly treasonable course of the *Record* ever since the war broke out; but most especially since the President issued his Emancipation Proclamation. The Archbishop supposed . . . that the anti-Catholic press would hereafter . . . quote these treasonable effusions of this "Secesh" editor . . . as emanating from Bishop Hughes, or that . . . they were published with his . . . approval. This has not been the case. The Archbishop has been disgusted with the course of the *Record* for some time past, but he has been too unwell of late to put his quietus on it.[27]

No longer associated with the Archbishop, the *Record* now became more bitterly anti-Lincoln as it joined the ranks of the Democratic opposition. Lincoln was now identified as the "jocular and anecdotal Chief Magistrate," the author of the Emancipation Proclamation that "could have its conception only in the brains of the perverted imagination of an Abolition fanatic."[28]

When Lincoln set aside April 30, 1863, as "a day of national humiliation, fasting, and prayer," Mullaly objected.

> With what special religious prerogative is the President invested that he should prescribe for any citizens of the Republic? Whatever fasting he thinks necessary let him do himself; and as for praying, the contractors and the other creatures of his administration have been *preying* with a vengeance upon the country for the past two years.[29]

---

26. Ibid., Mar. 14, 1863, 169; John Talbot Smith, *The Catholic Church In New York: A History of the New York Diocese from Its Establishment in 1808 to the Present Time* (New York, 1905), I, 273–74.

27. *New York Tribune*, Mar. 18, 1863. See also Albon P. Man Jr., "The Church And The New York Draft Riots Of 1863," *Records of the American Catholic Historical Society of Philadelphia*, LXII (Mar. 1951), 42.

28. *Metropolitan Record*, Mar. 28, 1863, 200–201.

29. Ibid., May 9, 1863, 296. Lincoln's Proclamation appears in Lincoln, *Works*, VI, 155–56.

Later that year Lincoln issued another proclamation, this time setting aside the last Thursday of November as a day of Thanksgiving. Again Mullaly did not approve. In recommending to his fellow citizens this special day of Thanksgiving, Lincoln asked of Americans

> that while offering up the ascriptions justly due to Him for such singular deliverances and blessings, they do also, with humble penitence for our national perverseness and disobedience, commend to His tender care all those who have become widows, orphans, mourners or sufferers in the lamentable civil strife in which we are unavoidably engaged, and fervently implore the interposition of the Almighty Hand to heal the wounds of the nation. . . . [30]

Mullaly found these Thanksgiving sentiments based on "pretentious zeal," and suggested spitefully that they "may have been inspired by some of those spiritual meetings which we are told, are of such frequent occurrence now-a-days at the White House." He did not comment on the Gettysburg Address until almost a year after its delivery, and then only to refer to "the heartless hilarity" by which Lincoln "disgusted the whole country on the field of Gettysburg." Surprisingly, the *Record* was one of the few contemporary newspapers to publish Lincoln's' letter to Mrs. Bixby, consoling her for the loss of five sons killed in action. In a dispatch from Boston dated November 25, 1864 (the same day the letter was printed in the *Boston Transcript*), Lydia Bixby was identified as a poor widow living in the eleventh ward and as the recipient of Lincoln's famous letter, which the *Record* reprinted. Textually, the *Record*'s version was similar to the one that appeared in the Transcript. No editorial comment accompanied the letter. Perhaps Mullaly reprinted it to stress the heavy loss of life occasioned by the war.[31]

The only way to end the war, to stop the killing, was to deprive Lincoln of a second term and to assure that a conservative Democrat would enter the White House in 1865. The *Record* would now play its role in achieving this end, and in doing so joined the ranks of the Copperhead press. Richard O. Curry has warned, and rightly so, that historians have too readily and unfairly pinned the label Copperhead on conservative Democrats who remained loyal to the Union even though they opposed the Administration. But Mullaly was a "peace at any

---

30. Ibid., VI, 496-97.
31. *Metropolitan Record*, Oct. 17, 1863, 665; ibid., July 2, 1864, 425; ibid., Dec. 3, 1864, 773. Lincoln's letter was dated Nov. 21, 1864. Still the best account of the Bixby letter is F. Lauriston Bullard, *Abraham Lincoln And The Widow Bixby* (New Brunswick, 1946).

price" Democrat who by 1863 was willing to have the North lose the war. In an article titled "Some Plain Talk," he wrote:

> Which do we prefer—to let the South go, or to lose our own liberties in an attempt to force it unwillingly into a union with us; and when to keep it in such a union we would require an army of occupation in every Southern State, numbering at least a million men. *For our part we must say that we prefer liberty to Union on such terms, and if that be treason make the most of it.*³²

The *Record* also predicted flatly that the Confederacy would win the war. "The Patriot's last hope," the dream of reconstruction "of the Union as it existed before Lincoln's Emancipation Proclamation," lay in depriving the President of reelection. Beginning in June 1864, the newspaper changed its name to become the *Metropolitan Record and New York Vindicator*. No longer did the masthead carry the subtitle, "A Catholic Family Paper." The *Record* was now a secular sheet espousing the "principles of Jeffersonian Democracy." Although now identified as a "Democratic and family weekly," the *Record*, as it was still popularly called, remained a journal catering to Irish Catholic readers.³³

Under its new title the *Record* continued to assault Lincoln. Mullaly argued that the President and his followers were waging war against American institutions, defended by Southerners. Had the Confederates lost, he argued, "their defeat would have been ours." Northerners were in debt to the South for the preservation of liberty. "The common enemy of the North and South," the foe of liberty, was to be found in Washington. "The arch conspirator against popular freedom" made "his lair in the White House." In his haste to drive this arch conspirator from his lair, Mullaly came dangerously close to ending up in a military prison.³⁴

---

32. *Metropolitan Record*, Apr. 18, 1863, 248 (italics supplied); Richard O. Curry, "The Union As It Was: A Critique Of Recent Interpretations Of The 'Copperheads,'" *Civil War History*, XIII (Mar. 1967), 25-39. Curry is not clear in distinguishing Copperheads from Peace Democrats. Mark E. Neely Jr., has offered some perceptive comments on Curry's essay in *Lincoln Lore*, No. 1632 (Feb. 1974), and No. 1633 (Mar. 1974). I have concluded that Mullaly was a Copperhead, an extreme Peace Democrat willing to lose the war and have the Union divided rather than see emancipation a reality. The *New York Times* once observed that the *Metropolitan Record* said in plain English "what was said in a more cautious and euphemistic way" by what the *Times* described as "other Copperhead papers." *New York Times*, Mar. 17, 1864.

33. *Metropolitan Record*, June 6, 1863, 360; Feb. 27, 1864, 136-37; *Metropolitan Record and New York Vindicator*, June 4, 1864, 360; ibid., Oct. 14, 1865, 13.

34. Ibid., June 18, 1864, 392.

In the summer of 1864, Mullaly denounced Lincoln's efforts to raise five hundred thousand additional troops for the Union armies. The draft had never been popular in New York City and a serious draft riot had broken out there in 1863. Taking advantage of this discontent and perhaps with an eye to the coming presidential election in November, Governor Horatio Seymour of New York had published in the form of a broadside a letter to the Secretary of War, objecting to the quotas established for New York City and Brooklyn, which the governor considered "excessive and injurious."[35]

Emboldened by Seymour's opposition, Mullaly published an article, 'The Coming Draft," that made him liable for "encouraging, counseling, and inciting resistance to the draft," action prohibited by an act of Congress signed into law in February 1864. Mullaly also warned in his article that New York would "never endorse" another draft that was aimed at putting Democratic voters in the army where "by the gentle manipulation of military satraps" they were changed into "Lincoln voters." The draft was a scheme of the Executive for depriving the people of a free election.[36]

The day of reckoning was August 19, 1864. Mullaly was arrested and brought before a Federal Commissioner, accused of willfully counseling "one Seymour and other persons to resist" the draft established by law. Examination of the charges was postponed until August 23, and Mullaly was freed on $2500 bail. By the time of Mullaly's hearing, the Democrats were meeting in Chicago to select a presidential candidate. Prosecution of a New York newspaper editor at this late date would only provide Democrats with another hero. Both the *New York Times* and the *New York Tribune* gave very little publicity to the Mullaly case, and the court ruled in the preliminary hearing to have the case dropped. The court decided that although Mullaly used language urging Governor Seymour "to resist the draft," the draft would not go into effect until September 5, 1864. In the eyes of the court what happened before that date were "mere preliminaries." The defendant was released.[37]

---

35. Horatio Seymour to Edwin M. Stanton, Aug. 3, 1864 (broadside), Robert Todd Lincoln Collection of the Papers of Abraham Lincoln, Library of Congress. See also Randall, *Lincoln the President*, III, 168–72.

36. *Metropolitan Record and New York Vindicator*, Aug. 6, 1864, 505–6; James G. Randall, "The Newspaper Problem In Its Bearing Upon Military Secrecy During The Civil War," *American Historical Review*, XXIII (Jan. 1918), 319n.

37. *New York Times*, Aug. 20, 1864; *Frank Leslie's Illustrated Newspaper*, XVIII (Sept. 3, 1864), 371; *Metropolitan Record and New York Vindicator*, Aug. 27, 1864, 553; *New York Tribune*, Aug. 27, 1864; *New York World*, Aug. 29, 1864.

Republican papers did not comment on Mullaly's release, but the *Record* denounced the judge's ruling. At the same time, however, the paper toned down its opposition to the draft. But other newsworthy activities now commanded Mullaly's attention. Lincoln was running for reelection, and the Democrats were about to nominate a candidate to run against him and a platform to run on.[38]

The Republicans had met in Baltimore in a convention of "Shoddyites and Loyal Leaguers," and chose a ticket of Abraham Lincoln, "autocrat of the White House," and Andrew Johnson, "his trusty henchman." The racial makeup of the Baltimore gathering had disgusted the *Record*.

> Truly we are approaching the millenium . . . when not only the lion and lamb, but the Caucasian and the African shall lie down together. . . . Ten negroes were among the delegates . . . Who could have thought that these sable sons of African descent, would have been called upon to represent South Carolina . . . But so it is.[39]

It was necessary to defeat this Baltimore ticket. Although Lincoln was showing signs of appreciating the horrors of war, he was no man of peace in Mullaly's eyes. At the Philadelphia Sanitary Fair, held in June 1864, the President had said that "war, at the best, is terrible, and this war of ours, in its magnitude and in its duration, is one of the most terrible." The words sounded good but they did not sway Mullaly. "Mr. Lincoln," he wrote, "enumerates the evils of war like a peace man, and yet no peaceman is he." Instead, he needed the war. "He is buoyant," Mullaly continued, "only in a sea of blood, and if he is borne again into the White House it must be cork like, on the tide of battle." It was important that Democrats stop his reelection bid.[40]

At the end of August the Democrats in Chicago named General George B. McClellan as their candidate to defeat Lincoln and adopted a platform urging immediate peace. Although the *Record* "frankly" announced that the General was not its choice, "there were several whom we preferred," the paper conceded that it could support McClellan upon "acceptance of the nomination and platform." McClellan accepted the nomination but not all of the platform. The General insisted that there must be union before there could be peace. He would support

---

38. *Metropolitan Record and New York Vindicator*, Sept. 3, 1864, 569–71.
39. Ibid., June 18, 1864, 395.
40. Lincoln, *Works*, VII, 394; *Metropolitan Record and New York Vindicator*, July 2, 1864.

the war. Mullaly was now bitter. He had had reservations about McClellan, he said, on account of the General's "many violations of the Constitution, while Commander of the Army of the Potomac," but had hoped that McClellan had seen the "futility of military force," and was now "prepared to accept the policy of Peace." But McClellan had not been converted. Mullaly would "stand upon the platform" and await a second convention.[41]

No second convention was forthcoming. Despite the pressure of "friends" to get the *Record* to endorse McClellan, Mullaly announced that he had "no heart in this campaign," no "faith in private assurances when they are in conflict with public professions and acts." Mullaly still supported the South.

> We believe that the South is entitled to the selection of her own form of government, and that the North, in the endeavor to force her into a compulsory Union is violating the principle of universal suffrage, which we claim to be the foundation of our democratic system. By this right we shall continue to stand, for it is a right older and more valuable than even the Union itself.... [42]

Yet, no matter how distasteful its candidate, the Democratic party was the only opposition Lincoln had. And Lincoln, the man who had disgraced the country "by his boorishness," who had displayed "callous indifference" to the sufferings of its people, and who was "as wicked as he was weak," had to be defeated. In an article titled, "Reasons Why Peace Men Should Vote for McClellan," Mullaly announced that he would no longer ignore the "appeals of numerous friends *from the Border States*" begging him to work for Lincoln's defeat and McClellan's victory. Mullaly now reasoned that a victorious McClellan would also mean a Democratic Congress and many Democratic governors. These would have an enormous influence on a President McClellan who would then be more responsible and less tyrannical than his predecessor in the White House.[43]

However, the efforts of a united Democratic party could not halt the Republican victory, gained, Mullaly was convinced, by fraudulent balloting among the soldiers. Lincoln's second term would bring with it a "Reign of Terror" and the silencing of the Democratic press.

---

41. Ibid., Sept. 10, 1864, 586; Sept. 17, 1864, 590.
42. Ibid., Sept. 24, 1864, 616.
43. Ibid., Oct. 1, 1864, 632; ibid., Oct. 15, 1864, 664.

As to the consequence of this election there can, we think, be no doubt. We shall have repeated conscriptions, increased taxation, and many years more of war. . . . As to the South, she shall be more united than ever. . . . And . . . [the South] will be independent when the North lies prostrate under intolerable oppression. . . . We shall continue to write as we have heretofore done until the pen be stricken from our hand.[44]

Lincoln's second term, when all these dire conditions would take place, began on March 4, 1865, with his famous second inaugural address. The *Record*'s evaluation of this masterpiece was as faulty as its prediction regarding the course of the second administration. The American people, Mullaly believed, had every reason "to feel mortified and chagrined at the painful and lamentable spectacle" presented at the inaugural. One needed only to call attention to the addresses of Lincoln and Johnson to produce this despair. Andrew Johnson "evidently did not shun Bourbon County, Kentucky" on his way to his inaugural. Lincoln's plea to "strive on to finish the work we are in" meant that the President intended to continue his "work of death and destruction." The address did not please Mullaly.

It was a remarkable and peculiar production, a strange blending of Abolitionism and Scripture, a curious medley of affected piety and patriotism. As to its style, it is only necessary to say that it was essentially Lincolnian and marked with all the originality which is claimed for everything that comes from his tongue or his pen. Its great recommendation is its brevity, for which the country can hardly be sufficiently thankful. . . . [45]

A month later the President was dead. Mullaly's reaction to Lincoln's assassination was proper. He called the action "a terrible tragedy" and a "horrid dream," and asked his readers to "unite in paying the last sad tribute of respect to which he was entitled. . . ." "History," Mullaly added, "would be the proper judge of Lincoln's character and policies." The murderer was denounced for substituting his own judgment for the law of the land.[46]

By the time of Lincoln's death the war was already over. Mullaly and the *Record* had supported a lost cause. The Emancipation Proclamation had triggered Mul-

---

44. Ibid., Nov. 12, 1864, 731.
45. Ibid., Mar. 11, 1865, 10; Mar. 18, 1865, 8–9. The text used in the *Record* varies slightly from that appearing in Lincoln, *Works*, VIII, 332–33.
46. *Metropolitan Record and New York Vindicator*, Apr. 22, 1865, 8; Apr. 29, 1865, 18.

laly's move toward Copperheadism and away from the position of his patron, Archbishop Hughes. These actions suggest strongly that Mullaly was motivated by racism, and the *Record* contained many articles demonstrating his hatred of blacks.

As early as December 1861, Mullaly had indicated in his private correspondence that he opposed emancipation schemes. As emancipation agitation increased in the North, so too did Mullaly's denunciations, both private and public. When still the "official organ" of the New York Archbishop, the *Record* published an article, "A Few Words Upon The Subject Of Slavery," which justified the institution of slavery on theological grounds. Another article denounced the "grand project" planned by Abolitionists "of social amalgamation and equality between blacks and whites. . . ."[47]

Later, after his break with Hughes, Mullaly wrote of his disgust at the sight of Negro troops in the uniform of American soldiers. In an article titled, "New York Disgraced," he wrote:

> On Saturday . . . a scene was presented on Broadway such as we trust will never again be witnessed in this great metropolis. It was the parade of a colored regiment, officered by white men, and with an escort of white men. It was the saddest proof that could be produced of the degeneracy of our Government, and of the depth of degradation into which the Republic has been plunged by the infamous party in power. . . . It was hard for a honest man to control his indignation at the sight, but it made the blood tingle to see some of our own race showing, by voice and gesture, their approbation of this infamous parody of patriotism.[48]

Mullaly's racial views were consistent with what many of his contemporaries, Catholic as well as non-Catholic, believed were commonly shared by Irish-American Catholics, an intense dislike of Negroes, emancipation, and abolitionists. Brownson had observed prejudice among Catholic immigrant groups and had deplored it. Administration newspapers in New York in July of 1863 bitterly condemned Irish anti-Negro feelings as responsible for the draft riots, and the *Tribune* later went so far as to blame the "Catholic-Copperhead" *Record* for instigating this bloodshed against New York's Negroes.[49]

47. Mullaly to Hughes, Dec. 17, 1861; Mullaly to Hughes, Apr. 10, 1862, Hughes Papers; *Metropolitan Record*, June 21, 1862, 392; June 28, 1862, 409.

48. Ibid., Mar. 12, 1864, 169.

49. *Brownson's Literary Review*, 3d Ser., III (Oct., 1862), 451–52; *Metropolitan Record*, July 25, 1863, 472; *New York Tribune*, July 23, 1863; Aug. 14, 1863.

Modern historians have agreed with the assessment that Irish-American Catholics were bitterly anti-Negro. Jay P. Dolan found that the "Irish community" had "an open dislike" for Negroes, an antagonism that erupted during the draft riots of 1863. And Adrian Cook, in his account of the rioting, concluded that "an overwhelming percentage of rioters were Irish." He found that of 184 rioters whose country of birth could be determined, 117 were born in Ireland. John Mullaly belonged to this community in New York and his newspaper reflected the views of New York City's Irish Catholics. He shared their racial prejudice.[50]

Yet, racial prejudice was perhaps not the only factor in causing Irish Catholics, like Mullaly, to oppose Republicans, the war, and emancipation. In looking for motives for the vicious rioting in 1863, Cook concluded that "intense racial prejudice of white New Yorkers in the 1860's is enough to explain all." He dismissed the argument that economic motivation might have played a role in causing the riots. But evidence does exist demonstrating that Irish and Negroes were competing for the same jobs in New York City. Negroes received less pay for the same jobs and were hired as strike breakers, which led to other riots before the most serious one of July 1863. Throughout the war anti-administration orators and writers had warned that black laborers would "move up into the North to steal the work and the bread" of white laborers. Although there was no mass migration northward of Negroes during the Civil War, many people believed the story. In several instances, duly reported in the New York press, fighting did break out between striking Irish laborers and Negroes brought in to replace them.[51]

On March 23, 1863, for example, workers on the piers used by the Erie Railroad went on strike, demanding $1.50 per day and no work on Sunday. Negroes were brought in to replace them and fighting broke out between whites and blacks. Several weeks later "about 300 Irish longshoremen" who had gone out on strike for higher wages attacked the Negroes used to replace them. Mullaly once complained in print that the New York papers, especially the *Tribune*, treated the Irish in a contemptible manner. He particularly objected to the *Tribune*'s referring to Irish laborers as "vagabonds," and noted in defense of the Irish that they faced the competition of Negro laborers willing to receive less money for the same tasks. The

---

50. Jay P. Dolan, *The Immigrant Church: New York's Irish And German Catholics, 1815-1865* (Baltimore, 1975), 24-25; Adrian Cook, *The Armies of The Streets: The New York City Draft Riots of 1863* (Lexington, 1974), 196.

51. Ibid., 204-6. See for example the remarks of Fernando Wood that Southern blacks would replace New York Irish and German laborers, in *Harper's Weekly*, V (Dec. 21, 1861), 802. See also *Metropolitan Record*, Dec. 14, 1861, 796; Aug. 9, 1862, 504; C. Chauncey Burr, "Slavery States Of The North," *The Old Guard*, I (1863), 252; *Age* (Philadelphia), Oct. 12, 1863.

fear that abolition would cause more Negroes to move North in search of jobs does in part explain the pro-slavery position of Mullaly and other Irish-Americans.⁵²

Also, Mullaly was very suspicious of both the *Times* and *Tribune*, Republican papers that managed on occasion to betray Know Nothing prejudices against Irish Catholics. Only three weeks after the war had begun, the *New York Times*, in an article on "The Progress of Population" predicted that both Slavery and Popery, incompatible as they were with "the spirit of the age"—liberty and civilization, were doomed to "speedy destruction." To an Irish Catholic immigrant, like Mullaly, who remembered the past conflicts with Know Nothings, these sentiments connected the new Republican party with the old enemy. Mullaly quickly denounced the item in the *Times* and repeated his deunuciation later, on several occasions.⁵³

The *New York Tribune* also was a Republican paper that displayed little sympathy for Irish Catholics. Shortly after the presidential election of 1864, the *Tribune* published an article, "The Irish Vote," that managed to insult Irish-Americans and Catholics. The article noted that ninety-nine out of every one hundred Irish-born Roman Catholics voted the Democratic ticket. It also observed that these voters were "not so well educated and informed" as American-born voters. Their votes in any given election could be "with perfect confidence inferred from their speech." The article then claimed that "the great body" of the Roman Catholic clergy in America sympathized with the slave holders and sought a "re-establishment" of "human bondage."

> And their influence over the laity, coinciding with that of the grogshops, wherein hate and scorn of 'the naygurs' is systematically inculcated as a source of political influence and power, is so potent and pervading that it is utterly idle to seek to indoctrinate the great mass of our Irish-born voters with those ideas and sentiments touching our great struggle . . . ⁵⁴

Mullaly had previously warned his readers that "Know Nothingism" was sleeping, not dead. Occasionally the bugbears of "Popery" and "Irishism" disturbed its

---

52. *New York Tribune*, Mar. 24, 1863; ibid., Apr. 14, 1863; *Metropolitan Record*, Apr. 25, 1863, 266. See also *New York Times*, Aug. 5, 1862. More examples are cited in Man, "Church and New York Draft Riots," 33-34.

53. *New York Times*, May 5, 1861; *Metropolitan Record*, May 25, 1861, 332; Aug. 9, 1862, 505; July 25, 1863, 473; Nov. 19, 1864, 745.

54. *New York Tribune*, Nov. 10, 1864. Later the *Tribune* stressed that it was condemning the Irish clergy and acknowledged that the attitude in Rome, where blacks had been consecrated bishops, was different. *New York Tribune*, Nov. 19, 1864; *Brownson's Quarterly Review*, 3d Ser., IV (Oct. 1863), 405-6.

slumber. "We have known people," he wrote, "to ascribe our national misfortunes to the influence of the 'Irish.'" As a response to these attacks Mullaly had listed and praised the record of Irish soldiers fighting for the North. The *Tribune*'s attack on Irish voters was only another Know Nothing attack and only assured that Irishmen would not support the *Tribune*'s politics.

> These attacks upon the intelligence and honesty of Irish-American voters are not calculated to gain many converts ... to Abolitionism, and we assure the *Tribune* that the low and vile innuendo against the Catholic priesthood, whose "influence over the laity," we are told, "coincides with that of the grog shops," will not dispose them towards affiliation with a party, one of whose principal organs slanders and vilifies both the Catholic laity and the Catholic clergy in the one breath.... [55]

Mullaly's newspaper reflected the suspicion of Republicans and antipathy to Know Nothings shared by Irish Catholic immigrants. It also reflected the concern of Irish laborers that emancipation policies of the federal government would threaten their jobs. Religious prejudice and economic self-interest both had their effects on Irish Catholics and John Mullaly. These motives do explain in part the editorial views of the *Record*. But only in part. It was racial prejudice more than anything else that made John Mullaly a Copperhead. Only once during the war did he show any sympathy for the plight of the Negroes. During the 1863 Draft Riots he reported that Negroes "were treated with horrible inhumanity by the rioters." He deplored this action and argued that a "superior race should disdain to vent its passions on ... poor wretches like the negroes, who are the footballs of every party...." He did not wish to have Negroes subjected to excessive cruelty, but he did not object to their bondage and opposed the Lincoln administration mostly on this one issue.[56]

In 1862 the *Record* had reprinted and commended Lincoln's letter to Horace Greeley in which the President advised the editor that his war aim was to save the Union and not free or protect Southern slaves. Mullaly liked Lincoln's statement but unfortunately never shared the sentiment Lincoln used to close that letter, his "oft-expressed *personal* wish that all men everywhere could be free."[57]

---

55. *Metropolitan Record*, Apr. 11, 1863, p. 234; *Metropolitan Record and New York Vindicator*, Nov. 19, 1864, 745-46. Professor David M. Potter has noted that anti-slavery and nativism "operated in partnership" and "drew their strength from the same religious and social constituencies." David M. Potter, *The Impending Crisis: 1848-1861* (New York, 1976), 251-52.

56. *Metropolitan Record*, July 25, 1863, 473.

57. Lincoln, *Works*, V, 388-89.

Abraham Lincoln on Labor and Capital

James A. Stevenson

Abraham Lincoln and virtually all of his frontier contemporaries were immersed in an inherited culture that extolled a hoary republican ideal. Lincoln, as a result, propounded economic ideas that were determined by his existence within a venerable and a compelling tradition. This tradition must be understood as an eighteenth- and nineteenth-century historical/cultural phenomenon that transcended specific political, economic, and social ideologies. As a blending of all those aspects of life and thought, the republican ideal had, for those individuals holding it, a political dimension (a belief in personal liberty and in the political ideology of republicanism), an economic dimension (a belief in the free labor system and in economic independence based on the ownership of productive private property), and a social dimension (a belief in a non-elite, egalitarian society of small, independent producers who have an equal opportunity for social mobility). Maturing within the matrix of that culture, Lincoln shared it with those of the small producing and working class who maintained and/or practiced an equal-rights tradition, mutualism,[1] an egalitarian-antimonopoly outlook, respect for the dignity of labor, faith in unlimited social mobility,

---

1. In the mid-nineteenth-century U.S. cultural context, mutualism may be defined as a social network of horizontal, socioeconomic personal relationships that have been established between independent but mutually helpful producers.

personal independence based on the ownership of productive private property, and, most importantly, the labor theory of value.

Given his life within such a cultural environment, Lincoln adopted an economic viewpoint which looked less to the future of a wholly industrial and hierarchical society than to the past of a largely rural and egalitarian society.[2] Capturing that aspect of Lincoln's outlook, Daniel Walker Howe has written:

> The triumph of the northern bourgeoisie [after the Civil War] ushered in an era very different from anything Lincoln could have expected or wanted. His objective, in the broadest sense, was to defend and extend the kind of free society he had known in Springfield. This was a society of small entrepreneurs, market-oriented farmers, young men working for others until they could save enough to set up for themselves, and striving professionals like himself.... In 1859, Lincoln described this society and [stated] "Let us hope... that by the best cultivation of the physical world beneath and around us, and the intellectual and moral world within us," that this society and the aspirations it embodies "shall not pass away."[3]

While, as Howe argued, Lincoln's model for the future was based on the past, the underpinning of Lincoln's economic ideas rested on the labor theory of value. It was a concept about which he thought deeply. One sign of this is found in his 1859 speech before the Wisconsin State Agricultural Society. In it,

---

2. Writers have differed greatly over Lincoln's economic prescience or lack of it. Following in the tradition of Charles Beard's belief that the pre–Civil War Republican party represented the "forces of emerging industrial capitalism," Gabor S. Boritt's touchstone economic interpretation has portrayed Lincoln as a forward-looking student of economic change. And, while David R. Wrone, fitting within Richard Hofstadter's view that Lincoln neither anticipated nor desired the form of the U.S. economy that arose after the Civil War, pictured Lincoln as a good man whose deficient economic knowledge allowed him to be overcome by the corporate property system, Melvin E. Bradford simply dismissed Lincoln as a politico who eschewed all principles, including economic principles. See William E. Gienapp, *The Origins of the Republican Party, 1852–1856* (New York: Oxford Univ. Press, 1987), 353; Gabor S. Boritt, "Lincoln and the Economics of the American Dream," 92, 91, 103, and Melvin E. Bradford, "Against Lincoln: An Address at Gettysburg—Commentary on 'Lincoln and the Economics of the American Dream,'" 109–10, both in *The Historian's Lincoln: Pseudohistory, Psychohistory and History*, ed. Gabor S. Boritt and Norman O. Forness (Chicago: Univ. of Illinois Press, 1988); Richard Hofstadter, *The American Political Tradition and the Men Who Made It* (New York: Vintage, 1958), 105–7; David R. Wrone, "Abraham Lincoln's Idea of Property," *Science & Society* 33 (Winter 1969): 69, 56; Melvin E. Bradford, "The Lincoln Legacy: A Long View," *Modern Age* 24 (1980): 357–58.

3. Daniel Walker Howe, *The Political Culture of the American Whigs* (Chicago: Univ. of Chicago Press, 1979), 297.

Lincoln acutely described some of the principal differences men had over this fundamental and divisive issue. As he rhetorically explored the subject, his own position was revealed by the weight of his argument. He began by stating,

> The world is agreed that *labor* is the source from which human wants are mainly supplied. There is no dispute upon this point. From this point, however, men immediately diverge. Much disputation is maintained as to the best way of applying and controlling the labor element. By some it is assumed that labor is available only in connection with capital—that nobody labors, unless somebody else, owning capital, somehow, by the use of that capital, induces him to do it. Having assumed this, they proceed to consider whether it is best that capital shall *hire* laborers, and thus induce them to work by their own consent; or *buy* them, and drive them to it without their consent.[4]

Considering Lincoln's free labor sympathies, he could be expected to condemn those who believed that slavery was the proper mechanism for extracting labor, but he went much further. Lincoln challenged both means of dominating labor, and he called the combined outlook a *"'mud-sill'* theory." He stated,

> Having proceeded so far they naturally conclude that all laborers are necessarily either *hired* laborers, or *slaves*. They further assume that whoever is once a *hired* laborer, is fatally fixed in that condition for life; and thence again that his condition is as bad as, or worse than that of a slave. This is the *"mud-sill"* theory.[5]

While the nature of these remarks reveals that Lincoln's outlook remained rooted in the practical experience of independent producers, the quality of his remarks also indicates that he embellished his youthful experiences of farming and shopkeeping with more sophisticated economic study.

In describing Lincoln's acquaintance with formal academic economic studies, Gabor S. Boritt noted that although Lincoln may have read or browsed through some of the economic writings of James R. McCullock and James and John Stuart Mill, Lincoln's own economic offerings reveal only the influence of Henry C. Carey and Francis Wayland. In Carey's 1835 *Essay on the Rate of Wages*,

---

4. Roy P. Basler et al., eds. *The Collected Works of Abraham Lincoln*, 9 vols. (New Brunswick, N.J.: Rutgers Univ. Press, 1953-55), 3:477.

5. Ibid., 477-78.

Lincoln could have found "many of the economic concepts he later adopted," i.e., pro-tariff arguments, wage and price ideas, and the notion that the security of capital promoted the interest of the workingman. As Boritt explained, "In other Carey works Lincoln could have seen demonstrated the identity of the interests of labor and capital. . . . Above all Carey tied protectionism, economic development, and democracy into a knot." As for the influence of Wayland's economic ideas, Boritt reported that Lincoln's longtime law partner, William Herndon, maintained that Lincoln had a "special liking" for Wayland's 1837 textbook *The Elements of Political Economy*. In Wayland's text, which Lincoln certainly read, Lincoln discovered the "dominant presence" of the labor theory of value. As a preacher-economist, Wayland held that any "involuntary exchange between capital and labor . . . was 'robbery.'" This outlook, rooted as it was in moral terms, made a strong impression on Lincoln, who was fond of associating moral arguments with economic positions.[6] In sum, Lincoln absorbed some key ideas from his perusal and study of economic works, but those ideas were always filtered through the practical experience of frontier living.

Working and living close to people who earned their livelihoods from farming or closely related industries for most of his life, Lincoln never read the economic writings of Karl Marx, but he developed a remarkably similar theoretical understanding of the antagonistic relationship between capital and labor. Lincoln's analysis (logical analysis and sociohistorical experience) was based, in part, on some of the same arguments Marx used to assert the validity of the labor theory of value (logical proof, analytical proof, sociohistorical experience, and argument by *reductio ad absurdum*). So, when Lincoln condemned the mud-sill theory as wrongheaded and shallow, he backed his words with the weight of a considered intellectual appraisal. His argument was used to uphold the thinkers who maintained that free labor need be neither coerced nor permanently subordinated to capital:

> But another class of reasoners [Lincoln included] hold the opinion that there is no *such* relationship between capital and labor [i.e., capital must induce labor to work], as assumed; and that there is no such thing as a freeman being fatally fixed for life, in the condition of a hired laborer, that both these assumptions are false, and all inferences from them groundless.[7]

6. Gabor S. Boritt, *Lincoln and the Economics of the American Dream* (Memphis, Tenn.: Memphis State Univ. Press, 1978), 121–25.

7. Basler et al. 3:478.

In Lincoln's opinion, the misconception(s) of the first set of "reasoners" was founded on an erroneous belief about the primacy of capital in the relationship between capital and labor. This error was basic because, in making labor inferior to capital, it reversed a fundamental economic truth. As Lincoln explained it, the correct judgment held that

> labor is prior to, and independent of, capital; that, in fact, capital is the fruit of labor, and could never have existed if labor had not first existed—that labor can exist without capital, but that capital could never have existed without labor. Hence . . . labor is the superior—greatly the superior—of capital.[8]

It is doubtful that either the Classical economists (who equivocated on the labor theory of value) or Marx supported the labor theory of value with as much clarity or emphasis. There is, as well, no indication that Lincoln ever altered his view of this crucial economic premise.

When in 1861, during his Annual Message to Congress, President Lincoln eliminated the oblique and third-person style that had characterized his 1859 analysis of the labor theory of value, he clearly was using the authority of his office to assert that capital was economically inferior to labor. After warning that the "rights of the people" were threatened by the antidemocratic forces of the South, he condemned the "effort to place *capital* on an equal footing with, if not above *labor*." Again, after denying the view that labor must exist only in a "fixed" and dependent relationship to capital, Lincoln repeated his 1859 labor theory of value assertions and added a revealing phrase that illuminated more of his pro-labor bias. "Labor is the superior of capital, *and deserves much the higher consideration*," he wrote. "Capital has rights," but those rights were only as "worthy of protection as any other rights."[9]

Lincoln, of course, could not ignore the potential for exploitation that his concept of the labor theory of value exposed. Still, he was so absorbed with pressing political matters that he never pursued an extensive theoretical discussion of the labor theory value. Such ideas as use-value, exchange value, necessary labor, surplus value, and prices remained for economists like Marx to explore. Yet, while Lincoln never used concepts like those, he did not skirt the issue of economic exploitation. According to him and from the perspective of the republican ideal and the free

---

8. Ibid.
9. Ibid., 5:51, 52 (emphasis added).

labor system of the North, however, three aspects of the American socioeconomic culture seemed to mitigate against the sort of irrepressible class struggle that Marx envisioned. Although two of these mitigating characteristics—the right to strike and social mobility—were intrinsically connected to the republican ideal, the third was based mostly on Lincoln's optimistic view that capital and free labor had no irreconcilable differences. For instance, after his 1861 statements regarding the labor theory of value, Lincoln explained, "Nor is it denied that there is, and probably always will be, a relation between labor and capital, producing mutual benefits."[10]

Still, as a practical politician, Lincoln met rapacious industrialists, brutal construction bosses, greedy landlords, and plenty of impoverished workers and farmers. In acknowledging such things, his view of labor's preeminent role in the free labor system inevitably led him to support the right to strike. His stand on this issue, however, consisted of a peculiarly Lincolnian-small producer admixture of striking, quitting, and moving. As Lincoln saw it, in the midst of the bounty offered by America, the free labor system not only permitted the right to strike, but also the right to move—both geographically and socially. His best expression of this outlook occurred in a pre-presidential speech in 1860, at New Haven, Connecticut. In contrasting the rights of free labor with slave labor, Lincoln described the virtues of a mobile wage-labor system in these words:

> *I am glad to see that a system of labor prevails in New England under which laborers CAN strike* when they want to [Cheers,] where they are not obliged to work under all circumstances, and are not tied down and obliged to labor whether you pay them or not! [Cheers.] I *like* the system which lets a man quit when he wants to, and wish it might prevail everywhere.[11]

In connecting striking, quitting, and moving, Lincoln revealed why he saw no irreconcilable conflict between labor and capital. After all, in America, except for the slaves in the South, labor had a tremendous opportunity for geographical mobility. Lincoln's own frontier existence confirmed this fact. As a boy, he had moved from Kentucky to Indiana; as a young man, he had moved to Illinois. For Lincoln, such mobility not only served to ameliorate poor or abusive working

---

10. Lyman Abbott, "Lincoln as a Labor Leader," *Outlook* (Feb. 27, 1909): 504-5; W. J. Ghent, "Lincoln and Labor," *Independent* 66 (Feb. II, 1909): 301; Basler et al., 5:52.

11. Basler et al., 4:24.

conditions, but it was essential for the performance of the capitalist system. His thinking on the matter becomes clear when during a speech to an audience composed partly of striking New Haven shoe workers, he stated,

> I desire that if you get too thick here, and find it hard to better your condition on this soil, you may have a chance to strike and go somewhere else, where you may not be degraded. . . . Then you can better your condition, and so it may go on and on in one ceaseless round so long as man exists on the face of the earth![12]

Lincoln's view that social mobility was closely linked to geographical mobility was shaped by more than his personal career. His personal experience was confirmed on the sociological level by the triumphant careers of his successful frontier neighbors. Many of them, after all, seemed to follow the path of Lincoln's own rise to fortune and/or fame. As David R. Wrone wrote,

> The majority of Lincoln's aristocratic associates originated, as he did, in the lower levels of society. . . . For example, C. H. Moore walked into Clinton in 1841 with all his possessions bundled in a stick over his shoulder. Tom Snell, like John Dean Gillett, was an orphaned, poor youth. David Davis . . . traveled West to seek a fortune, with less than fifty dollars in his purse. Richard Oglesby lived a harsh existence in the river bottoms until he made one fortune and married another. Robert Latham's father owned land when Logan County was a wilderness, but lived there to wait for its increase in value. John Warner came from the poor counties of Virginia, and like Isaac Funk, lived in a rude log cabin his first years in Illinois. The record continues in a similar manner with scores of other men.[13]

Like such rags-to-riches Illinois friends and acquaintances, Lincoln himself became a middle-class attorney who received considerable fees from Illinois railroad companies as well as less wealthy clients. And, while he had no ambition to acquire land, he did not dogmatically begrudge others' desire for large land holdings.[14] Such land ownership, as Lincoln perceived it, was impractical, but it also was due those who wanted it on the basis of their equal rights. It was even more justified on the basis of a system that promoted man's right to rise.

12. Ibid., 25.
13. Wrone, 68–69.
14. Abbott, 504; Wrone, 55, 57, 63–64.

Proud of such a system, it is no surprise that, between 1856 and 1861, Lincoln made several striking comments on the subject of American social mobility. Such comments were delivered in the context of his free labor attack on slavery and as part of his message that social mobility was the by-product of geographical mobility. For example, in 1856, Lincoln blasted the *Richmond Enquirer*'s claim that Southern slaves were better off than Northern laborers.

> What a mistaken view do these men have of Northern laborers! They think that men are always to remain laborers here—but there is no such class. The man who labored for another last year, this year labors for himself, and next year he will hire others to labor for him.[15]

Later, in 1860, when elaborating on this portrait of an economic system that encouraged unlimited social mobility, Lincoln told his New Haven audience:

> I take it that it is best for all to leave each man free to acquire property as fast as he can. Some will get wealthy. I don't believe in a law to prevent a man from getting rich; it would do more harm than good. So while we do not propose any war upon capital, we do wish to allow the humblest man an equal chance to get rich with everybody else. [Applause.] When one starts poor, as most do in the race of life, free society is such that he knows he can better his condition; he knows that there is no fixed condition of labor. . . .[16]

Lincoln followed these remarks with those that demonstrated his acute understanding of the more constructive principles underlying a dynamic capitalist system. Although he introduced his comments with a personal example of social mobility, his real message was that the whole system must permit anyone of merit—including a black man—to better himself. "I am not ashamed to confess," Lincoln stated,

> that twenty-five years ago I was a hired laborer, mauling rails, at work on a flatboat—just what might happen to any poor man's son! [Applause.] I want every man to have the chance—and I believe a black man is entitled to it—in which he can better his condition—when he may look forward and hope to be a hired

---

15. Basler et al., 2:364.
16. Ibid., 4:24.

laborer this year and the next, work for himself afterward, and finally to hire men to work for him! That is the true system.[17]

It is vital to note, however, that this emphasis on social mobility, when considered in isolation from other aspects of Lincoln's outlook, distorts his ideas by falsely suggesting that he advocated the development of a modern and highly acquisitive economy rather than one which was based on the experiences and principles of the republican past and which promoted small producer opportunities to earn a good living in a society of interdependent equals.

If left unbalanced by the countervailing small-producer/labor bias in Lincoln's thinking, the view that Lincoln's concept of equality only emphasized equality of opportunity (i.e., an American dream of no more than the right "to rise") makes Lincoln appear much too prescient in his economic outlook. Lincoln's concept of equality, a "society of equals," was never divorced from the Jeffersonian vision of a nation of yeomen farmers.[18] While arguing a wholly different thesis, Boritt, for one, has strengthened this view by acknowledging that, in the 1850s, Lincoln held a "very restricted" understanding of the "coming wage-earning society" and accepted factories as only a "somewhat peripheral part of the system." Such an observation is not only consistent with Lincoln's fundamentally Jeffersonian outlook but also with the socio-economic facts of Illinois in the 1850s. Lincoln always envisioned a society in which individuals and society would advance together. He imagined that such an opportunity would occur only within the context of an independent small-producer economy. Indeed, inferring from Boritt's comments, it is only within this context that Lincoln's anticapitalist bias becomes meaningful.[19]

Lincoln's uneasiness about unproductive capitalists becomes fully comprehensible when considered as a prejudice spawned by a republican antimonopoly outlook. Accordingly, while Lincoln extolled the free labor system as one in which "every man can make himself,"[20] he never actually advocated the goal of great wealth either for himself or for others. His emphasis on the right to rise was based on the inherited equal rights and antimonopoly tradition of the republican ideal. This outlook was brought into sharp focus when Lincoln forcefully argued against greedy, entrepreneurial ambition and vast disparities of wealth in society. Before the Wisconsin State Agricultural Society, he told his 1859 audience:

17. Ibid., 24–25.
18. Ibid., 3:462; Rose Strunsky, "Abraham Lincoln's Social Ideals," *Century* 87 (1914): 590.
19. Boritt, *Lincoln and the Economics of the American Dream*, 180–81, 176–77.
20. Basler et al., 2:364.

The ambition for broad acres leads to poor farming, even, with men of energy. I scarcely ever knew a mammoth farm to sustain itself; much less to return a profit upon the outlay. I have more than once known a man to spend a respectable fortune upon one; fail and leave it; and then some man of more modest aims, get a small fraction of the ground, and make a good living upon it. Mammoth farms are like tools or weapons, which are too heavy to be handled. Ere long they are thrown aside, at a great loss.

So, in keeping with the yeomen farmers' Jeffersonian aversion to monopolies, Lincoln condemned large-scale property ownership as both greedy and inefficient. While he advocated unlimited social mobility, he did not advocate it as a means to great wealth and certainly not as a means to dominate others. The egalitarian nature of his notion of social mobility was captured in his comment "Advancement—improvement in condition—is the order of things in a *society of equals*."[21]

Such a society, of course, reflected the culture from which Lincoln had sprung. As late as Lincoln's departure for the presidency, Illinois retained many of the economic and the social-psychological characteristics that marked the republicanism of a household economy. Hence, despite Wrone's assertion that Illinois already was dominated by a landed aristocracy in the 1850s, data reveal that rural and urban Illinois was still a largely small-producer society. The apparent paradox raised by Wrone's findings may be explained by the fact that, as opposed to the more numerous class of small producers, a few large-scale Illinois landowners could exercise a disproportionate share of economic and political influence. Agricultural historian Paul Wallace Gates, at any rate, noted that despite the existence of a few farms of astounding size, "it should be emphasized that large-scale farming in Illinois was the exception, not the rule."[22] And, amid the large cohort of rural and urban small producers, some memories of a lifestyle based on the former household economy were sustained by the continuing small-scale agrarian make up of the Illinois economy.

In Illinois, if not the northeast, the existence of numerous middling farmer, small shopkeepers and manufacturers, skilled laborers, and craftsmen formed a large cohort of independent small producers. Lincoln not only identified with these people, but he perceived them to be the heart and the soul of the free labor

---

21. Ibid., 3:475–76, 462 (emphasis added).
22. Wrone, 57; Paul W. Gates, "Large-Scale Farming in Illinois, 1850 to 1870," *Agricultural History* 6 (Jan. 1932): 22.

system. It is through his remarks about them that it is possible to learn why he thought that capitalism held such promise for the individual. And it is through his analysis of their economic existence that his concept of social mobility is put in its proper historical and egalitarian perspective.

Through remarks that he made in 1859, and which he repeated in 1861 during his Annual Message to Congress, Lincoln revealed that his concept of social mobility was inspired by a belief that the only decent society was the one in which any individual had an opportunity to become an independent, small-scale producer. After discussing and dismissing the role of the "few" capitalists and the "few" laborers in America, Lincoln offered Congress his opinion on those he considered to be the economic backbone of a just society. He began by noting that such people composed a majority of the people in both North and South:

> A large majority belong to neither class—neither work for others, nor have others working for them. In most of the southern States, a majority of the whole people of all colors are neither slaves nor masters; while in the northern [states] a large majority are neither hirers nor hired.

Continuing to define these people, Lincoln described their small-scale ownership of the means of production in words which perfectly captured the economic source of their fierce sense of independence and pride:

> Men with their families—wives, sons, and daughters—work for themselves, on their farms, in their houses, and in their shops, taking the whole product to themselves, and asking no favor of capital on the one hand, nor of hired laborers or slaves on the other.

While many of these people, as Lincoln carefully pointed out, were both owners and workers, this dual role did not alter anything fundamental in the capitalist system:

> It is not forgotten that a considerable number of persons mingle their own labor with capital—that is, they labor with their own hands, and also buy or hire others to labor for them.... No principle stated [i.e., the labor theory of value or right to rise] is disturbed by the existence of this mixed class.

Actually, far from disturbing any free labor "principle," the "mixed class" confirmed all such principles. That class, in short, was the socioeconomic magnet that not only drew industrious individuals out of poverty, but it kept the whole free labor system in dynamic motion:

> The prudent, penniless beginner in the world, labors for wages awhile, saves a surplus with which to buy tools or land for himself; then labors on his own account another while, and at length hires another new beginner to help him. This is the just, and generous, and prosperous system, which opens the way to all—gives hope to all, and consequent energy, and progress, and improvement of condition to all.[23]

With these eloquent words, Lincoln maintained that the American capitalist system was impelled forward not by ruthless competition but by the constantly renewed promise of small-scale, productive-property ownership.

Such an economic outlook was firmly rooted in a Jeffersonian vision of America and the egalitarian values and practices of the more comprehensive and amorphous republican ideal. So, despite the emergence of a competitive market economy in Illinois as well as in much of the nation, Lincoln virtually never used the word *competition* in connection with his notion of economic progress. Neither the socioeconomic nature of the pre-1861 Illinois economy nor his inherited concepts of equal rights and mutualism would allow him to believe that naked greed or rampant competition motivated the majority of men in the American economic environment. As far as Lincoln described it, the free labor system was motivated by the individual's aspiration to advance within the socially acceptable context of an egalitarian culture of independent, small-scale producers. And, as long as property ownership remained widespread and accessible to all, the system would function fine. Indeed, when, in the context of America's small-producer cornucopia, a hired laborer failed to acquire his rightful share of the means of production, Lincoln maintained that it was due less to the fault of the system than to the fault of the laborer. According to Lincoln: "If any continue through life in the condition of the hired laborer, it is not the fault of the system, but because of either a dependent nature which prefers it, or improvidence, folly, or singular misfortune."[24]

23. Basler et al., 5:52.
24. Ibid., 3:479.

Obviously, Lincoln cannot be identified as a severe critic of America's pre-1865 capitalist system, but neither was he a naive defender of a system that contained the potential for robbing producers of the value of their labor. In fact, his principal economic objection to slavery was founded on the belief that every man was entitled to the full fruit of his labor. In a compelling 1858 affirmation of that truth, Lincoln swept aside Stephen Douglas's racially inspired jabs with the equal rights language so dear to small producers:

> I hold that ... the negro ... is not my equal in many respects—certainly not in color, perhaps not in moral or intellectual endowment. But in the right to eat the bread, without the leave of anybody else, which his own hand earns, *he is my equal and the equal of Judge Douglas, and the equal of every living man.*[25]

By founding this argument on the labor theory of value, Lincoln not only concluded that every worker was due the whole product of his labor, but he rendered a moral judgment. Economic exploitation was immoral. Only seven years after the great debates with Douglas, the labor theory of value had led him to pass this providential judgment on a war that had sacrificed over six hundred thousand lives on the altar of "unrequited toil":

> Fondly do we hope—fervently do we pray—that this mighty scourge of war may speedily pass away. Yet, if God wills that it continue, until all the wealth piled by the bond-man's two hundred and fifty years of unrequited toil shall be sunk, and until every drop of blood drawn with the lash, shall be paid by another drawn with the sword, as was said three thousand years ago, so still it must be said "the judgments of the Lord, are true and righteous altogether."[26]

Committed to the labor theory of value and horrified by the economic implications of slavery, Lincoln developed an economic outlook, if not a theory, that was both critical and penetrating. Although the issue of slavery directed his attention away from a strict focus on the dangers future capitalist developments might pose for free labor, it did not eliminate his concern that capital had the potential to exploit free laborers. Guided by his attachment to the republican ideal, his acquaintance with the independent producer experience of the frontier, and his

---

25. Robert W. Johannsen, ed. *The Lincoln-Douglas Debates* (New York: Oxford Univ. Press, 1965), 52–53.
26. Basler et al., 8:333.

belief in the beneficial results of social mobility, he criticized that threatening potential. Even in wartime, Lincoln was concerned that untrammelled capital would corrupt or destroy the economic foundation (small-producer ownership of the means of production, equality of opportunity, and the ability to retain the fruit of one's labor) of individual independence and freedom. He, therefore, warned of capital's attempt to dominate government. In his First Annual Message to Congress, he stated,

> It is not needed, nor fitting here, that a general argument should be made in favor of popular institutions; but there is one point, with its connexions, not so hackneyed as most others, to which I ask a brief attention. It is the effort to place *capital* on an equal footing with, if not above labor, in the structure of government.
>
> No men living are more worthy to be trusted than those who toil up from poverty—none less inclined to take, or touch, aught which they have not honestly earned. Let them beware of surrendering a political power which they already possess, and which, if surrendered, will surely be used to close the door of advancement against such as they, and to fix new disabilities and burdens upon them, till all of liberty shall be lost.[27]

Considering these words and the influence of modern corporate lobbyists, giant bureaucracies, and the fact that over 88 percent of the U.S. work force now consists of people who are almost totally dependent upon their managerial superiors for their livelihoods, working conditions, and promotions, Lincoln's warning appears to have been disturbingly prophetic.

---

27. Ibid., 5:51–53.

Lincoln's Calvinist Transformation

Emancipation and War

Nicholas Parrillo

The role of religion in Abraham Lincoln's political leadership very much deserves to be studied, for, as Reinhold Niebuhr claims, Lincoln apprehended the religious meanings of political events more deeply than did almost any other American of his time.¹ Yet the sources available on the subject present serious difficulties. While Lincoln's statements on religion were at times profound, they were never lengthy or great in number. Some historians have tried to fill in the picture by using the reminiscences of people who knew Lincoln, but these sources entail problems of their own. Authors of reminiscences suffered from the tricks of memory. Further, they were especially tempted to bias their accounts when talking about religion, for after Lincoln was murdered and consequently canonized as a national saint, a heated controversy ensued over what religious group might claim him.²

One approach to this problem of sources is to put aside reminiscences and

---

I wish to thank John Stauffer for his excellent instruction in American cultural history and for his guidance as I wrote and edited this paper. I am grateful to David Herbert Donald and Lawrence Buell for their valuable criticisms of the manuscript.

1. Reinhold Niebuhr, "The Religion of Abraham Lincoln" in *Lincoln and the Gettysburg Address: Commemorative Papers*, ed. Allan Nevins (Urbana: Univ. of Illinois Press, 1964), 72-87.

2. For the confusion on Lincoln's religion after his death, see Merrill D. Peterson, *Lincoln in American Memory* (New York: Oxford Univ. Press, 1994), 68-69, 76, 226-30. For an overview of major reminiscences, see William E. Barton, *The Soul of Abraham Lincoln* (New York: George H. Doran, 1920), 101-221, 303-6, 309-57.

look at Lincoln's undisputed writings to see what they reveal about the shape of his beliefs. A whole line of scholars have followed this method.[3] While many have traced what Lincoln said, none has traced how he said it. Numerous writers, from Edmund Wilson to David Herbert Donald, have noted that Lincoln's references to God and religion became more frequent and profound in his later life,[4] but there has never been an attempt to chart comprehensively how the emphases, nuances, and shadings of his religious rhetoric developed over the years.[5]

The time has come for such an approach, for it sheds new light on one of the most confusing aspects of Lincoln's religion. He said throughout his life that he believed in *providence*, that is, the ordination of all earthly events by a higher power, which he frequently called God. Lincoln's lifelong use of this concept makes it hard to tell whether his beliefs on the subject ever changed, and if so, when and how.[6] Literary analysis reveals that, even though Lincoln

---

3. William J. Wolf was the first to call for a tighter focus on Lincoln's writings. Though Wolf looked more closely at Lincoln's works than had his predecessors, he still cited many reminiscences. See *The Almost Chosen People: A Study of the Religion of Abraham Lincoln* (Garden City, N.Y.: Doubleday, 1959). Elton Trueblood's use of sources was similar. See *Abraham Lincoln: Theologian of American Anguish* (New York: Harper and Row, 1973). Wolf's stated goal to focus on Lincoln's works was executed much more faithfully by Glen E. Thurow, *Abraham Lincoln and American Political Religion* (Albany: State Univ. of New York Press, 1976), and David Hein, "Lincoln's Theology and Political Ethics" in *Essays on Lincoln's Faith and Politics*, ed. Kenneth W Thompson (Lanham, Md.: Univ. Press of America, 1983). There are, of course, other strategies for dealing with the sources on Lincoln's religion. Wayne C. Temple's study includes a staggering number of sources of varying reliability and is quite useful as a catalogue of references to religion both in Lincoln's writings and in the reminiscence literature. See *Abraham Lincoln: From Skeptic to Prophet* (Mahomet, Ill.: Mayhaven Publishing, 1995). The most insightful analysis of the reminiscences (and the one that best integrates them with Lincoln's writings) appears in Allen C. Guelzo's intellectual biography, *Abraham Lincoln: Redeemer President* (Grand Rapids, Mich.: Eerdmans, 1999), which appeared after I completed this essay. Guelzo concludes, as I do, that Lincoln gravitated toward Calvinism in the course of the war, that providentialism superseded his liberal views to some extent, and that the change contributed to his decision about emancipation. However, where I consider this change to be a full-fledged transformation, Guelzo believes it was much more limited and that Lincoln retained a melancholy doubt about God's redemptive power (115–21, 149–60, 318–29, 341–45, 416–21, 447, 461–63).

4. Edmund Wilson, *Patriotic Gore: Studies in the Literature of the American Civil War* (New York: Oxford Univ. Press, 1966), 99–106; David Herbert Donald, *Lincoln* (New York: Simon and Schuster, 1995), 337.

5. This essay focuses as much as possible on Lincoln's own writings. The quotations in the text include three Lincoln utterances not included in Basler's *Collected Works*, but each of these comes from a contemporary account by a well-established source: in my note 60, Gideon Welles's diary entry on the cabinet meeting of Sept. 22, 1862; in my notes 60 and 62–63, Salmon P. Chase's diary entry on the same meeting; and in my note 69, Oville Hickman Browning's diary entry on his conversation with Lincoln on Dec. 18, 1862.

6. Barton states that Lincoln's religion went through an evolutionary process but does not give a time frame in *The Soul of Abraham Lincoln*, 260–90. In *The Almost Chosen People*, Wolf asserts that

always subscribed to the same technical definition of providence, the role that this concept played in his rhetoric underwent a gradual but dramatic change during his presidency. Before the Civil War, the understanding of providence that appeared in Lincoln's rhetoric was complacent and conveniently amenable to the existing arrangements of society. Lincoln's God lacked any palpable motive force or determinative power. Such a conception was made possible in part by perfectionist and postmillennial currents in the Protestantism of his day. Indeed, his portrayal of a relaxed and accommodating God was typical of his contemporaries, especially when they spoke on the potentially explosive subject of slavery. In the prewar years, it was not from religion but from secular republicanism that Lincoln's rhetoric and actions drew their energy. Throughout the 1850s, the principles of liberty, equality, and self-government had the force and weight of sacred doctrine in Lincoln's mind, while Christian ideas represented merely a corollary to republican principles, or at most a useful tool of argument for secular ends. But once Lincoln became president and began to prosecute war against the Confederacy, his statements on religion took on a different cast. The notion of God that appeared in his language gravitated ever closer to that of Calvinism: an activist, independent, and judgmental God whose designs informed every single earthly event but whose purposes often seemed inscrutable to human eyes. Linked to this notion was a Calvinist-like view of humanity as utterly sinful, deserving of retribution, and entirely dependent on God in all aspects of life. Lincoln's deep commitment to republicanism never lost its motive power, but by the end of the war, his new Calvinist tendencies acquired strength equal to that of his never-changing democratic beliefs.

Lincoln certainly was not the only American to invoke Calvinist ideas in response to the war. Americans in this period had at their disposal a longstanding Calvinist tradition originating with the Puritans of the colonial era. Though Puritan doctrine no longer possessed the dominance that it had exercised in colonial New England, it still carved out a significant place for itself in the pluralist religious culture of the nineteenth century.[7] For instance, the Baptist sermons that Lincoln

---

Lincoln's religious evolution was well under way by the early 1850s and that it continued through the end of the Civil War. Wilson says that the transformation was concurrent with the war in *Patriotic Gore*, 99–106. Trueblood argues that Lincoln's spiritual growth was confined to the first two years of the war in *Abraham Lincoln: Theologian of American Anguish*, 26–47, 118, while Hein claims that Lincoln's beliefs never changed in his "Lincoln's Theology and Political Ethics," 111–12.

7. For the pervasiveness of Calvinism and the increasing reaction against it during the first half of the 1800s, see Nathan O. Hatch, *The Democratization of American Christianity* (New Haven: Yale Univ. Press, 1989), 170–79. For a broad overview of the religious history of the period, see Sydney E. Ahlstrom, *A Religious History of the American People* (New Haven: Yale Univ. Press, 1972), 385–509.

heard at his parents' church in the 1810s and 1820s and the Presbyterian sermons that he heard at his wife's church in the 1850s and 1860s were all laced with Calvinist doctrine.[8] Northern preachers were in large part drawing on the American Calvinist tradition when, in their effort to explain the Civil War, they spoke ever more frequently of a judgmental and interventionist God.[9] Since the Puritans originated the American Calvinist tradition and gave it its most undiluted expression, I use their ideas, and those of their best-known theologian, Jonathan Edwards, as a clear marker by which to gauge changes in Lincoln's religious language. One might consider the citation of Puritans like Edwards to be anachronistic in a study of Lincoln, but we must remember that Edwards articulated ideas that were still usable for nineteenth-century believers. In fact, Edwards' writings achieved their greatest popularity not during his own lifetime, but during Lincoln's.[10]

Lincoln's wartime rhetoric drew on ancient traditions that remained popular in American religious culture and that achieved a special resurgence during the Civil War. But this does not mean that his words can be reduced to a simple mirroring of public opinion. Surely Lincoln's acute sensitivity to the public mind had something to do with the change in his language, yet his rhetorical development exhibited enough differences from the typical line of the Northern pulpit that it deserves to be read on its own terms. Though he did emphasize divine activism and human dependency, he never adopted other themes common among Northern preachers, such as their belief that the war was a premillennial event or that it was a holy crusade against Southern rebelliousness and slavery.[11]

Lincoln's religious transformation was closely interwoven with his policies

---

8. Barton, *The Soul of Abraham Lincoln*, 271-72; Wolf, "Abraham Lincoln and Calvinism" in *Calvinism and the Political Order*, eds. George L. Hunt and John T. McNeill (Philadelphia: Westminster Press, 1965), 141-43; Guelzo, *Abraham Lincoln: Redeemer President*, 36-38. Each scholar claims that this Calvinist preaching had a significant influence on Lincoln's beliefs.

9. For Northern invocations of an activist and judgmental God as a result of the Civil War, especially in the pulpit, see James H. Moorhead, *American Apocalypse: Yankee Protestants and the Civil War, 1860-1869* (New Haven: Yale Univ. Press, 1978), chaps. 1-3. For similar trends in the laity, see Anne C. Rose, *Victorian America and the Civil War* (Cambridge: Cambridge Univ. Press, 1992), 59-67.

10. For Edwards's popularity in the antebellum period, see Joseph A. Conforti, *Jonathan Edwards, Religious Tradition, and American Culture* (Chapel Hill: Univ. of North Carolina Press, 1995), chaps. 1-5. Conforti states that Edwards's Calvinist metaphysics, while of great importance to nineteenth-century scholars, were not as popular in the mainstream as his works on piety. Nevertheless, a reminiscence by Noah Brooks indicates that Lincoln knew of Edwards's *Freedom of the Will* and wished to read it. See *Lincoln Observed: Civil War Dispatches of Noah Brooks*, ed. Michael Burlingame (Baltimore: Johns Hopkins Univ. Press, 1998), 219.

11. For these themes in Northern religion, see Moorhead, *American Apocalypse*, 35-56; George M. Fredrickson, "The Coming of the Lord: The Northern Protestant Clergy and the Civil War Crisis"

regarding emancipation and war. He first departed from his old religious views because of the challenges of waging war, and he latched onto a Calvinist conception of providence when confronting his uncertainty over emancipation policy. He then discerned that freedom for the slaves and the redemptive bloodshed of war seemed to be features of providential design, and these realizations made it justifiable for him to stick by his emancipation policy and his relentless prosecution of the war, despite pressure to the contrary.

This reading of Lincoln's religious development gives us new angles on scholarly disputes. William J. Wolf and David Hein both assert that Lincoln's religious convictions were the foundation for his belief in democracy and his hatred of slavery, though they differ as to what those convictions were and what role they played. Both of their arguments cut against Lincoln's language.[12] This study argues instead that Lincoln's democratic and antislavery beliefs were fully formed in a secular fashion long before his religious ideas came into their own.

On the more fundamental question of Lincoln's belief in his own capacity to discern the divine will, there has been much confusion. Wolf makes moderate claims in this area, stating that Lincoln recognized the limits of his mortal perception but still worked to do the right thing by making provisional interpretations of God's purposes. Yet Wolf muddles his own model: he cites a questionable story about Lincoln receiving direct revelation, and he characterizes Lincoln

---

in *Religion and the American Civil War*, eds. Randall M. Miller, Harry S. Stout, and Charles Reagan Wilson (New York: Oxford Univ. Press, 1998), 119-22. For the uniqueness of Lincoln's views, see Mark A. Noll, "'Both Pray to the Same God': The Singularity of Lincoln's Faith in the Era of the Civil War," *Journal of the Abraham Lincoln Association* 18.1 (Winter 1997): 1-26.

12. Wolf says that Lincoln's prewar antislavery beliefs were derived from his religious convictions (*The Almost Chosen People*, 89-103, 110-14), but Melvin B. Endy Jr. rightly points out that the passage on which Wolf largely bases this claim turns out to be a rarity in the body of Lincoln's rhetoric in his "Abraham Lincoln and American Civil Religion: A Reinterpretation," *Church History* 44 (June 1975): 236. Further, Wolf argues that Lincoln considered America to have a special, divinely ordained destiny to realize democracy. See *The Almost Chosen People*, 24-25, 149-53, 184-85. Though Lincoln did speak somewhat along these lines in the prewar years, Wolf's interpretation conflates Lincoln's belief in American republicanism with his belief in God to a far greater extent than is justified by his wartime rhetoric. Further, Hein rightly points out that Lincoln always focused less on America's peculiar destiny as a special nation than on the universality of republican principles. But Hein then errs, I believe, when he claims that Lincoln's lifelong convictions about democratic equality and antislavery rested on his belief in a universal community of all humanity under God. See his "Lincoln's Theology and Political Ethics," 142-46. Lincoln's statements on the inevitability of racial division belied such a belief, as in his "Address on Colonization to a Committee of Colored Men, Washington, D.C.," Aug. 14, 1862, in *Abraham Lincoln: Speeches and Writings*, ed. Don E. Fehrenbacher, 2 vols. (New York: Library of America, 1989), 2:353 (hereafter cited as *SW*). Further, Hein gives not one quote from Lincoln in which universal community is expressed in religious terms.

as "one of God's latter-day prophets."[13] This has opened the door for Melvin B. Endy Jr. to assert that Lincoln thought he was communicating directly with God.[14] Hein reacts against Endy's bold interpretation by arguing the exact opposite: Lincoln considered God's will to be completely opaque and thought it pointless to try to discern it.[15] The rhetorical evidence suggests that we ought to walk a path between extremes and interpret Lincoln more along the lines of Wolf's moderate claims. In the tradition of discerning special providences initiated by the Puritans and continuing through much of American religious history, Lincoln came to believe that, while as a mortal he could never know God's mind with certainty, he could still search into God's purposes when those purposes seemed to be manifest, and he could allow his own mortal perceptions of God's will to inform his actions, especially when this helped him to face adverse circumstances or make difficult decisions.

As we embark on an in-depth examination of Lincoln's transformation, our first task is to contextualize his religious outlook on politics as it stood in the 1850s. In this period, many Americans—looking back on their remarkable Revolution, their explosive geographic expansion, and their material prosperity—explained these developments in the framework of postmillennialism, or the idea that God's kingdom would arrive on earth gradually by natural means. In this scheme, the U.S. was the new Israel, and it was God's design to improve the nation morally and materially. Sin was destined to fade away over time.[16] This perfectionist doctrine went hand-in-hand with a broad de-emphasis on sin by popular preachers such as Charles Finney, who claimed that human beings were capable of bringing about their own salvation, in contrast to the less popular and older view of Edwards and the Puritans, who insisted that only God could lift humans out of total depravity.[17]

Postmillennialism and perfectionism provided Americans with a way out of their moral dilemma over slavery. Many Americans considered slavery a great

---

13. For Wolf's moderate claims, see *The Almost Chosen People*, 186–87; for his more grandiose references to Lincoln's prophetic qualities, see 24–25, 184. Wolf cites an 1899 reminiscence about Lincoln and direct revelation on 124–25.

14. Endy, "Abraham Lincoln and American Civil Religion: A Reinterpretation." Though Endy makes some excellent criticisms of prevailing interpretations, his thesis is severely weakened by the use of unreliable sources.

15. Hein, "Lincoln's Theology and Political Ethics."

16. Moorhead, *American Apocalypse*, 9; Fredrickson, "The Coming of the Lord," 115.

17. Finney, *Lectures on Revivals of Religion by Charles Grandison Finney*, ed. William G. McLoughlin (Cambridge: Harvard Univ. Press, 1960), 13.

evil and yet saw no practical way to get rid of it, except over the course of many decades. The supposed inevitability of providential progress assured Americans that, even if they personally could do nothing to end slavery in the present, the ugly institution was sure to disappear in the grand scheme of history.[18] Henry Clay, Lincoln's model for how to deal with slavery, hated the peculiar institution, though his commitment to constitutional law and public order prevented him from attacking it in the states where it already existed. Providence made this a justifiable position for Clay. In an 1839 speech, he confronted the question of whether blacks were forever to remain slaves in the U.S., only to assure his listeners that "the same Providence who has hitherto guided and governed us" would slowly make slavery disappear.[19] In keeping with God's supposed method for ending slavery, Clay advocated gradual emancipation coupled with colonization of the freedmen in Africa. Such a scheme meant that African Americans would return to their ancestral homeland having been Christianized by their sojourn in America. Clay rhapsodized on the benevolence and symmetry of this divine plan in an 1827 oration: "May it not be one of the great designs of the Ruler of the Universe . . . thus to transform an original crime, into a signal blessing to that most unfortunate part of the globe?"[20]

This sunny prediction Lincoln quoted approvingly in his eulogy on Clay in 1852. He added that Clay's "suggestion of the possible ultimate redemption of the African race and African continent, was made twenty-five years ago. Every succeeding year has added strength to the hope of its realization. May it indeed be realized!" Lincoln inherited from Clay not only a dislike for slavery and an affinity for colonization, but also an optimistic hope that providence would take care of the entire problem. In Lincoln's words, colonization will hopefully be carried out "so gradually, that neither races nor individuals shall have suffered by the change." Despite slavery's ugliness in the present, the happy result can erase previous iniquity: Americans have the chance one day to restore "a captive people to their long-lost fatherland, with bright prospects for the future." The scheme of colonization needed to be implemented by "present and coming generations of our countrymen," a vague phrase that relieved Lincoln and his contemporaries from any specific burden of responsibility.

18. Moorhead, *American Apocalypse*, 87–89; Fredrickson, "The Coming of the Lord," 115–16.
19. Clay, "Petitions for the Abolition of Slavery" (1839) in *The Life and Speeches of Henry Clay*, ed. Daniel Mallory (New York: Van Amringe and Bixby, 1844), 372.
20. Quoted in Lincoln, "Eulogy on Henry Clay at Springfield, Illinois," July 6, 1852, in *SW*, 1:271.

Not only would the sinful practice of slavery be painlessly removed, but, Lincoln hoped, the nation would escape punishment for committing the sin. At one point in the eulogy on Clay, Lincoln acknowledged God's just wrath against the slaveholding Egyptians: "Pharaoh's country was cursed with plagues, and his hosts were drowned in the Red Sea for striving to retain a captive people who had already served them more than four hundred years." But in the same breath, Lincoln asked that his own country be excused from retribution: "May like disasters never befall us!" He thought it would be "glorious" for America to be redeemed from slavery if "neither races nor individuals shall have suffered by the change."[21]

Lincoln's words can be taken as a complacent rationalization for the status quo. Consequences are not faced head-on. The call for action is postponed to the future. Indeed, as of 1852, Lincoln had never demonstrated any serious resolve to act against slavery.[22] At every turn in his eulogy, complacent optimism clouds reality: he says that "every succeeding year has added strength to the hope for [the] realization" of God's positive design,[23] when in fact the American Colonization Society had established no colonies since its lackluster efforts in the 1820s.[24] Disliking slavery, but feeling unable to act against it, Lincoln found that his sense of providence could help make the national predicament acceptable.[25]

In keeping with this relatively complacent conception of providence, God did not constitute much of a motive force in Lincoln's prewar writing, even in discussions of religious issues. Take for example his most extensive utterance on religion during the 1850s: a fragment written to refute the biblical justification of slavery published by clergyman Frederick Ross in 1857. In Lincoln's whole statement, God never appeared as an active agent, and Lincoln in no way relied upon God to refute Ross's biblical justification of slavery. Rather, Lincoln pointed out that God and the Bible were not proper tools for resolving the slavery controversy: "the Almighty gives no audable answer to the question, and his revelation—the Bible—gives none—or, at most, none but such as admits of a squabble, as to it's meaning." Lincoln refuted Ross by exposing his self-interested motives: "If [Ross]

---

21. "Eulogy on Henry Clay at Springfield, Illinois."
22. Lincoln's antislavery activities were few before the Kansas-Nebraska bill of 1854. See Donald, *Lincoln*.
23. "Eulogy on Henry Clay at Springfield, Illinois."
24. On colonization as a rationalization for inaction on slavery, see Robert Abzug, *Cosmos Crumbling* (New York: Oxford Univ. Press, 1994), 134.
25. Endy, "Abraham Lincoln and American Civil Religion," makes a similar point about Lincoln's complacency regarding slavery in relation to providence (238); however, he uses this point to cast doubt on Lincoln's true commitment to the Declaration of Independence—a claim with which I disagree.

decides that God Wills [his slave] Sambo to continue a slave, he thereby retains his own comfortable position." Lincoln asked whether, under these circumstances, Ross will be "actuated by that perfect impartiality, which has ever been considered most favorable to correct decisions?" Neither God nor the Bible was needed to refute Ross. Lincoln used his skills as a lawyer to expose the groundless arguments of a selfish man who unfairly dragged Scripture into a controversy where it was not relevant. Even when Lincoln referred to the Bible, he did so more to expose the absurdity of proslavery theology than to invoke divine justice against slaveholders, as when he aped the claim that slavery benefits the slaves: "Wolves devouring lambs, not because it is good for their own greedy maws, but because it is good for the lambs!!!"[26] While Lincoln believed that slavery could not be justified on religious grounds, God was not at the center of his thinking.

Republicanism, not God or scripture, formed the true core of Lincoln's prewar thought and rhetoric. Nothing could override the ideals expressed in the Declaration of Independence. In a speech at Lewistown, Illinois, during his 1858 Senate campaign, Lincoln implored any listeners who ceased to believe that all men are created equal to drop all petty concerns and "come back to the truths that are in the Declaration of Independence."[27] In this wholly secular paean to the Declaration, Lincoln's language was more characteristic of religion than when he actually talked about God and scripture. The legal approach of his reply to Ross and the complacent rationalizations of his eulogy on Clay were swept aside. American republicanism took on attributes that might seem more appropriate for describing the Calvinist God before a devout congregation. Republican ideals constituted a kind of supernatural force: Lincoln called the Declaration "immortal" and its principles "sacred"; the doctrines at stake constituted "something higher" than "earthly honors." Further, he employed a pattern of declension and repentance among citizens in regard to the Declaration, just as there was among sinners in regard to God. Lincoln urged listeners who had strayed from the Declaration to return to the fold: "let me entreat you to come back"; "come back to the truths that are in the Declaration of Independence."

More important, the Declaration existed on its own terms to Lincoln; it was

---

26. "On Pro-slavery Theology," in *SW*, 1:685–86.

27. For the quotes given in this discussion of the "Speech at Lewistown, Illinois," Aug. 17, 1858, see Abraham Lincoln, *The Collected Works of Abraham Lincoln*, ed. Roy P. Basler, 9 vols. (New Brunswick, N.J.: Rutgers Univ. Press, 1953), 2:547 (hereafter cited as *CW*). For the appropriation of Puritan homiletics to express American national identity, see Sacvan Bercovitch, *The American Jeremiad* (Madison: Univ. of Wisconsin Press, 1978).

not to be modified by individuals. Lincoln insisted that no one could insert the word "not" into the phrase "all men are created equal." To do so would "take away from [the Declaration's] grandeur, and mutilate the fair symmetry of its proportions." The Calvinist God possessed a similarly complete independence from mortals. Edwards scoffed at humans' foolish hope that they have "power to move correspondent affections in God," and he acknowledged "man's absolute dependence on the operations of God's holy spirit."[28] In a further religious parallel, Lincoln recognized the Declaration as a forceful agent in people's lives. Using the passive voice, Lincoln claimed "to be actuated in this contest" by the agent of American republicanism. The Declaration itself obligated people to change their normal earthly ways—"to drop every paltry and insignificant thought for any man's success." It appeared as a supernatural force capable of changing the status quo, in contrast to Lincoln's description in the Clay eulogy of a subtle and invisible God who legitimizes the status quo.

Like the God of Calvin, the Declaration was so tremendous that all mortal beings were abased before it. Extolling the great document, Lincoln devalued all other things: "thought for any man's success" is "paltry and insignificant"; citizens must have "no thought for the political fate of any man whomsoever." In comparison with the Declaration, one man's political fortune "is nothing; I am nothing; Judge Douglas is nothing." Lincoln told his listeners that, if they would only preserve the Declaration, "you may not only defeat me for the Senate, but you may take me and put me to death." The Declaration was so awesome that Lincoln felt an urge to be humiliated and destroyed for its sake. Edwards had a similar reaction to God. Facing the supreme being, he wished for the worst abasement he could imagine: "Others speak of their longing to be humbled to the dust [before God]. Though that may be a proper expression for them, I always think to myself, that I ought to be humbled down below hell."[29]

For Lincoln, political ideals took on the force and weight of religious convictions. In many of his prewar speeches, America's free institutions demanded a religion-like commitment. As early as 1838, Lincoln hoped that the rule of law would become "the *political religion* of the nation."[30] In a speech against the Ne-

---

28. Edwards, "A Faithful Narrative of the Surprising Work of God" in *A Jonathan Edwards Reader*, eds. John E. Smith, Harry S. Stout, and Kenneth P. Minkema (New Haven: Yale Univ. Press, 1995), 71; "Personal Narrative" in *A Jonathan Edwards Reader*, 291.

29. Edwards, "Personal Narrative," 295.

30. "Address to the Young Men's Lyceum of Springfield, Illinois," Jan. 27, 1838, in *SW*, 1:32.

braska bill in 1854, he repeatedly referred to the preservation of liberty as the "ancient faith" of the nation.[31]

With secular political traditions taking on the seriousness of religion, Lincoln's actual references to God in his political speeches merely provided a corollary to his republican ideals. Such a reference occurred in an earlier section of the Lewistown speech. Lincoln quoted the "truths to be self-evident" passage from the Declaration and elaborated, "This was [the founders'] lofty, and wise, and noble understanding of the justice of the Creator to his creatures."[32] Wolf says that this sentence and those that follow demonstrate the "theological foundation" of the Declaration as Lincoln saw it.[33] This may be true at the level of step-by-step logic, but the language does not suggest that Lincoln's conception of the Declaration depended on his theological views. His focus was not on God; he was much more enthralled with the founders. God starts out as a noun ("Creator") in the sentence quoted above, then is reduced in Lincoln's next sentence to a possessive adjective: "Yes, gentlemen, to all His creatures, to the whole great family of man." In the sentence after, God is further reduced to the abstract adjective "Divine": "In [the founders'] enlightened belief, nothing stamped with the Divine image and likeness was sent into this world to be . . . imbruted by its fellows." God then disappears for the final ten sentences of the speech. Lincoln never makes God the subject of any clause. In fact, he directly passes over the agency of God with the passive construction "was sent into the world." Meanwhile, in the two sentences after the Creator has disappeared from view, the founders loom larger, empowered by strong verbs: "They grasped not only the whole race of man then living, but they reached forward and seized upon the farthest posterity. They erected a beacon to guide their children."[34] Rhetorically, God was squeezed toward the margin.

Though Lincoln thought slavery evil because it was incompatible with republicanism, he believed that Americans could justifiably tolerate the institution so long as they retained the ideal of universal liberty and remained on a trajectory, however gradual, toward emancipation. In an 1858 speech, Lincoln explained this idea through a biblical analogy. He closely paraphrased the Sermon on the

---

31. "Speech on the Kansas-Nebraska Act at Peoria, Illinois," Oct. 16, 1854, in *SW*, 1:328.
32. "Speech at Lewistown, Illinois," Aug. 17, 1858, in *CW*, 2:546.
33. Wolf, *The Almost Chosen People*, 96.
34. "Speech at Lewistown, Illinois." Endy, in "Abraham Lincoln and American Civil Religion: A Reinterpretation," points out that passages like this one, which place Lincoln's opposition to slavery in the context of universal humanity under God, are rare in Lincoln's speeches (236).

Mount: "As your Father in Heaven is perfect, be ye also perfect." According to Lincoln, God meant this admonition to be "a standard, and he who did most towards reaching that standard, attained the highest degree of moral perfection. So I say in relation to the principle that all men are created equal, let it be as nearly reached as we can." This principle argued for the non-extension of slavery: "If we cannot give freedom to every creature, let us do nothing that will impose slavery upon any other creature."[35] At first glance, these words might seem a religious justification for Lincoln's opposition to slavery. But, if we look closely at Lincoln's carefully composed sentences, we see that his opposition to slavery stands on its own secular terms. The religious reference appeared purely for the purpose of analogy. Lincoln drew a parallel between the manner in which a religious person must strive to be perfect like God and the manner in which an American citizen must strive to follow the principles of the Declaration. In both cases, persons worked toward an unrealizable ideal. But to construe the passage as anything other than an analogy muddles Lincoln's construction of language. If Lincoln had wanted to use religion as the basis for antislavery policy, he could have and he would have. He chose not to.

While for most of the 1850s Lincoln believed in a marginal God and a providential plan for emancipation far in the future, he displayed uncertainty about these issues when the slavery controversy reached new heights in 1859. In a speech attacking Douglas, Lincoln paraphrased Thomas Jefferson's famous warning on slavery, "I tremble for my country when I remember that God is just!" He then elaborated: "We know how [Jefferson] looked upon [slavery] when he thus expressed himself. There was danger . . . of the avenging justice of God in that little unimportant popular sovereignty question of Judge Douglas. He [Jefferson] supposed there was a question of God's eternal justice wrapped up in the enslaving of any race of men, or any man, and that those who did so braved the arm of Jehovah—that when a nation thus dared the Almighty every friend of that nation had cause to dread His wrath."[36] Where before Lincoln used biblical analysis or oblique references to the Creator, he now envisioned the deity as an active character opposing slavery. This new God interacted directly with people: he could be "dared" and could exercise "His wrath." Lincoln imbued God with a strong physical image, "the arm of Jehovah." Further, he mentioned "the avenging justice of God" in counterpoint to "that little unimportant popular

---

35. "Speech at Chicago, Illinois," July 10, 1858, in *SW*, 1:458.
36. "Speech at Columbus, Ohio," Sept. 16, 1859, in *SW*, 2:41-42.

sovereignty question of Judge Douglas," thus contrasting divine omnipotence with human weakness in a manner reminiscent of Calvinism—Edwards said that "all the kings of the earth before God are as grasshoppers."[37]

Yet Lincoln did not seem truly committed to this new rhetoric about God. The whole statement was, technically, not in Lincoln's own voice; rather, it served as an explication of Jefferson's ideas. Even the most powerful sentence began with the equivocal phrase: "He supposed." Further, Lincoln's description of God lacked immediacy because he phrased it entirely in the past tense: "there was danger"; "those who did so"; "a nation thus dared"; "every friend . . . had cause." Especially interesting is the sentence, "there was a question of God's eternal justice wrapped up in the enslaving of any race of men." The phrase "wrapped up" is vague and noncommittal, suggesting that Lincoln sensed some connection between God and slavery but felt unsure of the specifics. The model of an active God was in front of him, but he did not know yet what to make of it. Finally, the continued presence of Jefferson from the beginning of the passage to the end suggest that, although Lincoln made a new foray into religious language, he still relied on republicanism as the foundation of his rhetoric.

Starting in 1860, Lincoln faced the tremendous responsibility of leading the nation at a time of crisis. After his nomination, he felt "deeply, and even painfully sensible of the great responsibility which is inseparable from [the] honor."[38] After the election, he realized that he had "a task before [him] greater than that which rested upon Washington."[39] As a result, Lincoln now wanted God to be on his side, helping him. He began to consider God as an active agent. As Donald notes, Lincoln now invoked God's aid more frequently than ever before.[40] This was a significant departure. Yet, at the same time, we need to recognize that Lincoln's new invocations of God amounted to little more than devices of self-protection. Lincoln's language focused narrowly on his own success: "Without the assistance of [the] Divine Being . . . I cannot succeed. With that assistance I cannot fail."[41] His hope to become a "humble instrument in the hands of the Almighty"[42] likewise displayed his personal wish for divine help. Lincoln tried

---

37. Edwards, "Sinners in the Hands of an Angry God" in *A Jonathan Edwards Reader*, 99.
38. "Reply to Committee of the Republican National Convention, Springfield, Illinois," May 19, 1860, in *SW*, 2:157.
39. "Farewell Address at Springfield, Illinois," Feb. 11, 1861, in *SW*, 2:199.
40. Donald, *Lincoln*, 337.
41. "Farewell Address at Springfield, Illinois."
42. "Address to the New Jersey Senate at Trenton, New Jersey," Feb. 21, 1861, in *SW*, 2:209.

to imbue the American electorate with divine wisdom. In this way, he affirmed himself by defining his election as the work of God: "I must trust in that Supreme Being who has never forsaken this favored land, through the instrumentality of this great and intelligent people."[43] The same pattern appeared in the First Inaugural Address: "If the Almighty Ruler of nations . . . be on your side of the North, or on yours of the South, that truth, and that justice, will surely prevail, by the judgment of this great tribunal, the American people."[44] Lincoln's changing religious worldview was not yet solid enough to stand separate from republicanism as a force in its own right.

Lincoln saw no need for war, and he hoped that an active God would simply make the crisis disappear. At the inauguration, he wistfully predicted that a spiritual force would change the minds of the Rebels: "The mystic chords of memory . . . will yet swell the chorus of the Union, when again touched, as surely they will be, by the better angels of our nature."[45] He hoped in 1861 for a speedy providential resolution without consequences, just as he had hoped to avoid consequences for the sin of slavery in his eulogy on Clay in 1852.

As war broke out that spring, Lincoln's invocations of God continued in much the same vein. For the first few months, religious language served mainly as a channel through which to hope for success: "let us renew our trust in God, and go forward without fear."[46] After the Union defeat at Bull Run on July 21, however, it became clear that success would not come easily. Recognizing the seriousness of the crisis, Congress called for a national day of fasting and prayer, which Lincoln declared by proclamation. In some ways, the proclamation reflected familiar trends in Lincoln's religious rhetoric. The war was an act of providence: Americans must "recognize the hand of God in this terrible visitation."[47] Lincoln asked for divine aid to meet the challenges ahead, imploring God to confer "a blessing upon [the Union's] present and prospective action."

43. "Speech at Buffalo, New York," Feb. 16, 1861, in *CW,* 4:220-21.
44. "First Inaugural Address," Mar. 4, 1861, in *SW,* 2:223.
45. Ibid., 2:224.
46. "Message to Congress in Special Session," July 4, 1861, in *SW,* 2:261.
47. For all quotes from "Proclamation of a National Fast Day," Aug. 12, 1861, see *SW,* 2:264. This is the first of four presidential proclamations by Lincoln cited in this study, the other three being "Proclamation Appointing a National Fast Day," Mar. 30, 1863; "Proclamation of Thanksgiving," July 15, 1863; and "Proclamation of Thanksgiving and Prayer," Sept. 3, 1864. Hein believes it is better not to use Lincoln's proclamations in a study of his religion, for it is not certain that Lincoln composed them. See his "Lincoln's Theology and Political Ethics," 110-11, 120-23. Indeed, it is documented that Secretary of State William H. Seward wrote Lincoln's "Proclamation of Thanksgiving," of October 3, 1863. See *CW,* 6:497n. No one is sure to what degree Lincoln shared with

Then, for the first time, Lincoln added the dynamic of sin and chastisement: he acknowledged that the affliction of war was "most justly deserved." Further, he adopted the model of a national soul. Like Israel of old, the American people could sin, endure punishment, repent, and receive blessings as a collective body. "Our own beloved Country, once, by the blessing of God, united, prosperous and happy, is now afflicted with faction and civil war" due in part to "our own faults and crimes as a nation."

Despite these innovations, the proclamation also indicated that, for the most part, Lincoln's worldview had not changed much. His rhetoric demonstrated no close apprehension of sin or redemption. Countless preachers interpreted military defeat as a chastisement for collective sin in 1861.[48] Lincoln's proclamation sounded like an automatic repetition of this hackneyed theme, mainly because of his inadequate use of language. The tone was perfunctory: "Whereas it is fit and becoming in all people, at all times, to acknowledge and revere the Supreme Government of God; to bow in humble submission to his chastisements; to confess and deplore their sins and transgressions in the full conviction that the fear of the Lord is the beginning of wisdom; and to pray, with all fervency and contrition, for the pardon of their past offences, and for a blessing upon their present and prospective action." We have not even reached the main verb, and already the

---

Seward the authorship of the other proclamations. I argue that the proclamations that I cite differ markedly in their rhetorical strength and emphasis and that these differences correspond with the phases of religious development through which Lincoln was passing at the time he issued each one, as established by his other writings. This suggests that Lincoln did play a large role in the composition of these four documents. To support the opposite argument, Hein cites Carl Sandburg, *Abraham Lincoln: The War Years*, 4 vols. (New York: Harcourt, 1939), 2:359, 3:375, but Sandburg actually supports my case at least as much as he does Hein's. Sandburg thinks that Lincoln and Seward probably collaborated on these documents to varying degrees, but he adds that Lincoln seems to have taken a stronger hand in the authorship as the war progressed, as indicated by the "distinct trend toward a deeper religious tone" (3:375). I assume that Lincoln wrote all the documents and that the stronger religious sense of those from the latter half of the war (e.g., "Proclamation Appointing a National Fast Day," Mar. 30, 1863) indicates Lincoln's deepening apprehension of God's sovereignty; it is just as much in keeping with this interpretation to assume that Lincoln allowed others to write the early proclamations (resulting in the perfunctory and impersonal tone of "Proclamation of a National Fast Day," Aug. 12, 1861) and then took greater part in the authorship when he was ready. Even without taking such factors into account, one thing is certain: we risk distorting Lincoln's religion just as much by rejecting the documents as by accepting them, since, in the vacuum of conclusive documentary evidence, it is just as possible that Lincoln wrote the proclamations as that he did not. We ought to hear and weigh interpretations from both sides.

48. David B. Chesebrough, ed., *"God Ordained This War": Sermons on the Sectional Crisis, 1830-1865* (Columbia: Univ. of South Carolina Press, 1991), 6-7.

sentence seems tiresome. It sounds as if Lincoln had collected a bunch of religious catchphrases and pasted them together in the excessively clausal style of a legal brief. All the expected phrases are there—"Supreme Government of God"; "humble submission"; "fear of the Lord"; "beginning of wisdom"—but they pile up on each other so mechanically that the statement imparts no true sting. The numerous word pairs might be appropriate for a contract or a will, but in this context they make the language hopelessly artificial: "fit and becoming"; "acknowledge and revere"; "confess and deplore"; "sins and transgressions"; "fervency and contrition." Further, Lincoln was so quick to collect the benefits of God's forgiveness that his acknowledgments of guilt lost their gravity. In Lincoln's exhortation that people pray "for a pardon of their past offences, and for a blessing on their present and prospective action," the use of "and" placed the two phrases on an equal plane, making them seem like unconnected items in a list and thereby ignoring the process by which penitence leads to redemption. Worst of all, Lincoln said that America had committed "crimes" and "offences," but he presented no idea of the nature of these crimes and offences. His words do not reflect the reality or seriousness of sin. Considering that Lincoln as of 1861 conceived of God as little more than a source of assistance, this is not very surprising.

In the first months of the war, Lincoln's views on slavery in relation to providence shifted moderately, while remaining basically within their original framework. Previously, he had believed that providence would cause slavery to disappear gradually. Now, he believed that the war itself had provided the impetus to begin that gradual process: in his message to Congress that December, he anticipated that many slaves would be freed by the chances of war and by gradual emancipation plans that the states might adopt as a result of the crisis.[49] Yet he did not want Southern society to be overturned suddenly: he was "anxious and careful that the inevitable conflict . . . [would] not degenerate into a violent and remorseless revolutionary struggle."[50] While his views on providential emancipation had once been distant and vague, they were now immediate and real. Yet he still saw no reason to give up the view that emancipation would be gradual and controlled: the time was now right for the process to begin, but the process might take several decades. In this context, Lincoln had no qualms about revoking a proclamation of immediate emancipation by General John C. Fremont in

---

49. "Annual Message to Congress," Dec. 3, 1861, in *SW*, 2:291-92. See also Lincoln's emancipation proposals to the border states around the same time in Donald, *Lincoln*, 345-48.

50. "Annual Message to Congress," Dec. 3, 1861, 2:292.

September 1861.[51] Such a revocation did not clash with how Lincoln thought emancipation was meant to happen.

But circumstances changed. After major setbacks in the field during spring 1862, the Union began to consider extraordinary measures, including immediate emancipation of the Rebels' slaves. The president had to decide whether such a measure constituted a military necessity. This was a subjective question that left much to Lincoln's personal judgment.[52] In a vacuum of objective certainty, belief takes on a larger role,[53] and so it did in this case. Lincoln always had believed that God would appoint the proper time for emancipation. His outlook on this point never changed. What did change was that Lincoln now stood in a position to make decisions that might facilitate or obstruct the implementation of the divine plan. Thus, from summer 1862 to early 1863, while emancipation policy remained malleable, Lincoln had to face the question of what course God intended history to take.

He began searching for what God wanted him to do. Speaking to an abolitionist delegation in June 1862, he said that "it would be his earnest endeavor, with a firm reliance upon the Divine arm, and seeking light from above, to do his duty in the place to which he had been called."[54] Similar deference to God appeared in a private letter that October: "In the very responsible position in which I happen to be placed, being a humble instrument in the hands of our Heavenly Father . . . to work out his great purposes, I have desired that all my works and acts may be according to his will, and that it might be so, I have sought his aid."[55] Before the emancipation crisis, Lincoln's God appeared as an auxiliary to justify the status quo or to support preconceived human goals. Now the language reversed itself: Lincoln began with God's design, not presuming to know its ultimate intention; he then said that he wanted to follow that design and finally invoked God's aid toward that end.

As Lincoln deferred to God as an independent sovereign, he confronted the

---

51. Lincoln to John C. Fremont, Sept. 2, 1861, in *SW*, 2:266-68.

52. See the differing opinions within Lincoln's cabinet at different times in Donald, *Lincoln*, 365-66, 375-76. As Lincoln himself said, "the subject is difficult, and good men do not agree" ("Reply to Chicago Emancipation Memorial, Washington, D.C.," Sept. 13, 1862, in *SW*, 2:361). Looking back on the decision later, Lincoln admitted that he had not been certain: "I hoped for greater gain than loss; but of this, I was not entirely confident" (Lincoln to Albert G. Hodges, Apr. 4, 1864, in *SW*, 2:586).

53. William James, "The Will to Believe" (1896) in *William James: Writings 1878-1899*, ed. Gerald E. Myers (New York: Library of America, 1992), 473-74.

54. "Remarks to a Delegation of Progressive Friends," June 20, 1862, in *CW*, 5:279.

55. Lincoln to Eliza P. Gurney, Oct. 26, 1862, in *CW*, 5:478.

problem of how to discern God's will. Replying to an abolitionist memorial on September 13, he said that "it is my earnest desire to know the will of Providence in this matter. *And if I can learn what it is I will do it!*" But such a task was not easy, since "these are not . . . the days of miracles, and I suppose it will be granted that I am not to expect a direct revelation." The conflicting testimony of divines enhanced the difficulty of determining God's intention: "I am approached with the most opposite opinions and advice, and that by religious men, who are equally certain that they represent the Divine will." Revealing his frustration with this kind of theological wrestling, Lincoln said dryly, "I hope it will not be irreverent for me to say that if it is probable that God would reveal his will to others, on a point so connected with my duty, it might be supposed he would reveal it directly to me."

Throughout his interview with the abolitionists on September 13, Lincoln moved easily back and forth between the question of divine providence and the day-to-day events of the war. At one point, he promised that "whatever shall appear to be God's will I will do." At another point he insisted that "I view the matter as a practical war measure, to be decided upon according to the advantages or disadvantages it may offer to the suppression of the rebellion."[56] Readers today, more inclined toward religious skepticism and political cynicism than those of the nineteenth century, may interpret these two statements as contradictory—the former statement as an empty mouthing of religious language, and the latter as Lincoln's real intention. But we must consider the possibility that Lincoln saw these two statements as compatible: in a world ruled by a sovereign God, physical circumstances took on divine meaning and became potential indexes of providence. Calvinism runs in a similar vein: though the age of miracles and prophecy lies in the past, God continues to manifest his will by subtly manipulating worldly events.[57]

Lincoln searched for the will of providence through the events of the war. Edwards had taken a similar approach when he tried to discern, in the outcomes of contemporary wars between Catholic and Protestant powers, God's far-reaching plan for history.[58] In a similar way, the events of the Civil War became, for Lincoln, manifestations of God's intention for the future of slavery.

---

56. "Reply to Chicago Emancipation Memorial, Washington, D.C.," 2:361, 363, 367.

57. See Puritan efforts to catalogue special providences in Perry Miller, *The New England Mind: The Seventeenth Century* (Cambridge: Harvard Univ. Press, 1982), 230–31.

58. Edwards, "Notes on the Apocalypse," in *A Jonathan Edwards Reader*, 49–56. See also Edwards, *Apocalyptic Writings*, ed. Stephen J. Stein (New Haven: Yale Univ. Press, 1977), 254–57, 267, 261, 449, 459. Quoted in Bercovitch, *The American Jeremiad*, 116–17.

A week before Lincoln's conversation with the abolitionists on September 13, Robert E. Lee had invaded Maryland. A confrontation with George McClellan's forces was imminent. Lincoln decided that, if the Confederates lost the next battle, he would interpret the Union victory as a manifestation that God's will favored emancipation. On September 17, McClellan fought Lee at Antietam and sent him retreating to Virginia. Historians assert that Lincoln issued the preliminary Emancipation Proclamation directly after Antietam because, as Seward suggested, the victory would make the proclamation look like an act of strength in the eyes of the public and of foreign governments, rather than an act of desperation.[59] Though such a consideration surely influenced Lincoln's decision, the justification that he set forth in the cabinet meeting on September 22 had much more to it. Navy Secretary Gideon Welles recorded in his diary that Lincoln defined Antietam in religious terms: "[Lincoln] had made a vow, a covenant, that if God gave us the victory in the approaching battle, he would consider it an indication of Divine will, and that it was his duty to move forward in the cause of emancipation. It might be thought strange, he said, but there were times when he felt uncertain how to act; that he had in this way submitted the disposal of matters when the way was not clear to his mind what he should do. God had decided this question in favor of the slaves."[60] In the moment of

---

59. See for example Mark E. Neely Jr., *The Last, Best Hope of Earth: Abraham Lincoln and the Promise of America* (Cambridge: Harvard Univ. Press, 1995), 106–10.

60. Gideon Welles, *Diary of Gideon Welles*, ed. John T. Morse Jr., 3 vols. (Boston: Houghton Mifflin, 1911), 1:143. Arguing that Lincoln did not believe he could discern the divine will, Hein asserts that Welles's account of Lincoln's words should not be believed, partly because it differs from Treasury Secretary Salmon P. Chase's diary account of the same meeting, in which Lincoln says he "made a promise . . . to my Maker" to issue the proclamation once the Rebels were driven from Maryland. See *Inside Lincoln's Cabinet: The Civil War Diaries of Salmon P. Chase*, ed. David Donald (New York: Longmans, Green, 1954), 150. Hein states that, in Chase's account, Lincoln decides to issue the proclamation on his own and then adds a promise to God as an affirmation, whereas in the Welles's account, Lincoln reduces God to a "finite, wheeler-dealer divinity." See his "Lincoln's Theology and Political Ethics," 149. Hein misreads Welles: victory was not a reward for emancipation but "an indication of Divine will." Lincoln had "submitted the disposal of matters" to a higher power, not promised to do the right thing in exchange for good fortune. Further, the accounts by Chase and Welles are not, as Hein believes, mutually exclusive: Lincoln may have said at the outset of the meeting that he made a promise to God and then, at some other point "in the course of the discussion," as Welles says, elaborated on what he meant by this. To believe both accounts seems the better course, because it is highly unlikely that Welles simply misheard such strong statements about the agency of God. Further, Hein argues that Chase's account fits better with the fact that Lincoln had already decided on the course of emancipation as of July and was merely waiting for an opportune moment. See "Lincoln's Theology and Political Ethics," 150–51. The notion (adopted by several biographers) that in July Lincoln became irrevocably determined

decision, Lincoln did not rely on an analysis of military necessity. In fact, he felt "uncertain how to act," meaning that the question of military necessity was not clear to him. Therefore, he "submitted the disposal of matters" to providence.

Reading these words at a glance, one might think that Lincoln recognized the moral evil of slavery and initiated a holy crusade against it. Nothing could be further from the truth. When Lincoln performed "his duty," he merely fell in line with God's design for history instead of taking personal action on a moral question. Indeed, it was impossible for Lincoln to justify the Emancipation Proclamation as a moral attack on slavery, because it allowed thousands of slaves to remain in bondage in the border states and in the occupied parts of the Confederacy. For Lincoln, emancipation served as no holy crusade but merely fulfilled divine providence. "God had decided this question in favor of the slaves." God could just as easily have decided this question against the slaves and allowed the institution to survive for as many ages as he wished.[61]

Because he followed the design of God, rather than acted on his own, Lincoln downplayed himself to an extraordinary degree during the cabinet meeting. A man making one of the riskiest decisions in American history displayed little confidence in himself. In his diary, Treasury Secretary Salmon P. Chase quoted Lincoln as saying, "I know very well that many others might, in this matter, as in others, do better than I can; and if I were satisfied that the public confidence was more fully possessed by any one of them than by me, and knew of any Constitutional way in which he could be put in my place, he should have it. I would gladly yield it to him."[62] This unusual statement makes sense if we consider that Lincoln did not need self-confidence: the impetus of action came from outside of himself—from God. Over and over, his phraseology steered away from men-

---

to emancipate the slaves makes Lincoln seem more forthrightly committed to black freedom, but it is much more in keeping with his well-known pragmatism to assume that he was keeping all of his options open between July and Antietam. For the portrayal of Lincoln as less-than-certain about emancipation in this period, see Donald, *Lincoln*, 366-67, 373, 374. This interpretation of Lincoln's decision suggests greater uncertainty and makes it more probable that he would allow religious considerations to inform his actions.

61. Endy, in "Abraham Lincoln and American Civil Religion," argues rightly that Lincoln's decision to emancipate the slaves derived more from his belief that this was the course of providence than from his moral antipathy to slavery (238). Many Northerners viewed emancipation in the same way that Lincoln did, i.e., they ascribed its occurrence to providence and therefore found it easier to accept the radical change. See Moorhead, *American Apocalypse*, 96-98; Fredrickson, "The Coming of the Lord," 118-19.

62. Chase, *Inside Lincoln's Cabinet*, 150.

tion of his own agency: "I have thought all along that the time for acting on [emancipation] might very probably come. I think the time has come now."[63] God's initiative for emancipation contained a motive force of its own.

Though Lincoln tried to follow God's will, he was not sure that he had interpreted the design correctly. Lincoln was not a prophet in the nineteenth-century tradition of William Lloyd Garrison, John Brown, or Ralph Waldo Emerson. The president's perception of providence resembled that of the Puritans, who maintained an awareness of their own mortal limitations even as they tried to discern God's design through the faculties at their disposal.[64] Two days after the president issued the preliminary Emancipation Proclamation, enthusiastic supporters serenaded Lincoln at the White House. He responded less than enthusiastically. He claimed that he attempted to follow the will of God as best he could, but he admitted that his perception was imperfect: "I can only trust in God I have made no mistake." Despite the cheers of the crowd, Lincoln refused to say anything celebratory or even positive about the proclamation: "I shall make no attempt on this occasion to sustain what I have done or said by any comment." When he concluded by saying, "in my position I am environed with difficulties,"[65] it was clear that he still had doubts. Indeed, even if he had followed God's course correctly, he did not know where that course would lead. Lincoln wrote a few weeks later that God possessed "some wise purpose of his own, mysterious and unknown to us."[66] God might ordain a precipitous emancipation, or he might simply initiate the slow process in which Lincoln had believed so strongly during the 1850s. The providential gradualism of Clay still seemed possible. Lincoln tried to enact this course in December 1862, when he presented to Congress a scheme for compensated emancipation implemented over the course of thirty-seven years.[67]

However futile his actions seemed, and however confusing the situation became, Lincoln decided that he would not give up trying to follow the will of God. In October 1862 he wrote, "if after endeavoring to do my best in the light which [God] affords me, I find my efforts fail, I must believe that for some purpose unknown to me, He wills it otherwise."[68] Lincoln retained this attitude through

63. Ibid.
64. Puritan belief in the limitations of reason is one of the central themes in Miller, *The New England Mind*.
65. "Response to Serenade, Washington, D.C.," Sept. 24, 1862, in *SW*, 2:372.
66. Lincoln to Eliza P. Gurney, Oct. 26, 1862, 5:478.
67. "Annual Message to Congress," Dec. 1, 1862, in *SW*, 2:406-15.
68. Lincoln to Eliza P. Gurney, Oct. 26, 1862.

the worst days of the war. In early December, the Union army suffered a crushing defeat at Fredericksburg. A political crisis then erupted during which it became clear that many congressmen and members of the cabinet had lost confidence in the president. Referring to his opponents, Lincoln said, "they wish to get rid of me, and I am sometimes half disposed to gratify them," adding that "we are now on the brink of destruction. It appears to me the Almighty is against us, and I can hardly see a ray of hope."[69] God had become so active an agent that he seemed terrifying: he was "against" Lincoln and ready to rain down "destruction" on the administration. What is more, Lincoln submissively accepted God's independent and active nature. He recognized that there was not "a ray of hope" without God's approval, and he was "half disposed to gratify" what seemed to be God's wishes for his destruction. This intense conviction of God's sovereignty matched that of the Puritans, who put "more emphasis upon one attribute [of God] than upon any other—upon that of sovereignty."[70]

As Lincoln discerned divine meaning in particular events of the war, like the victory at Antietam, he likewise searched for God's purpose in the war as a whole. At some point in autumn 1862 (the exact date is unknown), Lincoln wrote a personal meditation which, according to his secretaries, was "not written to be seen of men."[71] An excerpt follows:

> The will of God prevails. In great contests each party claims to act in accordance with the will of God. Both *may* be, and one *must* be wrong. God can not be *for*, and *against* the same thing at the same time. In the present civil war it is quite possible that God's purpose is something different from the purpose of either party. . . . I am almost ready to say this is probably true—that God wills this contest, and wills that it shall not end yet. By his mere quiet power, on the minds of the now contestants, He could have either *saved* or *destroyed* the Union without a human contest. Yet the contest began. And having begun He could give the final victory to either side any day. Yet the contest proceeds.[72]

Now that he apprehended providence more immediately, Lincoln realized that he must assign divine meaning to everything that happens, including the bloodshed

---

69. Orville Hickman Browning, *The Diary of Orville Hickman Browning*, eds. Theodore Calvin Pease and James G. Randall, 2 vols. (Springfield: Illinois State Historical Library, 1925-33), 1:600.
70. Miller, *The New England Mind*, 14.
71. Quoted in *CW*, 5:404n.
72. "Meditation on the Divine Will," circa early September 1862, in *SW*, 2:359.

of war. In 1861, he believed the war was needless and hoped that God would make the controversy vanish by acting on the "minds" of the contestants. But since God had allowed the conflict to continue, it had to have a purpose of its own, beyond the objects for which either side was fighting. Lincoln did not guess at the purpose. He showed no inkling of the connection between war and slavery that he would make in later years. This was not surprising since, as we have seen, Lincoln was not sure whether God intended emancipation. But whatever Lincoln's uncertainties, he did, significantly, consider for the first time whether the war existed for some supernatural purpose.

Lincoln's new conception of God was coupled with a deeper awareness of national sin. This was logical, for a deep conviction of God's sovereignty usually imparts a sense of humanity's distance from God's height. As the war dragged on through spring 1863, Lincoln issued a proclamation for a national day of fasting. His only previous effort in this genre was the perfunctory fast proclamation of 1861 mentioned above, with its unconvincing statements about national sin and repentance. To this rhetorical flop, Lincoln's proclamation for March 1863 provided a stunning contrast:

> May we not justly fear that the awful calamity of civil war, which now desolates the land, may be but a punishment, inflicted upon us, for our presumptuous sins, to the needful end of our national reformation as a whole people? We have been the recipients of the choicest bounties of Heaven. We have been preserved, these many years, in peace and prosperity. We have grown in numbers, wealth and power, as no other nation has ever grown. But we have forgotten God. We have forgotten the gracious hand which preserved us in peace, and multiplied and enriched and strengthened us; and we have vainly imagined, in the deceitfulness of our hearts, that all these blessings were produced by some superior wisdom and virtue of our own. Intoxicated with unbroken success, we have become too self-sufficient to feel the necessity of redeeming and preserving grace, too proud to pray to the God that made us! It behooves us then, to humble ourselves before the offended Power, to confess our national sins, and to pray for clemency and forgiveness.[73]

This document burned with the conviction of sin far more than the proclamation of 1861. Where before Lincoln spouted a long list of unrelated clauses, he

---

73. "Proclamation Appointing a National Fast Day," Mar. 30, 1863, in *CW,* 6:156.

now put forth a connected and causative process: prosperity to forgetfulness to punishment to supplication. Forgiveness was relegated to the margin—a result that occurred only after the primary process of humiliation and penitence. Lincoln's language acquired force proportionate to his scathing message. America's sins were specific: the people were presumptuous, vain, deceitful, intoxicated, and proud. In the 1861 proclamation, Lincoln used label-words to indicate wrongdoing: "sins and transgressions"; "past offences." In this latter case, he put together phrases and sentences that actually embodied the emotional sting of sin: "the deceitfulness of our hearts"; "too proud to pray to the God that made us!"

It may seem strange that Lincoln focused on the sin of impious self-reliance without mentioning what, according to today's values, is a far more obvious sin—slavery. The choice makes sense if we consider Lincoln's place in his religious development. The results of emancipation were as uncertain in March 1863 as they had been the previous autumn. Judging from the physical signs of the war, Lincoln had no confirmation that God intended for America to throw off slavery right away. Because he did not know what God planned, it was premature for him to identify slavery as the sin that brought on the war. Impious self-reliance, on the other hand, was a sin with which Lincoln had firsthand experience. Starting life poor, he slowly accumulated "the choicest bounties of Heaven"—personal wealth, a successful career, and political fame. Having relied on himself for most of his life, Lincoln realized in autumn 1862 that he had to rely on God. The national sin of excessive self-reliance was Lincoln's sin, too. This helps explain why his religious rhetoric gained such resonance.

From spring 1863 to spring 1864, it seemed ever more evident to Lincoln that emancipation was meant to be. Believing that God's design might be discerned through the events of the war, he watched as black Union enlistees fought with great success and the Northern army won major victories at Gettysburg and Vicksburg.[74] When Lincoln viewed the nation in December 1863, in a panorama painted in his Annual Message to Congress, he found strong evidence that emancipation had taken on a life of its own. Looking back on the fall of 1862, Lincoln recalled that emancipation did not seem sure of success when first implemented: "The policy of emancipation . . . gave to the future a new aspect, about which hope, and fear, and doubt contended in uncertain conflict." But the situation had changed. Lincoln pointed out the advance of Union forces; the takeover of Arkansas and Tennessee, in which leading citizens were declaring "openly

74. For the success of black enlistment in Lincoln's eyes during the period, see James McPherson, *Battle Cry of Freedom* (New York: Ballantine, 1988), 686-87.

for emancipation in their respective States"; and the extraordinary reversal of public opinion in Maryland and Missouri, "neither of which three years ago would tolerate any restraint upon the extension of slavery into new territories," but which now "only dispute . . . as to the best mode of removing it within their own limits." To Lincoln, these "movements, by State action, for emancipation in several of the States, not included in the emancipation proclamation, are matters of profound gratulation."[75]

To a man so much aware of divine sovereignty, this spread of emancipation spirit even into places where he had not explicitly intended it to go seemed a clear manifestation of providence: as Lincoln said in April 1864, "the nation's condition is not what either party, or any man devised, or expected. God alone can claim it. Whither it is tending seems plain." He then postulated that "God now wills the removal of a great wrong," obviously slavery.[76] The following day, receiving a petition for the emancipation of all slave children, Lincoln said, "while I have not the power to grant all [the petitioners] ask, I trust they will remember that God has, and that, as it seems, He wills to do it."[77] Now that divine will had manifested itself, to fail in carrying it out would be to invite the wrath of God. This explains why Lincoln sometimes responded in religious language when people asked him to roll back emancipation. He said in August 1864 that the re-enslavement of black troops could not "escape the curses of Heaven."[78] In a meeting with leading Republicans that same month, Lincoln said, "There have been men who have proposed to me to return to slavery the black warriors . . . to their masters to conciliate the South. I should be damned in time [and] in eternity for so doing."[79]

The conception of emancipation as a preordained act of God, in addition to the continued need for black troops and the need to keep faith with the freedmen, provides additional motivation behind why Lincoln defended black liberty with unusual tenacity starting in December 1863. Before Congress that month, he said that "while I remain in my present position I shall not attempt to retract or modify the emancipation proclamation; nor shall I return to slavery any person who is free by the terms of that proclamation."[80] In summer 1864, he refused to negotiate peace with the Confederacy without abolition, despite pressure to

---

75. "Annual Message to Congress," Dec. 8, 1863, in *SW,* 2:550–51.
76. Lincoln to Albert G. Hodges, Apr. 4, 1864, 2:586.
77. Lincoln to Mrs. Horace Mann, Apr. 5, 1864, in *SW,* 2:587.
78. Lincoln to Charles D. Robinson, Aug. 17, 1864, in *SW,* 2:621.
79. "Interview with Alexander W. Randall and Joseph T. Mills," Aug. 19, 1864, in *CW,* 7:507.
80. "Annual Message to Congress," Dec. 8, 1863, 2:552.

the contrary in the midst of an election year. The following winter, he threw the full weight of his office behind the constitutional amendment abolishing slavery. These actions constituted a strikingly rigid stance for the normally flexible Lincoln, who often said that his motto was, "My policy is to have no policy."[81]

The religious underpinnings of Lincoln's commitment to emancipation explain his unusual statement on slavery in the Annual Message to Congress of December 1864. After once again refusing to modify the Emancipation Proclamation, he said that "if the people should, by whatever mode or means, make it an Executive duty to re-enslave [persons freed by the proclamation], another, and not I, must be their instrument to perform it."[82] In effect, Lincoln said that a higher principle than popular government existed. The American electorate, the lifeblood of Lincoln's beloved republicanism, could not move him to stand in the way of emancipation. This was a sharp reversal for a man who had said to a crowd of supporters only four years earlier that "in all the trying positions in which I shall be placed, . . . my reliance will be placed upon you and the people of the United States."[83] Before the war, Lincoln's belief in republicanism had the force of religion. Now, his convictions about the inevitability of God's providence, at least in some areas, had taken precedence over his faith in the popular will.

Nowhere did Lincoln's Calvinist tendencies assume greater importance than in his conception of the meaning of the war itself. In his private meditation on the divine will in autumn 1862, as we have seen, he postulated that the war might serve as a positive instrument through which God might effect some unknown purpose. But as Northern triumphs at Gettysburg and Vicksburg in summer 1863 made Northern victory an immediate possibility, Lincoln became anxious for peace and de-emphasized his conception of the war as a purposeful instrument. In a proclamation of thanksgiving for the two victories, issued on July 15, Lincoln hoped for divine intervention to end the bloodshed, hoping that God may "subdue the anger, which has produced, and so long sustained a needless and cruel rebellion, to change the hearts of the insurgents."[84] The war no longer seemed to be an event ordained by God for its own sake, but rather a "needless" problem caused by mortals alone.

Yet the fighting continued, and Lincoln's outlook changed to give meaning to events. His conception of the war as a purposeful phenomenon resurfaced

---

81. Donald, *Lincoln*, 15.
82. "Annual Message to Congress," Dec. 6, 1864, in *SW*, 2:661.
83. "Reply to Oliver P. Morton at Indianapolis, Indiana," Feb. 11, 1861, in *SW*, 2:200.
84. "Proclamation of Thanksgiving," July 15, 1863, in *CW*, 6:332.

with great energy during the Gettysburg Address of November 1863. Whereas Lincoln dismissed the war as "needless" in July, he showed at Gettysburg that the continual bloodshed contained a certain usefulness for the North. "From these honored dead we take increased devotion to that cause for which they gave the last full measure of devotion." Northerners' devotion to the cause of republican government was "increased" by the "honored dead"—that is, by the carnage of war—in other words, by the war itself. The Christian overtones of the speech reinforce this theme. Through the "honored dead" will come "a new birth of freedom."[85] As in Christianity, death served as the precondition for new life. Christ had to die on the cross in order for human souls to be redeemed.[86] As Christ's death became a positive instrument for the salvation of souls, war became a positive instrument for the salvation of republicanism. Lincoln saw the war as an event existing on its own terms with its own purpose. This formulation, though cast here in an overtly secular and political context, was about to play a major role in Lincoln's religious development.

In April 1864, Lincoln completed the synthesis of religious ideas that had developed over the past two years. The synthesis appeared in a letter to newspaper editor Albert Hodges. Three major themes converged: 1) the war as a positive and purposeful instrument, 2) national sin, and 3) God's design to end slavery immediately. "Whither [the nation's condition] is tending seems plain. If God now wills the removal of a great wrong, and wills also that we of the North as well as you of the South, shall pay fairly for our complicity in that wrong, impartial history will find therein new cause to attest and revere the justice and goodness of God."[87] As part of his design to extirpate the sin of slavery, God used the war as an instrument to punish the U.S. for its "complicity" in that sin. Lincoln always believed that the North and the South shared the responsibility for perpetuating slavery, so it seemed just that both sides should suffer.

Lincoln's synthesis steeled him for the trial ahead. Starting in spring 1864, he backed Lt. Gen. Ulysses S. Grant in a radical strategy of unrelenting combat to bring the material resources of the North to bear against the South. For the first several months, the effort produced nothing but stalemate and bloodshed. Despite immense pressure to dismiss the "butcher" Grant and stop the slaughter, Lincoln stood by his general. After its disastrous beginnings, Grant's approach

---

85. "Address at Gettysburg, Pennsylvania," Nov. 19, 1863, in *SW*, 2:536.
86. For New Testament resonances in the Gettysburg Address, see Wolf, *The Almost Chosen People*, 170.
87. Lincoln to Albert G. Hodges, Apr. 4, 1864.

ultimately exhausted the South and brought victory to the Union. If Lincoln had not withstood the pressure to remove Grant, the North might well have lost the war.[88] Lincoln's perseverance through great losses was reinforced by his belief that the war was not a senseless evil but an instrument of expiation. Suffering might be great, but under God's sovereignty, it could not be without positive meaning. Therefore, suffering had to be endured, understood, and embraced for whatever purpose it might have, not necessarily avoided. As Perry Miller explains, Puritan piety "requires not only that men endure afflictions, but that they find positive goodness in the worst of them.... No matter how exasperating, no matter how disastrous, because all experience is given of God, it must have some reason behind it."[89]

Thus, as the bloodshed mounted, Lincoln pleaded less and less for God to end the war. He began asking God only to *preserve* the Union so that it could continue to fight and to experience purposeful suffering for as long as God thought necessary. This change of focus from victory to preservation was apparent in Lincoln's reaction to the watershed Union victory at Atlanta on September 2. The capture of this important city vindicated Lincoln's aggressive war strategy and suddenly made him the favorite to win the November election.[90] Lincoln issued a special proclamation of thanksgiving. If ever there was a time to exult in victory and look forward to relief, it was now. But in contrast with the hopes for relief that he expressed in earlier proclamations, Lincoln asked only for God to "continue to uphold the Government of the United-States against all the efforts of public enemies and secret foes." He wanted only for the Union to be preserved so it could keep fighting. Americans ought to thank God "for His mercy in preserving our national existence against the insurgent rebels who so long have been waging a cruel war against the Government of the United-States." He did not request that God "change the hearts" of the insurgents. Whereas Lincoln called the war "needless and cruel" in the proclamation of July 1863, he retained the adjective "cruel," but, acknowledging that the war did fulfill a need for expiation, dropped the adjective "needless."[91] In his previous thanksgiving proclamation of July

88. On Grant and Union victory, see T. Harry Williams, "The Military Leadership of North and South" in *Why the North Won the Civil War*, ed. David Herbert Donald (New York: Simon and Schuster, 1996), 55–57. On the pressure to remove Grant amidst the slaughter, see Donald, *Lincoln*, 513–15.

89. Miller, *The New England Mind*, 39.

90. William E. Gienapp, lecture on the election of 1864, Historical Studies B-42, Harvard Univ., Cambridge, MA, Oct. 10, 1997.

91. "Proclamation of Thanksgiving and Prayer," Sept. 3, 1864, in *CW*, 7:533–34.

1863, Lincoln wistfully predicted victory: Gettysburg and Vicksburg furnished "augmented confidence that the Union of these States will be maintained . . . and their peace and prosperity permanently restored."[92] Yet after the far more decisive victory at Atlanta, he offered no predictions of victory at all.

After such a gratifying triumph, a different sort of man would have celebrated and looked forward to a happy future. Lincoln did not take this path. In October 1862, a Quaker woman named Eliza Gurney visited Lincoln at the White House and prayed with him. In August 1863, she sent him an encouraging letter. Lincoln received it but did not reply. Thirteen months later, in the wake of the great victory at Atlanta, Lincoln wrote back to Gurney and reaffirmed the justice of God's wrath: "we hoped for a happy termination of this terrible war long before this; but God knows best, and has ruled otherwise." A long war, senseless though it may seem, must be best for the country. Lincoln predicted that "we shall yet acknowledge [God's] wisdom [in prolonging the war] and our own error [in hoping for its termination]." God "intends some great good to follow this mighty convulsion, which no mortal could make, and no mortal could stay." The purposeful nature of the war justified and strengthened Lincoln's resolve to continue fighting: "we must work earnestly in the best light [God] gives us, trusting that so working still conduces to the great ends He ordains." He indicated how important this attitude had been to his war leadership by saying that he felt "much indebted" to Gurney for her efforts to "strengthen [his] reliance on God."[93]

Lincoln's Calvinist outlook shone forth even more strongly in his Annual Message to Congress in December 1864. In keeping with his recent writings, Lincoln did not express any hope for victory or relief. Rather, he collected numerous statistics to show that the population of the North had increased during the war. He then made a conclusion that sounds bizarre in the mouth of a politician: "We do not approach exhaustion in the most important branch of national resources—that of living men. While it is melancholy to reflect that the war has filled so many graves, and carried mourning to so many hearts, it is some relief to know that, compared with the surviving, the fallen have been so few. . . . The important fact remains demonstrated, that we have *more* men *now* than we had when the war *began;* that we are not exhausted, nor in process of exhaustion; that we are *gaining* strength, and may, if need be, maintain the contest indefinitely."[94]

---

92. "Proclamation of Thanksgiving," July 15, 1863, in *CW,* 6:332.
93. Lincoln to Eliza P. Gurney, Sept. 4, 1864, in *SW,* 2:627.
94. "Annual Message to Congress," Dec. 6, 1864, 2:659–60.

Though speaking to a people who had made enormous sacrifices, Lincoln gave minimal treatment to death and mourning, relegating these subjects to subordinate clauses. His message featured a grisly optimism about the huge number of living men who were still available to be expended. There was no wistful hope for resolution or closure, and no assurance of eventual triumph. The point was not that the Union's plentiful manpower would help it to win the war, but rather that the Union was strong enough to keep fighting even if the war never ended—to "maintain the contest indefinitely." The goal was not victory but preservation in the face of suffering. To the Calvinist mind, it was necessary to view even the most terrible sufferings in a wide perspective, so as not to dwell on seeming injustices in what was actually a completely just universe: "There was in the [Puritan] piety a strange tendency to calculate and measure human miseries . . . . because it was necessary for the child of God to know how much he was being disciplined and at what point he should put off sackcloth and ashes that he might be up and doing the Lord's work."[95] Just as Calvinists "calculate and measure" human suffering to keep it in perspective, Lincoln compared the Union's losses in population to its gains, thereby showing that the suffering was not so great as to cause despair and that the Union must keep fighting. It makes sense that Lincoln stood by Grant even through the bloodiest days.

Not that Lincoln was heartless. His conviction that the war represented the judgment of God did not stop him from recognizing that judgment as a terrible thing. As a mortal, it was natural, indeed unavoidable, for Lincoln to experience dread and sadness when looking upon the awful punishment wrought by God. But while the suffering was horrible, it was also just, and so it was acceptable to perpetuate it.

At his second inauguration, Lincoln shared his interpretation of the war with the nation. At the opening of the address, the theme of preservation, rather than victory, loomed large. Lincoln gave the army the quietest endorsement possible: "The progress of our arms. . . . is, I trust, reasonably satisfactory and encouraging to all."[96] He refused to predict the providential outcome: "With high hope for the future, no prediction in regard to [the progress of our arms] is ventured." Notably, Lincoln wrote himself out of the speech completely: aside from the inconsequential "I trust" in the sentence quoted above, he never used the first person singular. This speech was meant as an interpretation of God's design: for

---

95. Miller, *The New England Mind*, 39.
96. For all quotes from the Second Inaugural Address, Mar. 4, 1865, see *SW,* 2:686-87.

Lincoln to mention himself, when he was only a humble instrument used by God to effect purposes far beyond mortal capacity, would have been incongruous.

As a mortal with fears and sympathies, Lincoln hoped that God's punishment would end soon: "Fondly do we hope—fervently do we pray—that this mighty scourge of war may speedily pass away." But even as Lincoln prayed for mercy, the image of the scourge suggested the inexorable exactness of divine justice: God lashed white Americans with the scourge of war, just as they once lashed their slaves with the whip. Lincoln remained willing to endure the punishment until the sin was purged: "if God wills that [the war] continue, until all the wealth piled by the bond-man's two hundred and fifty years of unrequited toil shall be sunk, and until every drop of blood drawn with the lash, shall be paid by another drawn with the sword, as was said three thousand years ago, so still it must be said 'the judgments of the Lord are true and righteous altogether.'" The phrase "two hundred and fifty years" placed American slavery in the historical terms of the Old Testament, recalling the Hebrews' four hundred years of bondage. In both biblical Egypt and modern America, the justice of God came slowly, but with a vengeance.

Though his language reflected God's terrible judgment, Lincoln himself shied away from a personal condemnation of slavery. He said it was "strange that any men should dare to ask a just God's assistance in wringing their bread from the sweat of other men's faces; but let us judge not that we be not judged." Lincoln refused to commit to a moral attack. Technically, he did not even admonish the South for slavery. Rather, he admonished them because they asked a just God's assistance to perpetuate slavery—that is, because they invoked God for inappropriate purposes. Lincoln probably avoided a serious moral attack because, in his eyes, moral judgments need come only from God: the war itself was God's comment on slavery. There was no reason for Lincoln to underline so manifest a reproach.

In the Second Inaugural, Lincoln went further than ever before in his Calvinist conception of God. He postulated "that American Slavery is one of those offences which, in the providence of God, must needs come, but which, having continued through His appointed time, He now wills to remove, and that He gives to both North and South, this terrible war, as the woe due to those by whom the offence came." For some time, Lincoln had been saying that God was removing slavery and punishing the mortals who perpetuated the evil institution. But for the first time, he made it clear that providence caused slavery. Mortals had not initiated the offence; they were merely the instruments "by whom the offence came." And yet, mortals were still guilty of the offence and still deserve punishment for it. In true Calvinist fashion, Lincoln ascribed minimal agency to human beings and yet still held them accountable for their sins. Edwards made a similar argument in his treatise *Freedom of the Will*. If God determined that a man's motive was not to seek grace, then, based on that motive, the man would invariably fail to seek grace. Yet the sin of failing to seek grace was still justly blamed on the man.

By ascribing the offense of slavery to providence rather than to individuals, Lincoln's words imparted a strong sense of the universality of sin. Many observers have called Lincoln a charitable Christian because he refused to single out the South for blame. But we must recognize that Lincoln's charity made sense only in the larger context of his conviction that slavery was America's original sin—and that therefore all Americans were equal in being the people "by whom the offence came."[97]

Finally, the Second Inaugural is notable because it contains no references to American republicanism. This speech could be given by an absolute monarch just as easily as by an American president. The reversal from the 1850s, when republicanism provided the lifeblood of Lincoln's oratory, is impressive. Though republicanism remained important to Lincoln all his life, he found in the Calvinist ethos a new frame for understanding the world and a new source of rhetorical power.

Wolf calls the Second Inaugural "the climax of Lincoln's religious development."[98] Certainly the speech was Lincoln's most eloquent statement on religion. However, we should be careful not to spotlight the Second Inaugural too much, for it was merely one expression of religious ideas that had been an integral part of Lincoln's leadership throughout the war—ideas that were inseparable from his conduct on emancipation and military policy. Lincoln's Calvinist-like convictions strengthened and legitimized his uncompromising stands on emancipation, no matter how risky, and on strategy, no matter how costly. To the familiar factors of industrial capacity, generalship, political leadership, and diplomacy, historians might add Lincoln's Calvinist transformation as a reason why the North won the Civil War.

---

97. This idea was shared by James Madison, who referred to "the dreadful fruitfulness of the original sin of the African trade." Quoted in Matthew T. Mellon, *Early American Views on Negro Slavery* (Boston: Meador Publishing, 1934), 158.

98. Wolf, *The Almost Chosen People*, 183.

Only His Stepchildren

Lincoln and the Negro

Don E. Fehrenbacher

If the United States had a patron saint it would no doubt be Abraham Lincoln; and if one undertook to explain Lincoln's extraordinary hold on the national consciousness, it would be difficult to find a better starting-point than these lines from an undistinguished poem written in 1865:[1]

> One of the people! Born to be
> Their curious epitome;
> To share yet rise above
> Their shifting hate and love.

A man of the people and yet something much more, sharing popular passions and yet rising above them—here was the very ideal of a democratic leader, who in his person could somehow mute the natural antagonism between strong leadership and vigorous democracy. Amy Lowell, picking up the same theme half a century later, called Lincoln "an embodiment of the highest form of the

Presented at Gettysburg College, November 19, 1973, as the 12th Annual Robert Fortenbaugh Memorial Lecture, and at the College of William and Mary, November 28, 1973, as a James Pinckney Harrison Lecture.

1. Richard Henry Stoddard, *Abraham Lincoln; an Horatian Ode*, cited in Roy P. Basler, *The Lincoln Legend: A Study in Changing Conceptions* (Boston, 1935), 234.

Civil War History, Vol. XX No. 4 © 1974 by The Kent State University Press

typical American."[2] This paradox of the uncommon common man, splendidly heroic and at the same time appealingly representative, was by no means easy to sustain. The Lincoln tradition, as a consequence, came to embrace two distinct and seemingly incompatible legends—the awkward, amiable, robust, railsplitting, story-telling, frontier folklore hero; and the towering figure of the Great Emancipator and Savior of the Union, a man of sorrows, Christlike in his character and fate.

Biographers have struggled earnestly with this conspicuous dualism, but even when the excesses of reminiscence and myth are trimmed away, Lincoln remains a puzzling mixture of often conflicting qualities—drollness and melancholy, warmth and reserve, skepticism and piety, humbleness and self-assurance. Furthermore, he is doubly hard to get at because he did not readily reveal his inner self. He left us no diary or memoirs, and his closest friends called him "secretive" and "shut-mouthed." Billy Herndon in one of his modest moods declared, "Lincoln is unknown and possibly always will be."[3] Plainly, there is good reason for scholarly caution in any effort to take the measure of such a man.

No less plain is the intimate connection between the Lincoln legend and the myth of America. The ambiguities in his popular image and the whisper of enigma in his portraits have probably broadened the appeal of this homespun Westerner, self-made man, essential democrat, and national martyr. Almost anyone can find a way to identify with Lincoln, perhaps because "like Shakespeare . . . he seemed to run through the whole gamut of human nature."[4] Whatever the complex of reasons, successive generations of his countrymen have accepted Abraham Lincoln as the consummate American—the representative genius of the nation. One consequence is that he tends to serve as a mirror for Americans, who, when they write about him, frequently divulge a good deal about themselves.

Of course the recurring election of Lincoln as *Representative American* has never been unanimous. There was vehement dissent at first from many unreconstructed rebels, and later from iconoclasts like Edgar Lee Masters and cavaliers of the Lost Cause like Lyon Gardiner Tyler. In the mainstream of national life, however, it became increasingly fashionable for individuals and organizations to square themselves with Lincoln and enlist him in their enterprises. Often this required misquotation or misrepresentation or outright invention; but lobbyists and legislators, industrialists and labor leaders, reformers and bosses, Populists,

2. Ibid., 264-65.
3. David Donald, *Lincoln's Herndon* (New York, 1948), 305.
4. John T. Morse Jr., *Abraham Lincoln* (Boston, 1893), II, 355.

Progressives, Prohibitionists, and Presidents all wanted him on their side. New Deal Democrats tried to steal him from the Republicans, and the American Communist party bracketed him with Lenin. Lincoln, in the words of David Donald, had come to be "everybody's grandfather."[5]

Most remarkable of all was the growing recognition of Lincoln's greatness in the eleven states of the Confederacy, ten of which had never given him a single vote for President. This may have been a necessary symbolic aspect of sectional reconciliation. Returning to the Union meant coming to terms with the man who had saved the Union. No one took the step more unequivocally than Henry W. Grady, prophet of the New South, who told a New York audience in 1886 that Lincoln had been "the first typical American, the first who comprehended within himself all the strength and gentleness, all the majesty and grace of this Republic."[6] When Southerners talked to Southerners about it, they were usually more restrained. Nevertheless, by the early twentieth century, the Lincoln tradition was becoming a blend of blue and gray, as illustrated in *The Perfect Tribute*, a story from the pen of an Alabama woman about a dying Confederate soldier's admiration for the Gettysburg Address.[7]

Bonds of sympathy between Lincoln and the South had not been difficult to find. He was, after all, a native Southerner—implacable as an enemy, but magnanimous in victory and compassionate by nature. In his hands, nearly everyone agreed, the ordeal of Reconstruction would have been less severe. Even Jefferson Davis concluded that his death had been "a great misfortune to the South."[8]

In addition, Lincoln seemed to pass the supreme test. He could be assimilated to the racial doctrines and institutional arrangements associated with the era of segregation. The historical record, though not entirely consistent, indicated that his opposition to slavery had never included advocacy of racial equality. With a little editing here and some extra emphasis there, Lincoln came out "right" on the Negro question. This was a judgment more often understood than elaborated in Southern writing and oratory, but certain self-appointed guardians of white supremacy were sometimes painfully explicit in claiming Lincoln as one of their own. He had been willing, they said, to guarantee slavery forever in the states where it already existed. He had issued the Emancipation Proclamation with great reluctance. He had opposed the extension of slavery only in order to reserve the

---

5. David Donald, *Lincoln Reconsidered* (2nd ed.; New York, 1969), 16.
6. Michael Davis, *The Image of Lincoln in the South* (Knoxville, Tenn., 1971), 159.
7. Ibid., 138.
8. Ibid., 103.

western territories exclusively for white men. He had denied favoring political and social equality for Negroes, had endorsed separation of the races, and had persistently recommended colonization of Negroes abroad. This was the Lincoln eulogized by James K. Vardaman of Mississippi, perhaps the most notorious political racist in American history, and by the sensational Negrophobic novelist, Thomas Dixon. In his most famous work, *The Clansman,* Dixon had Lincoln as President parody himself during a discussion of colonization:

> We can never attain the ideal Union our fathers dreamed, with millions of an alien, inferior race among us, whose assimilation is neither possible nor desirable. The Nation cannot now exist half white and half black, any more than it could exist half slave and half free.[9]

When one remembers that all this time millions of black Americans were still paying homage to the Great Emancipator, dualism begins to seem pervasive in the Lincoln tradition. Racist elements, to be sure, were never very successful in promoting the image of Lincoln as a dedicated white supremacist, but support from an unlikely quarter would eventually give the idea not only new life but respectability in the centers of professional scholarship.

During the first half of the twentieth century, Lincoln studies became a functional part of the literature of the Civil War, in which the problem of race was present but not paramount. Titles of the 1940s indicate the general bent of interest: *Lincoln and His Party in the Secession Crisis; Lincoln and the Patronage; Lincoln's War Cabinet; Lincoln and the Radicals; Lincoln and the War Governors; Lincoln and the South.* There was, it should be observed, no *Lincoln and the Negro.* That would come, appropriately, in the 1960s.

The sweep of the modern civil rights movement, beginning with the Supreme Court's anti-segregation decision in 1954, inspired a new departure in American historical writing. Never has the psychological need for a usable past been more evident. Black history flourished and so did abolitionist history, but the most prestigious field of endeavor was white-over-black history. Attention shifted, for example, from slavery as a cause of the Civil War to slavery as one major form of racial oppression. With this change of emphasis, the antebellum years began to look different. A number of monographs appearing in the 1960s, such

---

9. Thomas Dixon, *The Clansman: An Historical Romance of the Ku Klux Klan* (New York, 1905), 46; Davis, *Image,* 147–52.

as Leon F. Litwack's *North of Slavery*, demonstrated the nationwide prevalence of white-superiority doctrines and white-supremacy practices. Many Republicans and even some abolitionists, when they talked about the Negro, had sounded curiously like the slaveholders whom they were so fiercely denouncing. In fact, it appeared that the North and the South, while bitterly at odds on the issue of slavery, were relatively close to one another in their attitudes toward race. And Lincoln, according to Litwack, "accurately and consistently reflected the thoughts and prejudices of most Americans."[10]

The racial consensus of the Civil War era made it easy enough to understand why black Americans failed to win the equality implicit in emancipation, but certain other historical problems became more difficult as a consequence. For instance, if most Northerners in 1860 were indeed racists who viewed the Negro with repugnance as an inferior order of creation, then why did so many of them have such strong feelings about slavery? And why did racist Southerners fear and distrust racist Republicans with an intensity sufficient to destroy the Union? And does not the achievement of emancipation by a people so morally crippled with racism seem almost miraculous—like a one-armed man swimming the English Channel? No amount of talk about overwrought emotions or ulterior purposes or unintended consequences will fully account for what appears to be a major historical paradox, with Lincoln as the central figure.

When the civil rights struggle got under way in the 1950s, both sides tried to enlist Lincoln's support, but the primary tendency at first was to regard desegregation as a belated resumption of the good work begun with the Emancipation Proclamation. Many leading historians agreed that during the presidential years there had been a "steady evolution of Lincoln's attitude toward Negro rights."[11] The changes carried him a long way from the narrow environmental influences of his youth and made him, in the words of Richard N. Current, more relevant and inspiring than ever "as a symbol of man's ability to outgrow his prejudices."[12]

This was the liberal interpretation of Lincoln's record on racial matters. It came under attack from several directions, but especially from the ranks of intellectual radicalism and black militancy, both academic and otherwise. New Left historians, many of them activists in the battle for racial justice, could find little

---

10. Leon F. Litwack, *North of Slavery: The Negro in the Free States, 1790–1860* (Chicago, 1961), 276.

11. Fawn M. Brodie, "Who Defends the Abolitionist?" in Martin Duberman (ed.), *The Antislavery Vanguard: New Essays on the Abolitionists* (Princeton, 1965), 63–64.

12. Richard N. Current, *The Lincoln Nobody Knows* (New York, 1958), 236.

to admire in Abraham Lincoln. Compared with abolitionists like William Lloyd Garrison and Wendell Phillips, he seemed unheroic, opportunistic, and somewhat insensitive to the suffering of black people in bondage. He was "the prototype of the political man in power, with views so moderate as to require the pressure of radicals to stimulate action."[13] His pre-war opposition to slavery, embracing the Republican policy of nonextension and the hope of ultimate extinction, reflected a "comfortable belief in the benevolence of history." It amounted to a "formula which promised in time to do everything while for the present risking nothing."[14]

Election to the presidency, in the radical view, produced no great transformation of his character. "Lincoln grew during the war—but he didn't grow much," wrote Lerone Bennett Jr., a senior editor of *Ebony*. "On every issue relating to the black man . . . he was the very essence of the white supremacist with good intentions."[15] He moved but slowly and reluctantly toward abolishing slavery, and his famous Proclamation not only lacked "moral grandeur," but it had been drafted "in such a way that it freed few, if any, slaves."[16] His reputation as the Great Emancipator is therefore "pure myth."[17] Most important of all, Lincoln probably believed in the inferiority of the Negro and certainly favored separation of the races. He was, in Bennett's words, "a tragically flawed figure who shared the racial prejudices of most of his white contemporaries."[18]

This, then, was the radical interpretation of Lincoln's record on racial matters, and what strikes one immediately is its similarity to the views of professional racists like Vardaman and Dixon. The portrait of A. Lincoln, Great White Supremacist, has been the work, it seems, of a strange collaboration.[19]

No less interesting is the amount of animus directed at a man who died over a hundred years ago. In the case of black militants, hostility to Lincoln has no doubt been part of the process of cutting loose from white America. Thus, there is little history but much purpose in the statement of Malcolm X: "He probably did more to trick Negroes than any other man in history."[20]

---

13. Howard Zinn, "Abolitionists, Freedom-Riders, and the Tactics of Agitation," in Duberman (ed.), *Antislavery Vanguard*, 438-39.
14. Martin Duberman, "The Northern Response to Slavery," in ibid., 396, 402.
15. Lerone Bennett Jr., "Was Abe Lincoln a White Supremacist?" *Ebony*, XXIII (Feb., 1968), 37.
16. Ibid., 37-38, 40.
17. Richard Claxton Gregory, *No More Lies: The Myth and the Reality of American History* (New York, 1971), 182.
18. Bennett, "Lincoln a White Supremacist," 36.
19. Davis, *Image*, 156: "'There is something sadly ironic in seeing black extremists and Ku Kluxers clasping hands over the grave of the Great Emancipator's reputation."
20. Robert Penn Warren, *Who Speaks for the Negro?* (New York, 1965), 262.

For white radicals too, rejection of Lincoln signified repudiation of the whole American cultural tradition, from the first massacre of Indians to the Vietnam War. In what might be called the "malign consensus" school of U.S. history, Lincoln remained the Representative American, but the America that he represented was a dark, ugly country, stained with injustice and cruelty. Plainly, there is much more at stake here than the reputation of a single historical figure.

James K. Vardaman, it is said, used to carry with him one particular Lincoln quotation that he would whip out and read at the slightest opportunity. This excerpt from the debate with Douglas in 1858 at Charleston, Illinois, is now fast becoming the most quoted passage in all of Lincoln's writings, outstripping even the Gettysburg Address and the Second Inaugural. Pick up any recent historical study of American race relations and somewhere in its pages you are likely to find the following words:

> I will say then that I am not, nor ever have been in favor of bringing about in any way the social and political equality of the white and black races,—that I am not nor ever have been in favor of making voters or jurors of negroes, nor of qualifying them to hold office, nor to intermarry with white people; and I will say in addition to this that there is a physical difference between the white and black races which I believe will forever forbid the two races living together on terms of social and political equality. And inasmuch as they cannot so live, while they do remain together there must be the position of superior and inferior, and I as much as any other man am in favor of having the superior position assigned to the white race.[21]

It is, of course, a quotation that bristles with relevancy. Problems that once preoccupied Lincoln's biographers, such as his part in bringing on the Civil War and the quality of his wartime leadership, have been more or less pushed aside by a question of newer fashion and greater urgency. It is well phrased in the preface to a collection of documents titled *Lincoln on Black and White* (1971): "Was Lincoln a racist? More important, how did Lincoln's racial views affect the course of our history."[22]

Anyone who sets out conscientiously to answer such a query will soon find himself deep in complexity and confronting some of the fundamental problems

---

21. Roy P. Basler (ed.), *The Collected Works of Abraham Lincoln* (New Brunswick, N.J., 1953–55), III, 145–46.
22. Arthur Zilversmit (ed.), *Lincoln on Black and White* (Belmont, Calif., 1971), n.p.

of historical investigation. In one category are various questions about the historian's relation to the past: Is his task properly one of careful reconstruction, or are there more important purposes to be served? Does his responsibility include rendering moral judgments? If so, using what standards—those of his own time or those of the period under study? Then there are all the complications encountered in any effort to read the mind of a man, especially a politician, from the surviving record of his words and actions. For instance, what he openly affirmed as a youth may have been silently discarded in maturity; what he believed on a certain subject may be less significant than the intensity of his belief; and what he said on a certain occasion may have been largely determined by the immediate historical context, including the composition of his audience.

Terminological difficulties may also arise in the study of history, and such is the case with the word "racist," which serves us badly as a concept because of its denunciatory tone and indiscriminate use.[23] Conducive neither to objectivity nor to precision, the word has been employed so broadly that it is now being subdivided. Thus we are invited to distinguish between ideological racism and institutional racism,[24] between scientific racism and folk racism,[25] between active racism and inactive racism,[26] between racism and racial prejudice,[27] between racism and racialism,[28] between hierarchical racism and romantic racialism.[29] In its strictest sense, racism is a doctrine, but by extension it has also come to signify an attitude, a mode of behavior, and a social system. The *doctrine*, a work of intellectuals, is a rationalized theory of inherent Negro inferiority. In a given person, however, it can be anything from a casual belief to a philosophy of life. As an *attitude*, racism is virtually synonymous with prejudice—a habitual feeling of repugnance, and perhaps of enmity, toward members of another race. It can be anything from a

---

23. See Michael Banton, "The Concept of Racism," in Sami Zubaida (ed.), *Race and Racialism* (London, 1970), 17-34. The indiscriminate use of the word is well illustrated in the assertion of Robert Froman, *Racism* (New York, 1972), 27-28, that there is a "racist overtone" to the statement that Columbus or Leif Ericson discovered America, because it implies that the Siberians who had arrived earlier "did not count."

24. David M. Reimers (ed.), *Racism in the United States: An American Dilemma?* (New York, 1972), 5.

25. Banton, "Concept of Racism," 18.

26. Forrest G. Wood, *Black Scare: The Racist Response to Emancipation and Reconstruction* (Berkeley, 1970), 15.

27. George M. Fredrickson, *The Black Image in the White Mind: The Debate on Afro-American Character and Destiny, 1817-1914* (New York, 1971), 2.

28. Margaret Nicholson, *A Dictionary of American-English Usage* (New York, 1958), 469.

29. Fredrickson, *Black Image*, 101.

mild tendency to a fierce obsession. Racism as a *mode of behavior* is prejudice activated in some way—a display of racial hostility that can be anything from mere avoidance of the other race to participation in a lynching. Racism as a *social system* means that law and custom combine to hold one race in subordination to another through institutional arrangements like slavery, segregation, discrimination, and disfranchisement. Individuals can help support such a system with anything from tacit acquiescence to strenuous public service in its defense. These multiple and graduated meanings of the word "racism" are important to remember in exploring the historical convergence of Abraham Lincoln and the American Negro.[30]

"One must see him first," says Bennett, "against the background of his times. Born into a poor white family in the slave state of Kentucky and raised in the anti-black environments of southern Indiana and Illinois, Lincoln was exposed from the very beginning to racism."[31] This is a familiar line of reasoning and credible enough on the surface. Any racial views encountered during his youth were likely to be unfavorable to the Negro. But more important is the question of how *often* he encountered such views and how *thoroughly* he absorbed them. Besides, the assumption that his racial attitudes were shaped more or less permanently by his early social environment does not take into account the fact that youth may rebel against established opinion. Lincoln did in a sense reject his father's world, leaving it behind him forever soon after reaching the age of twenty-one. Certainly his personal knowledge of black people was very limited. After catching a few glimpses of slavery as a small boy in Kentucky, he had little contact with Negroes while growing up in backwoods Indiana or as a young man in New Salem, Illinois. Those first twenty-eight years of his life take up just three pages in Benjamin Quarles's book, *Lincoln and the Negro*.[32]

If Lincoln entered manhood with strong feelings about race already implanted in his breast, one might expect to find indications of it in his earlier letters and speeches. For instance, on a steamboat carrying him home from a visit to Kentucky in 1841, there were a dozen slaves in chains. They had been, literally, sold down the river to a new master, and yet they seemed the most cheerful persons

---

30. *Webster's Third New International Dictionary* (Unabridged) defines "racism" as: "*1*. the assumption that psychocultural traits and capacities are determined by biological race and that races differ decisively from one another, which is usually coupled with a belief in the inherent superiority of a particular race and its right to domination over others. *2a*. a doctrine or political program based on the assumption of racism and designed to execute its principles. *2b*. a political or social system founded on racism. *3*. racialism."
31. Bennett, "Lincoln a White Supremacist," 36.
32. Benjamin Quarles, *Lincoln and the Negro* (New York, 1962), 16–18.

on board. Here was inspiration for some racist remarks in the "Sambo" vein, but Lincoln, describing the scene to a friend, chose instead to philosophize about the dubious effect of "condition upon human happiness." That is, he pictured Negroes behaving, as George M. Fredrickson puts it, "in a way that could be understood in terms of a common humanity and not as the result of peculiar racial characteristics."[33] Although one scholar may insist that Lincoln's racial beliefs were "matters of deep conviction,"[34] and another may talk about "the deep-rooted attitudes and ideas of a lifetime,"[35] there is scarcely any record of his thoughts on race until he was past forty years of age. Long before then, of course, he had taken a stand against slavery, and it was the struggle over slavery that eventually compelled him to consider publicly the problem of race.

There is no escape from the dilemma that "relevance" makes the past worth studying and at the same time distorts it. We tend to see antebellum race and slavery in the wrong perspective. Race itself was not then the critical public issue that it has become for us. Only widespread emancipation could make it so, and until the outbreak of the Civil War, that contingency seemed extremely remote. Our own preoccupation with race probably leads us to overestimate the importance of racial feeling in the antislavery movement.[36] In fact, there is a current disposition to assume that if a Republican did not have strong pro-Negro motives, he must have acted for strong anti-Negro reasons, such as a desire to keep the Western territories lily-white.[37]

Actually, much of the motivation for antislavery agitation was only indirectly connected with the Negro. For example, the prime target often seemed to be, not so much slavery as the "slave power," arrogant, belligerent, and overrepresented in all branches of the Federal government.[38] In Lincoln's case, no one can doubt

---

33. Fredrickson, "A Man but Not a Brother: Abraham Lincoln and Racial Equality," *Journal of Southern History*, in press.

34. George Sinkler, *The Racial Attitudes of American Presidents, from Abraham Lincoln to Theodore Roosevelt* (Garden City, N.Y., 1971), 75.

35. Fredrickson, "A Man but Not a Brother."

36. See Banton, "Concept of Racism," 22–24, for the "inductivist explanation" of racism, which, he says, "is chiefly found in the writings of American sociologists. They are acquainted with racism in its modern forms and work backwards, viewing earlier statements about race from a modern standpoint instead of setting them in the intellectual context of the time in which they were made."

37. For example, although he carefully qualifies his stated conclusions, this is the effect of Eugene H. Berwanger's *The Frontier Against Slavery: Western Anti-Negro Prejudice and the Slavery Extension Controversy* (Urbana, Ill., 1967).

38. See Larry Gara, "Slavery and the Slave Power: A Crucial Distinction," *Civil War History*, XV (1969), 5–18.

his profound, though perhaps intermittent, sympathy for the slave. Yet he also hated slavery in a more abstract way as an evil principle and as a stain on the national honor, incompatible with the mission of America.[39]

It is a mistake to assume that Lincoln's actions in relation to the Negro were determined or even strongly influenced by his racial outlook. He based his antislavery philosophy, after all, squarely upon perception of the slave as a man, not as a Negro. According to the Declaration of Independence, he declared, all men, including black men, are created equal, at least to the extent that none has a right to enslave another. This became a point at issue in the famous debates with Stephen A. Douglas, who vehemently denied that the Declaration had anything to do with the African race. Lincoln, in turn, accused his rival of trying to "dehumanize" the Negro. But he had constructed an argument against slavery which, carried to its logical conclusion, seemed to spell complete racial equality. So Douglas insisted, anyhow, while Lincoln protested: "I do not understand that because I do not want a negro woman for a slave I must necessarily want her for a wife."[40]

Opponents of slavery everywhere had to contend with the charge that they advocated Negro equality. In the Democratic press, Republicans almost invariably became "Black Republicans," and political survival more often than not appeared to depend upon repudiation of the epithet. Thus the race question was most prominent in the antebellum period as a rhetorical and largely spurious feature of the slavery controversy.

Lincoln's first general remarks about racial equality on record were made in 1854, when the repeal of the Missouri Compromise drew him back to the center of Illinois politics. What to do, ideally, with southern slaves, he pondered in a speech at Peoria. "Free them, and make them politically and socially our equals? My own feelings will not admit of this; and if mine would, we well know that those of the great mass of white people will not."[41] More often that year, however, he talked about the humanity of the Negro in denouncing the extension of slavery. Then came the election of 1856 and Fremont's defeat, which Lincoln analyzed with some bitterness: "We were constantly charged with seeking an amalgamation of the white and black races; and thousands turned from us, not

---

39. "Our republican robe is soiled, and trailed in the dust," said Lincoln in 1854. In the same speech, he called slavery a "monstrous injustice," and then added, "I hate it because it deprives our republican example of its just influence in the world." *Collected Works*, II, 255, 276. Duberman, "Northern Response to Slavery," 399-401, points to nationalism as one reason for opposition to abolitionism; but it should also be emphasized that national pride fortified the antislavery movement.

40. *Collected Works*, III, 9-10, 29, 80, 95, 112-113, 146, 216, 280, 300-304, 470.

41. Ibid., II, 255-256.

believing the charge ... but *fearing* to face it themselves."[42] It was at this point, significantly, that he became more aggressive and explicit in disavowing racial equality. He began using census figures to show that miscegenation was a by-product of slavery. He spoke of the "natural disgust" with which most white people viewed "the idea of indiscriminate amalgamation of the white and black races." And, under heavy pounding from Douglas during the senatorial campaign of 1858, he answered again and again in the manner of the notorious Charleston passage quoted above.[43] Indeed, his strongest feeling about race appears to have been his vexation with those who kept bringing the subject up. "Negro equality! Fudge!!" he scribbled on a piece of paper. "How long, in the government of a God great enough to make and maintain this Universe, shall there continue knaves to vend and fools to gulp, so low a piece of demagoguism as this?"[44]

Most of Lincoln's recorded generalizations about race were public statements made in the late 1850s as part of his running oratorical battle with Douglas.[45] Furthermore, nearly all of those statements were essentially disclaimers rather than affirmations. They indicated, for political reasons, the *maximum* that he was willing to deny the Negro and the *minimum* that he claimed for the Negro. They were concessions on points not at issue, designed to fortify him on the point that *was* at issue—namely, the extension of slavery. If he had responded differently at Charleston and elsewhere, the Lincoln of history simply would not exist. And words uttered in a context of such pressure may be less than reliable as indications of a man's lifetime attitude.

At least it seems possible that Lincoln's remarks in middle age on the subject of race were shaped more by his political realism than by impressions stamped on his mind in childhood. The principal intellectual influence, as Frederickson has demonstrated, was Henry Clay, Lincoln's political hero, whom he studied anew for a eulogy delivered in 1852. Clay, in his attitude toward slavery, represented a link with the Founding Fathers. A slaveholder himself who nevertheless believed that the institution was a "curse," he began and ended his career working for a program of gradual emancipation in Kentucky. He helped found and steadily supported the American Colonization Society. In his racial views, moreover, Clay emphasized the Negro's humanity and reserved judgment on the question

---

42. Ibid., 391.
43. Ibid., II, 405, 408; III, 16, 88, 249.
44. Ibid., III, 399.
45. The principal exceptions are the Peoria speech of October 16, 1854, and the statement to the delegation of Negroes of August 14, 1862.

of innate black inferiority. Lincoln not only adopted Clay's tentative, moderate outlook but extensively paraphrased and sometimes parroted his words.[46]

Considering, then, the peculiar context of his most significant remarks on the subject of race, and considering also his dependence on Clay, it seems unwise to assert flatly, as some scholars do, that Lincoln embraced the doctrine of racism. Not that it would be astonishing to find that he did so. The assumption of inherent white superiority was almost universal and rested upon observation as well as prejudice. Comparison of European civilization and African "savagery" made it extremely difficult to believe in the natural equality of white and black races. Yet Lincoln's strongest statements, even if taken at face value and out of context, prove to be tentative and equivocal. He conceded that the Negro *might not* be his equal, or he said that the Negro *was not* his equal *in certain respects*. As an example, he named *color*, which certainly has a biological implication. But we cannot be certain that he was not merely expressing an aesthetic judgment or noting the social disadvantages of being black. He never used the word "inherent," or any of its equivalents, in discussing the alleged inferiority of the Negro, and it is not unlikely that he regarded such inferiority as resulting primarily from social oppression. In 1862, he compared blacks whose minds had been "clouded by slavery" with free Negroes "capable of thinking as white men." His last recorded disclaimer appears in a letter written as President-elect to a New York editor. He did not, it declared, "hold the black man to be the equal of the white, unqualifiedly." The final word throws away most of the declaration and scarcely suits a true ideological racist. Here there is a doubleness in the man as in the legend. It appears that he may have both absorbed and doubted, both shared and risen above, the racial doctrines of his time.[47]

Lincoln, who had four sons and no other children, was presumably never asked the ultimate racist question. He did indicate a disinclination to take a Negro woman for his wife, agreeing with most of his white contemporaries in their aversion to miscegenation. Otherwise, there is little evidence of racism as an attitude or racism as a mode of behavior in his relations with Negroes. Frederick Douglass, sometimes a severe critic of his policies, said emphatically: "In all my interviews with Mr. Lincoln I was impressed with his entire freedom from popular prejudice

---

46. Fredrickson, "A Man but Not a Brother." But for an argument belittling Clay's influence on Lincoln, see Marvin R. Cain, "Lincoln's Views on Slavery and the Negro: A Suggestion," *Historian*, XXVI (1964), 502–20.

47. *Collected Works*, III, 16; IV, 156; V, 372–73.

against the colored race."⁴⁸ During the war years in Washington, the social status of Negroes underwent a minor revolution, exemplified in the arrival of a black diplomat from the newly recognized republic of Haiti. Lincoln, according to Current, "opened the White House to colored visitors as no President had done before, and he received them in a spirit which no President has matched since."⁴⁹ Douglass and others appreciated not only his friendliness but his restraint. There was no effusiveness, no condescension. "He treated Negroes," says Quarles, "as they wanted to be treated—as human beings."⁵⁰

On the other hand, Lincoln in the 1850s did plainly endorse the existing system of white supremacy, except for slavery. He defended it, however, on grounds of expediency rather than principle, and on grounds of the incompatibility rather than the inequality of the races. Assuming that one race or the other must be on top, he admitted preferring that the superior position be *assigned* to the white race. Thus there was little association of institutional racism with ideological racism in his thinking.

Although Lincoln was by no means insensitive to the deprivation suffered by free Negroes,⁵¹ he saw little hope of improving their condition and in any case regarded slavery as a far greater wrong. Moreover, it appeared that any serious attack on institutional racism would raise the cry of "Negro equality," and thereby damage the antislavery cause.

But then, if he hated slavery so much, why did Lincoln not become an abolitionist? There are several obvious reasons: fear for the safety of the Union, political prudence, constitutional scruples, a personal distaste for extremism, and perplexity over what to do with freed slaves.⁵² In addition, it must be emphasized that Lincoln, as Lord Charnwood observed, "accepted the institutions to which he was born, and he enjoyed them."⁵³ Social reform was a fairly new phenomenon in antebellum America. Only a relatively small number of persons had adopted it as a lifestyle, and Lincoln cannot be counted among them. This author of the greatest reform in American history was simply not a reformer by nature. He even acquiesced in the retention of slavery, provided that it should not be allowed to

---

48. Allen Thorndike Rice (ed.), *Reminiscences of Abraham Lincoln* (New York, 1888), 193.
49. J. G. Randall and Richard N. Current, *Lincoln the President* (New York, 1945-55), IV, 316.
50. Quarles, *Lincoln and the Negro*, 204.
51. See especially his comment on an assertion by Roger B. Taney alleging that the Negro's status had improved since the framing of the Constitution, *Collected Works*, II, 403-4.
52. See discussion of factors discouraging abolitionism in Duberman, "The Northern Response to Slavery," 398-401.
53. Lord Charnwood, *Abraham Lincoln* (New York, 1917), 455.

expand. For him, the paramount importance of the Republican anti-extension program lay in its symbolic meaning as a commitment to the principle of ultimate extinction. Some later generation, he thought, would then convert the principle into practice. What this amounted to, in a sense, was antislavery tokenism, but it also proved to be a formula for the achievement of political power, and with it, the opportunity to issue a proclamation of emancipation.

Of course, it has been said that Lincoln deserves little credit for emancipation—that he came to it tardily and reluctantly, under Radical duress. "Blacks have no reason to feel grateful to Abraham Lincoln," writes Julius Lester in *Look Out, Whitey! Black Power's Gon' Get Your Mama!* "How come it took him two whole years to free the slaves? His pen was sitting on his desk the whole time. All he had to do was get up one morning and say, 'Doggonnit! I think I'm gon' free the slaves today.'"[54] But *which* morning? That turned out to be the real question.

Lincoln, it should be remembered, was under strong pressure from *both* sides on the issue of emancipation, and so the Radical clamor alone will not explain his ultimate decision. Nevertheless, when the war began, many Americans quickly realized that the fate of slavery might be in the balance. Veteran abolitionists rejoiced that history was at last marching to their beat, and Lincoln did not fail to read what he called "the signs of the times." Emancipation itself, as he virtually acknowledged, came out of the logic of events, not his personal volition, but the time and manner of its coming were largely his choice.

There had been enough Republicans to win the presidential election, but there were not enough to win the war. They needed help from Northern Democrats and border-state loyalists, who were willing to fight for the Union, but not for abolition. A premature effort at emancipation might alienate enough support to make victory impossible. It would then be self-defeating, because there could be no emancipation without victory. Lincoln's remarkable achievement, whether he fully intended it or not, was to proclaim emancipation in such a way as to minimize disaffection. He did so by allowing enough time for the prospect to become domesticated in the public mind, and by adhering scrupulously to the fiction that this momentous step was strictly a military measure. Much of the confusion about the Emancipation Proclamation results from taking too seriously Lincoln's verbal bowings and scrapings to the conservatives while all the time he was backing steadily away from them.[55]

---

54. Julius Lester, *Look Out, Whitey! Black Power's Gon' Get Your Mama!* (New York, 1968), 58.
55. For a good statement of Lincoln's strategy, see Hans L. Trefousse, *The Radical Republicans, Lincoln's Vanguard for Racial Justice* (New York, 1969), 182.

The best illustration is his famous reply of August 22, 1862, to the harsh criticism of Horace Greeley, in which he said that his "paramount object" was to save the Union. "What I do about slavery, and the colored race," he declared, "I do because I believe it helps to save the Union; and what I forbear, I forbear because I do *not* believe it would help to save the Union."[56] The most striking thing about the entire document is its dissimulation. Although Lincoln gave the impression that options were still open, he had in fact already made up his mind, had committed himself to a number of persons, had drafted the Proclamation. Why, then, write such a letter? Because it was not a statement of policy but instead a brilliant piece of propaganda in which Lincoln, as Benjamin P. Thomas says, "used Greeley's outburst to prepare the people for what was coming."[57]

There were constitutional as well as political reasons, of course, for casting the Proclamation in military language and also for limiting its scope to those states and parts of states still in rebellion. In a sense, as historians fond of paradox are forever pointing out, it did not immediately liberate any slaves at all. And the Declaration of Independence, it might be added, did not immediately liberate a single colony from British rule. The people of Lincoln's time apparently had little doubt about the significance of the Proclamation. Jefferson Davis did not regard it as a mere scrap of paper, and neither did that most famous of former slaves, Frederick Douglass. He called it "the greatest event in our nation's history."[58]

In the long sweep of that history, emancipation had come on, not sluggishly, but with a rush and a roar—over a period of scarcely eighteen months. Given more time to reflect on its racial implications, white America might have recoiled from the act. Lincoln himself had never been anything but a pessimist about the consequences of emancipation. Knowing full well the prejudices of his countrymen, he doubted that blacks and whites could ever live together amicably and on terms of equality. Over a century later, it is still too early to say that he was wrong.

With stark realism, Lincoln told a delegation of free Negroes in August 1862: "On this broad continent, not a single man of your race is made the equal of a single man of ours. Go where you are treated the best, and the ban is still upon you." And while blacks suffered from discrimination, whites suffered from the discord caused by the presence of blacks. "It is better for us both, therefore, to

---

56. *Collected Works*, V, 388–89.
57. Benjamin P. Thomas, *Abraham Lincoln* (New York, 1952), 342.
58. Speech at Cooper Institute, February 1863, quoted in Zilversmit, *Lincoln on Black and White*, 133.

be separated," he said.[59] But Lincoln apparently never visualized a segregated America. For him, separation meant colonization, which, as a disciple of Henry Clay, he had been advocating at least since 1852. Perhaps the strangest feature of Lincoln's presidential career was the zeal with which he tried to promote voluntary emigration of free Negroes to Africa or Latin America. He recommended it in his first two annual messages, urged it upon Washington's black leadership, and endorsed it in his Preliminary Emancipation Proclamation. He had foreign capitals circulated in a search for likely places of settlement. Furthermore, with funds supplied by Congress, he launched colonization enterprises in Haiti and Panama, both of which proved abortive.[60]

What surprises one the most about these almost frantic activities is their petty scale. Lincoln implored the delegation of Washington Negroes to find him a hundred, or fifty, or even twenty-five families willing to emigrate. The Haitian project, if completely successful, would have accommodated just five thousand persons—about the number of Negroes born every two weeks in the United States. It would have required an enormous effort even to hold the black population stable at four and one-half million, let alone reduce it appreciably. Back in 1854, Lincoln had admitted the impracticability of colonization as anything but a long-range program.[61] Why, then, did he betray such feverish haste to make a token beginning in 1862?

One interesting answer emerges from the chronology. Most of the colonization flurry took place during the second half of 1862. After that, Lincoln's interest waned, although according to the dubious testimony of Benjamin F. Butler, it revived near the end of the war.[62] After issuing the Emancipation Proclamation on January 1, 1863, Lincoln never made another public appeal for colonization. It appears that his spirited activity in the preceding six months may have been part of the process of conditioning the public mind for the day of jubilee. The promise of colonization had always been in part a means of quieting fears about the racial consequences of manumission. Offered as the ultimate solution to the problem of the black population, it could also serve as a psychological safety valve for the problem of white racism. This combination of purposes had inspired a number of Republican leaders to take up the cause of colonization in

---

59. *Collected Works*, V, 372.
60. Quarles, *Lincoln and the Negro*, 108-23, 191-94.
61. *Collected Works*, II, 255.
62. Benjamin F. Butler, *Butler's Book* (Boston, 1892), 903-8.

the late 1850s. One of them, the brother of his future postmaster-general, had told Lincoln then that the movement would "ward off the attacks made upon us about Negro equality."[63]

In his second annual message of December 1, 1862, Lincoln said, "I cannot make it better known than it already is, that I strongly favor colonization." Then he continued in a passage that has received far less attention: "And yet I wish to say there is an objection urged against free colored persons remaining in the country, which is largely imaginary, if not sometimes malicious." He went on to discuss and minimize the fear that freedmen would displace white laborers, after which he wrote:

> But it is dreaded that the freed people will swarm forth, and cover the whole land? Are they not already in the land? Will liberation make them any more numerous? Equally distributed among the whites of the whole country, and there would be but one colored to seven whites. Could the one, in any way, greatly disturb the seven? There are many communities now, having more than one free colored person, to seven whites; and this, without any apparent consciousness of evil from it.[64]

Here, along with his last public endorsement of colonization, was an eloquent plea for racial accommodation at home. The one might remain his ideal ultimate solution, but the other, he knew, offered the only hope in the immediate future.

Yet, if his plans for Reconstruction are an accurate indication, Lincoln at the time of his death had given too little consideration to the problem of racial adjustment and to the needs of four million freedmen. How much that would have changed if he had not been killed, has been the subject of lively controversy.[65] Certainly his policies by 1865 no longer reflected all the views expressed in 1858, when he had repudiated both Negro citizenship and Negro suffrage. Now, by fiat

---

63. Eric Foner, *Free Soil, Free Labor, Free Men: The Ideology of the Republican Party before the Civil War* (New York, 1970), 271. See also, Harry V. Jaffa, *Crisis of the House Divided: An Interpretation of the Issues in the Lincoln-Douglas Debates* (Garden City, N.Y., 1959), 61.

64. *Collected Works*, V, 534-35. See also Lincoln's letter to John A. Andrew, February 18, 1864, in ibid., VII, 191.

65. See especially, William B. Hesseltine, *Lincoln's Plan of Reconstruction* (Tuscaloosa, Ala., 1960); Ludwell H. Johnson, "Lincoln and Equal Rights: The Authenticity of the Wadsworth Letter," *Journal of Southern History*, XXXII (1966), 83-87; Harold Hyman, "Lincoln and Equal Rights for Negroes: The Irrelevancy of the 'Wadsworth Letter,'" *Civil War History*, XII (1966), 258-66; Ludwell H. Johnson, "Lincoln and Equal Rights: A Reply," *Civil War History*, XIII (1967), 66-73.

of his administration in defiance of the Dred Scott Decision, blacks were citizens of the United States, and he had begun in a gentle way to press for limited black enfranchisement. He had overcome his initial doubts about enlisting Negroes as fighting soldiers, was impressed by their overall performance, and thought they had earned the right to vote.

Lincoln once told Charles Sumner that on the issue of emancipation they were only four to six weeks apart.[66] The relative earliness of his first favorable remarks about Negro enfranchisement suggests that he had again read the "signs of the times." It is not difficult to believe that after the war he would have continued closer to the Sumners than to the conservatives whom he had placated but never followed for long. And one can scarcely doubt that his postwar administration would have been more responsive to Negro aspirations than Andrew Johnson's proved to be.

But for several reasons Lincoln's role was likely to be more subdued than we might expect from the Great Emancipator. First, during peacetime, with his powers and responsibilities as Commander-in-Chief greatly reduced, he probably would have yielded more leadership to Congress in the old Whig tradition. Second, at the time of his death, he still regarded race relations as primarily a local matter, just as he had maintained during the debates with Douglas: "I do not understand there is any place where an alteration of the social and political relations of the Negro and white man can be made except in the State Legislature."[67] Third, Negroes as Negroes were nearly always connotative in Lincoln's thinking. Their welfare, though by no means a matter of indifference to him, had never been, and was not likely to become, his "paramount object." They were, in the words of Frederick Douglass, "only his stepchildren."[68]

Finally, in his attitude toward the wrongs of the free Negro, Lincoln had none of the moral conviction that inspired his opposition to slavery. He never seems to have suspected that systematic racial discrimination might be, like slavery, a stain on the national honor and a crime against mankind. Whether that is the measure of his greatness must be left to each one's personal taste. Of Copernicus we might say: What a genius! He revolutionized our understanding of the solar system. Or: What an ignoramus! He did not understand the rest of the universe at all.

---

66. Trefousse, *Radical Republicans*, 210–11.
67. *Collected Works*, III, 146.
68. *Life and Times of Frederick Douglass, Written by Himself* (New York, 1962 reprint of 1892 edition), 485.

Defending Emancipation
Abraham Lincoln and the Conkling Letter, 1863

ALLEN C. GUELZO

Abraham Lincoln might well have believed that "I never in my life was more certain that I was doing right than I do in signing" the Emancipation Proclamation into military law on January 1, 1863. But doing what was right and what was politically viable were two different things. "At no time during the war was the depression among the people of the North so great as in the spring of 1863," remembered James G. Blaine, and largely because "the anti-slavery policy of the President was ... tending to a fatal division among the people." The simple fact of announcing his intention to proclaim emancipation back in September had created more public anger than Lincoln had anticipated. William O. Stoddard, one of Lincoln's White House staffers, gloomily recalled "how many editors and how many other penmen within these past few days" rose in anger to remind Lincoln

> that this is a war for the Union only, and they never gave him any authority to run it as an Abolition war. They never, never told him that he might set the negroes free, and, now that he has done so, or futilely pretended to do so, he

---

The author wishes to acknowledge the invaluable assistance given him in the making of this article by Michael Burlingame, Thomas F. Schwartz (Illinois State Historical Preservation Agency), Kim Bauer (Illinois State Historical Library), John Sellers (Library of Congress), and William C. Harris (North Carolina State University).

is a more unconstitutional tyrant and a more odious dictator than ever he was before. They tell him, however, that his edict, his ukase, his decree, his firman, his venomous blow at the sacred liberty of white men to own black men is mere *brutem fulmen*, and a dead letter and a poison which will not work. They tell him many other things, and, among them, they tell him that the army will fight no more, and that the hosts of the Union will indignantly disband rather than be sacrificed upon the bloody altar of fanatical Abolitionism.[1]

It was not that Lincoln or the Proclamation lacked defenders. A long queue of prominent Republicans—George Boker, Francis Lieber, Grosvenor Lowrey, and Robert Dale Owen—promptly entered the lists with pamphlets and articles. But an equally formidable roster of Northern Democratic critics and jurists— including Benjamin Curtis, Montgomery Throop, and Joel Parker—were there waiting for them. Agitation mounted in many places for a negotiated settlement to the war or a national peace convention that would avoid emancipation. "The Darkest hour of our Country's trial is yet to come," warned Benjamin F. Butler. "Nothing is surer than an assembly to settle this struggle on the basis of the *Union as it was!*" Even worse, it was rumored "that the President will recoil from his Emancipation Proclamation" because of the heavy political costs it imposed.[2] In the end, if Lincoln had any hope of turning public opinion in favor of emancipation by argument, the arguments would have to be his, and he would have to be his own best apologist for the Proclamation.

The surest mark of how Lincoln rose to that challenge is the public letter he wrote on August 26, 1863, for James Cook Conkling and a "mass meeting of unconditional Union men" in Lincoln's own home town of Springfield, Illinois. After months of uncertainty, the Conkling letter signaled that Lincoln's commitment to emancipation was absolute and would not be bargained away in return for concessions by the Confederates. Thus, a straight line runs from

---

1. Frederick Seward, in *Recollected Words of Abraham Lincoln*, eds. Don and Virginia Fehrenbacher (Stanford: Stanford Univ. Press, 1996), 397; James G. Blaine, *Twenty Years of Congress: from Lincoln to Garfield*, 2 vols. (Norwich, Conn.: Henry Bill, 1884-86), 1:488; "To Hannibal Hamlin," Sept. 28, 1862, in *Collected Works of Abraham Lincoln*, ed. Roy P. Basler, 9 vols. (New Brunswick, N.J.: Rutgers Univ. Press, 1953-55), 5:444 (hereafter cited as *CW*); William O. Stoddard, *Inside the White House in War Times: Memoirs and Reports of Lincoln's Secretary* (1890), ed. Michael Burlingame (Lincoln: Univ. of Nebraska Press, 2000), 97.

2. Butler to Edward L. Pierce, July 20, 1863, Edward L. Pierce Papers, Houghton Library, Harvard University; Benjamin Flanders to Salmon P. Chase, Nov. 29, 1862, Abraham Lincoln Papers, Library of Congress.

the Proclamation through the Conkling letter to the Thirteenth Amendment and the final abolition of slavery.

It also speaks directly to the legion of skeptics who have doubted the tenacity or the sincerity of Lincoln's pledges of freedom in the Proclamation. The prose style itself has raised this skepticism, beginning with Lincoln's own time. Adam Gurowski, the curmudgeonly Polish expatriate who labored as a translator in the State Department, growled into his diary that the Proclamation was "written in the meanest and the most dry routine style; not a word to evoke a generous thrill." "This all-important paper," wrote Daniel Kirkham Dodge sixty years later, in friendly bewilderment, "is as lacking in literary qualities as the calls for troops and the formal communications to Congress on routine business." But the most famous dismissal of Lincoln's purposes in emancipation was undoubtedly Richard Hofstadter, who was also irritated at the Proclamation's stylistic flaccidity, and who found in that flaccidity the key to understanding the secret emptiness of Lincoln's motives. "Had the political strategy of the moment called for a momentous human document of the stature of the Declaration of Independence, Lincoln could have risen to the occasion." Instead, what Lincoln composed on New Year's Day 1863 "had all the moral grandeur of a bill of lading." It accomplished nothing because it was intended to accomplish nothing "beyond its propaganda value."[3] The influence of Hofstadter's easily repeatable quip about "the moral grandeur of a bill of lading" has had long endurance, and even the most favorably disposed of modern Lincoln biographers, like David Donald, have found themselves forced to concede that the Proclamation "lacks the memorable rhetoric of his most notable utterances."[4]

The tradition of the public letter—a personal commentary on policy or events cast in the ostensibly private form of a letter but intended for official or newspaper publication—had a long history in antebellum politics for presidents and presidential candidates. It stood more or less in the place of what might today be described journalistically as a "news conference." Lincoln's skill with the public

---

3. Adam Gurowski, *Diary: from March 4, 1861 to November 12, 1862* (Boston: Lee & Shepherd, 1862), 278; Daniel Kirkham Dodge, *Abraham Lincoln: Master of Words* (New York: D. Appleton, 1924), 130–31; Richard Hofstadter, "Abraham Lincoln and the Self-Made Myth," *The American Political Tradition and the Men Who Made It* (1948; reprint, New York: Knopf, 1973), 117, 129, 131.

4. David Donald, *Lincoln* (New York: Simon & Shuster, 1995), 375. A notable exception is Stephen B. Oates, who declared in a 1976 essay that "I do not agree with Richard Hofstadter's view," even though it was "hugely popular both in and out of the academies." See his "Lincoln's Journey to Emancipation," in *Our Fiery Trial: Abraham Lincoln, John Brown and the Civil War Era* (Amherst: Univ. of Massachusetts Press, 1979), 137.

letter was second only to the rhetorical skills he manifested in his formal and informal speeches. One of his most famous documents—his reply to Horace Greeley's own impatient pre-emancipation public letter, "The Prayer of Twenty Millions"—was cast in the form of a public letter and never sent to Greeley at all as a personal communication. Instead, it was published in the columns of John W. Forney's pro-administration *Washington Daily Chronicle*. Chauncey M. Depew believed that Lincoln's "series of letters were remarkable documents. He had the ear of the public; he commanded the front page of the press, and he defended his administration and its acts and replied to his enemies with skill, tact, and extreme moderation." As one historian has observed, the public letter became Lincoln's most perfect vehicle "to explain his views, counter criticism, and manifest his humanity."[5]

Lincoln actually wrote four important public letters in the eight months following the formal issue of the Emancipation Proclamation. The first was a brief reply to a series of resolutions passed by a workingmen's convention in Manchester, England, on January 19, 1863; the second was the letter written in response to Erastus Corning and a convention of New York Democrats on June 12, 1863; the third responded to the resolutions of the Ohio Democratic State Convention two weeks later; and the fourth was to James C. Conkling and the Springfield Union meeting on August 26, 1863. Like the Greeley letter, these four letters also achieved independent lives of their own. The Corning letter was republished as a Union League pamphlet under the title *Truth from an Honest Man: The Letter of the President*, provoking a pamphlet reply by the New York Democrats it had been addressed to. The others were published under the title *The Letters of President Lincoln on Questions of National Policy* by Benjamin B. Russell. The Corning and Ohio letters, however, were preoccupied with justifying Lincoln's use of martial law in the arrest of Clement Vallandigham in May 1863 rather than with emancipation. It was the Conkling letter that addressed the public opposition to emancipation most directly.

Lincoln's first concern about that opposition fell on the Border States. "When I issued that proclamation, I was in great doubt about it myself," Lincoln later told John McClintock, the Methodist educator and editor. "I did not think that

---

5. "To the Workingmen of Manchester, England," *CW* 6:63–64; "To Erastus Corning and Others," ibid., 260–69; "To Matthew Birchard and Others," ibid., 300–306; and "To James C. Conkling," ibid., 406–11; Chauncey M. Depew, *My Memories of Eighty Years* (New York: Charles Scribner's Sons, 1922), 30; James A. Rawley, *Abraham Lincoln and a Nation Worth Fighting For* (Wheeling, Ill.: Harlan-Davidson, 1996), 53.

the people had been quite educated up to it, and I feared its effects upon the border states." He had more than good reason for concern. In Missouri, one of Lincoln's listening-post correspondents irritably warned him that "your [most] substantial friends about here feel almost disposed to give up the contest, or trying to sustain you." Little more than a week after Lincoln signed the Proclamation, William G. "Parson" Brownlow warned Montgomery Blair that "things are not working . . . in Kentucky. I fear the Legislature will take strong action against the proclamation, and even against the Administration." James Garfield thought that in Washington, "All the men who are worth talking to are in favor of it, now that it has been promulgated." As an Ohioan, however, he was sure that "it can only have an adverse effect in Ky. and Tenn." And that was only from Lincoln's friends; the Democratic opposition in the Border States was far less self-contained. "The President's proclamation has come to hand at last," complained the *Louisville Daily Democrat*. "We scarcely know how to express our indignation at this flagrant outrage of all constitutional law, all human justice, all Christian feeling." Kentucky Democrats, sniffing the opportunity to overturn the Unionist majorities in the Kentucky legislature, called a state convention in February, for the purpose of "preparing the Kentucky Mind for revolt against the Union," and had to be forcibly dispersed by Federal troops.[6]

But the "Border" embraced a larger space than merely the four loyal slave states. The attitudes that characterized the Border—a general but not absolute unionism, a marked hostility to free blacks and a refusal to surrender slavery as a legal institution, a hesitation to commit the lives of its people or its material to either side in the war—belong to a far wider band of territory than what was contained within the Border *States*. The Border, in conceptual terms, ran through the Union in a fat seam stretching on the north from northern New Jersey through Harrisburg and Pittsburgh and from there to Columbus, Indianapolis, and Springfield; while on the South it included northern and western Virginia and eastern and central Tennessee. Within that larger Border, the nearest the Proclamation came to touching off a legislative rebellion occurred, not in Kentucky or Missouri, but in Lincoln's own home state of Illinois.

---

6. John McClintock, in Fehrenbacher, ed., *Recollected Words*, 314; Truman Woodruff to AL, Apr. 12, 1863, Lincoln Papers; Brownlow to Montgomery Blair, Jan. 9, 1863, in Blair Family Papers, Library of Congress; Theodore Clarke Smith, *The Life and Letters of James Abram Garfield*, 2 vols. (New Haven: Yale Univ. Press, 1925), 1:244–45; "The President's Proclamation," *Louisville Daily Democrat*, Jan. 3, 1863; E. Merton Coulter, *The Civil War and Readjustment in Kentucky* (Chapel Hill: Univ. of North Carolina Press, 1926), 173–79; Lowell H. Harrison, *Lincoln of Kentucky* (Lexington: Univ. Press of Kentucky, 2000), 176–77.

Illinois went Republican in the 1860 election, with Lincoln's party winning control of the legislature. One of Lincoln's old political associates, Richard Yates, captured the governor's mansion by more than 12,000 votes. When the senior Democratic senator, Stephen A. Douglas, died in June 1861, Yates appointed a Republican (and longtime personal friend of Lincoln's), Orville Hickman Browning, to give the state two Republican senators (the other was Lyman Trumbull). But Illinois's political history was Democratic, especially in the southernmost districts of the state, where a heavy proportion of the population were either Southern-born immigrants or else considerably less than enthusiastic about opposition to slavery. Illinois might be technically a free state, but its commitment to Free Soil was more a matter of small-farmer hostility to the economic scale of the plantation economy rather than to slavery itself. If anything, Illinois was notoriously hostile to free blacks and made generous allowances to slaveowners to use slave labor on Illinois farms under the state's slave transit laws.[7]

By mid-1861, signs of resistance to Republican war policies were already appearing. The battered Illinois Democrats cleared their heads and resolved ominously at the party's state convention "that the perilous condition of the country had been produced by the agitation of the slavery question, creating discord and enmity between the different sections, which had been aggravated by the election of a sectional president." In 1862, the decision of Secretary of War Stanton to establish a "contraband" camp at Cairo, Illinois, and begin hiring out blacks as agricultural workers caused uproar in southern Illinois. "The Germans & Irish are told that they are to interfere with their employment by taking their places," wrote one anxious Republican congressional candidate, and Democratic congressman William Allen complained on the floor of the House of Representatives that "thousands of negroes have been taken, decoyed or stolen" and transported to Illinois to compete with white workingmen. "Southern Illinois must either be the home of white men or black men—They cannot dwell together!"[8]

The 1862 legislative elections, following hard on the heels of Lincoln's preliminary announcement of the Proclamation on September 22, were an un-

---

7. Paul Finkelman, "Slavery, the 'More Perfect Union,' and the Prairie State," *Illinois Historical Journal* 80 (Winter 1987): 248-69; on the dearth of antislavery feeling especially in southern Illinois, see Edgar F. Raines, "The American Missionary Association in Southern Illinois, 1856-1862," *Journal of the Illinois State Historical Society* 65 (1972): 250-51, and Suzanne Cooper Guasco, "'The Deadly Influence of Negro Capitalists': Southern Yeomen and Resistance to the Expansion of Slavery in Illinois," *Civil War History* 47 (Mar. 2001): 7-29; George W. Smith, *A History of Southern Illinois: A Narrative Account of its Historical Progress*, 3 vols. (Chicago: Lewis Publishing, 1912), 1:317.

8. Robert Smith to Richard Yates, Oct. 13, 1862, Lincoln Papers; *Congressional Globe*, 37th Cong., 3d sess., Dec. 23, 1862 (Washington, D.C.: Congressional Globe Office, 1863), 182.

nerving disappointment for the Republicans across the North, and especially in Illinois. The Democrats owned the Illinois Senate by a margin of one (thirteen seats to twelve), and the House of Representatives by 54 to 32. Lincoln's own home congressional district defeated a Lincoln friend, Leonard Swett, and sent to Washington instead John Todd Stuart, Lincoln's onetime law partner and mentor but now a Democrat. The U.S. Senate seat that Browning had inherited by appointment was up for reelection in the Illinois Senate and would now obviously be pulled out from under Browning as quickly as it had been put beneath him. "It is very mortifying to the true American," mourned the *Alton Telegraph* on December 19, 1862: "to be forced to acknowledge that there is a large and influential party, which in this trying hour, is either so unwise or so lost to all patriotic feeling, as to play into the hands of both our foreign and domestic enemies. The Democratic party may claim to be loyal, and denounce all who question its sincerity as much as it pleases, but it has pursued such a course in the last political campaign, as to cause the common sense of mankind . . . to pronounce it unfaithful to the Government."[9]

The Proclamation gave both an edge and a target to the newly renascent Illinois Democrats. There was already substantial disaffection among soldiers in Illinois regiments about the Proclamation, and the Democratic victory at the polls back home fanned it higher. "I have been engaged to day in reading letters written by Citizens of Illinois to different members of my Regiment," reported one officer in the 54th Illinois near Jackson, Tennessee, "advising them to desert & offering protection to them if they will. . . . I am really afraid that if something is not done at once to put a stop to this thing that the fire in the rear . . . will yet form a serious affair." A lieutenant in the 86th Illinois surveyed his company and found to his shock that "only 8 men in Co. K. approve the policy and proclamation of Mr. Lincoln." One relative of an Illinois cavalryman confidently promised that "every man that has got the sand will throw off on the Lincoln Government now after the proclamation setting the nigger free. Ill's is bound to go with the Southland." Of the more than 13,000 desertions that Illinois regiments suffered during the war, the single largest number occurred immediately after the Proclamation was issued; one regiment, the 109th Illinois, had to be disbanded for disloyalty.[10]

---

9. George W. Smith, *History of Illinois and Her People*, 6 vols. (Chicago: American Historical Society, 1927), 3:28; J. G. Randall, *Lincoln the President: Springfield to Gettysburg*, 2 vols. (New York: Dodd, Mead, 1945), 2:234–35; Paul Angle, *"Here I Have Lived": A History of Lincoln's Springfield, 1821-1865* (Chicago: Abraham Lincoln Bookshop, 1971), 274; "Influence of the Democratic Victory," *Alton Telegraph*, Dec. 19, 1862.

10. G. M. Mitchell to Ozias Mather Hatch, Apr. 14, 1863, in O. M. Hatch Papers, Illinois State

Even among the Republican faithful, there was disharmony and discouragement that made key supporters think of leaving the party. Paul Selby recalled that "it has been charged that there was a conspiracy among leading Republican politicians of Illinois, including those intimately connected with the State administration at that time, 'to remove Mr. Lincoln by fair means or foul from his exalted position as leader of the political and military forces of the country and replace him with one of its own creatures.'" Orville Hickman Browning, facing the inevitable recall to Illinois, was convinced that the Proclamation was an ill-timed political gesture and concluded to withdraw from Republican politics: "The counsels of myself and those who sympathize with me are no longer heeded. I am despondent, and have but little hope left for the Republic." One of Browning's neighbors, Jackson Grimshaw, warned that Browning was planning "to build up a great 'third' party" in Illinois as an alternative, and Joseph Medill accused Browning of defecting to "the secesh of Illinois." But this was only what Grimshaw himself was coming to expect as the result of the way Republicans were managing their own cause:

> Our movement is . . . kind to all but its *friends*. It *has* dug up *snakes* and it *cant* kill them, it has fostered d-d rascals & crushed honest men. If [it] were not that our country, our homes, our all is at stake, that you and I have all, all our blood in this fight–Lincoln, Baker, Bailhache Edwards & all might go to—. . . . God help us all but it looks blue. . . . Cotton & family speculations, concessions to army rascals—arrests one day & releases the next—Kentucky policy and all that have shit us to hell. . . . There are some loyal men amongst our democrats, but the Government must *use force* and crush out treason at home or we are used up.[11]

Historical Library; Charles W. Wills, *Army Life of an Illinois Soldier, Including a Day by Day Record of Sherman's March to the Sea* (Washington, D.C.: Globe Printing, 1906), 125-26; Joseph Miller to Pvt. William Wilmoth, Jan. 25, 1863, in Lincoln Research Files ("Emancipation Proclamation"), Illinois State Historical Library; Victor Hicken, *Illinois in the Civil War* (Urbana: Univ. of Illinois Press, 1966), 128-29, 139.

11. George Julian, *Political Recollections, 1840-1872* (1884; reprint, Westport, Conn.: Negro Univ. Press, 1970), 223; Paul Selby, "Light On A Famous Lincoln Letter," *Transactions of the Illinois State Historical Society for the Year 1908* (Springfield: Illinois State Journal, 1909), 243; Browning diary entry, Jan. 30, 1863, in *Diary of Orville Hickman Browning*, ed. T. C. Pease and J. G. Randall, 2 vols. (Springfield: Illinois State Historical Library, 1925-33), 1:621; Jackson Grimshaw to Ozias M. Hatch, Sept. 8, 1862, Feb. 12, 1863, O. M. Hatch Papers, Illinois State Historical Library; David M. Silver, *Lincoln's Supreme Court* (Urbana: Univ. of Illinois Press, 1957), 72. Zachariah Chandler also warned Lyman Trumbull that Browning was plotting "to get up an anti-confiscation, no-party Union, with the Locos." See Wilmer C. Harris, *Public Life of Zachariah Chandler, 1851-1875* (Lansing: Michigan Historical Commission, 1917), 66.

But when the new Illinois legislature convened in Springfield on January 3, 1863, the initiative was seized at once by the revived Democrats, and their principal target was Lincoln's Proclamation. The leading Democratic newspaper, the *Illinois State Register*, rejoiced that the Proclamation would be the first item to come under legislative scrutiny. "There can be no question of the popular condemnation of this measure.... If Mr. Lincoln will trample on the Constitution the people will not stand by him. They will become disheartened in fighting the battles of the country, and they will utterly withdraw from him the affection and respect which every ruler should, by upright conduct, command." Governor Yates stubbornly sent in a strongly pro-administration message to open the session on January 6, but the Democratic majority refused to receive it and limited the customary publication of the message to two thousand copies so that they could "send it forth into the world, entering their solemn protest against its revolutionary and unconstitutional doctrines." Two days later, Elias Wenger from the 37th District offered a hostile resolution, condemning the Proclamation in almost frantic terms: "WHEREAS the Government of the United States has been engaged for nearly two years in an unsuccessful attempt to suppress the Southern rebellion ... and whereas our country is becoming almost a nation of widows and orphans, who, if the President's emancipation proclamation be carried into effect, will become prey to the lusts of freed negroes who will overrun our country ... we are in favor of an immediate suspension of hostilities, and recommend the holding of a national convention, for an amicable settlement of our difficulties." This was no mere state-house squabble. The Illinois legislature was clearly trying to mobilize national discontent, and in such a way that Lincoln could not easily ignore. "All the democratic members of the legislature are open secessionists," wrote one anxious observer. "They talked about going to Washington, hurling Mr Lincoln from the presidential chair, and inaugurating civil war north."[12]

And on it went, throughout the legislative session, with emancipation invariably the primary target. The Proclamation was "unconstitutional, contrary to the rules and usages of civilized warfare, calculated to bring shame, disgrace and eternal infamy upon the hitherto unsullied flag of the Republic, and Illinois ... will protest against any war which has for its object the execution or enforcement of said proclamations." On February 4, shortly before the session ended, one last resolution announced, "we believe the further prosecution of the present war cannot result in the restoration of the Union and the preservation of the Constitution as our

---

12. *Illinois State Register*, Jan. 3, 1863; Mercy Levering Conkling to Clinton Conkling, Jan. 11, 1863, in James C. & Clinton L. Conkling Papers, Illinois State Historical Library.

fathers made it, unless the President's emancipation proclamation be withdrawn" and asked for the naming of five commissioners to go to Washington and urge Congress to issue an armistice and arrange for a peace convention.[13]

The mischief the legislature could cause was not limited to provocative resolutions. Three of Lincoln's old Illinois political allies wrote that spring that the legislature "will, we think pass an act taking the military power out of the hands of the Governor abolish the adjutant generals office and . . . resist a draft or any attempt to apprehend & return deserters to their Regiments in the field." Just as bad, "We cannot sell any Bonds, as the Legislature has not authorized any more to be sold," reported Conkling to Lincoln on April 10, 1863, "and have not made even the ordinary appropriations for supporting the State Government so as to be available." As the legislature's second session neared in June, Conkling's wife, Mercy Levering Conkling, looked on disapprovingly as "the democrats" arrived, "copperheads largely in the majority, boldly expressing their disloyalty, and plotting treason."[14]

This time, however, Yates found a weapon with which to strike back. The legislative session opened on June 3, only two days after the anti-administration *Chicago Times* was temporarily shut down by Gen. Ambrose Burnside for its "repeated expression of disloyal and incendiary sentiments" and a week after Clement Vallandigham was expelled to the Confederacy on Lincoln's order. Both incidents provided fresh tinder to incendiary anti-administration speech-making in the Illinois House. But on June 10, citing an obscure provision in the Illinois Constitution, Yates prorogued the legislature (and in fact would govern without the legislature's help until the very end of the legislature's term in 1864). The astounded representatives fumed against this "monstrous and revolutionary usurpation of power," but after two weeks of helpless protest they conceded. "Well knowing that their peace resolutions were pending, and lots more were being 'hatched up,'" Yates chortled. "I sent my polite note to them, telling them in the language of the soldiers to the rebels, to 'skeedaddle.' They had been in session for nine days, and it was a sight good for sore eyes to see them leaving with their nine dollars and postage stamps."[15]

---

13. *Journal of the House of Representatives of the Twenty-Third General Assembly of the State of Illinois* (Springfield: Baker & Phillips, 1865), 66, 78, 83, 373.

14. Jesse K. Dubois, Ozias M. Hatch, William Butler to AL, Mar. 1, 1863, and Conkling to AL, Apr. 10, 1863, Lincoln Papers; Mercy Levering Conkling to Clinton Conkling, June 7, 1863, in James C. & Clinton L. Conkling Papers, Illinois State Historical Library.

15. Camilla A. Quinn, *Lincoln's Springfield in the Civil War,* Western Illinois Monograph Series, No. 8 (Macomb: Western Illinois Univ., 1991), 47; Melvin W. Fuller, in *Journal of the House of Representa-*

This did not prevent the enraged Illinois Democrats from finding another stage with which to capture national attention, the mass political meeting. Like the public letter, the mass meeting was a staple of antebellum politics, and though the definition of *mass* could be stretched to include everything from a few hundred flag-wavers at a county seat to a major metropolitan quasi-convention, they were organized and staged with extraordinary frequency and partisan absolutism by Republicans and Democrats alike during the war years, as a way of connecting local political interests with national issues and national political figures. Even if, as Glenn Altschuler and Stuart Blumin have suggested, these rallies were largely stage-managed by over-motivated political activists before crowds who had more interest in the circuslike atmosphere of the rally than its ideological content, every pretense of popular spontaneity had to be maintained. "It was a period rife with popular assemblies," recalled Indiana Democrat David Turpie. "These were called Union or War meetings" and "were held in every town and city, in almost every township of the state."[16] The centerpiece of mass meetings was usually a roster of nationally known speakers who were set up at separate stands or platforms at the meeting grounds, while the people were free to move from one to the other, sampling the oratory. The conclusion of the meetings usually involved a series of resolutions whose general purpose was to offer public encouragement to the leaders of the cause or, alternately, by a show of numbers to offer as much political intimidation to the opposition as possible. Both the Republicans and Democrats had staged "mass meetings" in Springfield at the opening of the legislature in January 1863, and the proroguing of the legislature became the occasion for the calling of a Democratic mass meeting by the party's state committee at the Springfield fairgrounds on June 17, 1863.

True to form, the Democratic meeting would be a local event, but with a na-

---

tives of the Twenty-Third General Assembly of the State of Illinois (Springfield: Baker & Phillips, 1865), 728; William B. Hesseltine, *Lincoln and the War Governors* (New York: Knopf, 1948), 318; "Speech of Richard Yates," *Illinois State Journal*, July 13, 1863.

16. Glenn Altschuler and Stuart Blumin, "Limits of Political Engagement in Antebellum America: A New Look at the Golden Age of Participatory Democracy," *Journal of American History* 84 (Dec. 1997): 855–85; Turpie, *Sketches of My Own Times* (Indianapolis: Bobbs-Merrill Co., 1903), 189. Politician-general John A. McClernand reported to Lincoln on a Democratic meeting in Chatham, Illinois, where "a number hurrahed for John Morgan—the same Morgan who is now burning the houses and wasting the fields of peaceful citizens in the loyal state of Ohio." Judging by that meeting, McClernand was alarmed that a "bold demagogue, or a reckless inebriate, in my opinion, has it in his power to precipitate fearful strife and great bloodshed" in Illinois. See McClernand to AL, July 23, 1863, Lincoln Papers.

tional audience and national participants. The organizers, chaired by William A. Richardson, invited two of Lincoln's most prominent congressional critics, Samuel S. Cox of Ohio and Daniel Vorhees of Indiana, as the marquee speakers. When it was over, the *Illinois State Register* proudly announced, "The meeting yesterday was the most tremendous gathering of the people ever witnessed in Illinois," with attendance estimates varying from 75,000 (Democratic) to 15,000 (Republican). The resolutions denounced Yates, the arrest and banishment of Clement Vallandigham, and "the further offensive prosecution of this war." And almost as though the legislature was still in session, the meeting proposed "a national convention, to settle the terms of peace, which shall have in view the restoration of the Union as it was, and the securing by constitutional amendments such rights"—and here, the *rights* jeopardized by the Emancipation Proclamation were clearly in view—"to the several states and the people thereof, as honor and justice demand."[17]

Illinois Republicans tried to blunt the impact of the Democratic rally by staging a number of mass meetings of their own. These were held in Duquoin on July 17, in South Macon on July 23, in Havana on July 28, a "Grand Union Meeting" at Pleasant Plains (north of Springfield) on August 10, and a tremendous "Grand Union Demonstration" at the state capitol on July 8 that celebrated the fall of Vicksburg with a thirty-five-gun salute. Just as Yates's daring proroguing of the legislature could never quite wipe out the humiliation Illinois Republicans felt over the legislature's demand for a peace convention, none of these subsequent meetings could quite wipe away the irritation they felt at the size and celebrity of the June 17 Democratic meeting. By the beginning of August, Republicans had prepared a gigantic riposte, a mass meeting for September 3 at the Springfield fairgrounds designed to overshadow even the great June 17 meeting. It would distinguish itself from the Democratic meeting by being a "Union" meeting, inviting both Republicans and War Democrats, thus impugning the June 17 meeting as a purely selfish, partisan affair. True, the bulk of the meeting's leadership would be Republican, but it would feature (or so the organizers hoped) a wish list of national Republican and War Democrat heroes: Generals Benjamin Butler, John A. Logan, John A. McClernand; Governors David Tod of Ohio, Oliver P. Morton of Indiana, Andrew Johnson of Tennessee, and Andrew Gregg Curtin of Pennsylvania; plus U.S. speaker of the house Schuyler Colfax. "The meeting will be the largest ever held in the State," the *Journal* promised, "and will be a

---

17. "The Meeting Yesterday," *Illinois State Register*, June 18, 1863; *History of Sangamon County, Illinois* (Chicago: Inter-State Publishing, 1881), 315.

most impressive demonstration of the sentiment of loyal Illinois," Republican and Democrat alike.[18] Indeed, it would be that, and more, if the organizing committee's chairman, James Conkling, could get his way. He wanted as the principal speaker to be no one less than Abraham Lincoln.

James Cook Conkling was, like Lincoln, a Springfield lawyer, and his wife, Mercy Levering, had been a close friend of Mary Todd Lincoln's. Born in New York in 1816 and a graduate of Princeton, Conkling had clerked briefly in New Jersey then moved to Illinois in 1838 and was admitted to the bar that October. Like Lincoln, he had been an ardent Whig and successfully ran for both mayor of Springfield in 1845 and then the state legislature in 1851, where "he was identified with a small group of able men who were prominent in anti-slavery legislation." He joined the Republicans, became a member of the state Republican committee in 1856, but lost a race for the U.S. House. Conkling was one of fifteen Sangamon County delegates to the 1860 state nominating convention in Decatur that pledged itself to Lincoln's nomination for the presidency, and he prided himself on having "voted regularly for Mr. Lincoln for more than a quarter century whenever he aspired to any office." He strongly defended Lincoln's policies, including military arrests. "While the Government is contending against armed traitors it must also crush incipient treason," he icily wrote to one former Democratic acquaintance who had been imprisoned in Fort Warren as a Confederate sympathizer. "It is therefore...justified in arresting those who refuse to take the oath of allegiance." Lincoln, for his part, spoke well and highly of Conkling. When Conkling was appointed by Yates as Illinois's state agent to oversee the state accounts with the federal government, Lincoln endorsed Conkling to Secretary of War Stanton as "a good man" and described him to Quartermaster General Montgomery Meigs as having "ample business qualification, is entirely trustworthy; and with all is my personal friend of long standing." Yet none of this made Conkling much more than an important Illinois political operative. It was revealing of the disarray and anxiety of Illinois Republicans that the most crucial invitation of all would come not from key Illinois party figures and Lincoln allies like Joseph Medill, Leonard Swett, Browning, Isaac Arnold, or "Long John" Wentworth but from a comparatively minor political player from Springfield like Conkling. And yet, just

---

18. "Enthusiastic Union Meeting in Macon County," *Illinois State Journal,* July 25, 1863; "Grand Union Meeting," ibid., Aug. 10, 1863; "Grand Union Demonstration," ibid., July 9, 1863; "State Union Mass Convention," ibid., Aug. 8, 1863.

as Altschuler and Blumin suggested, the organization of the rally would be held tightly in the hands of men like Conkling—not, perhaps, the Illinois party elite but still an influential mid-level cadre of Springfield Republicans who were, for all practical purposes, the Republican leadership of central Illinois.[19]

Given the lack of sponsorship from the great names of Illinois Republicanism, neither Conkling nor his Springfield associates were taking any chances that the "Great Union Mass Meeting" would fall short of the mark set by the June 17 Democratic meeting. The *Illinois State Journal* began running notices for the meeting under its own editorial banner on August 13, announcing, "The Invitations for the great Union Mass Meeting are nearly all issued and the call with a large number of names appended, will appear in a few days." The next day, the *Journal* ran a still-larger notice, followed by a list of endorsements from local Republicans and War Democrats, including Yates, Jesse Dubois, Newton Bateman, Isaac Keyes, Paul Selby, and Conkling himself. By August 16, the number of endorsements had grown by 300, and the call for the meeting was moved to the *Journal's* front page, where it ran until August 31 (by which time, the list of endorsements consumed a column and a quarter of names in agate type).[20]

On August 21, the plan was beginning to catch national fire. The organizing committee happily announced that Radical Republican senator Zachariah Chandler had agreed to be a speaker, and on successive days the *Journal* added that Wisconsin senator James R. Doolittle, Maj. Gen. Richard J. Oglesby, McClernand, and Yates would join him. The *Journal* further expected public letters from Edward Everett and others. "Every county will be represented by its hundreds of delegates, and some by thousands," so much so that fears of overcrowding in Springfield were causing the organizers to ask loyal Springfielders to open private homes. But the attraction that Conkling hoped would secure the kind of

---

19. Frederick B. Crossley, *Courts and Lawyers of Illinois* (Chicago: American Historical Society, 1916), 191–92; *The United States Biographical Dictionary and Portrait Gallery of Eminent and Self-Made Men: Illinois Volume* (Chicago: American Biographical Publishing Co., 1876), 159–60; Joseph Wallace, *Past and Present of the City of Springfield and Sangamon County* (Chicago: S. J. Clarke Publishing, 1904), 54–55; Victor B. Howard, "The Illinois Republican Party," *Journal of the Illinois State Historical Society* 64 (Autumn 1971): 303; Wayne C. Temple, "Delegates to the Illinois State Republican Nominating Convention in 1860," *Journal of the Illinois State Historical Society* 92 (Autumn 1999): 296; Conkling to George Bancroft, Feb. 19, 1866, and Conkling to Robert Hall, July 31, 1862, in James C. & Clinton L. Conkling Papers, Illinois State Historical Library; "To Edwin M. Stanton," Feb. 3, 1863, and "To Montgomery C. Meigs," Jan. 31, 1863, *CW* 6:85, 90; Altschuler and Blumin, "Limits of Political Engagement," 868.

20. "The Great Union Mass Meeting," *Illinois State Journal*, Aug. 13, 1863; "Preparing for the Great Mass Meeting," ibid., Aug. 25, 1863.

crowd that would erase all memory of the embarrassments of the preceding eight months was Lincoln himself. On August 14, Conkling extended the invitation to the president, adding reasons why Lincoln should accept:

> The unconditional union men in our State are to hold a Grand Mass Meeting at Springfield on the 3rd Day of September next. It would be gratifying to the many thousands who will be present on that occasion if you would also meet with them.
> ... A visit to your old home would not be inappropriate if you can break away from the pressure of public duties. We intend to make the most imposing demonstration that has ever been held in the Northwest. Many of the most distinguished men in the country have been, and will be invited to attend and I know that nothing could add more to the interest of the occasion than your presence.

Conkling later explained, "We hardly expected he would be present, but we hoped to receive some communication which would indicate his future policy and give encouragement to his friends."[21] At that moment, however, Conkling was evidently very much in earnest about the possibility of Lincoln's presence in Springfield.

And so, for the moment, was the president. Lincoln had traveled comparatively little outside of Washington during the war, but the crisis in Illinois was nearly impossible for him to ignore. On August 20, he telegraphed Conkling: "Your letter of the 14th is received. I think I will go, or send a letter—probably the latter." Even the barest suggestion of Lincoln's attendance was enough to delight Conkling. The next day, the *Illinois State Journal* confidently proclaimed, "President Lincoln Will Probably Be Here.... President Lincoln has given assurances justifying a strong hope that he will be here.... Nothing could be more fitting ... in this hour of national triumph and hope, than that he should visit his old home and receive the greetings of his friends of the Prairie State." Privately, however, Conkling realized that this was a conditioned promise, and on August 21 he sent Lincoln a second letter, plying him with additional arguments for coming personally to Springfield. Lincoln toyed just seriously enough with the idea to write his old Springfield law partner, William Herndon, about the advisability of committing himself to the meeting. Herndon, replying to Lincoln on August 26, saw no reason for Lincoln to hold back. "[We] will have a great time here on the 3rd September and it is

---

21. Conkling to AL, Aug. 14, 1863, Lincoln Papers. See also *Dear Mr. Lincoln: Letters to the President*, ed. Harold Holzer (Reading: Addison-Wesley, 1993), 281; Conkling to George Bancroft, Feb. 19, 1866, in James C. & Clinton L. Conkling Papers, Illinois State Historical Library.

thought it will be the largest Convt. ever convened here. There is no doubt but it will be a large meeting. I hope it will—hope it will give us confidence, back-bone vigor & energy. The Union men are busy at work all over the State to meet any Emergency. They are determined—cool—not hasty—not rash."[22]

By August 23, Lincoln had decided not to make the journey. Part of the motivation was his anxiety over the uncertain military situation in Virginia and Tennessee, where Lincoln hoped that both Maj. Gen. George G. Meade and Maj. Gen. William S. Rosecrans would pursue the Confederate armies. Part of his reasoning also may have been due to a reluctance to feed the accusations of critics like Vallandigham by looking as though, by personal appearance in Springfield, he endorsed Yates's unilateral dismissal of the legislature as a good way of dealing with opposition. However, Lincoln could not disengage himself entirely from the Illinois situation, and so he chose instead to write a public letter for Conkling to read to the meeting on his behalf. (Curiously, it would make no allusion at all to Yates's proroguing of the legislature.) John Hay noted that afternoon that Lincoln "went to the library to write a letter to Conkling & I went to pack my trunk for the North." He worked on it intermittently over three days (William Stoddard noted that Lincoln "composed somewhat slowly and with care, making few erasures or corrections" and usually worked "alone by himself in his room"), completing a rough draft on August 26, followed by a finished draft the same day, and a final version in a copyist's hand on the 27th. The copyist's version contained some last-minute corrections in Lincoln's hand and a cover note to Conkling by Lincoln himself: "I can not leave here now. Herewith is a letter instead. You are one of the best public readers. I have but one suggestion. Read it very slowly. And now God bless you, and all good Union-men." Lincoln himself leaked the news to the press that he would not be going west after all, but would instead "address to his fellow-citizens another of those homely but powerful appeals which may have more than once been almost equal to battles won."[23]

---

22. "To James C. Conkling," Aug. 20, 1863, *CW* 6:399; "President Lincoln Will Probably Be Here," *Illinois State Journal*, Aug. 21, 1863; "The Great Meeting in Illinois. The President Expected," *Washington National Republican*, Aug. 22, 1863. The possibility of Lincoln absenting himself from Washington in the late summer of 1863 seems to have had general currency, since New Hampshire governor Joseph Gilmore had written him on Aug. 4, "I see from the public prints that you are intending to spend a few weeks among the Mountains of New Hampshire. May we not have the privilege of welcoming you to our state capital?" But it was actually Mary Lincoln, not her husband, who was planning a New Hampshire summer vacation. See Gilmore to AL, Conkling to AL, Aug. 21, 1863, and Herndon to AL, in Lincoln Papers.

23. Hay, diary entry, Aug. 23, 1863, in *Inside Lincoln's White House: The Complete Civil War Diary of John Hay*, ed. Michael Burlingame and J. R. T. Ettlinger (Carbondale: Southern Illinois Univ.

The letter arrived in Springfield on August 31, and while it deflated Conkling's hopes for a personal presidential appearance, it set off new speculation as to what the letter would say. "President Lincoln has written a letter to the Mass Convention to meet in this city," wrote the pro-administration *Chicago Tribune's* Springfield correspondent. "Its perusal will gladden the heart of every true Union man in the country, vindicate the President's fame and character, and be the keynote of the next Presidential campaign." Or it might, observed the once-more-restored *Chicago Times*, include a repudiation of the emancipation proclamation and "a statement" of "an amnesty to the great mass of the Southern people."[24]

Whatever mystery the letter contained, the meeting itself was everything that the organizers had hoped for. "Never, perhaps, in the history of Illinois, has such a gathering of men been seen," rejoiced the *Illinois State Journal*. "The State of Illinois has redeemed herself. The glory of the 3rd of September has effaced the stain of the 17th of June." The *Journal* wanted to estimate the crowds as high as two hundred thousand, although Conkling himself thought it was more reasonable to estimate "50000 to 75000 present." The Democratic press was more dismissive of the estimates: the *Illinois State Register* estimated 12,096, and the *Chicago Times'* correspondent "puts it at not exceeding 10,000, the greater portion of whom were women and children." But there was no doubt that Springfield was thronged with people. "The hotels are full," gushed the *Journal*. "Every house in the city, in which a Union family resides, is full to overflowing. Some of our leading citizens are boarding and sleeping more than fifty to one

---

Press, 1997), 76; "To James C. Conkling," Aug. 27, 1863, *CW* 6:414. Lincoln's rough draft of Aug. 26, 1863, survives in the Abraham Lincoln Papers at the Library of Congress as seven sheets, five of them in pencil, the final two in ink, with a few cross-outs; the formal draft, also August 26 and also extant in the Abraham Lincoln Papers, is written in ink on eight sheets of Executive Mansion stationery, with one of them, the fifth, pasted together where Lincoln probably removed a section he had originally planned to include on the futility of an armistice or peace convention, and a quick conclusion promising that "the government will return no person to slavery who is free according to the proclamation." See "Fragment," Aug. 26, 1863, *CW* 6:410-11. The actual letter sent to Conkling was recopied in another hand on four double sheets of Executive Mansion stationery, on which Lincoln made one notable alteration in his own hand, changing a phrase near the conclusion from "well-born bayonet" to "well-poised bayonet." AL's cover note to Conkling, marked "Private," was written on War Department stationery. Both the copyist's draft and Lincoln's cover note are in the Illinois State Historical Library. On Lincoln's composing habits, see Stoddard, *Inside the White House in War Times*, 171-72. Stoddard included this news as part of his Washington despatch for the Sept. 3, 1863, edition of the *New York Examiner*. Lincoln regularly used his staffers to leak significant news to the press through columns and letters they themselves contributed anonymously to a variety of Northern newspapers.

24. "From Springfield," *Chicago Tribune*, Sept. 1, 1863; "The News," *Chicago Times*, Sept. 2, 1863.

hundred people." At nine o'clock that morning, a great procession formed up at the state capitol and, led by "A magnificent flag and a band of music" and "a blue banner, with a portrait of President Lincoln in the center," it wound its way up and down Springfield's numbered streets, and finally west on Washington Street to the fairgrounds. "So vast was the crowd that speaking was had at five different stands at the same time," with a regular schedule of invited speakers at four of them and a fifth reserved for "volunteer speakers." Zachariah Chandler held forth at the first stand. He was followed by former Brig. Gen. Isham Haynie, Yates, and Doolittle, plus the reading of letters from Edward Everett, Daniel Dickenson, and Schuyler Colfax. The second stand featured McClernand and Chicago congressman Isaac Arnold. Oglesby spoke at the third stand, while the fourth stand was "set apart exclusively for German speakers."[25]

The set-piece of the meeting, however, was the reading of Lincoln's letter. Lincoln had addressed the letter *to* Conkling, but with the purpose that it should be read *by* Conkling to the meeting. (In fact, there was next to nothing in the letter that meant anything to Conkling personally.) Nevertheless, Conkling was determined to make the most of being the recipient of a letter from the president, and so he arranged for the letter to be read aloud publicly to himself at his speaking platform in a kind of staged tableau, with the crowd as a sort of secondary audience. Consequently, Lincoln's letter was read not by Conkling to the people but by Jacksonville lawyer I. J. Ketchum; it was read by Ketchum to Conkling, seated and beaming on the platform as though Ketchum was impersonating Lincoln for Conkling's benefit, while the rest of Springfield listened. Probably at no other point in the "mass meeting" was it clearer that the letter and the rally were the possession of the Republican elite. No matter how it was delivered, though, the letter "was received with great enthusiasm, particularly the portion of it announcing that a retraction of the proclamation of emancipation was as impossible as the raising of the dead." It was Conkling's moment to bask in the glory of being the mediator between Springfield and the nation, and he was not about to have his role in it missed.[26]

---

25. *Illinois State Journal*, Sept. 4, 1863.
26. Conkling to AL, Sept. 4, 1863, Lincoln Papers; "The Great Meeting," *Illinois State Register*, Sept. 9, 1863; "The News," *Chicago Times*, Sept. 4, 1863; "From Springfield," *Chicago Tribune*, Sept. 3, 1863; "The Great Union Mass Meeting," *Illinois State Journal*, Sept. 4, 1863. Lincoln's letter was printed in full as the first document in the *Journal*'s article, followed by the texts of the letters from Everett, Colfax, and Dickenson, and the speeches of Chandler and Oglesby. The speeches of McClernand and Doolittle were published in the *Journal* on September 7 and 9.

Despite the *Chicago Times'* prediction, the letter was Lincoln's most extensive and forthright defense of emancipation since the issuance of the Proclamation itself. The letter, all of 1,662 words long, falls logically into six sections. The first was a simple salutation to Conkling and to the organizers of the meeting, "my old political friends"; but it also made an opening political gesture of recognition to War Democrats, "those other noble men, whom no partizan malice, or partizan hope, can make false to the nation's life."[27]

That much said, Lincoln plunged bluntly into the second section, where it was clear at once that he intended to speak over the heads of the loyalists at the mass meeting to the very anti-emancipation Democrats who had triggered the legislative rumpus of the past spring, in the evident hope that they might be willing to keep supporting the war if they could have their anger at emancipation reasoned away. "There are those who are dissatisfied with me," he said simply, adding that their dissatisfaction came down to one thing: "You desire peace; and you blame me that we do not have it." What he asked the dissatisfied to do at that point was to reflect on how peace could actually be obtained. "There are but three conceivable ways." First was to keep on with the war and "suppress the rebellion by force of arms. This I am trying to do." Could there be any disagreement with that? "Are you for it?" he asked rhetorically. Lincoln presumed so, but he accepted for the moment that they did not and moved on to suggest a second way to bring peace: "give up the Union." Were there any takers for that? "Are you for it?" This time, he presumed not. In that case, "If you are not for *force*, nor yet for *dissolution*, there only remains some imaginable compromise." Could anyone really imagine from where such a Union-saving compromise would come? Not from anyone in the South. "The strength of the rebellion, is its military—its army," Lincoln explained, and the Rebel military showed no inclination at all to compromise. Even if the Confederate politicians in Richmond would announce their interest in negotiations, "no paper compromise, to which the controllers of Lee's army are not agreed, can, at all, affect that army," and "no word or intimation, from that rebel army, or from any of the men controlling it, in relation to any peace compromise, has ever come to my knowledge of belief." Moreover, any efforts by well-intentioned Northerners to propose an armistice would only "waste time, which the enemy would improve to our disadvantage; and that would be all." There was, in other words, no way forward for saving the Union except to fight

---

27. "To James C. Conkling," Aug. 26, 1863, in *CW* 6:406–7. Lincoln's own final draft wrote out the salutation on the top half of a sheet of Executive Mansion stationery.

determinedly and unitedly to victory over the Confederacy. All the wild talk of national peace conventions weakened that resolve.[28]

Lincoln understood that this was not the real grounds for the "dissatisfaction," or even the calls for national compromise. He began the third section of the letter with an accusation: "But, to be plain, you are dissatisfied with me about the negro." Indeed they were, and he knew that this "difference of opinion between you and myself upon that subject" was the issue before which all the other dissatisfactions were little more than smoke screens. Lincoln's gambit was to seize the moral high ground and turn the debate from a vicious argument about race to a more imposing argument about the Union. "I certainly wish that all men could be free," Lincoln wrote, which was an assertion so disarming that no one could easily object—and knowing that the president turned the knife deftly on his critics by adding, "while I suppose you do not." Having cast them neatly to the disadvantage, Lincoln still protested that he did not propose to make even that an issue: "Yet I have neither adopted, nor proposed any measure, which is not consistent with even your view." He then added the proviso that would be crucial to the entire development of his argument: "provided you are for the Union." The strategy of the letter was now becoming apparent. By establishing a common commitment to saving the Union as paramount, Lincoln was now ready (after the irresistible suggestion that the anti-emancipation Democrats had put their party over the last six months in the place of denouncing both union *and* freedom) to ask whether any of his emancipation policies had been anything else except services to the cause of the Union. He had not, he reminded them, acted wildly or irresponsibly on the subject of emancipation. "I suggested compensated emancipation; to which you replied you wished not to be taxed to buy negroes." Lincoln here referred to the compensated emancipation plans he had designed in the spring of 1862, offering federally financed funds for buying the freedom of slaves in the Border States. This would have meant taxing Northerners to subsidize the purchase of enslaved blacks, but this was only "to save you from greater taxation to save the Union" by means of war. The logical corollary he was hoping to trigger in their minds would be, "If it is really true that *you are for the Union*, then there should be no reason to grumble at the costs of compensated emancipation, because it would save the Union and do it at far less expense than taxing Northerners to support a war." By forcing his hearers into agreement to a common condition—being *for the Union*—he planned to pull them along into agreement with his deduction from

28. "To James C. Conkling," Aug. 26, 1863, *CW* 6:407.

that premise: the need for emancipation. The use of the if/then conditional would from this point be his principal literary weapon.²⁹

A counterargument lurked here that the Proclamation was so radical a gesture that it was the principal reason why the Union was becoming impossible to restore. "Some of you profess to think its retraction would operate favorably for the Union." But practically speaking, the truth was that "the war has certainly progressed as favorably for us, since the issue of the proclamation as before." (Corollary: if really *you are for the Union*, there is no reason to retract the Emancipation Proclamation.) The irony of these protests, Lincoln pointed out, is that all the while "you say you will not fight to free negroes," there were large numbers of emancipated blacks who "seem willing to fight for you." Every one of them who is willing to subtract himself or herself from the Confederate war-making effort by running away to the Union lines, or who is willing to don a Union uniform and carry a rifle against the Rebels, is providing just so much more aid in saving the Union. "I thought that in your struggle for the Union, to whatever extent the negroes should cease helping the enemy, to that extent it weakened the enemy in his resistance to you. Do you think differently?" Lincoln again jabbed rhetorically.³⁰

For those who swept aside the practical benefits of emancipation on the grounds that it was unconstitutional, Lincoln was ready with a related response. "You dislike the emancipation proclamation; and, perhaps, would have it retracted. You say it is unconstitutional." This was a matter of interpretation, however, not constitutional fact. The constitution, after all, designates the president as commander in chief in time of war, and under international law, emancipations of an opponents' slaves were perfectly within the legal category of military actions that could be taken

---

29. Lincoln was sufficiently anxious to prove the favorable impact of the Proclamation on the course of military events that on August 31 he telegraphed Conkling with a paragraph to insert in the reading of the letter, attesting "that some of the commanders of our armies in the field who have given us our most important successes, believe the emancipation policy, and the use of colored troops, constitute the heaviest blow yet dealt to the rebellion; and that at least one of those important successes, could not have been achieved when it was, but for the aid of black soldiers." See, "To James C. Conkling," Aug. 31, 1863, *CW* 6:423. Lincoln was quoting a letter he had received from Ulysses S. Grant shortly after sending his own letter to Conkling, in which Grant described emancipation and "arming the negro" as "the heavyest blow yet given the Confederacy." See "To Abraham Lincoln," Aug. 23, 1863, *The Papers of Ulysses S. Grant*, ed. John Y. Simon, 24 vols. (Carbondale: Southern Illinois Univ. Press, 1967-), 9:195-97. This, and a similar letter from Nathaniel Banks, "gave much satisfaction to the President," according to Salmon Chase, to whom Lincoln showed the letters on August 30. See, David Donald, ed., *Inside Lincoln's Cabinet: The Civil War Diaries of Salmon P. Chase* (New York: Longmans, Green, 1954), 178. Conkling marked his copyists' version of Lincoln's letter with a caret, "Here insert Telegram," to note the place where the telegraphed paragraph was to be read.

30. "To James C. Conkling," Aug. 26, 1863, *CW* 6:408.

to weaken the enemy. "The most that can be said, is, that slaves are property. Is there—has there ever been—any question that by the law of war, property, both of enemies and friends, may be taken when needed? And is it not needed whenever taking it, helps us, or hurts the enemy?" Of course, it was possible to quibble whether such a confiscation proclamation in time of war should be considered valid "as law"—in other words, as a measure that would hold up under examination in a court. If it wasn't, there was no use calling for the Proclamation's retraction now, because litigation would find out whatever defects it had in the law's own good time; if, however, the Proclamation is valid, then what point would be served by retracting it? "If it is valid, it needs no retraction. If it is valid, it can not be retracted, any more than the dead can be brought back to life."[31]

Significantly, these two points—the Proclamation's constitutionality as a wartime measure and its technical legal standing before the federal courts thereafter—were more bothersome to Lincoln than this simple either/or treatment suggested. He had told Maj. Gen. Stephen A. Hurlbut in July, "I think [the Proclamation] is valid in law, and will be so held by the courts," but even if not, "I think I shall not retract or repudiate it. Those who shall have tasted actual freedom I believe can never be slaves, or quasi slaves again." While he was determined that "while I remain in my present position I shall not attempt to retract or modify the emancipation proclamation, nor shall I return to slavery any person who is free by the terms of that proclamation, or by any of the Acts of Congress"; nevertheless, he acknowledged that "the Executive power itself would be greatly diminished by the cessation of actual war." He admitted to Confederate vice president Alexander Stephens as late as the Hampton Roads Conference in February 1865, "His own opinion was that as the proclamation was a war measure and would have effect only from its being an exercise of the war power, as soon as the war ceased, it would be inoperative." He insisted that he would make it apply "to such slaves as had come under its operation while it was in active exercise," including slaves de facto liberated by the Union armies. But he was aware that "the courts might decide the other way." This helps to explain Lincoln's eagerness as early as 1864 for a constitutional amendment that would put emancipation beyond the reach even of the federal courts.[32]

---

31. Ibid., 409.
32. "To Stephen A. Hurlbut," July 31, 1863, *CW* 6:358; "Annual Message to Congress," Dec. 8, 1864, ibid., 8:151-52; Alexander Stephens, *A Constitutional View of the Late War Between the States*, 2 vols. (Philadelphia: National Publishing Co., 1868-70), 2:610-11; William C. Harris, "The Hampton Roads Peace Conference: A Final Test of Lincoln's Presidential Leadership," *Journal of the Abraham Lincoln Association* 21 (Winter 2000): 50.

Lincoln would grant this much to his political critics. If they wished "exclusively to save the Union" and not to emancipate slaves, their love for the Union (if really *you are for the Union*) was quite acceptable and should carry them forward with him to the goal of saving it. "Fight you, then, exclusively to save the Union," the president encouraged. Whenever they had succeeded in conquering "all resistance to the Union," if Lincoln should ask them to fight any longer after that, then "it will be an apt time, then, for you to declare you will not fight to free negroes." All this, of course, was a highly subtle joke. By the time such critics had fought and saved the Union, the war for black freedom would also be over. But while the war was still on, there was no other way to get black help to save the Union than through offering blacks freedom. "Negroes, like other people, act upon motives." If, for the sake of saving the Union, "they stake their lives for us, they must be prompted by the strongest motive—even the promise of freedom." Here, Lincoln added ominously, "the promise being made, must be kept."[33] There would, in other words, be no taking back of the Emancipation Proclamation. A pledge of life had to be balanced with a pledge of freedom, a pledge so solemn that it would balance forever the risk of life.

Then, abruptly, the argument for emancipation seemed spent. Lincoln turned quickly and briefly in the fourth section of the letter to what many at the fairgrounds might have imagined would have been the longer subject of his letter, a review of the progress of the war. "The signs look better." The Mississippi was now open with the fall of Vicksburg, and the "Father of Waters again goes unvexed to the sea." The northwest and the northeast had all contributed their strength, and so even had the unionist South, "in black and white." Victories at "Antietam, Murfreesboro, Gettysburg, and on many fields of lesser note" had been won, while the navy—"Uncle Sam's Web-feet"—had imposed a blockade that covered the deep sea as well as "wherever the ground was a little damp." Thanks went to all, "For the great republic—for the principle it lives by, and keeps alive—for man's great future,—thanks to all."[34]

Lincoln had one more round to fire on behalf of emancipation in the fifth and most acerbic section. "Peace does not appear so distant as it did," he concluded, and when it did, the peace would prove the basic point he had been struggling to make since his July 4, 1861, special message to Congress: "that among free men, there can be no successful appeal from the ballot to the bullet," that in

---

33. "To James C. Conkling," Aug. 26, 1863, *CW* 6:409.
34. Ibid., 6:409-10.

democracies, minorities cannot willfully destroy a polity because they have not triumphed, and still pretend that they are functioning democratically. When that case is proved—and if really Democrats really were for the Union—then it will be discovered that "there will be some black men who can remember that, with silent tongue, and clenched teeth, and steady eye, and well-poised bayonet, they have helped mankind on to this great consummation." What, then, would the critics have to say to such men, who had helped them make their own case for the Union and democracy? "While, I fear," Lincoln continued, "there will be some white ones, unable to forget that, with malignant heart, and deceitful speech, they have strove to hinder it."[35] If any of them happened to have been sitting in the Illinois legislature that spring, they knew now what conclusions Lincoln expected them to draw about their own role in history.[36]

The meeting went on until the evening, concluding with resolutions, fireworks, and a final torchlight procession. The next morning, even the hostile *Illinois State Register* had to concede that "crowded into the narrow amphitheatre of the fair ground, the crowd made a respectable enough appearance," and Conkling jubilantly informed Lincoln by letter that "Our mass meeting was a magnificent success ... and the largest meeting by far that ever assembled together in the State." But the focus of national attention, from the following morning on, was less on the meeting itself and more on Lincoln's letter. Corrected copies were picked up and reprinted across the North—Simon Hanscom's *Washington National Republican* was given the "only correct and authorized copy" to print—and it was even read aloud again at another mass Union meeting in Syracuse, New York, the same day. Congratulations poured in on Lincoln from John Goodrich, Henry Wilson,

---

35. Ibid., 6:410.
36. Ibid. Lincoln actually had one more telegram to send to Conkling about the letter, but it was not for public reading. Lincoln had guarded the letter jealously, choosing not to leak it to the press and sending it out of the White House by private messenger, according to Noah Brooks (*Washington in Lincoln's Time* [New York: Century, 1895], 62–63). However, a "Botched up" version of the letter promptly appeared Sept. 3 in the *Washington Daily Chronicle, Chicago Tribune,* and *New York Evening Post*. Lincoln was "mad enough to cry," and John W. Forney, editor of the *Chronicle*, promptly fobbed responsibility onto L. A. Gobright of the Associated Press (Forney to AL, Sept. 3, 1863, Lincoln Papers). That morning, Lincoln telegraphed Conkling with a demand for an explanation ("To James C. Conkling," Sept. 3, 1863, *CW* 6:430). The telegram caught up with Conkling as the meeting was in progress, and Conkling admitted rather lamely the next day to Lincoln that copies had been sent simultaneously to the St. Louis, Chicago, and Springfield newspapers with instructions not to print them before the meeting. Conkling presumed the breach came from the *Chicago Tribune* (Conkling to AL, Sept. 4, 1863, Lincoln Papers).

John Murray Forbes, and Charles Sumner. (Goodrich, the collector of the Port of Boston, at least had gotten Lincoln's joke: "What a contrast—the black man trying to save, & the white man trying to destroy his country. I think Copperheads must feel that they are compared to the Negro quite to their disadvantage.") Before the end of the year, the Conkling letter was reprinted as a pamphlet at least twice. Lincoln was particularly anxious that his declarations about the permanence of emancipation had been clearly heard, and he quizzed Illinoisan Anson Miller about it when Miller reported to the White House later that month. "He wanted to know all about [the] great political meeting that had then just been held in Springfield," Miller wrote, adding, "I told him that the passage in the letter which was most vehemently cheered was the one about the colored men; and I quoted it to him: 'We have promised the colored men their rights; and, by the help of God, that promise shall be kept.' When I told him this, he replied, very earnestly, 'Well God helping me, that promise shall be fulfilled.'"[37]

The newspapers, like the crowd, also discerned the core of Lincoln's letter on emancipation. The *Chicago Tribune*, especially, saw in the letter Lincoln's reaffirmation of the permanence of emancipation, no matter what. "It has been feared that even he looked upon his Proclamation as a temporary expedient, born of the necessities of the situation, to be adhered to or retracted as a short-sighted or time-serving policy dictated; and that when the moment for attempting compromise might come, he would put it aside," the *Tribune* editorialized, adding: "In a few plain sentences, than which none more important were ever uttered in this country, Mr. Lincoln exonerates himself from the crimes urged against him, shows the untenableness of the position that his enemies occupy, and gives the world assurance that that great measure of policy and justice, which ... guarantees freedom to three millions of slaves, is to remain the law of the republic. ... The battle is to be fought out. No miserable compromise ... is to stop the progress of

---

37. *Washington National Republican*, Sept. 3, 1863; on the Syracuse meeting, see *New York Times*, Sept. 4, 1863. The planner of the Syracuse meeting, Benjamin Field, had written to Lincoln on August 26 asking for a copy of the letter that he had heard Lincoln was preparing for the Springfield meeting. Lincoln sent a copy of the letter, with the same injunction to "not let it become public until your meeting shall have come off." See Field to Lincoln, Lincoln Papers; AL, "To Ben Field," Aug. 29, 1863, *CW* 6:420; "The 'Union' Mass Meeting," in *Illinois State Register*, Sept. 4, 1863; Conkling to AL, Sept. 4, 1863, Lincoln Papers; Quinn, *Lincoln's Springfield in the Civil War*, 53; "The Springfield Mass Meeting," *Chicago Tribune*, Sept. 4, 1863; John Z. Goodrich to AL, Sept. 3, 1863, Lincoln Papers; Moses Coit Tyler, "One of Mr. Lincoln's Old Friends," *Journal of the Illinois State Historical Society* 29 (Jan. 1936): 256–57. The Conkling letter was reprinted as *The War Policy of the Administration: Letter of the President to Union Mass Convention at Springfield, Illinois* (Albany: Albany Journal, 1863), and in *The Letters of President Lincoln on Questions of National Policy* (New York: H. H. Lloyd, 1863).

our arms.... God bless Old Abe!" Even the *Chicago Times* conceded that Lincoln had now made emancipation irrevocable. "The President does not believe that any compromise embracing the maintenance of the Union is now possible.... The arming of negroes is defended ... and a puff is given to the sable warriors, the promise of freedom to whom 'being made, must be kept.'"[38]

The *Times* might have drawn some consolation from what the Conkling letter does *not* say, because there were some significant omissions. Lincoln would defend emancipation, but he made no mention of what the ultimate fate of slavery would be in the places where it remained legal, or even whether renunciation of slavery would be the price of re-union. While Lincoln vigorously defended the enlistment of black soldiers, he avoided any announcement of what direction he thought the issue of black civil rights ought to take. Nevertheless, the *Times* returned angrily to the same theme two days later, still unwilling to accept that Lincoln had drawn his line at the Proclamation. "We have here an assumption that the President, who is a creature of the constitution, may, by proclamation, fasten upon the people an irrevocable law which subverts the constitution. If the proclamation cannot be retracted, then every provision in the constitution pertaining to slavery is abrogated.... If it cannot be retracted any more than the dead can be brought back to life (by human agency), then the soul of the Constitution has been murdered—assassinated—by him who solemnly swore to 'preserve, protect and defend it.'" The *Louisville Daily Democrat*, the mouthpiece of anti-administration sentiment in Kentucky, saw Lincoln's adamant defense of emancipation as the promise that "we must go on until there is no power to resist left in the South—not a remnant," and "at the end, if there ever be an end, we shall have, not a restoration of the Union, but something else, which may be desirable or not, no one can foresee." In New York, the anti-administration journal *The Old Guard* bitterly remarked, "If it has any meaning at all it means that the object of this struggle is to free negroes. And to do this he is willing to shed the blood of a quarter of a million of white men, and to tax all the white men who survive to a degree that will be the torture of their existence." But the friendlier *New York Times* rejoiced, indicating "that it is plain that the President has no power to make a man once legally free again legally a slave. The President's argument for the employment of colored troops is unanswerable."[39]

---

38. *Chicago Tribune*, Sept. 3, 1863; *Chicago Times*, Sept. 3, 1863.

39. *Chicago Times*, Sept. 5, 1863; *Louisville Daily Democrat*, Sept. 8, 1863; "Does Mr. Lincoln Wish to Save the Union," *The Old Guard* 1 (Oct./Dec. 1863): 278; *New York Times*, Sept. 3, 1863.

What struck even a few of Lincoln's admirers as odd, however, was the style of the letter. For one thing, there were some unusual grammatical lapses and some overstrained metaphors: "Uncle Sam's Web-feet," the "Father of Waters," "the Sunny South," "apply the means" (an old theological phrase about the constant use of preaching and other "means" to religious conversion), and a particularly *outre* misconstruction at the close of *they have striven* as "they have strove." The *New York Times* half-praised the letter for its "downright directness of sentiment and style," which appealed to "the real people." The *North American Review* thought that Lincoln has "been reproached with Americanisms by some not unfriendly British critics," but the *Review* decided that "we cannot say that we like him any the worse for it." George Templeton Strong believed, "There are sentences that a critic would like to eliminate, but they are delightfully characteristic of the man," while the letter itself was "likely to be a conspicuous document in the history of our times." The *Illinois State Register* was more brutal: "Mr. Lincoln speaks of 'Uncle Sam's webbed feet' as if the government were a goose," and "in the radical view of who constitutes 'the government,' perhaps he is right." Even one of the president's secretaries wondered if Lincoln's stylistic gifts had momentarily deserted him. "His last letter is a great thing," John Hay wrote to his colleague, John Nicolay, but it was marred by "hideously bad rhetoric—some indecorums that are infamous—yet the whole letter takes its solid place in history, as a great utterance of a great man."[40]

The Conkling letter was also noticeable for the prominence of one particular rhetorical device: the repeated, jabbing interrogatory—*Are you for it? Does it appear otherwise to you?*—and the semi-interrogatory that jumps ahead to put a response to a question into the hearers' mouths—*You desire peace, you are dissatisfied with me about the negro, I suppose you do not, You say you will not fight to free negroes*. This use of prolepsis (the anticipation of a question or objection) was a favorite of Lincoln's as early as his Lyceum Speech of 1838 and figures largely in many of the speeches he gave in 1859, when he was stumping for Ohio gubernatorial candidate Salmon Chase, and the 1860 Cooper Union Address. Obviously, it was a technique that would come easily to a lawyer like Lincoln, for whom interrogation and cross-examination were necessary tools of the trade (and Lincoln, as Isaac Arnold remembered, "had no equal . . . in the examination and cross-examination of a

---

40. *New York Times*, Sept. 3, 1863; *North American Review* 98 (Jan. 1864): 244; George Templeton Strong, *Diary of the Civil War, 1860-1865*, ed. Allan Nevins (New York: Macmillan, 1962), 355; *Illinois State Register*, Sept. 8, 1863; Hay to John G. Nicolay, Sept. 11, 1863, in *At Lincoln's Side: John Hay's Civil War Correspondence and Selected Writings*, ed. Michael Burlingame (Carbondale: Southern Illinois Univ. Press, 2000), 54.

witness").[41] The device, however, played only an infrequent role in his presidential state papers. Where it showed much more frequently were in the public letters of 1863, especially in the reply to the Ohio Democrats, and it was at its peak in the Conkling letter.

One reason beyond Lincoln's habitual fondness for prolepsis, and why it should play so large a role in the Conkling letter, may be connected to another practical influence on Lincoln in the summer of 1863. In addition to the situation in Illinois, Lincoln had to keep a continuously anxious eye on emancipation's impact on Kentucky, and especially the Kentucky gubernatorial election in August. The resistance to emancipation that "Parson" Brownlow had detected in January had little abated by the summer, and anti-emancipationists had succeeded in persuading former governor Charles A. Wickliffe to run against the Unionist candidate, Thomas Bramlette. Another reason why Lincoln was reluctant to leave Washington in August 1863 was his concern with the Kentucky election, which, as he put it, "got ugly." Bramlette had no reputation for being pro-emancipation, but he staged a surprisingly strong campaign. On June 25 at Carlisle, Kentucky, Bramlette delivered an aggressive speech, which was republished as a pamphlet and became the centerpiece of his campaign. It has some unusual resonances with the Conkling letter, especially in its repeated use of prolepsis. "You sympathize with the cotton gentlemen, do you?" asked Bramlette. "This was their plan, and it still is their malignant plan." It added:

> You say the Emancipation Proclamation is all wrong, and Kentucky should not sanction it. You are a Kentuckian, and let us see where you stand. The president carefully excluded from his Emancipation proclamation all the border States....
>
> You object to negro soldiers. Who began this business? Who raised the first negro regiment? Did Lincoln? Don't you know that in the beginning of this strife, in New Orleans, they heralded it abroad that they had already organized two negro regiments to fight the Yankees with . . . ? Why is it you have grown so terribly repugnant to negro aid? You are willing it should be employed against us, but now that it is being employed to help us, you are terribly disturbed. . . . At this point I am met by a certain class of men who call themselves "constitutional Union men. . . . You say you don't approve of the measures or policy of the Administration

---

41. Michael Leff and Jean Goodwin, "Dialogic Figures and Dialectical Argument in Lincoln's Rhetoric," in *Rhetoric and Public Affairs* 3 (Spring 2000): 59–69; Isaac N. Arnold, *The Life of Abraham Lincoln*, ed. James A. Rawley (1884; Lincoln: Univ. of Nebraska Press, 1994), 84.

in the prosecution of the war.... Suppose one of you were assaulted by robbers, who threatened to burn your house and murder your family ... [and] that while you are engaged in a close hand to hand conflict with one of them you should see that brawny negro having one of them down, would you say, "Hold on! I don't want any negro to help me...." Is this what any sane man would do?

The Carlisle speech is far more personal and denunciatory in tone than Lincoln's Conkling letter, but the rhetorical similarities are remarkable, especially given their overlap in the summer of 1863 and Lincoln's concern for the responses to emancipation in both Kentucky and Illinois. Further underscoring Lincoln's interest in the Carlisle speech, one of Hay's anonymous editorials on August 7, 1863, for John Forney's *Washington Daily Chronicle* on the Kentucky election, featured long extracts from the Bramlette speech. The awareness in the Lincoln White House of the importance of the Carlisle speech suggests that Lincoln may have had more than just examples of cross-examination in the back of his mind as he composed the Conkling letter.[42]

For all of its complicated and colorful context, the Conkling letter has not received nearly so much attention as the other public letters of 1863, just as Lincoln's use of the genre of the public letter is usually overshadowed by the greatness of his public speeches. Few Lincoln biographers have paid it serious attention, and while some early biographers reprinted large extracts in their works, the volume of modern notice has dwindled to a few citations, at best.[43] This, in itself, tracks the extent to which Lincoln biography gradually shifted attention away from Lincoln's role as racial emancipator to the great reunifier or wartime chieftain. This neglect misses the significance of a document which, as

---

42. AL to Mary Todd Lincoln, Aug. 8, 1863, *CW* 6:372. The full text of the Carlisle speech was printed as "Speech of Judge Bramlette on the Conduct of the War and the Duty of Kentuckians, Delivered at Carlisle," *Louisville Daily Democrat*, July 1, 1863; Hay, "Editorial," Aug. 7, 1863, in *Lincoln's Journalist: John Hay's Anonymous Writings for the Press, 1860-1864*, ed. Michael Burlingame (Carbondale: Southern Illinois Univ. Press, 1998), 334-37.

43. Francis Fisher Browne, *The Every-Day Life of Abraham Lincoln*, ed. John Y. Simon (1887; reprint, Lincoln: Univ. of Nebraska Press, 1995), 600-602; Josiah Gilbert Holland, *Holland's Life of Lincoln*, ed. Allen C. Guelzo (1866; Lincoln: Univ. of Nebraska Press, 1998), 420-21; and Arnold, *Life of Abraham Lincoln*, 336-40, all give substantial citations from the Conkling letter. Modern writers are scantier in their treatment of it, as in Stephen B. Oates, *With Malice Toward None: The Life of Abraham Lincoln* (New York: Harper & Row, 1977), 358-60; Phillip Shaw Paludan, *The Presidency of Abraham Lincoln* (Lawrence: Univ. of Kansas Press, 1994), 222-23, and David Donald, *Lincoln* (New York: Simon & Shuster, 1995), 456-57.

Conkling himself noted, signaled that "the Presidential Campaign for your successor (*if any*) has already commenced in Illinois." More than that, the Conkling letter underscored the central place that Lincoln insisted emancipation would have in that campaign, especially as he pressed forward in 1864 to secure the legal permanence of emancipation through the Thirteenth Amendment. It also offered the most extended and eloquent defense of emancipation as both policy and principle that Lincoln would compose. (In fact, it would be one of the few documents of his own composing that he would afterward quote to illustrate his position.) "The letter to Conkling is one of Lincoln's most intense exertions of political mind," writes literary critic David Bromwich, "and in it we see not only a skilled but a great lawyer arguing."[44] Above all, it was the Conkling letter that had the longest lasting political impact, since it made clear, finally and beyond any question, that Lincoln had no intention whatsoever of backing off from, or negotiating around, emancipation. This makes the Conkling letter a reminder, even as Lincoln's reputation as an emancipator has become clouded over time, that the Emancipation Proclamation had made slaves, not merely pawns in a political game, but "thenceforwards and forever free."

44. Conkling to AL, Aug. 21, 1863, Lincoln Papers; "To Charles D. Robinson," Aug. 17, 1864, *CW* 7:499; Bromwich, "Lincoln's Constitutional Necessity," *Raritan* 20 (Winter 2001): 23.

The Historian as Gamesman

Otto Eisenschiml, 1880–1963

WILLIAM HANCHETT

Otto Eisenschiml lived the classic American success story. He arrived in the United States from his native Austria in 1901 at the age of twenty-one, penniless and barely able to speak English. When he died in 1963 he was rich and famous and was listed as author or editor of thirteen books and pamphlets in *Who's Who in America*. One of the books, *Why Was Lincoln Murdered?* (1937), had profoundly influenced how the American people thought about one of the most important periods in their history.

With the equivalent of an American undergraduate degree in chemistry from the Vienna Polytechnic School, Eisenschiml first worked in America in a boiler factory in Pittsburgh and then in a linseed oil plant in Chicago. Because he was ambitious and had a quick and eager mind, he found the routine work unsatisfying, and he soon began to act as a consultant for businessmen with chemical problems—how to keep the transparent address windows in envelopes from cracking and clouding over, for example, and what kind of oil was most effective in keeping leather gloves soft and pliable. Solving such problems was both challenging and remunerative, and Eisenschiml soon recognized that a career in business offered more opportunities for advancement than one in chemistry. Shortly after World War I, he left the laboratory and, as president of the Scientific Oil Compounding Company, became the distributor of raw materials used in the manufacture of paints, varnishes, and fungicides. He patented some discoveries in the infant plastics industry, invented the formula for one of the first deodorants, invested shrewdly, and within a few years had made a fortune.

As a boy in Vienna, Eisenschiml's interest in American history had been aroused by the stories of his father, who had served as an officer in an Illinois regiment during the Civil War and become an American citizen before returning to Austria to marry. As a man in the United States, his interest was stimulated by his own travels. With time, money, and almost superhuman energy, Eisenschiml embraced the study of the Civil War, especially Lincoln's death, not merely as a hobby but as another career. Trained in scientific method as a student of chemistry, he resolved to apply it in his historical investigations, though he recognized that historians and scientists faced different problems. "In chemistry," he noted, "one dealt with elements and compounds that could be depended on; whether neutral or corrosive, harmless or poisonous, they always were honest. In history one dealt with human beings and their testimony. Neither was ever quite dependable or quite honest." As human beings themselves, furthermore, historians were often unable to divest themselves of their prejudices, a problem seldom encountered in the laboratory. Still, historians, like scientists, could investigate problems and propose hypotheses which further research might either establish as historical truths or demolish forever. Solving problems in history was, after all, "not unlike the solving of chemical problems."[1]

As a chemist and consultant, Eisenschiml had discovered that each of the tasks he undertook consisted of three distinct and obvious steps: the first was to find a good problem, the second was to solve it, and the third was to sell the solution.[2] In Lincoln's murder, which he began to study in the 1920s, Eisenschiml found a good problem, for the books and articles on the subject were superficial and amateurish, and there was no convincing interpretation of the motivations of John Wilkes Booth. Eisenschiml did not believe that a desire to avenge the South and be hailed as the last champion of the Lost Cause—the most commonly accepted explanation of Booth's action—was sufficient. As he saw it, "a great political crime was committed without an adequate motive."[3] So, he asked, why had Lincoln been murdered?

In attempting to solve this problem, step number two, Eisenschiml engaged

---

1. Otto Eisenschiml, *Without Fame. The Romance of a Profession* (Chicago: Alliance Book Corp., 1942), 345; *Why Was Lincoln Murdered?* (New York: Grosset & Dunlap, 1937), 307.
2. *Without Fame*, 226.
3. *Why Was Lincoln Murdered?*, 379-80.

in the most thorough and systematic search for assassination-related material yet undertaken. He prided himself upon having discovered the documentary evidence, now known as "Investigation and Trial Papers Relating to the Assassination of President Lincoln," collected by the War Department in 1865 (though these documents had been consulted by previous researchers). He purchased collections of private papers, and with the help of a research staff he turned up hundreds of government documents, memoirs, and magazine and newspaper articles, many of them never before studied. As he and his staff sifted through these thousands of pages, he later recalled, a pattern began to emerge. As the pattern "grew in size and distinctness, we became almost frightened at the form it was taking. Could it be that Lincoln's murder had been an inside job?"[4]

In *Why Was Lincoln Murdered?* Eisenschiml proposed with stunning forcefulness that the assassination had indeed been an inside job: it had been masterminded by U.S. Secretary of War Edwin M. Stanton! His hypothesis was that Stanton and other Radical Republicans who opposed Lincoln's compassionate program for peace and reunion had had the president killed so they could proceed with a reconstruction policy that would make the South pay for its rebellion and assure the permanent supremacy of their political party. In addition, according to Eisenschiml, Stanton believed that with Lincoln dead, he would emerge as the nation's most popular leader and be rewarded by the people with the presidency.[5]

No fair-minded person, let alone a scientist striving for scholarly objectivity, could possibly maintain that this pattern emerged from the evidence. It did not. It was imposed upon the evidence, which was stretched and twisted to establish the pattern. Six examples of how Eisenschiml manufactured his case against Stanton, each of which was supported by extensive documentation and pages of exposition, must suffice here:[6]

1. Why did not the War Department take the strictest measures to protect the president?
2. Why did Stanton deny Lincoln the escort he had requested to the theater that fatal evening?
3. Why was the guard who deserted his post outside Lincoln's box never punished?

---

4. *Without Fame*, 349.
5. *Why Was Lincoln Murdered?*, 411, 419.
6. For a detailed critique of Eisenschiml's methods, see William Hanchett, "The Eisenschiml Thesis," *Civil War History*, XXV, No. 3 (Sept. 1979), 196–217, and *The Lincoln Murder Conspiracies* (Urbana: Univ. of Illinois Press, 1983), Chaps. 6, 7.

4. Why was the telegraphic service out of Washington interrupted at about the same time as the assassination?
5. Why did Stanton send out telegrams blocking all the roads out of Washington except the road Booth took?
6. When Booth's co-conspirators were captured and held in prison for trial, why were they cut off from communication with the world and forced to wear canvas hoods to assure their silence?

These were dishonest questions deliberately framed to cause unwary readers to jump to conclusions that Eisenschiml knew were unfounded.

1. Presidents cannot be strictly protected unless they want to be. Despite frequent and urgent pleas from Stanton and others, Lincoln did not want to be.
2. Stanton denied Lincoln the officer whose company he had requested because he did not want the president to go to the theater. The officer was to have been a guest inside the box, not a guard outside it, a distinction Eisenschiml blurred by referring to him as an "escort" for Lincoln and his "guests."
3. The guard who took a seat so he could watch the play, a member of the Washington metropolitan police force, was tried before the police board, which dismissed the case against him. Perhaps he could show that he had not been ordered to remain at the door of the box, where, in fact, it had not been the habit to station a guard; perhaps the board understood that he would have had no reason to deny Booth entrance to the box, Lincoln's interest in actors and the theater being well known.
4. Only the commercial telegraph between Washington and Baltimore went out of operation. Other commercial lines and the military lines were not interrupted.
5. Stanton could not order the blocking of the road Booth took out of Washington because there were no telegraphic facilities along it or at the end of it. He did notify the nearest stations.
6. The conspirators (except Mary E. Surratt) may have been treated cruelly by being forced to wear the hoods for a few weeks, but they were not silenced or denied communication with the world. Each was interrogated repeatedly by civilian and military authorities, and each was represented by counsel at the conspiracy trial. Those who were hanged spent their last nights in the company of family or clergy; those sentenced to prison had unlimited opportunities to talk in prison and after their pardons in 1869.

Eisenschiml freely admitted that he could not prove his case against Stanton because it was based exclusively on circumstantial evidence, but he never admitted that he had tampered with the circumstantial evidence. The allegation that without Lincoln, Stanton believed his popularity as architect of the Union victory would make him president was malicious fiction. Never a popular figure, Stanton cared nothing for popularity and never held or sought an elective office.

In the third step of his problem-solving technique, the selling of his solution, Eisenschiml experienced a degree of success that must have surprised him. Published simultaneously in England and America, *Why Was Lincoln Murdered?* was a Book-of-the-Month Club selection and enjoyed a large sale as a paperback. Even more gratifying, all or parts of the sensational Eisenschiml thesis were immediately picked up by writers who understood the market value of stories of conspiracy and betrayal involving the nation's best-loved hero. They eagerly searched for additional facts and incidents by which to arouse suspicion against Stanton and the Radicals. Eisenschiml's solution to the Lincoln murder was so extensively sold to the public in books, articles in newspapers and mass circulation magazines like *Reader's Digest* and, later, *Playboy*, and in radio and television dramatizations, that within a generation it is probable that a majority of Americans who had an opinion on the assassination accepted it as true. Novelist Gore Vidal could not resist it in his 1984 *Lincoln*.

If a large part of the literate public bought the Eisenschiml thesis, most professional historians did not. Recognizing that in *Why Was Lincoln Murdered?*, and in most of his subsequent books, as well, Eisenschiml violated the conventions of historical scholarship and simple fair play, historians said so to each other in short reviews published in their journals. Not until 1979 did there appear a close analysis of the methods by which he had fabricated his case against Stanton. Had it not been for his success with the public, exposure would not have been worthwhile, for scholars have more important things to do than to occupy themselves with every crackpot theory that comes along. Yet it was precisely because historians, rejecting Eisenschiml among themselves, ignored him, that his thesis was able to obtain such a powerful hold over the public imagination.

How did so brilliant a man come to write such bad history? Part of the explanation is that at the time Eisenschiml began to study and write about the Civil War a revisionist movement critical of the leadership provided by the Radical Republicans during and after the war was in full flood, and he was carried along. In suggesting that Stanton, one of the leading Radical villains, might have been guilty of the ultimate villainy, he simply carried anti-Radical revisionism to its furthest extreme.

Another clue to Eisenschiml's work is found in his disdain for the professionalism produced by American universities. "As knowledge is pumped into a man's head in college," he wrote, "a proportionate amount of natural shrewdness and incentive goes out of him. . . . What one could do did not count so much as the kind of degree one had acquired. Creative ability and inventiveness, those rarest and most precious of all mental qualities, were being forced into a straitjacket." When Eisenschiml asked chemists with advanced degrees who applied to him for jobs if they had a problem they wished to solve, they stared at him blankly. When he asked if they could make practical use of the solution to a problem after they had found it, they stared some more. The best of them were capable only of finding the answers to questions asked by someone else.[7]

In this criticism of higher education there is more than the smugness of a self-made man for inferiors with degrees more advanced than his own. There is, as well, testimony of Eisenschiml's admiration for the intellectual virtues of originality and inventiveness, both in the asking of questions and in the search for answers. In everything he did, Eisenschiml was determined to be original and inventive, a determination that was the basis of his fortune and was perhaps the very essence of his character.

Eisenschiml's experience as a chemist helps in still another way to explain the kind of history he wrote. Although chemists were responsible for revolutionary improvements in medicine and agriculture and in a multitude of ways that bettered peoples' lives, they were looked down upon by their employers and paid the wages of stenographers. They lived in poverty and obscurity. In the chapter of his autobiography that explains why he left chemistry for business—the chapter was entitled "A Servant Leaves the Kitchen"—he said, "I wanted to get out of a profession whose members were considered second-class citizens." He rejoiced that in business he was treated like a first-class citizen, that the men in high places with whom he associated treated him as an equal. He rejoiced that "The former servant . . . was acclaimed a gentleman."[8] Eisenschiml craved wealth, recognition, acceptance. But because he was both brighter and more self-assertive than other people, he craved something else. He explained it in

7. *Without Fame*, 230, 362-64.
8. Ibid., 317.

his autobiography, indeed in the book's title. As a youth and as a chemist, the periods of his life with which the work is principally concerned, he was *Without Fame*. Eisenschiml longed obsessively for fame.

Why Was Lincoln Murdered? made him famous, but its dismissal by most historians as an advocate's brief, rather than a judicious effort to discover truth, infuriated him, and he retaliated by denouncing the historical profession. Like professional chemists, historians lacked imagination and curiosity. They sat in their comfortable armchairs, rewrote each other's books, and resisted new ideas, especially if they came from an outsider. "No union card, no historian,"[9] was their attitude, he charged, ignoring the respect shown by academicians for the American histories and biographies of so many of his non-cardholding contemporaries, including James Truslow Adams, Frederick Lewis Allen, Paul Angle, William E. Barton, Catherine Drinker Bowen, Claude G. Bowers, Irving Brant, Bruce Catton, George Dangerfield, Bernard DeVoto, Marquis James, Mathew Josephson, Margaret Leech, Lloyd Lewis, E. B. Long, R. Gerald McMurtry, George Fort Milton, Jay Monaghan, Allan Nevins, Ralph G. Newman, Henry F. Pringle, Carleton Putman, Ruth Painter Randall, Carl Sandburg, Mark Sullivan, Ida Tarbell, Louise Hall Tharp, Benjamin P. Thomas, William H. Townshend, Louis A. Warren, and others. It was not prejudice against those lacking professional training as historians that denied Eisenschiml membership in this distinguished group.

Priding himself on being a *Historian Without an Armchair*, Eisenschiml asserted that with a few exceptions the "college Olympians" rejected his thesis because "They had declared Lincoln's death a closed chapter. How dare anyone reopen a chapter which they had declared closed, especially if he carried no professional union card? They would not debate the issue with me. . . . They acted like street gamins who, having run out of arguments, hide behind their mothers' skirts and become abusive. They must be right at any cost; the last thing in the world that seemed to worry them was the truth. Like many other grownup men, they were in reality only little boys in long pants."[10]

The fact is that so far from having declared the chapter on Lincoln's death closed in 1937, historians had not yet even opened it. The amateurishness of published accounts is what had attracted Eisenschiml's attention in the first place, and the first book on the subject by a professionally trained historian

---

9. Otto Eisenschiml, *O. E., Historian Without an Armchair* (Indianapolis: Bobbs-Merrill, 1963), 80, 122; Eisenschiml, *Reviewers Reviewed* (Ann Arbor: William L. Clements Library, 1940), 12.

10. *O. E., Historian*, 122.

did not appear until 1982.[11] There was thus no orthodoxy, no historiographic establishment, for Eisenschiml's thesis to offend. Indeed, the anti-Radical bias of the profession at the time Eisenschiml wrote would have inclined it to be sympathetic in his favor. Nor was there among historians an emotional pro-Stanton commitment that might cause some of them to rush to the secretary's defense by disparaging the character of his attacker. Stanton was anything but a beloved figure, and Eisenschiml's character was never abused, although it is true that some reviewers, repeating information learned from his book's dust jacket, identified him as a chemist. With some justification, the irrelevancy angered him as much as if it had been a personal insult.

In a 1940 rebuttal to his critics Eisenschiml told what else he found objectionable in their reviews. Of the seven *Reviewers Reviewed*, four were professional historians, and they did indeed have more critical things to say about the book than a new author would enjoy reading. One of the four was certainly guilty of unprofessional flippancy and condescension, and his parting advice to chemist Eisenschiml was the arrogant, "Shoemaker, stick to your last." Eisenschiml accused another reviewer of engaging in "author-hunting," and expressed surprise that the tone adopted by the others could have originated with "people who brush their teeth."[12] The critique, published as a pamphlet, created a certain sympathy for Eisenschiml among those historians who accepted it at face value. It appeared that the amateur had indeed been unfairly treated by the professionals. But in fact only one of the reviewers engaged in the kind of derision Eisenschiml claimed characterized all seven, and none of them matched him in the abusive terms he applied over a long period of time to members of the historical profession.

Historians rejected the Eisenschiml thesis because it was unreasonable and wrong. Eisenschiml freely admitted that there was no evidence of the kind admissible in court to establish a relationship between Stanton and the assassination conspiracy, thus protecting his incessant pretensions of scientific objectivity. But by implication and innuendo and by the raising and phrasing of questions like those used above as examples, he insinuated throughout his book that such a relationship had existed. When reviewers observed that that was what he had done, he became indignant. "May I point out to these sensitive souls," he asked testily, "that science knows no insinuations—only possibilities and probabilities worthy

---

11. Thomas R. Turner, *Beware the People Weeping. Public Opinion and the Assassination of Abraham Lincoln* (Baton Rouge: Louisiana State Univ. Press, 1982).

12. *Reviewers Reviewed*, 9, 14.

of further investigations?" He then proceeded to instruct his critics on the nature of scientific method. "A physician finds that a certain treatment benefits typhoid patients; his results cover only a limited number of cases, and he hesitates to draw definite inferences. He publishes his results so that others may take over from that point. If that be insinuation, let them make the most of it."[13] Eisenschiml thus compared himself to a scientist presenting a progress report. But if the physician in his illustration knew that it was not his treatment that benefited his patients but something else, known or unknown, and if he proceeded to publish the details of his treatment anyway, would he not be making a dishonest insinuation?

Eisenschiml's enjoyment of the fame that resulted from his writing was diminished by his extreme sensitivity to the criticism that also resulted from it. To compensate, he pretended that he thought he was too creative for his own good, that his originality was a liability, even a curse. "Tell the people something they already know," he remarked, "and they will love you for it; tell them something new, and they will resent it, for to make yourself look superior is an unforgivable offense." "Verily, verily, uneasy lies the head of the pioneer who strays from the beaten paths of orthodox history, and ventures into unexplored fields, because they are overgrown with thorns, thistles and poison ivy." "Searching for truth in history," he wrote toward the end of his life, "is a thankless task. . . . If your findings run contrary to tradition and public belief, you are a heretic and are treated accordingly. Few people, even intelligent ones, are interested in truth, although none will admit it."[14]

But that was only a pose. Eisenschiml was less interested in searching for truth in history than he was in being original, inventive, and famous. Nevertheless, the martyr's role was effective on the lecture circuit, to which he was addicted for many years. Audiences, impressed by his foreign accent and authoritative manner—tempered as it was by a certain impishness that won their affections and prompted them to frequent sympathetic laughter—felt themselves privileged to be in the presence of a truly original thinker who had been ostracized for his creativity by the stuffy historical establishment. He reveled in the public's applause; otherwise he would never have endured so many uncomfortable trips, eaten so many indigestible meals, and met so many anonymous people whose company he did not enjoy. Hearing himself talk so often about the need for

---

13. Ibid., 18.
14. Otto Eisenschiml, "Too Many Civil War Books?," *Civil War History*, VI, No. 3 (Sept. 1960), 251; O. E., *Historian*, 102, 120.

scientific objectivity in the acquisition and evaluation of historical evidence and about the lack of receptivity to new ideas typical of historians, he may truly have come to believe he was a modern Galileo, to whom he more than once compared himself. If so, he was not the first salesman to buy his own spiel.

The fact is that Eisenschiml thrived on controversy and cultivated the role of outsider, of maverick, of nonconformist, for it was one sure way to prove that he was what he most admired—an original. On the lecture circuit he refused to join in the community singing which so often preceded his talks, and made no effort to disguise his impatience. He prided himself on speaking without a prepared speech or even notes because, he explained, such aids were impolite to audiences. (Perhaps so, but his impromptu delivery could not have failed to be impressive, and it could have been convenient as an explanation of possible misstatements of fact.) He believed he had the gift of premonition, and wished he had not; he was interested in phrenology; he boasted of braving Chicago winters without an overcoat. He was an eccentric who played to the part. A reputation for eccentricity, he observed, "is the ultimate goal of human freedom. If you are known as odd, peculiar—cracked, when you are out of earshot—you can do anything you like. You can defy conventions, make your own rules, and still remain reasonably popular. Verily, it is great to be known as an eccentric."[15]

Eisenschiml was so eccentric that in 1961 he delivered an impassioned address before the Civil War Round Table of Chicago, of which he had been a cofounder in 1940, advocating the adoption of a code of ethics for historians. The carefully prepared speech (which he apologized to the audience for reading from manuscript) accused historians of having engaged in a merciless vendetta against him, and charged them with many other ethical and scholarly offenses, including the presentation of facts in such a way as to mislead readers, the interpretation of events to conform to a preconceived point of view, and the use of only those sources that supported their hypotheses.[16] Since he could not have described more accurately his own major transgressions against scholarship, it is tempting to suspect that he was playing a colossal joke on the historical profession. But he was not joking; he was showing the truly pathetic degree to which he had personalized criticism and exposing his inability to look at himself objectively.

---

15. *Without Fame*, 3, 45, 82-84, 87-88, 191-92.

16. Otto Eisenschiml, "Ethics and the Civil War Historians. Do We Need a Code for Historical Writers?," mimeograph copy of address delivered Sept. 15, 1961, 29. Special thanks to James O. Hall, McLean, Va., who provided the copy, and to Arthur F. Loux, Stilwell, Kans., who supplied a tape recording of this talk and of one other.

If Eisenschiml was deficient in self-understanding, readers can gain an embarrassing insight into his mind and character in one of his least well known books, *The Art of Worldly Wisdom. Three Hundred Precepts for Success Based on the Original Work of Baltasar Gracian*, published in 1947. Though clearly inspired by Gracian—a seventeenth-century Spanish Jesuit, some of whose concise maxims for getting along in the world Eisenschiml liberally paraphrased or rewrote—the book was, as its title page proclaimed, Eisenschiml's own. Another source of inspiration may have been the mottoes, epigrams, and orphic sayings of the writer and self-promoter Elbert Hubbard, whose work Eisenschiml and other businessmen of his generation admired.

In *The Art of Worldly Wisdom* Eisenschiml instructed his readers how to become successful, how to overcome enemies, and how to impress others with displays of wisdom and learning. He did not always follow his own advice, as when he wrote, "Let moderation in everything be your guide," and "If you want to make your arguments impressive, deal in understatements, not in overstatements." Some advice he did follow: "If you want to be known, choose an occupation where you meet the public. . . . Unless people meet you, see you, or hear you, you never gather more than respect, if that. Applause is reserved for those who stand in the spotlight." Some of the precepts may have given him personal comfort at times when he felt the sting of his rejection by professional historians: "What is condemned by one is praised by someone else. No matter what you do, you will be complimented by some and abused by others. Do not feel overly elated by approval, or too downcast by condemnation."[17]

But Eisenschiml's supply of worldly wisdom taught him that neither praise nor condemnation mattered very much. What did matter was success. "The world bows to success," he wrote in a passage for which there is no equivalent in Gracian, "and cares little how it has been won. The well-paid servant attends to you whether your money was earned or stolen. The luster of a conquering general is not dimmed by the means he used to gain victory. The loser must explain; the winner twirls his thumbs and smiles."[18]

As a winner, Eisenschiml may be excused if he occasionally stood twirling his thumbs at the window of his apartment in the Belden-Stratford Hotel overlooking Lincoln Park and Lake Michigan. If he did, the success he was justified in celebrating was won as a chemist and businessman, for in the writing of

---

17. Otto Eisenschiml, *The Art of Worldly Wisdom* (New York: Essential Books, 1947), 20, 35, 44, 53.
18. Ibid., 35.

history he was not a historian but a gamesman. He developed his inspiration that Stanton might have been behind the conspiracy that took Lincoln's life as a kind of intellectual exercise, a sophisticated parlor game, the point of which was to see how strong a case he could make. If the asking of misleading questions and the manipulation of facts was involved, well, who else had ever been so imaginative and so provocative, and was not that what daring and original thinkers were supposed to be? Furthermore, did he not freely admit that he had not solved the mystery, that an indictment against Stanton would not stand up in court? He often pointed out that he had entitled his book *Why Was Lincoln Murdered?*, not *Why Lincoln Was Murdered;* the sophism allowed him to maintain his self-respect, and at the same time it tricked his popularizers and, through them, the American people into thinking him an honest man.

But playing games with history is a dangerous pastime, as Eisenschiml well knew. "Interest in our history," he told his adopted countrymen in 1960, "is precious and should not be abused.... Appreciation of one's national history is an effectual protection against subversive influences. If this be admitted,... its correct and intelligent interpretation transcends in importance all other considerations. In the long run a clear understanding of our past may prove a stronger defense ... than the military weapons our scientists and technologists may design."[19]

Yet the Eisenschiml thesis was a deliberate falsification of the American past. It dishonored the reputation of a great secretary of war and true friend of Lincoln and distorted the nature of political controversy in the wartime North. In short, it misrepresented the history of the country's most traumatic incident, Lincoln's murder, and of its most profound experience, the Civil War. Further, it helped condition Americans to assume the existence of sinister conspiracies behind other events, past and present, great and small, and thus encouraged irrationality and the simplistic search for villains upon whom to blame all difficulties.

If history is too precious to be abused, if its "correct and intelligent interpretation" is of transcendent importance, if "a clear understanding of our past" is a major bulwark of national security, then Eisenschiml committed a grievous offense against the nation. He did it out of eccentricity and flamboyance rather than ill-will, but that does not make it less real. Generations will be required to undo the damage. In the meantime, a constructive lesson may be learned if it serves to remind those who write history of what is perhaps their most solemn responsibility: "Historian, know thyself."

19. "Too Many Civil War Books?," 257.

Contributors

Don E. Fehrenbacher (1920–1987) was Professor of History at Stanford University.

Joseph George Jr. is Professor of History Emeritus at Villanova University.

Allen C. Guelzo is the Henry R. Luce III Professor of the Civil War Era at Gettysburg College.

William Hanchett is Professor of History Emeritus at San Diego State University.

John T. Hubbell is Professor of History Emeritus at Kent State University.

Herman Hattaway is Professor of History Emeritus at the University of Missouri-Kansas City.

Ludwell H. Johnson is Professor of History Emeritus at the College of William and Mary.

Archer Jones (1926–2006) was Professor of History at North Dakota State University.

Mark E. Neely Jr. is the McCabe Greer Professor in the American Civil War Era at Pennsylvania State University.

Otto H. Olsen is Professor of History Emeritus at Northern Illinois University.

NICHOLAS PARILLO is Associate Professor at Yale Law School.

At the time his article was published, JAMES A. STEVENSON was Associate Professor of History at East Georgia State College.

CHARLES B. STROZIER is Professor of History at the John Jay College of Criminal Justice.

CRAIG D. TENNEY is Professor of Journalism Emeritus at Pennsylvania State University.

DOUGLAS L. WILSON is Professor of English Emeritus at Knox College

MAJOR L. WILSON is Professor of History Emeritus at Memphis State University.

Index

Abell, Mrs. E. H., 52-53
abolitionism: called threat to republic, 15, 24-25; Lincoln and, 27, 176, 246; *Metropolitan Record* on, 168-70, 176; nationalism and, 243n39; as requirement for peace negotiations, 225-26; Storey's hatred of, 155-56; Van Buren on, 15, 25-26, 28; vs. Union preservation in Civil War goals, 154-55, 170-71, 247-48, 252-53
abolitionists, 237; Lincoln and, 4, 9, 238; mob action against, 27-28, 34
Abraham Lincoln: Quest for Immortality (Anderson), 37
African Americans, 180; competing for jobs, 184-86, 250, 256; freedom and rights promised for fighting for Union, 274, 277; hostility to free, 183, 256-57; humanity of, 243-46; Lincoln on, 225, 241, 249; rights for, 237, 276, 277; Storey's hatred of, 155-56; in Union Army, 132-34, 174, 183, 224, 251, 272, 279
Altschuler, Glenn, 262
ambition: Lincoln's, 19, 38-39, 116-17; Mary Todd Lincoln's, 76
American Colonization Society, 244
Ammen, Jacob, 157-58
amnesty, in Lincoln's Civil War strategy, 132-33
Anderson, Dwight G., 20, 37
Angle, Paul M.: on documentation for Ann Rutledge story, 44-45, 48, 51, 58, 60-61; on Lincoln's broken engagement, 69, 89, 94
Antietam, Battle of, 125, 129, 219
aristocracy, Lincoln's marriage into, 78-79
Armstrong, Jack, 64-66
Army of the Potomac, 126-30
Arnold, Isaac N., 264, 278-79; suppression of *Chicago Times* and, 158-60, 162-63, 164n63
The Art of Worldly Wisdom (Eisenschiml), 292
Ashmun, George, 101-2, 107-9, 115
assassination, Lincoln's, 283; effects of, 235; Eisenschiml accusing Stanton of masterminding, 284-87, 289-90, 292-93; War Department report on, 284
Atlanta, Union victory at, 228-29

Baker, Edward D., 79, 102-3, 116, 118
Bale, Hardin, 50
banking system, 23, 31
Banks, Nathaniel P., 144, 272n29
Barton, William E., 202n6
Basler, Roy, 163
Bateman, Norman, 265
Beard, Charles, 188n2
Beauregard, P. G. T., 127, 141-43
Bell, Ann, 81
Bell, James, 82, 94
Bell, Jane D., 81-82, 87, 91
Bell, Lizzie Herndon, 52, 54
Benjamin, Judah P., 138

296

INDEX

Bennett, Lerone, Jr., 238, 241
Bennett, William, 52
Beveridge, Albert J., 45, 49, 65, 100
Bible, influence on Lincoln, 32–33
Bixby, Lydia, 177
Black, Chauncey (Lamon's ghost), 78n20, 80
black militants, hostility to Lincoln, 237–39, 247
Black Republicans, 243
Blaine, James G., 252
Blair, Montgomery, 152, 256
Bledsoe, Albert Taylor, 100–101
blockade, and cotton trade, 149
Blumin, Stuart, 262
Boker, George, 253
Bonaparte, Napoleon, 36
Booth, John Wilkes, 283, 285
Border States, and Emancipation Proclamation, 255–56, 279
Boritt, Gabor S., 100–101, 188n2, 189–90, 195
Bradford, Melvin E., 188n2
Bragg, Braxton, 142, 144, 146
Bramlette, Thomas, 279–80
Bromwich, David, 281
Brown, William, 116–17
Browning, Orville Hickman, 92, 257–59, 264
Brownlow, William G. "Parson," 256, 279
Brownson, Orestes A., 171–73, 183
Buell, Don Carlos, 127–28
Burnside, Ambrose E., 125, 127, 129, 154; *Chicago Times* criticism of, 156–57; Lincoln revoking suppression of *Chicago Times* by, 151–52, 157, 160–62; quashing opposition press, 151–53; suppression of *Chicago Times* by, 151, 157–60
Butler, Benjamin F., 144, 253, 263
Butler, Elizabeth, 93–94, 98
Butler, William, 98–99

cabinet, Davis's, 138–40
cabinet, Lincoln's, 138–40, 153, 217n52, 220–21
Caesarism, 20; attributed to Lincoln, 21, 37; Jackson accused of, 16, 18–19, 21, 23; Lincoln warning against, 15, 18–19, 34–35
Calhoun, John C., 4, 24, 109, 113–15
Calvinism, 218, 232; conception of God in, 203, 231; influence on other religions, 203–4; Lincoln moving toward, 202n3, 203, 205, 229–30
Cameron, Simon, 139, 152, 170
Campbell, John A., 148
capital, 191; labor's relation to, 190–92, 199; Lincoln warning against domination of government by, 200; small producers as owners and workers, 197–98
capitalism: industrial, 188n2; Lincoln on, 3, 195, 197
Carey, Henry C., 189–90
Cass, Lewis, 120
Catholics: called pro-slavery, 173, 183; Irish, 183–86; *Metropolitan Record* appealing to Irish, 167–68, 178; *Metropolitan Record* as official organ of NY archbishop, 168, 171, 174–76; *Metropolitan Record* as secular vs. associated with, 174–76, 178; newspapers of, 167–68. See also *Metropolitan Record*
Chandler, Zachariah, 157, 259n11, 269
Charnwood, Lord, 246
Chase, Salmon P., 219n60, 220
Chicago Times: criticism of Civil War policies in, 154–56; Lincoln revoking suppression of, 157–61; responses to suppression of, 158–60; suppression of, 151, 157, 261
Chicago Tribune, 162n54
citizenship, of African Americans, 250–51
civil rights: for African Americans, 237, 277; infringements on, 156, 173, 175–76
civil rights movement, 236–37
Civil War: Davis as leader during, 136–37, 140, 141–42, 145; Davis's military mistakes in, 145–47; effects of, 2–3, 29, 216, 227, 247; effects on Lincoln, 41–42, 203; emancipation's effects on, 218, 260–61, 272; goals for, 154–55, 168–70, 247–48, 252–53, 277; God's will for slavery and, 42, 218–19; as instrument of God, 203, 204, 214, 226, 227–29; Lincoln on casualties of, 229–30; Lincoln trying to discern God's will in, 222–25; Lincoln's determination to keep fighting, 228–30; Lincoln's goals in, 126–28, 173, 186, 248; Lincoln's leadership in, 12–13,

Civil War (*cont.*)
127–28, 136, 141–42, 147, 273; needlessness of, 20, 214; policies of, 154–55, 204–5, 256; political strategy in, 132–34, 247–48; pressure to end, 177–78, 180, 182, 253, 270–71; progress of, 149, 226, 228–29, 274; as punishment for sins, 42, 223–24, 227, 230–31; Republicans politicizing, 144–45; resistance to, 156, 260–61. *See also* military strategy
The Clansman (Dixon), 236
Clark, Henry, 65
class, social, 187–88, 197–98. *See also* social mobility
class struggle, 192
Clay, Henry, 22, 207; influence on Lincoln's stance on race, 244–45; Lincoln's eulogy for, 4, 207–9, 244; on Mexican War, 120; on slavery, 7, 221, 249
Cogdal, Isaac, 58–59
Colfax, Schuyler, 263, 269
colonization, of freed slaves, 155; Clay promoting, 207, 244; Lincoln promoting, 148, 207, 236, 249; Republicans promoting, 249–50
Compromise of 1850, 4, 7
Confederacy, 147, 174, 178; cabinet criticized, 138–40; Davis as president of, 135–36; foreign policy of, 149–50; peace negotiations with, 225–26, 253–54; problems of, 139, 147; resources of, 147, 149–50; respect for Lincoln in, 235; sympathy for, 153; unwillingness to compromise, 270–71; Vallandigham expelled to, 153, 261; War Department of, 139–40
Confederate Army, 126–27; Davis and, 136, 141–45; Davis's mistakes with, 145–47; Lee's, 129, 134; Lincoln hoping to lure rebels away from allegiance to, 132–33; strengths of, 124
Congress, U.S., 148, 221; Lincoln not running for reelection to, 115–16, 119–20; Lincoln's boredom in, 117–18, 121; Lincoln's election to, 103–4; Lincoln's opposition to Mexican War in, 100, 105; unregularized elections to, 103–4; Whigs' Mexican War stance in, 105–7
Conkling, James C., 89–90, 261, 281; background of, 264–65; on Lincoln's love affairs, 91, 93; Lincoln's private telegram to, 275n36; organizing Republicans' Union meeting in Springfield, 264, 275; wanting Lincoln to speak at Union meeting in Springfield, 264–66
Conkling, Mercy Levering, 261, 264–65
Conkling letter, 268; Bramlette's Carlisle speech compared to, 279–80; Conkling expected to read at mass meeting, 267, 269; as defense of emancipation, 269–71, 281; dissemination of, 275, 276n37; Lincoln's commitment to emancipation in, 253–54, 276–77; Lincoln's composition of, 267; Lincoln's telegraphed addition to, 272n29; not describing ultimate fate of slaves or African Americans, 277; responses to, 275–76; rhetorical strategies in, 270–74, 278–79
conscription, 174–75, 179. *See also* draft riots
Constitution, U.S., 11; acceptance of slavery in, 25; emancipation said to violate, 260, 272–73, 277; Lincoln on, 9, 35, 41; Lincoln wanting amendment to abolish slavery, 13, 226, 273, 281; Mexican War said to violate, 101–2, 115
Cook, Adrian, 184
Cooper Union speech, 10
Copperheadism, 154, 165, 177, 183, 186
Corning, Erastus, 255
Corwin, Thomas, 107, 109
cotton, in Confederate finances, 149–50
Cox, Samuel S., 263
Crittenden proposals, as compromise over expanding slavery, 11
culture, republican ideal in, 187–88
currency, Lincoln on, 23
Current, Richard N., 37, 237
Curry, Richard O., 177
Curtin, Andrew Gregg, 263
Curtis, Benjamin, 253

Davis, David, 158–60
Davis, Jefferson, 135, 235, 248; criticisms of cabinet of, 138–40; generals and, 141–45; Lincoln compared to, 137, 141–42, 147; personality of, 136–38, 140, 147, 150; political influences on, 144–45
death, Lincoln said to desire triumph over, 20

Declaration of Independence, 35; applicability to blacks, 3, 5; equality in, 28–29; Lincoln's commitment to, 41, 208n25, 209–12, 243; as Lincoln's ideal, 7, 40n22
defensive advantage, Lincoln recognizing, 122–23, 126–28, 130, 133–34
Defrees, John D., 104
democracy: Lincoln's commitment to, 205; use of force in, 274–75. *See also* republic; republicanism
Democratic Party, 26, 180, 185; Lincoln's criticism of wars under, 112; Lincoln's public letters to, 255; *Metropolitan Record* promoting, 176–77; on Mexican War, 103, 104–5, 107–9; opposition to Lincoln's policies, 161, 262–63; peace platform of, 180; Republicans needing support of to win war, 247; response to Emancipation Proclamation, 256, 260; split of, 168; strength in Illinois, 257–58, 262–63; use of mass meetings, 262–63; Van Buren's contributions to, 15, 25–26
Depew, Chauncey M., 255
derangement, Lincoln's, 99; after broken engagement, 71–72; after Rutledge's death, 44–45, 51–53, 58, 63; from being jilted, 89–91; leap from church window, 83–84; over conflict in feelings for Mary Todd and Matilda Edwards, 75, 78, 81, 88; over insecurity about marriage, 76–77; timing of, 74, 85, 91–92; varying opinions on seriousness of, 92–93
Dickenson, Daniel, 269
Dixon, Thomas, 236
Dodge, Daniel Kirkham, 254
Dolan, Jay P., 184
Donald, David, 47, 50n22, 213, 235, 254
Doolittle, James R., 265, 269
Douglas, Stephen A., 19, 147, 199, 243; death of, 257; Lincoln vs., 7–8, 17, 212–13; Matilda Edwards and, 75, 88; popular sovereignty doctrine of, 28–29; on Republicans, 8–9, 244
Douglass, Frederick, 245–46, 248
draft riots, 179, 183–84, 186
Drake, Daniel, 91
Dred Scott decision, 5
dualism, Lincoln's, 234, 236, 245

Dubois, Jesse, 265
Dunn, George G., 107–9, 114–15

economy, 198; exploitation in, 191–93, 199; influence on Irish Catholics' opposition to emancipation, 184–86; labor's relation to capital in, 190–92; Lincoln's ideals on, 187, 193–94; Lincoln's knowledge of, 188n2, 189–90; mud-sill theory of, 189–90; panic of 1837, 33
education, Lincoln's, 32–33
Edwards, Albert S., 69, 80
Edwards, Cyrus, 74–75, 88–89
Edwards, Elizabeth, 69, 82; on Lincoln and Mary Todd, 75–79; on Lincoln's broken engagement, 77, 79
Edwards, Jonathan, 218, 232
Edwards, Matilda, 70–72, 74, 93; Lincoln's broken engagement and, 75–80, 83; Lincoln's feelings for, 79–82, 85, 87–88; Lincoln's rejection by, 89–91; Mary Todd and, 82–83, 86, 88; Speed and Lincoln's rivalry for, 87, 91, 99; Speed's feelings for, 82–83; suitors of, 86, 88, 90, 99
Edwards, Ninian W.: on Lincoln and Mary Todd, 75, 77–79; Mary Todd and Matilda Edwards both living with, 74–75; on Speed courting Matilda Edwards, 82
egalitarianism, in republican ideal, 187–88, 195–96, 198
Eisenschiml, Otto: background of, 282–83; business acumen of, 282–83, 287; on lecture circuit, 290–91; manufacturing evidence against Stanton, 284–87, 289–90; motives for presenting Stanton as mastermind of assassination, 286–88, 290, 292–93
elections: 1860, 11, 213–14; 1864, 228
Ellis, A. Y., 94n49
emancipation: in Civil War goals, 169–70, 173; Civil War leading to, 216; colonization to ward off fear of effects of, 249–50; compensated, 221, 271; Conkling letter as defense of, 269–72, 281; effects of, 242, 248; Fremont ordering, 170, 216–17; gradual, 148, 207, 211, 216–17, 221, 244, 247; influence of Lincoln's religion on, 202n3, 204–5, 232; lack of peaceful path to, 6; Lincoln preparing

emancipation (*cont.*)
  public for, 247-49; Lincoln revoking Hunter's, 170; Lincoln trying to discern God's will about, 217-19, 224-25; Lincoln's commitment to, 253-54, 269-70, 276-77, 281; Lincoln's conservatism about, 2, 173-74, 247; as military strategy, 217; opposition to, 183, 184, 186, 261, 279; public opinion on, 220n61, 252; timing of, 219-21, 247-48
Emancipation Proclamation: called unconstitutional, 260, 272-73, 277; effects of, 255-56, 258, 272; limited effects of, 238, 248, 279; Lincoln's certainty about, 252; in Lincoln's Civil War strategy, 133; Lincoln's hesitation about, 235, 255-56; Lincoln's public letters following, 255; Lincoln's refusal to modify, 226, 273; Lincoln's rhetoric in, 254; not moral attack on slavery, 220-21; opposition to, 155-56, 173-74, 182-83, 263; political effects of, 252-53, 256-61, 280-81; timing of, 219, 247-48
Embree, Elisha, 106-8, 114-15
Emery, Edwin and Michael, 152
Endy, Melvin B., Jr., 205n12, 206, 208n25
entrepreneurship, in republican ideal, 187-88
equality, 212; colonization to ward off accusations about, 249-50; in Declaration of Independence, 28-29, 209-11; Lincoln not advocating racial, 235-36, 238-39, 243-45; Lincoln's commitment to ideal of, 203, 209-11; racial, 243
Europe, demand for southern cotton, 149
Everett, Edward, 265, 269
expansionism: Lincoln on, 109, 111-12; political pressure for, 113-14; Whigs on, 111, 114-15, 121

Fehrenbacher, Don, 37
filiopiety, 29; Lincoln's, 17, 19-20, 27, 30; Van Buren's, 16-18, 30
First Amendment, defense of, 151
Foote, Henry S., 148
Forbes, John Murray, 276
foreign policy, Whigs', 111
Forgie, George B., 19-20, 37
Forney, John W., 255
founding fathers: Lincoln on, 16-17, 19-20, 35; Lincoln's desire to replace, 36-37; Lincoln's idealization of, 40-42; on slavery, 5, 25; on threats to republican experiment, 23-24; Van Buren on, 16, 26
Fredericksburg, Union defeat at, 222
Fredrickson, George M., 136-37, 141, 242
free enterprise. *See* capitalism
free labor system: based on small producers, 196-97; labor's relation to capital in, 190-92; Lincoln's belief in, 3, 7, 199; as Northern value, 9-10, 12; in republican ideal, 187-88; social mobility through, 193-95, 198
Fremont, John C., 170, 216-17, 243
friendships, Lincoln's, 92; with Ann Rutledge, 46; with Cogdal, 58-60; love affairs and, 92-93; Speed as closest, 70-71, 95-98; with Thompson, 119-20

Gallatin, Albert, 109
Garfield, James, 256
Gates, Paul Wallace, 196
General Orders, No. 38, 153
Gettysburg, Battle of, 224
Gettysburg Address, 3, 41, 177, 227
God, 42; Calvinist, 209-10, 231; Civil War as instrument of, 227-29; conceptions of, 204, 212-13; Lincoln hoping for intervention in war by, 214, 226, 228; Lincoln trying to discern will in Union Army victories and defeats, 219, 222, 224-25; Lincoln trying to discern will of, 205-6, 222-24; Lincoln trying to discern will of about emancipation, 217-19, 221, 224-25; Lincoln's conception of, 203, 208, 211, 216, 223; Lincoln's desire for help from, 213-14; plan to end slavery, 217, 227; in slavery debate, 212-13
Goodrich, John, 275-76
Goudy, Jane, 93
government: fear of overthrow for authoritarianism, 34-35; Hughes's support for, 175-76; Lincoln warning against capital's domination of, 200; press treatment of, 151
Grady, Henry W., 235
Graham, Mentor, 50, 57-58
grandiosity, Lincoln's, 38-39

Grant, Ulysses S., 125, 134, 227–28, 272n29
Greeley, Horace: criticism of *Metropolitan Record*, 171–72; Lincoln's response to, 173, 186, 248, 255
Green, Bowling, 58
Green, Nancy, 58, 61
Greene, William G., 50
Grimshaw, Jackson, 259
Guelzo, Allen C., 202n3
Gurney, Eliza, 229
Gurowski, Adam, 254

Haiti, Lincoln promoting emigration to, 249
Halleck, Henry W., 147; influence on Lincoln's military strategy, 122, 126–27, 133; using simultaneous advance strategy, 124–25; on Virginia campaign against Lee, 128–29
Hanks, Dennis, 32
Hanscom, Simon, 275
Hardee, W. J., 143
Hardin, John J., 88–89, 93, 116
Hardin, Martinette, 93
Hardin, Sarah, 93
Harrison, William Henry, 22
Harvey, J. S., 105
Hathaway, R. L., 106
Hay, John, 267, 278, 280
Haynie, Isham, 269
Hein, David, 205n12, 206, 214n47, 219n60
Helm, Katherine, 69
Henry, John, 116–17
Herndon, J. Rowan, 49
Herndon, William, 32, 75n16, 78n20, 82; awareness of Ann Rutledge story by, 49–50; basis for Ann Rutledge story by, 44–45, 47–48, 51–60, 66; credibility of, 50, 77; criticism of Ann Rutledge story by, 44–47, 60–63; gathering information for biography, 48–49, 50n22; on Lincoln and Jack Armstrong, 65; on Lincoln and Mary Todd, 47, 75; on Lincoln's ambition, 38, 115–16; on Lincoln's broken engagement, 68–69, 70–71, 77, 79–80, 83; on Lincoln's relationship with Ann Rutledge, 43, 51; on Lincoln's speeches, 3–4; political influence on Lincoln, 101, 266–67; response to suppression of *Chicago Times*, 158–60;

Speed giving information about Lincoln's love affairs, 70–71, 97–98
Herndon's Lincoln, 43, 48–49
Higgins, Judge, 162
Hill, A. P., 145
Hill, John, 47n13, 52
Hill, Mrs. Samuel, 54n37
Hilton, H. G., 106
historians, 293; Eisenschiml denouncing, 288, 291; Eisenschiml violating conventions of, 286, 289–90, 291; Eisenschiml's investigation of Lincoln's murder, 283–84; lack of attention to Lincoln's assassination by, 283, 288–89; scientific method of, 283, 290; treatment of Eisenschiml by, 289, 291
Hodges, Albert, 227
Hofstadter, Richard, 188n2, 254
Holmes, Theophilus, 143
Hood, John Bell, 143, 146
Hooker, Joseph, 125, 129–30
Howe, Daniel Walker, 188
Howells, William Dean, 65
Hughes, John J., 171; *Metropolitan Record* and, 167–68, 174–75; support for government and conscription, 175–76; tolerance for slavery, 175
human rights, to fruits of labor, 3
Hunter, David, 170

icon, Lincoln as, 233–35
identity crisis, Lincoln's, 39–40
Illinois, 262; internal improvements in, 31–32; political effects of Emancipation Proclamation in, 256–61, 280–81; socioeconomic culture of, 193, 196; Yates proroguing legislature of, 261, 263, 267
immortality, Lincoln's desire for, 20, 37
indemnity, in Mexican War, 112–14
industry, in Lincoln's economic views, 195
Irish, 185–86. *See also* Catholics, Irish
Irwin, B. F., 52

Jackson, Andrew, 36, 129; accused of Caesarism, 18–19, 21; Van Buren including in founding fathers, 16–17; Whigs' fears about mob action under, 22–23
Jackson, Thomas "Stonewall," 124
Jaffa, Harry V., 28–29

Jefferson, Thomas, 40n22, 212–13
Jeffersonian ideal, 195–96, 198
jobs, competition for, 184–86, 250, 256
Johnson, Andrew, 182, 263
Johnston, Albert Sidney, 142–43, 145
Johnston, Joseph E., 141–43, 145
Jomini, Baron de, 122, 125, 132
Jones, John, 62
justice, Lincoln's vision of, 3

Kansas, rejecting slavery, 7
Kansas-Nebraska Act, popular sovereignty in, 4–5, 7
Kean, Robert G. H., 139–40
Kentucky, effects of Emancipation Proclamation on, 277, 279–80
Ketchum, I. J., 269
Keyes, Isaac, 265
Know Nothingism, of *New York Times* and *Tribune*, 185–86

labor, 189; mobility of, 192–93; relation to capital, 190–92, 199; small producers as owners and workers, 197–98
Lamon, Ward Hill, 78, 80
law: growing disregard for, 33–34; Lincoln studying, 53n34, 55; Lincoln's practice of, 121, 278–79; rule of, 1, 14–15, 26–28
leadership, Lincoln's idealized, 233–34
lecture circuit, Eisenschiml on, 290–91
Lee, Robert E.: campaigns against, 126–30, 134; Davis and, 143, 145; incursion into the North, 125, 129–30, 219; Lincoln's strategy against, 129, 131
left, criticisms of Lincoln by, 1–2
legislature, Illinois, 257; Lincoln in, 31, 83–84, 91–92, 116; Yates proroguing, 261, 263, 267
Lester, Julius, 247
Levering, Mercy, 86, 89–91, 93
liberty: for African Americans, 225, 274, 277; Lincoln's commitment to, 203, 211; in republican ideal, 187–88
Lieber, Francis, 253
Lincoln, Mary Todd (wife), 117, 264, 267n22; broken engagement of, 68, 74–75, 86–87, 94; confusion about initiator of broken engagement of, 89–90, 94; courtship of, 39, 71–74, 83, 99; effects of Ann Rutledge story on, 46–47; family's opposition to marriage of, 69–70; interest in love affairs of, 82, 93; letter releasing Lincoln from engagement to, 79, 83–84; Lincoln telling Speed about, 70–71; Lincoln's guilt about broken engagement to, 94, 96; Lincoln's reluctance to marry, 71–72, 74, 78–79, 85, 94; Matilda Edwards and, 82–83, 86, 88–89; other suitors of, 84, 86, 90; relationship with Lincoln, 69–70; sources of information about broken engagement of, 69–72, 76–77, 79–80, 83, 89
Lincoln, Nancy Hanks (mother), 32–33
Lincoln, Thomas (father), 40–42
Lincoln tradition, 233–34
Linder, Usher F., 113
Litwach, Leon F., 237
Logan, John A., 263
Logan, Stephen T., 103, 120–21
Lovejoy, Elijah P., 27–28, 34
Lowrey, Grosvenor, 253
Luraghi, Raimondo, 135–36, 150
Lyceum Address, Lincoln's, 14–15; disparagement of Van Buren and Jackson in, 22–23; filiopiety in, 17, 19–20, 41; lack of manuscript copy of, 35–36; Lincoln's grandiosity in, 38–39; political philosophy in, 31–32; presaging Lincoln's move toward Caesarism, 21, 37; reflecting internal turmoil, 38–42; rhetoric of, 33, 278; on threats to Union, 27, 33–34, 39; warnings against Caesarism in, 18–19, 34–35

Malcolm X, hostility to Lincoln, 238
Mallory, Secretary of the Navy, 140
Manifest Destiny, 112. *See also* expansionism
marriage, Lincolns', 20n10, 76; Lincoln's reluctance about, 71–72, 74, 78–79, 85, 94; rumors of Lincoln's not showing for wedding before, 77, 78n21; rumors of social climbing motive for, 78–79
Marsh, Mathew S., 63–64
martial law, Lincoln justifying, 255
Marx, Karl, 190, 192
mass meetings, 262–65
Master, Edgar Lee, 44
Matheny, James H., 78–79, 84–85

McClellan, George B., 180; battles of, 123–25, 219; Lincoln and, 125–28, 141–42, 174; military strategy and, 122–25, 133
McClernand, John A., 262n16, 263, 265
McClintock, John, 255–56
McDowell, Irvin, 129
McGaughey, Edward, 106
McHenry, Henry, 53n34, 63, 65
McNamar, John, 51–56, 61
McNeely, William, 52
Meade, George G., 133, 267
Medill, Joseph, 259, 264
Memminger, Christopher, 150
Metropolitan Record, 165, 171, 178n32; becoming anti-administration paper, 172, 174, 176–78, 182; breaking from Hughes, 174–76; goals of, 167–68; initial support for Lincoln and war, 169–70; Mullaly launching, 166–67; politics of, 177, 181, 186
Mexican War: called unconstitutional, 101–2; defensive-line strategy for, 112–13, 115; Democrats on, 107–9; indemnity in, 112–14; Lincoln's opposition to, 100–101, 105, 110; political effects of opposition to, 103, 120–21; proposals for ending, 106–8, 114; seen as inevitable, 111–12; slavery's relation to, 111, 113; Whigs on, 114–15, 118–19, 120; Whigs' opposition to, 103–6, 115, 121
Mexico, slavery forbidden in, 110
Miles, G. U., 49–50, 54n37, 58
military strategy: anaconda strategy in, 132–33; Davis and, 145–47; differing among theatres, 132; emancipation in, 217, 248, 272–73; goals of Lincoln's, 126–29, 129n130; Grant's total war, 227–28; influences on Lincoln's, 125, 133; Jackson's, in Valley Campaign, 124; Lincoln accused of interfering with commanders', 132; Lincoln's, 122–23, 126, 147, 228; Peninsular school of, 132; Scott's western offensive strategy of, 134; simultaneous advance in, 124–25; suppression of *Chicago Times* in, 151; turning enemy in, 125; Union morale in, 123–24; Virginia and, 131–32; in the West, 127, 129, 134
Miller, Anson, 276

Miller, Perry, 228
Mississippi River, in Lincoln's military strategy, 126–27, 132
Missouri Compromise (1820), 4–5, 28–29
mob action: against abolitionists, 27–28, 34; antidotes to, 24, 39–40; as threat to Union, 14, 33–34; Whigs' fears of, 22–23
moderation, Lincoln's, 1
Monroe, James, 25
morale: effects of abolitionism on, 154–55; effects of black Union soldiers on, 133; effects of Lee's incursion to Pennsylvania on, 129–30; failure of Confederate, 137n5; Northern, 252
morality: Declaration of Independence as ideal for, 212; Lincoln's not attacking slavery on, 220–21, 231; Whigs' desire to Christianize America, 26–27
Morgan, John, 262n16
Morton, Oliver P., 263
Mullaly, John, 185; arrest of, 179–80; becoming more fiercely anti-Lincoln, 174, 176–78, 181–82; breaking from Hughes, 174–76; initial support for Lincoln and war, 169–70; on Lincoln's assassination, 182; *Metropolitan Record* of, 166–67, 172; mistrust of abolitionists, 168–69; opposition to conscription, 179–80; as pro-slavery, 171, 173; racism of, 182–84, 186; trying to maintain hope for Lincoln's conservatism, 173–74; varied interests of, 165–66; willingness for North to lose Civil War, 177–78

nationalism, in abolitionism debate, 243n39
Nevins, Allan, 137
New Left historians, 237–38
New Salem, Illinois, 58n53; residents' memories about Lincoln and Rutledge, 51–57; rumors of Lincoln's relationship with Ann Rutledge in, 47–48, 51
New York City: Catholic newspapers in, 167; draft riots in, 179, 183–84; Tweed Ring in, 166n2
New York Herald, 166–67
New York Times, 178n32, 185
New York Tribune: Greeley's criticism of *Metropolitan Record* in, 171–72; Know Nothingism of, 184–86

New York World, Burnside suppressing, 157
newspapers, 121, 168, 269n26; Catholic, 167, 172-73; Conkling letter and, 275-78; Copperheadism in, 165, 177; Lincoln's news leaked to, 267, 275n36; on Mexican War, 103-4, 120; Mullaly working for, 165-66; on Republicans' Union meeting in Springfield, 268-69. See also *Metropolitan Record*
Niebuhr, Reinhold, 201
North: Lee's incursion into, 125, 129-30, 219; values of, 9-10, 12
Northwest Ordinance (1787), 5

Ogden, William B., 158
Oglesby, Richard J., 265
"On the Perpetuation of Our Political Institutions." *See* Lyceum Address, Lincoln's
order, concern for, 26-27, 30
Owen, Robert Dale, 107, 253
Owens, Mary, 39

Parick, Rembert, 135
Parker, Joel, 253
Parks, Samuel, 65n76
patronage, influence on Northern decisions, 145
peace convention, 271; proposed to avoid emancipation, 253, 261, 263
Peace Democrats. *See* Copperheadism
Peck, John, 111-12
Pemberton, John C., 144
Peninsular school of military strategy, 132
Pennsylvania, in strategy against Lee, 125, 128-29
perfectionism, in American culture, 206-7
personality, Lincoln's: ambition in, 19, 38-39, 116-17; capacity for growth and change, 40, 42; in Civil War, 12; coldness, 76; compared to Davis's, 137-38; conflict over intimacy, 70; criticisms of, 181; dualities of, 234; grandiosity *vs.* healthy self-assertiveness, 38-39; in Lincoln tradition, 233-34; melancholy, 43-44, 46, 92; moderation, 9; pragmatism, 10, 13, 219n60; reasonableness, 1-2; reticence in, 9, 58-59; rigidity in, 11-12; sources of information on, 64
Plato, 36

political parties: Republicans politicizing war for supremacy in, 144-45; Van Buren and, 24-25
political process, Lincoln's faith in, 11-12, 23. *See also* two-party system
political religion: Lincoln called prophet of, 15, 28-30; Lincoln's desire for veneration of law to be, 27; Van Buren in, 26, 28
politics, 146, 148; effects of Emancipation Proclamation in, 252-53, 256-61, 277, 279-81; effects of opposition to Mexican War in, 100-101, 103, 120-21; Herndon advising Lincoln on, 101-2; influence on Lincoln's decisions, 144, 147; Lincoln's cabinet and, 139-40; in Lincoln's Civil War strategy, 132-34; Lincoln's ideals in, 209-11; in Lincoln's revocation of suppression of *Chicago Times*, 160-61, 163; in Lincoln's stance on race, 243-44; *Metropolitan Record* becoming increasingly vocal on, 172, 174; *Metropolitan Record* initially avoiding, 168, 171; pressure for expansionism in, 113-14; Republicans politicizing Civil War for, 144-45; suppression of opposition press and, 152, 158-61, 162-63; use of mass meetings in, 262-63; use of public letters in, 254-55
Polk, James K., 20; annexation of Texas under, 109, 111; Mexican War under, 4, 115, 119
Pope, John, 141
popular sovereignty, 19, 22; in Kansas-Nebraska Act, 4-5, 7; Lincoln seeing as threat to Union, 28-29
postmillennialism, in American culture, 203, 206-7
Potter, David, 11, 136, 138
press, freedom of, 151-53, 163-64
Prewitt, Nancy Rutledge, 56n44
procedural community, Whigs on, 26-27
progress, 6, 27
prolepsis, as Lincoln's rhetorical strategy, 278-79
property rights, 191; forfeited in war, 272-173; in republican ideal, 187-88
providence, 214, 225; Calvinism's conception of, 205; influence on attitudes

toward slavery, 206-8, 216, 231-32; Lincoln's belief in, 202-3; Lincoln's conception of, 205, 221-22; in timing of emancipation, 219-21
psychohistory: difficulty of, 20-21; on Lincoln's filiopiety, 19-20; Lincoln's Lyceum Address reflecting internal turmoil, 38-42; on Lincoln's "towering genius," 36-37
public letters, 254-55; Lincoln's rhetorical strategies in, 278-79; Lincoln's use of, 267, 280; newspapers printing text of, 269n26; sent for Union meeting in Springfield, 265, 269. *See also* Conkling letter
public opinion: on emancipation, 220n61, 247-48, 252-53; Lincoln's sensitivity to, 204; to suppression of *Chicago Times*, 158
Putnam, James S., 158

Quarles, Benjamin, 241
Quigley, Alice Edwards, 80

race: attitudes about slavery and, 237; civil rights movement's influence on historical writing about, 236-37; effects of Lincoln's beliefs about, 239-40; emancipation making a bigger issue, 242; equality of, 243, 249-50; evolution of Lincoln's attitudes on, 241-42, 244-45, 250-51; Lincoln endorsing system of white supremacy, 239, 246; Lincoln not believing in equality of, 235-36, 238-39, 243-45; Lincoln promoting separation of, 205n12, 236, 238, 243-44, 246, 248-49; separation of, 256
race relations: discord in, 248-49; Lincoln considering local issue, 251
race war, projected as result of emancipation, 174
racism, 251; of Irish Catholics, 183-84; Lincoln's, 238, 239-40, 245; Mullaly's, 182-83, 186; multiple meanings of, 240-41, 242n36; pervasiveness of, 237
Radical Republicans, 247, 265, 284; Eisenschiml manufacturing evidence against, 286-87; revisionist movement vilifying, 286-87, 289
railroads, strategic importance of, 132, 146

Ramsdell, Charles, 150
Randall, James G., 9, 152; on Ann Rutledge story, 45, 47-48, 57-66; on Lincoln and Jack Armstrong, 65-66; on New Salem residents' memories about Lincoln, 51-52
Randall, Ruth Painter, 79n23; on Lincoln's broken engagement, 69, 73n13; on Lincoln's love affairs, 47, 70, 74, 81-82, 93n47
Randolph, George W., 139-40
Reagan, Postmaster General, 140
reason, as antidote to mob action, 33-35, 39-40
reasonableness, Lincoln's, 1-2
reconstruction, 132-34, 148, 284; Lincoln's plan for, 235, 250
religion: Calvinism's influence on other, 203-4; competition to claim Lincoln's, 201; influence of Lincoln's, 201, 205, 232; Lincoln's, 42, 203, 227; Lincoln's republicanism equaling influence of, 209-11, 226, 232; in Lincoln's rhetoric, 202, 209, 214-16, 223-24; postmillennialism in American culture, 206-7; variety of, 203-4; Whigs' desire to Christianize America, 26-27
Representative American, Lincoln as, 234, 239
republic, 27, 30; concerns about saving, 14, 23; Declaration of Independence as basis for, 28-29; as experiment, 14-15, 23; lack of need for heroics in, 17, 19; Lincoln's commitment to continuation of, 25, 41; successes of, 23-24; threats to, 14, 23-25
Republic (Plato), 36
republican ideal, 227; Lincoln's, 187-88, 191-92, 195, 199, 203; small producers in, 197-98. *See also* republicanism
republican institutions, 15-16
Republican Party, 148, 155, 172, 185, 188n2; attendance at Springfield Union meeting of, 268-69, 275; as first deliberately sectional party, 8; in Illinois, 257, 264-65; opposition to expansion of slavery, 5, 8, 247; promoting colonization, 249-50; race and, 180, 237, 243-44; response to Emancipation Proclamation,

Republican Party (*cont.*)
253, 259; response to suppression of *Chicago Times*, 159, 161–63; as revolutionary or not, 9–10; sponsoring Union meeting at Springfield, 263–68; support for Douglas among, 7–8; use of mass meetings, 262–63; war and, 144–45, 247
republicanism, 211, 227; influence on Lincoln, 203, 226, 232; Lincoln's commitment to, 205n12, 209–11. *See also* republican ideal
revolution, Civil War as, 2–3, 12
revolutionaries: Lincoln as, 13; qualities of, 1–3; Republicans as, 9–10
Rhodes, James Ford, 139, 147–48
Richardson, William A., 263
Richmond, Virginia, 126, 129; Lincoln recognizing difficulty of taking, 127–28, 130–31, 134
Rickard, Sarah, 80, 93, 97–99
Roberts, Octavia, 80
Rosecrans, William S., 125, 146, 267
Ross, Frederick, 208–9
Russell, Benjamin B., 255
Rutledge, Ann, 39; basis for story of Lincoln and, 66; cause of death of, 57; documentation of Lincoln's relationship with, 44–45, 47–49, 50n22, 56–59; Herndon on, 43, 49–50; Lincoln's reaction to death of, 52–54, 57–59, 61–62; New Salem residents' memories about Lincoln and, 51–57; Randall's treatment of story of Lincoln and, 60–63; romanticization of Lincoln and, 43–46, 51
Rutledge, David, 55
Rutledge, James McGrady, 54–55, 56n44, 57, 62
Rutledge, John, 56n44
Rutledge, Mrs. William, 54
Rutledge, Robert B., 53–57, 62, 65

Sandburg, Carl, 44, 46, 69, 214n47
Scott, Winfield, 134
secession crisis (1860–1861), 11, 168
Second Inaugural address, 42
sectionalism, political parties counteracting influence of, 25
security, Lincoln's, 284–85
Seddon, James A., 139

segregation, 249
Selby, Paul, 259, 265
self-government, Lincoln's commitment to, 203
Seven Days Battles, 123–24, 127
Seward, William H., 12, 139, 152, 214n47, 219
Seymour, Horatio, 179
Sherman, F. C., 158
Sherman, William Tecumseh, 146–47
Short, James, 50, 53, 60–62, 65
Simon, John Y., 39; on Ann Rutledge story, 46–47, 52–53, 60, 63, 66–67
sin: Civil War as punishment for, 42, 223–24, 227, 230–31; Lincoln increasing using in rhetoric, 215, 223; national, 227; slavery as, 232
slave power, antislavery agitation against, 242
slavery: acceptance of, 5, 25, 171–73, 175, 186; as America's sin, 224, 232; biblical justification for, 208–9; Catholic newspapers on, 172–73; Civil War as punishment for, 42, 231; Civil War ending, 247; Conkling letter not describing ultimate fate of, 277; constitutional amendment abolishing, 13, 226, 273, 281; Douglas accused of supporting, 7, 19; effects of, 245; efforts to outlaw in Washington DC, 24–25; equality in Declaration of Independence applied to, 28–29; free labor system *vs.*, 6–7, 189, 193–94; God used in debate over, 212–13, 227; influences on attitudes about, 205–8, 216, 231–32, 241–42; lack of compromise over, 6, 10, 11–12; lack of moral attack on, 220–21, 231; Lincoln trying to discern God's will about, 217–21, 224; Lincoln's acceptance of, 235, 238, 246–47; Lincoln's expectation of end of, 9; Lincoln's hatred for, 243, 246; Lincoln's limited experience with, 241; Lincoln's motives for ending, 4, 6; Lincoln's reasons for opposition to, 4, 193–94, 199, 212, 243, 243n39; Lincoln's refusal to compromise over, 11–12; Mexican War's relation to, 109–11, 113; moderation's threat to, 10; North's complicity in, 227; public split over Lincoln's policies on, 252; racial at-

titudes and, 237; reasons for opposition to, 6, 211; Republican hatred of, 8
slavery, expansion of: as issue without substance, 20; lack of compromise over, 11-12; legislation allowing, 5, 28-29; Lincoln's concern about, 4-5; Lincoln's opposition to, 212, 235-36, 244, 246-47; as purported motive for Mexican War, 110; Republican opposition to, 5, 8
slaves: confiscation of, 172, 273; Lincoln on, 6, 243; in Union Army, 170, 274, 277
slaves, freed: debate on fate of, 243, 246, 250; in Union Army, 132-34. *See also* African Americans
Smith, Caleb Blood, 104, 109, 114-15
Smith, E. Kirby, 143
social mobility: geographical mobility and, 192-93; Lincoln on, 194-95, 197-200; in republican ideal, 187-88, 192
social reform, Lincoln not involved in, 246
South, 11-12; compassion for, 235, 284; Republicans as threat to, 8-9; social order of, 3
Spears, George, 48
speeches, Lincoln's: in Congress, 117-18; development of style, 31-33, 35; in newspapers, 35-36, 121; orality of, 33; proclamation for national day of fasting, 223-24; rhetoric of, 254, 255, 278; uncertain authorship of, 214n47; use of religious catchphrases in, 215-16. *See also specific speeches*
Speed, Fanny Henning, 94
Speed, Joshua Fry: leaving Springfield, 90-91, 94; Lincoln advising on engagement and marriage of, 94-96; on Lincoln's broken engagement, 70-71, 79, 83-84, 86, 89, 94; as Lincoln's confidant on courtships, 70-71, 95-96; on Lincoln's courtships, 74, 81; Lincoln's relationship with, 40, 95-98; marriage to Fanny Henning, 94; Matilda Edwards and, 75, 82-83, 86, 88; rivalry with Lincoln over Matilda Edwards, 87, 91, 99; Sarah Rickard and, 97-99
Springer, John G., 71n11
Springfield, Illinois: attendance at Republicans' Union meeting in, 268-69, 275; becoming state capital, 31; Conkling letter to be read at Union meeting in, 255, 267-68; mass meetings in, 262-64; Republicans' Union meeting in, 264-67
Stanton, Edwin M., 139, 170; accused of masterminding Lincoln's assassination, 284, 286-88, 290, 292-93; Eisenschiml manufacturing evidence against, 284-87, 289-90; Lincoln's security and, 285; suppression of opposition press and, 152, 157, 160-62
Stewart, A. P., 143
Stoddard, William O., 252-53, 267
Storey, Wilbur F.: criticism of Civil War policies, 155-56; discouraging Union enlistment, 154-55; racism of, 155-56; suppression of *Chicago Times* of, 157, 158
strike, right to, 192
Strong, George Templeton, 278
Strong, Newton D., 88
Strozier, Charles B., 20n10, 70
Stuart, John Todd, 92, 116, 258
suffrage: black, 250-51; women's, 4
Sumner, Charles, 157, 251, 276
Surratt, Mary E., 285
Swett, Leonard, 258, 264
Syracuse, New York, Conkling letter read in, 276n37

Tarbell, Ida M., 68-69, 77n18
Taylor, Zachary, 101, 110, 120; Mexican War and, 107-8, 111-13
Temple, Wayne C., 202n3
Test, Charles, 104
Texas: annexation of, 109-10, 111; in proposals for ending Mexican War, 106-8, 114
Thirteenth Amendment, 13, 226; Lincoln wanting, 273, 281
Thomas, Benjamin P., 65, 248
Thompson, Richard W., 105-7, 114-15, 119-20
Thornton, H. W., 92
Throop, Montgomery, 253
Thurow, Glen E., 202n3
Tod, David, 263
Toombs, Robert, 144
treason, Burnside threatening charges of, 153
Trumbull, Lyman, 91, 158-60, 162-63
Turpie, David, 262

Tweed Ring, 166n2
two-party system, maturation of, 15, 23
Tyler, John, 109

Union: abolitionism as threat to, 5–6, 25–26, 28; Lincoln's refusal to allow disruption of, 12; McClellan not choosing peace over, 180–81; plural nature of, 25–27, 29; in possible ends of Civil War, 270–71; slavery as compromise in formation of, 5–6; threats to, 28–29, 33–34; Van Buren's commitment to, 25
Union, preservation of: in Civil War goals, 247–48, 252–53; as common goal, 271–74; Lincoln asking God for, 228; as Lincoln's goal, 111, 173, 186; *Metropolitan Record* on, 168–69, 177–78; political parties' role in, 25–26
Union Army, 273; African Americans in, 132–34, 170, 174, 183, 251, 272, 279; *Chicago Times* discouraging enlistment in, 154–55; conscription for, 179; defeats of, 123, 215, 222; Emancipation Proclamation's effects on, 253, 258; Lincoln and generals of, 129, 141–44; Lincoln trying to discern God's will in victories and defeats of, 219, 221, 224–25; morale of, 154–55, 253; politics in appointments in, 144; simultaneous advance strategy by, 124–25; in suppression of *Chicago Times*, 157–58; victories of, 124, 226, 228–29, 274
Union Leagues, 162, 255
United States Catholic Miscellany, 169

Vallandigham, Clement L., 152, 255; arrest criticized, 156, 263; expelled to Confederacy, 153, 261
Valley Campaign, Jackson's strategy in, 124
values, Lincoln's, 3–4
Van Buren, Martin, 28; contributions to Democratic Party, 15, 25–26; filiopiety of, 16–18, 30; Inaugural Address of, 23–25, 27; Lincoln compared to, 14–15, 16–17, 30; Lincoln's Lyceum Address echoing, 21–22; opposition to abolitionism, 27, 28; political party system and, 24–25; respect for Jackson, 16–19; on threats to the republic, 14–15, 23–25; on Union's plural nature, 25–27; Whig characterizations of, 21–22
Van Higgins, Judge, 158
Vardaman, James K., 236, 239
Vicksburg, Battle of, 224, 263
Vidal, Gore, 286
Virginia: importance in military strategy, 126–27, 131; Lincoln's strategy in, 131–32
Vorhees, Daniel, 263

Wade, Benjamin, 157
Wallace, Frances, 69
war, Lincoln's dislike for, 112
War Democrats, 263, 265, 270
Warner, Ezra, 144
Warren, Louis A., 46
Washington, D.C., 24–25, 124
Washington, George, 40n22
Wayland, Francis, 189–90
Webb, Edwin B., 84, 86, 90n43
Webster, Daniel, 118
Weik, Jesse W., 45, 55n43, 77, 78n21, 83
Welles, Gideon, 159, 219
Wenger, Elias, 260
Wentworth, "Long John," 264
Whigs, 7; characterizations of Van Buren by, 21–22; desire to Christianize America, 26–27; on expansionism, 109, 111, 114–15, 121; Lincoln as, 15, 21, 26–27, 31, 115; Lincoln's opposition to Mexican War and, 100, 102–3; Mexican War and, 114–15, 118–20; opposition to Mexican War among, 103–6, 115, 121; sectionalism among, 118–19, 121; strength in Illinois and Indiana, 103, 107, 114, 116
Why Was Lincoln Murdered? (Eisenschiml), 282, 284; author's response to reviews of, 289–90; popularity of, 286; significance of title's wording, 293
Wickliffe, Charles A., 277
Wigfall, Louis T., 144
Williams, Kenneth P., 143–44
Wilson, Edmund, 19, 36–37
Wilson, Henry, 275
Wisconsin State Agricultural Society, Lincoln's speech before, 188–89, 195–96
Wolf, William J., 202n3, 202n6, 205–6, 211

women's suffrage, 4
Worden, Ananias, 158
Wright, Joseph A., 106
Wrone, David R., 188n2, 193, 196

Yates, Richard, 257; proroguing legislature, 261, 263, 267; support for Lincoln by, 260–61; Union meeting in Springfield and, 265, 269
Yearns, William B., 148
yeoman farmers, as Jeffersonian ideal, 195–96
Young Men's Lyceum (Springfield, Illinois). *See* Lyceum Address, Lincoln's

www.ingramcontent.com/pod-product-compliance
Lightning Source LLC
Chambersburg PA
CBHW030733250426
43671CB00034B/123